A LIFE IN POLITICS

A LIFE IN POLITICS

Selected Speeches and Lectures, 1979–2004

P.A. Sangma

Foreword by

A.P.J. Abdul Kalam

HarperCollins *Publishers* India
a joint venture with
THE INDIA TODAY GROUP
New Delhi

First published in India in 2012 by
HarperCollins *Publishers* India
a joint venture with
The India Today Group

ISBN: 978-93-5029-151-1

2 4 6 8 10 9 7 5 3 1

HarperCollins *Publishers*
A-53, Sector 57, Noida 201301, India
77-85 Fulham Palace Road, London W6 8JB, United Kingdom
Hazelton Lanes, 55 Avenue Road, Suite 2900, Toronto, Ontario M5R 3L2
and 1995 Markham Road, Scarborough, Ontario M1B 5M8, Canada
25 Ryde Road, Pymble, Sydney, NSW 2073, Australia
31 View Road, Glenfield, Auckland 10, New Zealand
10 East 53rd Street, New York NY 10022, USA

Typeset in 11.5/14 Adobe Garamond at
SÜRYA

Printed and bound at
Thomson Press (India) Ltd

CONTENTS

ACKNOWLEDGEMENTS

I have always believed in and admired the potential, talent and strength of India's younger generation. This book is written for them. I hope that it will give them, particularly young politicians, an opportunity to familiarize themselves with our socioeconomic problems, important political developments, and some effective policy decisions undertaken in the last few decades. I welcome all of them to analyse and think about these and, if need be, even criticize.

I owe special thanks to Kalpana Sharma, Director, Lok Sabha Secretariat, who offered honest, constructive and valuable suggestions to improve the manuscript. Her immeasurable strength, selfless attitude and tremendous patience are responsible for making this book a reality. A few words of appreciation will not be enough for her dedication and commitment.

I also thank B.N. Mohapatra, Research Officer, Lok Sabha Secretariat, for his consistent help and cooperation in preparing the manuscript. Thanks to the family and the P.A. Sangma Foundation for the inspiration and the encouragement to pen the book. A word of gratitude for my well wishers and the officials in the North Eastern states, in New Delhi and other parts of the country who have extended and are still extending their support in all my endeavours.

My thanks to the Publisher and the entire team of HarperCollins *Publishers* India for being so professional and friendly through the process.

P.A. SANGMA

A NOTE ON THE P.A. SANGMA FOUNDATION

The P.A. Sangma Foundation (PASF) is a registered society founded in June 2005 with its headquarters at Walbalgre, Tura, West Garo Hills, Meghalaya. The Foundation is essentially a platform committed to impart humanitarian services to the people, safeguarding and promoting social, cultural and environmental aspects of the society at large.

The Foundation is a purely non-political and non-partisan body. Its vision is to be an 'Agent of Change' to empower people socially, economically, through education, training and awareness programmes. One of the many objectives of the Foundation is to publish books, journals, magazines and other such materials that are considered necessary for the attainment of human development, on charitable basis without profit. The income of the publications will be utilized for the development of institutions of learning and culture.

LIST OF ABBREVIATIONS

AASU	: All Assam Students Union
ADA	: Additional Dearness Allowance
AICC	: All India Congress Committee
APC	: Agricultural Prices Commission
APHLC	: All Party Hill Leaders' Conference
BALCO	: Bharat Aluminium Company Limited
BICP	: Bureau of Industrial Costs and Prices
BJD	: Biju Janata Dal
BJP	: Bharatiya Janata Party
C&AG	: Comptroller and Auditor General
CBI	: Central Bureau of Investigation
CCEA	: Cabinet Committee on Economic Affairs
CEO	: Chief Executive Officer
CIL	: Coal India Limited
CPA	: Commonwealth Parliamentary Association
CPI	: Communist Party of India
CPI(M)	: Communist Party of India (Marxist)
CPWD	: Central Public Works Department
CrPC	: Criminal Procedure Code
CTBT	: Comprehensive Test Ban Treaty
CVC	: Chief Vigilance Commissioner
DA	: Dearness Allowance
DMK	: Dravida Munnetra Kazhagam
DRDO	: Defence Research and Development Organization
DTC	: Delhi Transport Corporation
ESCAP	: United Nations Economic and Social Commission for Asia and the Pacific
ESIC	: Employees' State Insurance Corporation

FCI	:	Food Corporation of India
FDI	:	Foreign Direct Investment
FMCT	:	Fissile Material Cut-off Treaty
GDP	:	Gross Domestic Product
HRD	:	Human Resource Development
IAS	:	Indian Administrative Service
ICAR	:	Indian Council of Agricultural Research
ICHR	:	Indian Council of Historical Research
IDPL	:	Indian Drugs and Pharmaceuticals Limited
IFS	:	Indian Foreign Service
ILO	:	International Labour Organization
IMDT Act	:	Illegal Migrants (Determination by Tribunal) Act
INC	:	Indian National Congress
INC(I)	:	Indian National Congress (Indira)
INTUC	:	Indian National Trade Union Congress
IPC	:	Indian Penal Code
IPG	:	Indian Parliamentary Group
IPU	:	Inter Parliamentary Union
ISRO	:	Indian Space Research Organization
ITI	:	Industrial Training Institute
L.P. Schools	:	Lower Primary Schools
LIC	:	Life Insurance Corporation
LoC	:	Line of Control
MBOSE	:	Meghalaya State Board of School Education
MDMK	:	Marumalarchi Dravida Munnetra Kazhagam
MLA	:	Member of Legislative Assembly
MP	:	Member of Parliament
MTNL	:	Mahanagar Telephone Nigam Limited
NAFED	:	National Agricultural Cooperative Marketing Federation of India Ltd
NCP	:	Nationalist Congress Party
NCVT	:	National Council for Vocational Training
NDA	:	National Democratic Alliance
NEC	:	North Eastern Council
NPT	:	Non-Proliferation Treaty
NSC	:	National Security Council
NTC	:	National Textile Corporation
OBC	:	Other Backward Castes
PAC	:	Public Accounts Committee

PCC	:	Pradesh Congress Committee
PDS	:	Public Distribution System
PF	:	Provident Fund
PMK	:	Pattali Makkal Katchi
PMO	:	Prime Minister's Office
POTA	:	Prevention of Terrorism Act
POTO	:	Prevention of Terrorism Ordinance
PSU	:	Public Sector Undertaking
RSS	:	Rashtriya Swayamsevak Sangh
SAARC	:	South Asian Association for Regional Cooperation
SAFTA	:	South Asian Free Trade Area
SAPTA	:	SAARC Preferential Trading Arrangement
SC	:	Scheduled Caste
ST	:	Scheduled Tribe
TADA	:	Terrorist and Disruptive Activities (Prevention) Act
TDP	:	Telugu Desam Party
UN	:	United Nations
UNDP	:	United Nations Development Programme
UNIDO	:	United Nations Industrial Development Organization
UPA	:	United Progressive Alliance
UPSC	:	Union Public Service Commission
VHP	:	Vishwa Hindu Parishad
WTO	:	World Trade Organization

FOREWORD

I am glad that the publication titled *A Life in Politics* is being brought out portraying the life and achievements of Shri P.A. Sangma. The publication includes select speeches of Shri Sangma on wide-ranging topics relevant to the nation and messages from several leaders on his unique personality traits. Reading about him, I am sure, will inspire young minds with the confidence that they can also climb to new heights in life by continuous acquisition of knowledge and ceaseless work. His well-thought-out speeches on various subjects including regional aspirations of the North East, national issues and possible approaches for accelerated development have great reference value.

I see in Sangmaji a great leader from the North East who has transformed into a national leader. His vision and thoughts have become very important for the country and particularly for the state of Meghalaya. Sangma's Gandhian approach on matters relating to industrialization and economic development of the state, his role in setting up of Shillong Development Authority and beautification of the popular hill station, and his approach in solving the problems faced by farmers of the state bring out his deep love for the state and its people.

I greet Shri P.A. Sangma for his role as an able parliamentarian and a great national leader. I wish him success in all his endeavours.

17 January 2012
New Delhi

(A.P.J. Abdul Kalam)

MESSAGES

Prime Minister

I have known Shri P.A. Sangma for many years and we have often made common cause in promoting the interests of the North Eastern Region. Shri Sangma has a long and distinguished record in Parliament having served eight terms. I recall his tenure as Speaker of the Lok Sabha when I interacted with him in my capacity as leader of the Opposition in the Rajya Sabha. He discharged his duties with impartiality and earned the respect of the members of the House. Shri Sangma served as the chief minister of Meghalaya in the late eighties and worked hard not only for the development of the state but also to focus the attention of the Government of India on the problems of Meghalaya and the North East. These are no small achievements for somebody who began his life in a small village in Meghalaya. Shri Sangma's rise in public life is a testimony to his qualities of head and heart and also his affable and informal disposition.

I convey my best wishes to Shri Sangma and wish him many more years of good health and prosperity.

(Manmohan Singh)

New Delhi

अटल बिहारी वाजपेयी

संदेश

यह जानकर प्रसन्नता हुई कि पूर्व लोकसभाध्यक्ष, केन्द्रीय मंत्री और जनप्रतिनिधि श्री पी.ए.संगमा के व्यक्तित्व और कृतित्व पर पुस्तक का प्रकाशन किया जा रहा है।

छठी लोक सभा से मुझे उनके साथ काम करने का अवसर मिला। लोक सभा में एक जागरूक जनप्रतिनिधि के रूप में, केन्द्रीय मंत्री और लोकसभाध्यक्ष के रूप में मैंने उन्हें कार्य करते देखा है। भूमिका चाहे जो भी रही हो, उन्होंने उसे बखूवी और बेबाकी से निभाया है। विषयों पर उनकी पकड़, संसदीय, संवैधानिक एवं कानूनी मामलों पर उनका विशुद्ध ज्ञान और उनकी वाकपटुता ने सभी पर अपनी अमिट छाप छोड़ी है। सहजता, सरलता और सादगी ने उनके व्यक्तित्व को गढ़ा है। देखने में वे जरूर छोटे दिखते हैं, मगर वड़े व्यक्तित्व के धनी है। संक्षेप में कहना हो तो - छोटी काया, वड़ा व्यक्तित्व।

विषयों और मुद्दों के प्रति उनकी अडिगता और निर्भीकता प्रशंसा की पात्र बनी। भारत के उत्तर-पूर्व क्षेत्र से आए श्री संगमा ने अपने व्यक्तित्व और कृतित्व से सिद्ध कर दिया कि देश के कोने-कोने में प्रतिभाएं छिपी हैं। आवश्यकता है उनको सामने लाने और अवसर देने की। श्री संगमा को राजधानी नई दिल्ली में यदि उत्तर-पूर्व का दूत कहा जाए तो अतिशयोक्ति नहीं होगी।

विरले गुणों के विरले श्री पी.ए. संगमा के स्वस्थ, समृद्ध, सफल और सक्रिय भविष्य एवं दीर्घायु के लिए मेरी शुभकामनाएं।

अटल बिहारी वाजपेयी

(अटल बिहारी वाजपेयी)

नई दिल्ली

Former Speaker Lok Sabha

An outstanding parliamentarian and a leader of great stature, Shri Sangma has added lustre to the many public offices he has held all through his political career. My distinguished predecessor in the office of the Speaker, Lok Sabha, he enhanced the prestige of the office in more ways than one. Always concerned about the decorum and dignity of the House and of its public image, he laid great stress on its orderly conduct and commanded respect from all sections of the House in his endeavours in that direction. His commendable initiative in holding a Special Session of the Lok Sabha in August 1997, as part of the celebrations marking the golden jubilee of our Independence, helped the nation in reminding itself of the values that guided our freedom movement besides providing an opportunity for national self-introspection, particularly about the health of the institutions of the republic and to identify the challenges before the country, at a crucial juncture in its history.

Authentically representing the simplicity, honesty and the innate goodness of the people of North East India, he carries these qualities abundantly into the stage of national politics in New Delhi where he is a much respected public figure. His abiding concern for the weaker sections, women and the working class has endeared him to vast sections of our people across the country. Endowed as he is with a spontaneous sense of humour, always well equipped with relevant facts and figures and entertaining a broad national vision, the whole House listens with rapt attention to his learned interventions during its proceedings.

Greeting him on this occasion, I convey him my best wishes for good health and longer years of constructive public life in the service of the whole country.

(Somnath Chatterjee)

New Delhi

Minister of Road Transport and Highways

It is heartening to learn that a book is being brought out on Shri P.A. Sangma, one of the most popular and friendly parliamentarians of our times. Mr Sangma's popularity is amply borne from his unanimous election as the Speaker of the eleventh Lok Sabha, even as an Opposition member. His quest for maintaining decorum, dignity and autonomy of the House with meticulous impartiality earned him respect nationwide and the reputation of an outstanding parliamentarian. Mr Sangma was an extremely popular Presiding Officer, respected for his knowledge of rules and even more for his innate understanding of parliamentary traditions.

The journey of Mr Sangma from the West Garo Hills district of the state of Meghalaya to the Indian Parliament is truly inspiring. During his early years, he worked as a lecturer, a lawyer and a journalist before joining politics as a worker of the Congress party. Since his first election to the sixth Lok Sabha, Mr Sangma has been re-elected to the Lok Sabha seven more times. In the government, Mr Sangma held key responsibilities including as Minister of Labour and Minister of Information and Broadcasting.

Mr Sangma has always maintained a deep connection with the people of Meghalaya and served the state as a chief minister. The people of Meghalaya still fondly remember him for his editorial skill during his stint as the editor of the Meghalaya daily, *Chandambeni Kalrang*.

At a personal level, he has been a warm and affable friend for long. I wish Mr Sangma and his family happiness and success in their future endeavours.

(Kamal Nath)

New Delhi

Minister of Defence

I am happy to learn that a book is being brought on Shri P.A. Sangma. Shri Sangma has held several important positions and has been known as an able parliamentarian. He was unanimously elected as Speaker of the eleventh Lok Sabha. He has ably manned various ministerial posts at the Central and state level. Shri Sangma is known as a humble person and a soft-spoken person and has a definite way with words.

I am sure that the book being brought out will bring out various other facets of his life that are not widely known. I hope the book will be read and liked widely.

I convey my best wishes to the endeavour.

(A.K. Antony)

New Delhi

Minister of Health and Family Welfare

I am glad to know that a book is being brought out on Shri P.A. Sangma, former Speaker, Lok Sabha.

Shri Sangma has been a lecturer, an eminent lawyer, a journalist, a great parliamentarian and a political stalwart. Blessed with an affable personality and phlegmatic temperament, he has always left a mark in everyone's heart. He has also been a great philanthropist and social activist engaged in doing yeoman's service to socially and economically backward people of Meghalaya. He has held prestigious positions in the Congress party and in the Government of India. Gifted with power of intellect and understanding, he is known for his wit and for handling meticulously and tactfully the transaction of business in the Lok Sabha.

Bringing out a book on Shri Sangma will not only be a fitting tribute to the services rendered by him to the nation and the people of this country, but will also help in discovering untold contributions made by him.

I extent my best wishes from the depths of my heart for every success in accomplishing this noble task.

Yours sincerely,

(Ghulam Nabi Azad)

New Delhi

Minister of New and Renewable Energy

I am delighted to know that a book is being brought out on Shri P.A. Sangma, eminent parliamentarian, former Speaker and eight-time member of the Lok Sabha.

I have the privilege of having known Shri Sangma for a very long time. Shri Sangma established himself on the national political scenario despite his humble beginnings and despite belonging to a place which is geographically remote. He started his early career as an expert on constitutional law and served as a lawyer and a journalist but soon found his real calling in politics. Starting from the very beginning, he served in almost all the positions in the Congress party, both at the state and at the national levels. Sensing his deep commitment and intelligence, his party chose to bestow him with various ministerial assignments in the Union government. He served as minister in nearly every important ministry including industry, commerce, coal and information and broadcasting. His finest hour came when he became the first-ever person to be unanimously elected as Speaker of Lok Sabha, with universal support cutting across all political parties. He also obtained the unique distinction of becoming the first-ever leader from the Opposition rank to hold this office, of being the youngest Speaker and the first-ever from the tribal community of the country to hold the august office.

Besides his many achievements, he will be best known for the progressive issues that he espoused. Empowerment of women, ethics in public life, social security measures for the downtrodden, pension for industrial workers and elimination of child labour were some of the many noble causes that he not only believed in but also supported through policy initiatives in every assignment that he handled.

His life is a lesson in the enduring human values of hard work, ethics, simplicity and fairness. My personal interactions with him too have borne out these very virtues and traits. I also take this occasion to fondly recollect my many pleasant interactions and meetings with him, both officially and personally, and wish him many more years of healthy, active and meaningful life devoted to the service of the nation and his people.

(Farooq Abdullah)

New Delhi

Governor of Uttarakhand

I have known Shri Purno Sangma for over a quarter of a century and have worked closely with him at various levels. A man of conviction and courage, he has held various positions in the state, in the party and in the Central government including the prestigious post of the Speaker of the Lok Sabha. A man of determination – nothing could stop him in his rise to power and fame. I do believe that he has still a long way to go and that the future will bring him many more laurels.

I wish him many more fruitful years in the service of the nation.

(Margaret Alva)

Dehradun

Governor of Assam

When I was the chief minister last, Shri Sangma had occupied a higher position in the Congress party hierarchy and was loved by everyone. He continued in that position for quite some time. He is good friend of mine and a very amiable personality.

Shri Sangma, before joining politics, worked in the capacity of a lecturer, a lawyer and a journalist. Hence, he is a man of many parts. He started his political career as a worker of the Congress party in the state of Meghalaya and his rise through the ranks of the party has been meteoric.

Shri P.A. Sangma came to national politics in 1977, when the country was preparing for the sixth General Elections. He was elected to the Lok Sabha from the Tura constituency of Meghalaya, his home state, on Congress ticket. Shri Sangma, as a thirty-year-old, entered the portals of Parliament at a time when the nation was witnessing a major political change, with the Congress party losing power at the Centre for the first time since Independence. In 1980, Shri Sangma was re-elected to the Lok Sabha from the same constituency.

In the party organization, too, Shri Sangma moved up fast and became the Joint Secretary of the All India Congress Committee in 1980, before he was inducted into the Union Cabinet. He has served our nation as honourable minister in the ministries of industry, commerce, supply, home, labour, coal and information and broadcasting.

It was Shri Sangma's thorough understanding of state politics which prompted the Congress party leadership to requisition his services for Meghalaya in 1988.

After being elected for the fifth time to Parliament, Shri Sangma was unanimously elected as the Speaker of the eleventh Lok Sabha with universal support, and maintained his reputation for impartiality, transparency, humility and wit and wisdom during his tenure as the Speaker of the Lok Sabha. From the time he assumed the office of the Speaker, he executed his responsibilities with much panache and assurance.

He had a unique approach to parliamentary reforms. As a Speaker, he ensured that rules were observed by the members even in the midst of stormy debates. Shri Sangma, as Speaker, ensured free debate, objective deliberations and healthy criticism in Parliament. Shri Sangma won the admiration of both the ruling coalition and the Opposition within a short span of time. He also displayed a tremendous sense of timing and history when he took laudable initiatives towards facilitating greater partnership between men and women in politics and in stressing the importance of ethics and probity in public life.

Shri P.A. Sangma is a multifaceted personality. His concern for decorum, freedom and dignity of the House earned him the reputation of being an exceptional parliamentarian.

I pray for his good health and wish that he continues to work for the society and the nation.

(Janaki Ballav Patnaik)

Guwahati

Chief Minister
Sikkim

It gives me immense happiness to know that a book on Shri P.A. Sangma is being written. To me, for that matter to anyone in the North East, the ability of Shri Sangma to reach the exalted position of the Speaker of the Lok Sabha is a subject of great marvel, sacred awe and reverence. It is a matter of great pride to me that a person of the North East, through his sheer hard work, knowledge, professionalism and sincerity, has contributed so much to the nation and commands respect as a great son of India. His handling of the proceedings in the Lok Sabha was superb and dexterous.

I have had the privilege of working with Shri Sangma on a number of occasions, both as political workers and as chief minister for the last many decades. A man of clean and pure heart, Shri Sangma's presence exudes friendliness and mutual respect. My interactions with him on issues of regional and national importance which take place on a regular basis have benefited me immensely, especially because of his rich knowledge and wisdom in serving the people in great measure and in innovative ways.

Needless to say that it is a great honour for me to pen my few thoughts for which I am very thankful to Shri Sangma and also Ms Agatha Sangma. I wish him good health and pray for his continued involvement in active politics at the regional and national level.

With best wishes.

(Pawan Chamling)

Gangtok

Chief Minister
Nagaland

I am happy to learn that a book on Mr Purno Agitok Sangma is being published. If I were to use only a single adjective to describe Sangma, I would probably use 'dynamic' because, like dynamite, he has packed in so much power and energy within his diminutive frame. And if I were to compare him with any one person, it would be no person other than Napoleon Bonaparte, who, in spite of his small physical stature, had held the whole European continent under his thrall at one point of history. It used to be said that 'when Napoleon stamped his feet, the European continent shook'. Sangma is one person who, in spite of his physical stature, and in spite of his humble background with a tribal tag, worked his way to the top through hard work and single-minded determination.

As a close associate in politics and a family friend, I have seen Sangma from close range as a politician, as a person and as a family man, and found him worthy of admiration and emulation in all these aspects. He is a practical, simple and down-to-earth man who can adjust to any situation, and who mingles freely with people, earning respect and admiration from friend and foe alike. He is truly a man of the masses. He is equally at ease in the company of the top leaders. He reads and understands the minds of the masses, and therefore, communicates well with them. That, in my view, is the secret of his successful bonding with the people. He has such a keen sense of humour, combined with a lively and positive personality that there never is a dull moment in his company. I also found him to be bit of a political maverick, with a multifaceted personality, difficult to emulate, and definitely not capable of duplication. He is not only frank and outspoken, but straightforward in his dealings. As a typical tribal, hypocrisy is alien to him. For his guts in expressing his beliefs and opinions openly, he might have suffered politically at certain times. But as leader, I respect and admire him all the more for it. He is always warm and generous to his friends, as he is fair and forgiving to his opponents.

In the realm of politics, he has been the brightest star of the North East, having been elected eight times to the Lok Sabha, and having served as a Union minister and Speaker of the Lok Sabha, in addition to having been a chief minister and member of the Legislative Assembly of Meghalaya. His performance as Union Labour Minister and Speaker of the Lok Sabha were particularly brilliant and spoke volumes about his leadership and statesman-like qualities, his dexterity in handling and resolving tricky situations, and his skill at consensus building. It will be really difficult for anyone from the North East to reach the level of his popularity, not to speak of breaking his record.

I have been with Sangma at several election campaigns in Nagaland, Assam, Meghalaya and West Bengal. I observed how easily he established a rapport with the audience or any other party worker he came into contact with. During one of his election campaigns for Tura Lok Sabha constituency, I happened to be with him at Tura. I observed that his big residential compound was turned into a campaign ground, where people from the villages came and pitched their tents, bringing with them their own beddings, rice, meat and vegetables, etc. This shows the people's trust and love for him as also his magnanimity, hospitality and humanity beyond measure.

Another remarkable achievement of Sangma is his success as a homemaker, in spite of his full-time engagement in politics and public affairs. I have seen him in action as a loving and caring husband, and as a doting and nurturing father. The way he has brought up all his children is admirable, as everyone can see. I am particularly happy the way he has groomed his daughter, Agatha Sangma, to be his worthy successor and to represent the new and youthful face of the North East in the Central government. And I have no doubt that Agatha will shine as another bright star of the North East, and prove to be a worthy daughter and successor to her illustrious father. I am confident that his two sons James Pangsang K. Sangma and Conrad K. Sangma who are honourable members of the Meghalaya Legislative Assembly will follow the footsteps of their father and continue to dedicate their time and energy in the service of the people. Though he is my senior both in age and in politics, I will always value and cherish his association with me and in accepting me as a comrade and a friend.

It is my prayer that the Almighty bless him richly with good health and long life so that he continues to serve the people of the region and the country at large for many years to come.

(Neiphiu Rio)

Kohima

मुख्यमंत्री
राजस्थान

संदेश

मुझे यह जानकर प्रसन्नता है कि लोक सभा के पूर्व अध्यक्ष एवं संसद सदस्य, श्री पी.ए. संगमा के व्यक्तित्व एवं कृतित्व और उपलब्धियों पर केन्द्रित एक पुस्तक का प्रकाशन किया जा रहा है।

राजनीति और सार्वजनिक जीवन में लोकप्रिय व्यक्तित्व पर पुस्तक का लेखन एवं प्रकाशन अपने आप में महत्वपूर्ण है। इससे नई पीढ़ी को उनके जीवन आदर्शो से प्रेरणा प्राप्त करने का अवसर मिलता है।

आशा है कि पुस्तक की सामग्री श्री संगमाजी के जीवन आदर्शो के साथ उनके लोक सभा अध्यक्ष, आठ बार लोक सभा सदस्य, राज्य सभा एवं मेघालय विधान सभा सदस्य के रूप में देश-प्रदेश के विकास, जनकल्याण और संसदीय परम्पराओं के निर्वहन की दिशा में निभाई गई भूमिका तथा अपने क्षेत्र के सांस्कृतिक, सामाजिक, आर्थिक एवं सामुदायिक विकास में योगदान को प्रकाशमान करने वाली होगी।

मैं श्री संगमाजी के स्वस्थ एवं सुदीर्घ जीवन की मंगला कामना करते हुए इस पुस्तक के प्रकाशन की सफलता के लिए अपनी शुभकामनाएं प्रेषित करता हूं।

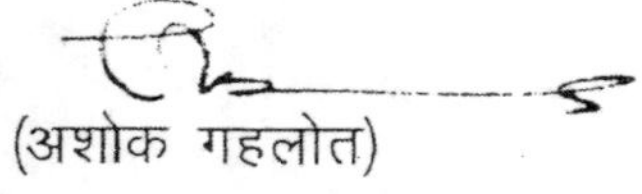

(अशोक गहलोत)

जयपुर

मुलायम सिंह यादव
संसद सदस्य (लोक सभा)
नेता, समाजवादी संसदीय पार्टी

मुझे यह जानकर अत्यन्त प्रसन्नता हो रही है कि श्री पी0ए0 संगमा के जीवन पर एक पुस्तक प्रकाशित हो रही है। श्री संगमा ने बहुत साधारण परिवार में जन्म लेकर असाधरण उपलब्धियाँ प्राप्त की हैं। केन्द्र में लम्बे समय तक मंत्री रहने के अलावा श्री संगमा मेघालय के मुख्यमंत्री रहे । 1989-90 में जब श्री संगमा मेघालय के मुख्यमंत्री थे तो मैं उत्तर प्रदेश का मुख्यमंत्री था। दिल्ली में अनेक बैठकों में संगमा जी के साथ काम करने का अवसर मिलता था। श्री संगमा जी की वक्तव्य शैली एवं उनकी प्रबन्धन कार्यक्षमता से सभी मुख्यमंत्री प्रभावित होते थे।

संयोगवश 11वीं लोक सभा (1996-98) में श्री संगमा जी लोक सभा अध्यक्ष बने। इस कार्यकाल के दौरान मैं केन्द्रीय सरकार में रक्षा मंत्री था। श्री संगमा जी अपने हॅसमुख स्वभाव से सदन का संचालन बहुत अच्छे ढंग से करते थे। जब भी मुझे संसद में श्री संगमा जी से मिलना होता था तो वे तुरन्त मुझे समय देते थे और समस्याओं का समाधान बताते थे। लोक सभा अध्यक्ष के रूप में वे कभी भी किसी पार्टी का पक्ष नहीं लेते थे।

राजनीति में समकालीन होने के नाते मुझे संगमा जी को निकट से देखने का अवसर मिलता रहा है। वे बहुत ही लोकप्रिय रहे हैं। पिछले कुछ समय से उन्होंने अपने प्रदेश मेघालय में काम करने का निश्चय किया है और मैं इस निर्णय से सहमत हूं। वे अपने परिश्रम एवं कुशलता से न केवल उत्तर-पूर्वी राज्यों में अपितु राष्ट्रीय स्तर पर एक राष्ट्रीयवादी उदार, कुशल प्रबन्धक, परिपक्व राजनीतिज्ञ नेता के रूप में उभरे हैं। उनका

चार दशकों का राजनीतिक अनुभव एवं परिपक्वता उन्हें राष्ट्र के बड़े पदों की जिम्मेवारी उठाने के लिए उपयोगी पात्र बनाता है।

मुझे आशा है कि आने वाले लम्बे समय तक श्री संगमा जी देश की सेवा करते रहेंगे। मैं पुनः श्री संगमा जी के उज्जवल भविष्य एवं सफलता की कामना करता हूं।

सादर,

आपका,

(मुलायम सिंह यादव)

लखनऊ

PREFACE

In one of the many interactions I have had with students in the course of my political career, I was asked to describe the strength of the Indian parliamentary system. I responded with a beautiful story from my life. When I became Cabinet minister, I took oath along with Madhavrao Scindia and Buta Singh. Whereas Scindia had a royal lineage, Buta Singh was the son of a commoner from Punjab, and I was as an ordinary person, a tribal, from the remote North East of India. Now, all three of us had become equals, irrespective of our backgrounds. This is the beauty of the Indian parliamentary system. It opens the doors of opportunities to persons from the remotest part of the country and provides a level playing field for their growth.

I am a strong believer in the institution of parliamentary democracy. I feel that given the size and complexities of India and its composite character, parliamentary democracy is the system best suited for the country's need. Parliamentary democracy works on the cardinal principle that people are the ultimate source of legitimacy. A government is legitimate because it is elected, elected by the people. I have watched the Parliament of India for almost thirty years, having being elected to the Lok Sabha nine times. During this period, I have seen ten prime ministers, starting from Indira Gandhi to Morarji Desai, Charan Singh, Chandrashekhar, Rajiv Gandhi, V.P. Singh, Deva Gowda, I.K. Gujral, A.B. Vajpayee and Dr Manmohan Singh. Within the Lok Sabha, I have also come across learned Speakers like N. Sanjeeva Reddy, K.S. Hegde, Rabi Ray, Shivraj Patil, Balram Jakhar, G.M.C. Balayogi, Manohar Joshi and Somnath Chatterjee. I have seen many parliamentarians working tirelessly day in and day out to serve the people and preserve the democratic institutions of the country. The list is very long. These include Bhupesh Gupta, Piloo Mody, Indrajit Gupta, L.K. Advani,

H.N. Bahuguna, Jagjivan Ram, Sushma Swaraj, Madhavrao Scindia, Rajesh Pilot, Madhu Dandavate, Sharad Pawar, Biju Patnaik, Prof. N.G. Ranga, Nitish Kumar, Sharad Yadav, Nirmal Chandra Chatterjee, Y.B. Chavan, C.M. Stephen, S.B. Chavan, Vasant Sathe, Mulayam Singh Yadav, Omar Abdullah and Jaswant Singh. Besides these eminent personalities, there are many parliamentarians, cutting across party lines, who have inspired me.

Today, I am deeply concerned about the decline of this great institution, among other institutions in the country. The way Parliament is being denigrated is a cause for worry for all of us. The general perception is that the authority of Parliament is no longer sacrosanct. I don't agree with this perception in its entirety. I feel it is the style of functioning of the legislature that has changed; not the legitimacy and authority of the Parliament of India. This change in the style of functioning is partly because of the changing composition of the legislature. During the initial years of independence, our Parliament was represented by urban-based intellectuals who valued policies, programmes and intellectual, issue-based debates. Today's legislators are mainly rural based. The individual voices which shaped many important policies of the government in the past are now absent. Nowadays, Members of Parliament run to the well of the House, disturbing the business of the House, primarily to get themselves noticed. Live telecast of the House proceedings has increased this tendency among the MPs.

MPs who are genuinely concerned about the people's problems find it difficult to express themselves in the House. They struggle for time. As former Speaker of the Lok Sabha, I feel the Lok Sabha is a hallowed hall of democracy. The ideal for all of us, therefore, should be to give it the sanctity of a place of worship. In the House there should be debate and dissent with dignity, compromise with courtesy and respect without rancour. The mandate as well as the basic terms of reference of the House is legislation. It is through legislation that we reflect the will of the people, lay down policies and establish rule of law. Time being the constraining factor we should deploy the same to produce optimum results in terms of good governance and fulfilling the aspirations of the people. Parliament business is serious but need not be tense. People will not watch parliamentary proceedings if they are not interesting, if not laced with wit and humour. When I was the Speaker, I endeavoured my utmost to be guided by transparency and impartiality and tried to provide equal opportunity to all in expressing their views.

Today, I am worried about certain things happening in the country. We have not been able to preserve and strengthen our institutions. We have systems in place but they do not work. Our institutions are in a state of decay. I am particularly worried about the institution of the prime minister. I strongly feel that the prime minister being subjugated to an extra-constitutional 'super' authority is a dangerous precedent. Without any personal bias, I also feel that since India is the largest democracy, it would be in the fitness of the things if the prime minister is elected by the House from members of the Lok Sabha. We should also start thinking and debating the desirability and possibility of electing the prime minister directly by the people. With a population of more than 1.2 billion people, India is capable enough of producing an able prime minister.

Against this background, I have made a humble attempt to put forth my views, experiences and interactions with the people of this country. This publication includes my selected speeches in the Lok Sabha, the Rajya Sabha, as a minister, the blessings and affections of my colleagues on being unanimously elected as the Speaker, Lok Sabha, rulings and announcements during my tenure as Speaker and some selected speeches in conferences and seminars held during the period I was Speaker. I hope readers will get a glimpse of the concerns that have motivated my public life as a politician and parliamentarian.

P.A. SANGMA

January 2012

PART I

Profile

PERSONAL LIFE

Purno Agitok Sangma, a dynamic and one of the most popular personalities of the Indian political scenario, was born on 1 September 1947 in a tiny village, Chapahati, in the West Garo Hills, Meghalaya, in the North East of India. His parents Dipchon Ch. Marak and Chimri A. Sangma came from a humble background. Growing up in the small tribal village in an equally small tribal Christian minority community of Garos, who constitute slightly over half a million of India's total population of more than 1,200 million, young Sangma had realized early in life that he would have to struggle hard to rise. It is said that social structure defines the mental faculty of a person living in that society. As a typical tribal, hypocrisy is alien to him. By nature, Sangma is a soft-spoken but determined personality. He is a man of few words who prefers to be known for his work and this distinguishes him from other politicians of the present generation. The Garos in Meghalaya are a classic example of a matrilineal society. The children in these regions are traditionally more inspired by their mothers and sisters than by their fathers and brothers. The young Sangma was no exception. Inspired by his mother Chimri A. Sangma, who inculcated in him the values of diligence, humility and honesty, he learnt that education was the only way to progress in life. He did his honours and master's degree in political science with specialization in international relations from the Dibrugarh University in Assam. Subsequently, he also obtained a degree in law from the same university.

P.A. Sangma married Soradini Kongkal Sangma of his own community on 6 June 1973. He has four children – two sons and two daughters. All his children are highly educated, qualified and established in their respective fields. The elder son, James, has completed a master's degree in mass communication from Brunel University, London, and is engaged in the production of documentary films. The eldest daughter, Christi, has completed her bachelor of architecture course from J.J. College of Architecture, Mumbai, and has done her Ph.D in architecture from Cardiff University in the United Kingdom. The second son, Conrad, after completing BBA from the Wharton School of Management, USA, and MBA from the Royal College of Management, London, is currently the leader of the Opposition in the Meghalaya Legislative Assembly and is also engaged in his own business in Shillong. The second daughter and the youngest of all, Agatha, is a law graduate from the Indian Law School, Pune, and has completed a master's degree from Nottingham University, United Kingdom. Agatha was elected to the fifteenth Lok Sabha from the Tura constituency, the same constituency nurtured by her father over the years. She is the youngest minister of state in the current Cabinet. Sangma has always believed that the inherent qualities of children should be nurtured and they should be given utmost freedom to choose their life and career.

EARLY CAREER

Sangma is a multifaceted personality endowed with scientific knowledge, logical thinking and passion for truth and service to the nation and its people. He is a man of many parts, having been, in the course of his career, an academician, a lawyer and a journalist before he joined politics. He started his early career as an expert on constitutional law and served as a lawyer and a journalist. As an advocate and as a journalist, he has always professed truth as a religion but soon found his real calling in politics and stood by the causes of the masses in the country.

He started his political life as a grass-roots worker of the Congress (I), and his rise through the ranks of the party has been phenomenal. When he joined the Congress party, a national party, most of the people in the hills were surprised. Regional parties were reigning supreme and in Meghalaya there was no hope for Congress at that time. No youth with political aspirations in those days would ever look at a national political party. Sangma's first choice, therefore, was a clear indication that he had from the very beginning a different vision of India in which he visualized a place of honour for his people. As a Youth Congress leader, he fought tooth and nail against Captain W.A. Sangma and his All-Party Hill Leaders' Conference (APHLC), denouncing regionalism as a creed that could only lead to communalism and localism, emotions that are the prime causes inhibiting progress. In recognition of his commitment to the party's ideals and also taking into account his organizational skills, Sangma was appointed the general secretary of the Meghalaya Pradesh Congress Committee in 1975 and held that post till 1980. He was associated with the building up of the Congress in Meghalaya and the merger of the APHLC with the Congress. He became the joint secretary of the All India Congress Committee in 1980. Sangma's rise in public life is a testimony to his qualities of head and heart and also his affable and informal disposition.

ENTRY INTO THE NATIONAL POLITICAL SCENE

Sangma came to the national political scene in 1977 when the country was preparing for the sixth General Elections and remained a member of Parliament for almost thirty years. He was elected to the Lok Sabha from the Tura constituency in his home state on a Congress ticket in the midst of the worst-ever defeat suffered by the Congress party in history. The thirty-year-old Sangma entered the portals of Parliament at a time when the nation was witnessing a major political change with the Congress party losing power at the Centre for the first time since Independence. It was an opportune moment for a budding parliamentarian to make his mark, and the articulate Sangma made full use of the opportunity to make an impact as a sincere and hard-working member.

In less than two years, national politics took a full turn and the Janata Party went out of office. The Charan Singh government which assumed office subsequently lasted but a few months. In the mid-term elections of 1980, the Indira Gandhi-led Congress party returned to power at the Centre. Sangma was re-elected to the Lok Sabha from the same constituency.

He was inducted into the Union Cabinet and assumed the office of the deputy minister in charge of industry in November 1980. As deputy minister, he found, to his dismay, that no papers were being presented to him for decision making. But Sangma was a fighter, and true to his courage to face the challenges head on, he did something which others normally would not do. Instead of being a fifth wheel to the wagon, he told Indira Gandhi, 'Madam, there is no work for me. I should better be working in the AICC where there is a lot of work.' Remedy followed quickly and papers started coming in. After two years, he was shifted to the Ministry of Commerce as deputy minister and held that post till December 1984.

Sangma was returned to the eighth Lok Sabha in the General Elections of 1984. Recognizing his potential and dedication to Congress ideals, the then prime minister, Rajiv Gandhi, inducted him into his Cabinet, this time as a minister of state in charge of commerce and supply. For a short while, he also functioned as the minister of state for home affairs. Sangma took over as the minister of state for labour with independent charge in October 1986.

Sangma established himself on the national political scenario despite his humble beginnings and his domicile in a place which is geographically remote. Throughout his life, he never pushed himself forward and preferred to remain in the background. All these honours came to him unsought. His humility, affability, sincerity, integrity of character, selflessness and devotion to the nation are the chief factors that pushed him up the ladder and earned him well-deserved popularity and love among the people. Ever amenable to reason and conciliatory in attitude, Sangma, however, was uncompromising when it came to safeguarding the fundamentals of national interests. It was no wonder then that during his tenure as labour minister, there was a sharp decline in industrial strikes and lockouts. Sangma is an inspirational force for politicians of the future for his discipline and hard work and genuine feelings for the marginalized and the downtrodden. His simplicity and utter disregard for pompous paraphernalia has won him admiration from the people of the country.

Throughout his political life, Sangma would always have the trust of his party leadership. During his tenure in the Congress, he was instrumental as a troubleshooter and a crisis manager. Whenever the party was in dilemma over any political situation, Sangma was deputed to resolve the crisis because the leadership knew that with his mature political thinking, organizational skill and the ability to judge the situation in an objective manner, he could provide a long-term solution to the crisis. He was the key man in the Congress so far as politics in the North East was concerned.

Known for his meticulous homework, complete mastery of the subject at hand and phenomenal memory for facts and details, Sangma was one minister who could reply to a heated debate in Parliament without the aid of officials' slips from the officers' gallery. He took his parliamentary job extremely seriously. His amiability, thorough knowledge of the functioning of his ministry and an inimitable sense of humour enabled him to tackle all challenges in Parliament. The Question Hour particularly brought out the best in him as he handled the most ticklish matters with consummate ease. Throughout his ministerial tenure, he retained the image of an honest and conscientious executive and always steered clear of any controversy. As a parliamentarian, he espoused ideas which had current relevance for the country. As early as in 1979, Sangma had mooted the idea of smaller states. He had said that if the cause of the tribals were to be served, formation of smaller states, in those areas where scheduled castes and scheduled tribes were prominent, was a solution, particularly as that would help people run the administration better. This idea can no doubt be debated now in the context of the present conditions in Jharkhand, Uttarakhand and Chhattisgarh. He had also warned the national parties that if they failed to respond to the aspirations of the people, the regional aspirations of people in different parts of the country would develop and that would pave the way for mushrooming of regional parties in India with demands for more and more divisions within the country. Today, we can see the dominance of regional parties and their growing clout in the political arena. Indeed, the composition of the legislative bodies reflects the strong presence of regional parties.

Another important idea mooted by Sangma as early as in 2005 was that of issuing unique identity cards to the genuine citizens of India to differentiate them from illegal migrants and foreigners. He suggested this on the floor of the Lok Sabha while participating in an adjournment motion on the issue of massive immigration from Bangladesh. He advised that the government should examine the possibility of amending the Citizenship Act instead of going for an amendment of the then proposed Foreigners Act to protect the rights of the genuine citizens of India. According to him, identity cards should be issued to genuine citizens of India so that they would have no fear psychosis and no policemen would go and question them about their identity and about their Indianness. His ideas are going to be put into practice by the Government of India through the unique identification drive.

Sangma had also endorsed the idea of downsizing ministries and downsizing the government. Throughout his life, he has been guided by four self-stipulated principles, namely, to keep thinking, keep working, keep smiling and keep praying.

BACK TO MEGHALAYA

Sangma had a remarkable understanding of the political realities of the entire North East, particularly his home state. Though, starting in 1977, he was in Delhi and busy with national politics, he never cut himself off from his roots and always kept track of political developments back home. It was this thorough understanding of state politics which made the Congress leadership requisition his services for Meghalaya in 1988. That year, he returned to Meghalaya politics, this time as chief minister. He headed a forty-eight-member coalition government during a tumultuous period in the state's political history. In 1990, following the resignation of his government, Sangma became the leader of the Opposition in the State Legislative Assembly.

CALL OF THE NATION

Being a top-rank national leader, his fame and acceptability transcend the geographical barriers of the North East. He could not resist the call of the nation and returned to national politics very soon. He returned to the Lok Sabha in 1991 following the General Elections and was inducted into the Union cabinet, this time by Prime Minister P.V. Narasimha Rao. Sangma was given independent charge of the Ministry of Coal. Despite being a young minister, he could understand at that point in time that an environment of harassment caused by avoidable vigilance and inquiries against public sector executives had demoralized them and diverted their attention from productively contributing to the PSU. As minister for coal, he played down the punitive approach to human resource management. The result was for everybody to see. The day he assumed office, Coal India was losing Rs 2,800 crore and within six months' time, the same Coal India would earn a net profit to the tune of Rs 164 crore. It was possible because he allowed the officers to work with genuine accountability.

In February 1992, he was given the additional responsibility of assisting the prime minister in the Ministry of Labour. In the context of the economic reforms and liberalization policy announced by the Union government, his principal challenge was to sell the idea of economic reforms to a restive and apprehensive labour force. Tirelessly presiding over tripartite Industrial Committee meetings, he made tenacious efforts at convincing the labour of the inevitability of economic reforms. He emphasized the need for a new management and work culture, the hallmark of which was generation of wealth through efficiency, productivity and modernization and sharing of wealth equitably. As a labour minister, he displayed inordinate patience in dealing with workers and labour unions and he accepted this as a part of his job. Smiling was a weapon in his armoury to meet the criticism of the trade unions.

Sangma assumed independent charge of the Ministry of Labour in January 1993. He was elevated to the Cabinet rank (the first tribal to be elevated as such) in the Ministry of Labour in February 1995. As the Union labour minister, he headed the Tripartite Indian Delegation to the International Labour Conference in Geneva six times where he proved his mettle repeatedly. He was also elected chairman of the Asia and Pacific Region for the International Labour Ministers' Conference, 1994–95. When foreign investors had just begun to favour India as their destination and a furore was raised in some quarters over the so-called 'social clause' issue, Sangma, as labour minister, organized a Conference of Labour Ministers from non-aligned and other developing countries in 1994–95. He brought about unanimity amongst them to hold the position that the leverage of international trade should not be used in respect of social issues like labour standards as that would be coercive.

Sangma was a rare labour minister who was and is still admired by the working class and the trade union leaders. He always tried to give the maximum welfare to the labour class within the framework of the official policies of the government. His message to the trade union leaders was: 'If you are not satisfied with my steps you are free to criticize and I will not object to that.'

In September 1995, Sangma took over as minister of information and broadcasting, a post he held till the General Elections to the eleventh Lok Sabha. Besides the ministerial portfolios, as a parliamentarian, Sangma, by virtue of his interest as well as the offices he held, was active in several committees. He was a member of the Committee on Subordinate Legislation, Committee on Communications and Committee on Government Assurances; he was also chairman of the Parliamentary Consultative Committees on Labour, Coal and Communications during his tenure as a Member of Parliament at different points in time. As an active member of the committees he made significant contributions to each and every one of them. Owing to his expertise in constitutional matters and ethics in public life, he was appointed a member of the National Commission to Review the Working of the Constitution from 2000 to 2002. He also served as the vice-president of the Indian Institute of Public Administration from 1998 to 2004 and was a member of the National Commission on Population from June 2002.

MAJOR POLICY INITIATIVES

During his uninterrupted political career of over three decades, with diversified experience at the Central and state levels and in varied important portfolios, Sangma is reputed and recognized in India for several of his policy initiatives. Important among these initiatives are:

As industry minister: Enhancement of production capability of the cement industry of India to the level of self-sufficiency.

As coal minister: Turning Coal India Limited (CIL), a giant public sector corporation of 700,000 workers, into a profit-making enterprise.

As commerce minister: Introduction of plantation crops of export importance like tea, rubber and cashew in non-traditional areas of the North East. He also took several policy measures towards professional management of the tea, coffee and rubber boards. His ministry introduced the auction system in tobacco which benefited the growers and made them capable of coping with increasing cost of production.

As labour minister: Initiation of social security and other measures in the liberalization phase of the Indian economy since 1991, in particular:

- Introduction of pensions for eighteen million industrial workers.
- Rationalization of wages and employment injury compensation for unorganized labour such as agricultural and construction workers.
- Creating and chairing of seven Special Industrial Tripartites to look into the social and economic impact of the reforms and structural adjustment on working people so as to maintain industrial peace side by side with reforms.
- Generation of awareness about enhancement of productivity amongst trade unions and working people. Sangma strongly believed that trade unions should work towards increasing productivity of the companies and at the same time the management should take welfare measures for workers so that welfare of the workers can indirectly lead to welfare of the economy.
- Holding an International Tripartite Conference in Delhi under his presidentship which evolved a common understanding among a large number of developing countries to oppose linking of trade with a social clause relating to the ratification of ILO conventions.

- Setting up a National Renewal Fund to train retrenched workers for new avenues.
- Skill development and retraining respectively amongst job seekers and working people through vocational training.
- Elimination of discrimination against women amongst working people.
- Protection of child rights.

Sangma was a protagonist of child rights. As labour minister, he placed elimination of child labour high on the national agenda and mobilized political resources for curbing child labour and protection of child rights at the national and state levels. He introduced the Child Labour (Prohibition and Regulation) Bill, 1986, which later became a landmark Act. It prohibits the engagement of children below the age of fourteen years in certain hazardous employments and regulates the conditions of work of children in certain other employments. He was criticized both in the Parliament and outside it for not totally banning child labour and for making it industry-specific. But Sangma understands the background in which a child is driven to work as labourer. He himself has come from a background which makes him humble enough to understand the reality that a total ban on child labour might not be practicable in an environment of abject poverty. Therefore, the concern of the government should be protection of child rights and maximization of child welfare. In this direction, his ministry formulated the National Policy on Child Labour which not only addressed the required legal action plan but also focussed on general welfare and development programmes for child workers and their families and a project-based plan of action for the purpose. During his tenure, the labour ministry invested substantial resources for free education of the children of beedi workers which proved to be very effective. Because of the free education that was given, a number of children of beedi workers could become doctors and engineers and the beedi workers themselves started working as a satisfied team which increased the productivity and profit of the industry. Identity cards were issued to the beedi workers so that they could be identified for accurate targeted delivery of welfare services.

PROTECTION OF WOMEN WORKERS

Another area of attention of Sangma as labour minister was welfare of women workers. In 1987, 86 per cent of the women workers in our country belonged to the unorganized sector and this caught his attention. The Equal Remuneration (Amendment) Bill, 1987, was passed during his tenure. Whereas the Equal Remuneration Act, 1976, provided for prohibiting discrimination against women in recruitment, there was no specific clause prohibiting such discrimination during employment. The penalties provided in the 1976 Act were also comparatively lighter which was one of the main reasons for ineffective implementation of this important piece of legislation. The 1987 amendment rectified these lacunae and made the Act effective. Sangma also urged voluntary organizations, trade unions and the citizens of this country to involve themselves in implementation of the labour laws because he was fully aware of the limitations of the government and the inspectors. Welfare of labour and their families has always been very close to Sangma's heart.

As information and broadcasting minister, Sangma initiated the preparation of the draft of the broadcasting law so as to liberalize the usage of airwaves and investments in the electronic media.

Besides his many achievements, Sangma will be best known for the progressive issues that he espoused in whichever capacity he worked. Empowerment of women, ethics in public life, social security measures for the downtrodden, pensions for industrial workers, elimination of child labour were some of the many noble causes that he not only believed in but also supported through policy initiatives in every assignment that he handled.

SPEAKER OF ALL AND FOR ALL

The finest moment in Sangma's life came when in a significant departure from the forty-nine-year-old Indian parliamentary experience, the eleventh Lok Sabha unanimously elected Sangma, a member of the Opposition, as the Speaker. From humble beginnings in a small tribal village in Meghalaya, he rose to the exalted office of the Speaker of the Lok Sabha by sheer dint of his merit, determination and industry. Affable, friendly, smiling and more often informal in disposition and endowed with a spontaneous sense of wit and humour, but firm when it came to ensuring orderly conduct of the House, Speaker Sangma had a charming personality which won him unstinted cooperation from all shades of political opinion represented in the Lok Sabha. His quest for maintaining decorum, dignity and autonomy of the House with meticulous impartiality earned him approbation nationwide.

Sangma's election to the august office of the Speaker, Lok Sabha, was historical from many points of view. In the history of the Lok Sabha, Sangma was the first to be unanimously elected Speaker with universal support cutting across all political parties. He is the first tribal, and that too from the North East, to occupy this post. He was the first from the Opposition to hold the office of Speaker and he was the youngest Speaker. After the unanimous election as Speaker, Lok Sabha, the *Tribune* wrote that in the post-election scenario, the best thing to happen till then was the exhibition of unanimity among all political parties on the choice of the Speaker for the eleventh Lok Sabha.

Sangma, undoubtedly, had all the credentials for the august office – legal training, long experience as a parliamentarian as well as a minister, reputation for impartiality, transparency, pragmatic temperament, humility, wit and wisdom. From the time he assumed the office of the Speaker, he executed his responsibility with such flair and assurance, it seemed that expertise on the job came to him instinctively. He had a unique approach to parliamentary reforms. As Speaker, he ensured that rules were observed by the members even in the midst of stormy debates. Parliamentary democracy, he observed, meant free debate, objective deliberations and healthy criticism, and it was for the Speaker to ensure that these objectives were achieved.

As someone who went from holding the balance between the Treasury and the Opposition benches to holding the balance of every individual member, Speaker Sangma won the admiration of both the ruling coalition and the Opposition within a short span of time. He respected the differences of opinion in the House 'which is the first element of democracy'. He also displayed a tremendous sense of timing and history when he took laudable initiatives towards facilitating greater partnership between men and women in politics and in stressing the importance of ethics and probity in public life. During his speakership, he guided the formation of a Standing Joint Parliamentary Committee on Empowerment of Women and also the constitution of a Joint Parliamentary Committee for considering the Constitution (Eighty-first Amendment) Bill, 1996, which sought to provide for 33 per cent reservation for women in the Lok Sabha and the state legislative assemblies. He also urged the government on the occasion of his address to the joint sitting of Parliament to celebrate the Golden Jubilee of India's Independence by formulating a national policy on empowerment of women.

In order to maintain high traditions in parliamentary life, Sangma believed that members of Parliament should maintain certain standards of conduct, both inside the House and outside. He was of the considered view that the ethical values that ought to permeate the legislative, the executive and the judicial wings of the constitutional system had a deep and lasting impact on the character, direction, credibility and future of democratic governance. During Sangma's tenure as Speaker, in a move which won encomiums from all quarters, an eight-member Study Group of the Committee of Privileges was constituted to report on Ethics and Standards in Public Life. The Study Group's report was considered by the Committee of Privileges and adopted with some amendments. The report was later presented to the twelfth Lok Sabha. It was under his speakership that the Parliament adopted a resolution, through a joint sitting of both the Houses, a truly historical document about how the members of Parliament ought to conduct themselves in the House and what their responsibilities are in the august legislature and also to the country and to the people.

Another major initiative taken by Speaker Sangma was the convening of a special session of both the Houses of Parliament from 26 August to 1 September 1997 as part of the Golden Jubilee celebrations of India's Independence. The session took stock of the achievements and also set a national agenda for the future. Opening the special session, for the first time in Indian parliamentary history, the Speaker addressed the House and stressed the need for a second freedom struggle –'freedom from our own internal contradictions, between our prosperity and poverty, between the plenty of our resource endowments and the scarcity of their prudent management, between peace and tolerance and the current conduct sliding towards violence, intolerance and discrimination'. After the speech, there was an absolute agreement between the members that there might not have been a better way for things to come about. The members not only appreciated his call for the second freedom struggle but also the width and depth of issues covered by him. The *Observer* compared him with Lord Buddha. The headline of the *Observer* dated 1 September 1997 was: 'Cheerful and smiling Buddha makes an Indian tribe proud.'

After an intervention by him, the government had to include a recording of one of Netaji Subhash Chandra Bose's speeches in the programme for Parliament during the midnight sitting on 14–15 August. Only recordings of Mahatma Gandhi's and Jawaharlal Nehru's speeches had been planned. This announcement that a speech by Netaji would be played was greeted with a thunderous roar from the audience and a continuous thumping of desks. Then there was Netaji speaking in Hindustani. During the two-minute speech the entire House burst into spontaneous applause at the end of every sentence.

Women's empowerment and reservation of seats for women in the legislature are hotly debated nowadays. The initial platform for empowerment of women through political representation was laid by Sangma. He is a strong advocate of women empowerment. It may be partly because he belongs to a community which is matrilineal in nature and he has seen how women not only in his community but also in his state contribute to economic development and nation building. It is because of this inner urge to give women a greater political platform that Sangma had guided the constitution of a Joint Parliamentary Committee for considering the eighty-first constitutional amendment which seeks to enhance the presence of women in Parliament. He also advocated the formation of a Standing Joint Parliamentary Committee on Empowerment of Women. On his initiative, the Specialized Inter-Parliamentary Conference of the Inter-Parliamentary Union (IPU) on Partnership between Men and Women in Politics was hosted by the Indian Parliament in 1997. He also chaired the sixtieth Conference of the Presiding Officers of Legislative Bodies in India held in New Delhi in March 1997, and the sixty-first Presiding Officers Conference in Shimla in March 1998. He was strictly of the opinion that the chair in the legislative bodies, whether the Speaker himself or the deputy Speaker or any other, was a highly sanctified institution. Its occupant should not yield to undesirable temptations and should especially take care that the exercise of his authority did not disrupt the due processes of the Constitution and the law. He also emphasized the need for time management in the House by the presiding officers and advised them to learn the art of transacting business through consensus. He was of the opinion that the presiding officers should calculate the cost of each second of their House time and give wide publicity for this so that public awareness about and resentment against wastage of House time were generated.

As Speaker, Sangma also led Indian parliamentary delegations to various important international forums. He led the delegations to the forty-second and forty-third Commonwealth Parliamentary Association Conferences in Kuala Lumpur in August 1996 and in Port Louis in September 1997, respectively. He also led Indian parliamentary delegations to the ninety-sixth Inter-Parliamentary Union Conference in Beijing in September 1996 and the ninety-eighth Conference in Cairo in September 1997. Sangma also headed the Indian parliamentary delegation to the second Conference of the Association of SAARC Speakers and Parliamentarians held in Islamabad in October 1997. He chaired the Inter-Parliamentary Specialized Conference of the IPU on 'Towards Partnership between Men and Women in Politics'. The first ever Conference of the Chairmen and Members of the Public Accounts Committees of SAARC Parliaments was also held in New Delhi in August 1997 during his eventful tenure.

Sangma was an extremely popular presiding officer, respected for his knowledge of rules and even more for his innate understanding of parliamentary traditions. He was equally at his best outside the House. He participated in many social gatherings and intellectual interactions organized by activist groups with great enthusiasm, guided objective and non-partisan debates on national issues, and added a new social and public dimension to the office of the Speaker.

His concern for decorum, freedom and dignity of the House earned him the reputation of an outstanding parliamentarian. His smiling face had a great impact on the minds of the members of the House. What, however, made Sangma acceptable to political parties of all shades, as a Speaker, was his ability to earn the confidence of people on both sides of the House. His abiding concern for the underprivileged and his tireless endeavours to eradicate poverty and remove socio-economic inequalities have endeared him to the masses. Indeed, he is a man of the masses with an international standing. It is the humane side of Sangma which has brought him a large number of friends amongst the people at large.

By virtue of his vast experience as a parliamentarian, knowledge of rules of parliamentary business and practices and his knack of handling tricky situations with wit and common sense, Sangma left an indelible imprint of his personality on the office of the Speaker of the Lok Sabha in a short span of less than two years. His cherubic face, hearty laugh, quick wit, boundless enthusiasm, impeccable demeanour and earthy wisdom made him a household name, with people from all over the country showering compliments for the rare skill with which he conducted the proceedings of the House. In the media, too, his tenure as Speaker was highly appreciated.

Sangma was also a good administrator. During his stint as Speaker, he exerted a positive influence on the administration of the Lok Sabha secretariat and its most prestigious component – the Parliament Library. Any member of the staff was free to meet him to air any grievance and to offer suggestions for improvement, and if found correct and acceptable, prompt decisions were taken. This created a picture of happiness and efficiency in the Lok Sabha secretariat. He is still fondly remembered by the officers and staff of the secretariat for the steps taken by him and for the care he had shown towards them. This is a measure of the love Sangma enjoys from people of any strata of our social and political life.

LIFE BEYOND OFFICE

The General Elections of 1998 saw Sangma returning to the Lok Sabha once again. He has been elected to the Lok Sabha a record consecutive nine times in 1977, 1980, 1984, 1991, 1996, 1998, 1999, 2004 and 2006 (by-election). During these years, he held important portfolios in the government like commerce, industry, home, coal, labour and information and broadcasting, and took several policy initiatives which were by and large people-centric. He spent his longest span as a minister in the labour ministry and took many labour welfare measures. During his stint as labour minister there was a sharp decline in industrial strikes and lockouts because of his sensitivity towards the labour and the working class. He was one of the most articulate and dignified Speakers irrespective of whether in the government or in the Opposition benches, listened to by all with respect and attention. He resigned from the Lok Sabha on 10 October 2005 on the issue of bifurcation of the Meghalaya State Board of School Education (MBOSE) and the police firing on innocent people which resulted in the death of nine persons.

Sangma is a nationalist from the core of his heart and this feeling of nationalism and Indianness led him to part with his own party to join the Nationalist Congress Party (NCP) on the issue of a nationalized citizen being projected as the prime minister of India. He defended his action on issues of principle of nationality. Without personal rancour, Sangma said that manning the high office of the head of the government was not merely an exercise in fulfilling legal requirements. Transcending law, the incumbent's roots in the country and the genus and values going with them were equally important. To put his thought in simple words, Sangma is an Indian from the core of his heart and he wanted a natural-born citizen of India as prime minister. Being a true tribal, he has complete faith in indigenous leadership.

Besides this nationalist spirit, another area which is very close to his heart is ethics and morality in public life. He created a group of parliamentarians to report on ethics and standards in public life. He said that we should be concerned with ethics in governance for its own sake and proactively. The first principle of ethics in our democracy should be that political parties and legislators stand accountable to the people in terms of their manifesto promises. Political ethics, according to Sangma, demand that there should be understanding amongst all political parties for the abolition of the 'mass transfer industry'. Sangma holds that otherwise the clone of politicians and civil servants will come to wield authority without responsibility or accountability, undermining the very basis of our parliamentary democracy. Corruption becomes rampant when service providers become financiers of elections. Sangma also advocates that laws relating to qualifications for and disqualification of members of legislative bodies on the grounds of criminality need to be comprehensively reviewed and re-established, leaving no scope for doubts and interpretations or for arbitrary exercise of powers by election officials. Further, he urges the political parties to play their role in this regard. A strong advocate of integrity of democratic institutions, Sangma worries about trends of institutional decay which could undermine good governance in the country. He is particular about safeguarding the integrity of the institutions of governorship, the prime minister's office, Election Commission, Central Bureau of Investigation, Vigilance Commission and law-and-order and allied formations like the police and the internal security systems. He has openly criticized the setting up of the National Advisory Council and feels that the subjugation of the office of the prime minister to a supervisory body is a dangerous precedent. For his guts in expressing his beliefs and opinions openly, he might have suffered politically at certain times. But his qualities are rarely to be seen in the more advanced parts of India where, under the influence of ideas and isms which are foreign to our philosophy, we have forgotten our own heritage, our own system of governance and faith in our own leadership.

Sangma has specialized knowledge about population research. His speeches on the population problem are not only scientific but also loaded with practical solutions to the problem. He is very conscious of the fact that whatever development takes place in this country, whatever be the efforts at employment generation that we make, until and unless we are able to check population growth, these will not amount to much. He understands the difference between the rate of growth and pattern of growth of population, and according to him, if we are talking about arresting the present growth rate by overall stabilization, we are not correcting the trend. He could see the pattern of population growth in the BIMARU states (Bihar, Madhya Pradesh, Rajasthan and Uttar Pradesh) and its possible political implications as quite disturbing and therefore needing special area-specific strategies. He had also urged upon the government on the floor of the House to have an all-party conference on population growth and to convene a special sitting of Parliament to discuss this problem and to reach a consensus on the New Population Policy in our country.

QUOTA CONUNDRUM

Sangma is highly concerned about the representation of tribals in political and judicial domains. However, his stand on the highly sensitive issue of reservation policy is a unique example of political courage. Though he is a member of a scheduled tribe community which is a direct beneficiary of that policy, and though he believes in the necessity of reservation for protection of the weaker sections of the society, he is unhappy about its adverse effects on the social psyche of his people. Reservation, for him, can be used as a ladder provided the person who is riding has the willingness and the capability to reach the destination. He has always warned the tribals against complacency and their overdependence on the quota system. He believes that instead of unceasingly depending on reservation, the tribals, or for that purpose any underprivileged section, need to become capable enough to come on par with their counterparts. He warns the tribals that their 'psychology of dependence' on the quota system can give them medicine and engineering degrees, but it may not necessarily give them the knowledge to be good doctors and good engineers which will work against them. He believes that facilities in terms of schools, colleges and training centres should be provided to them but the tribals themselves should make proper use of these resources and stand on their own feet. He exhorts tribal students to use the opportunity given by reservation to come up and be at par with their advanced brothers and sisters without asking for lowering of qualifying marks either for admissions or for jobs. He lays strong emphasis on imbibing the spirit of competition in the minds of the tribal students. During his tenure as chief minister, Sangma strongly emphasized vocationalizing of education. He is one of the few politicians of the present generation who has always favoured reservation on the basis of economic criteria. The facilities of reservation, he believes, can be extended to those who are not scheduled castes or scheduled tribes but on the basis of economic criteria. This will not only bring parity in social and economic terms but also bring down the resentment level against the system of reservation itself. As a role model, Sangma has never used nor has he allowed his children to avail of the reservation system during their education and career. If P.A. Sangma or his children are in the limelight today, it is because of their ability to reach that level by virtue of their own efforts and merits and their proactive commitment to serve the people of the country. His family is a classic example of how tribal children can compete with others, and even surpass them, if groomed properly.

From many a platform, Sangma, without being constrained by his ministerial responsibilities and extreme caution, aired his views openly, clearly and boldly. He did stand for constitutional safeguards for rapid advancement of historically backward social groups like the ST, SC and OBC. But he wanted the safeguards in a way that would not divide the Indian society into 'we' and 'they', avoiding the strains they brought into inter-tribe and tribal/non-tribal relations which had tended to morph into 'ethnic conflicts' and 'caste wars'. He appreciated the plight of non-tribal students hard hit by the quota system and went forward to help them as generously as possible. He has helped a large number of non-tribal students financially and has even provided them with jobs after completion of their studies. This is possible only for a man with a vision and with a heart set on unity among all sections of the people.

A CRUSADER OF NUCLEAR NON-PROLIFERATION

Sangma believes that weapons of mass destruction such as nuclear weapons should never be used and they must be eliminated from the earth. The principles that can be adopted to reduce and eliminate nuclear arsenal and other conventional weapons of mass destruction should be non-discriminatory and reassuring of prosperity and peace for all people of the world. The view subscribed by Sangma regarding Pokhran II in May 1998 was that the test was not driven by considerations of peace but by security threats from the neighbouring countries. He favoured the separation of civil nuclear energy from military nuclear energy, and felt that non-separation would mean that all nuclear reactors were being used for military purpose thereby causing difficulties in access to nuclear fuel.

He felt that India must get over the cold war syndrome. We cannot afford to blow hot and cold between non-aligned theology and liberal diplomacy. In our own national interest, we must be pragmatic. We are not only the largest democracy but also the largest functioning democracy. Therefore, it is important that India should be respected at the international level.

PRIDE OF THE NORTH EAST

The entry of Sangma into Meghalaya politics from the Centre was not only a turning point in the life of this gentleman politician but in the development process and direction of the state as well. People are backward in Meghalaya only because they have not been given the opportunity and because there are no facilities. The visionary eyes of Sangma could see that the state of Meghalaya has tremendous potential for development, be it in the field of human resources or natural resources, including land resources available in the state. He had felt that establishment of railway links to the state would not only bring the isolation of its people to an end but also unleash the potentialities of exploring its mineral resources. Besides, the establishment of railway links to Meghalaya is crucial from a strategic point of view. From the defence and trade point of view also the railway network is important as the state borders Bangladesh, and so it should have a direct link with the rest of the country. Therefore, in the interest of the state of Meghalaya and its people and also in the national interest, Sangma participated in almost all debates on the demands for grants in the railways and categorically placed his demands for the railway link in the North East before the government through Parliament. His continuous pursuit of the matter on the floor of the House forced the government to put forth a proposal of constructing new lines in the six hill states of the North Eastern Region and construct a second bridge over the River Brahmaputra.

So far as the approach to the problems of the North East is concerned, Sangma believes that it should be 'peace through development'. Peace which is enforced on the people is not realized by them. Peace has to come from within, naturally. He has been quite critical about the implementation of the Armed Forces (Special Powers) Act, 1958, in Manipur. He has demanded that this Act be repealed because the Act has not only failed to achieve its objectives but has also become a symbol of state domination and repression. He fears that this may further isolate the tribals and prevent them from joining the mainstream. He has urged the people of Meghalaya and the North East to actively cooperate with the government in the overall development of the state and the region and at the same time to retain the natural simplicity, courage, honesty and confidence of the tribals. The role played by him for protection of the rights of the non-tribals in the state of Meghalaya is unparalleled in the history of the state.

The North East political scenario in the 1980s and early 1990s was quite different from the contemporary political scenario. In 1980, Sangma proposed formation of a separate ministry for the North Eastern Region or alternatively, if that was not possible for some reason or the other, formation of a separate ministry under the charge of the prime minister for the welfare of scheduled castes, scheduled tribes and minorities. In that ministry, there should be a separate cell to look after the North Eastern Region because a major part of that region is inhabited by scheduled tribes. Further, during that time there used to be a common governor for the five states in the North Eastern Region which created not only administrative inconvenience but constitutional difficulties also. It so happened that the governor would address the Assam Assembly talking against Meghalaya, in Manipur he would speak against Nagaland, in Nagaland against the Assam government and so on. Sangma took up this matter with the government and also on the floor of the House that separate governors may be appointed for all the five North Eastern states. These states now have separate governors. Indeed, political developments in the entire North East owe a lot to Sangma.

During his brief stint as chief minister, Sangma took several pragmatic measures to solve the state's problems. The Sangma government's prime concern was investment in infrastructure. As a member of Parliament, Sangma had urged the Centre to increase investments in the infrastructure of his state and the entire North East. He had realized that improvement in the transport and the communication system within the state and between the neighbouring states could solve the problem of price rise in Meghalaya. He, therefore, pleaded with the Central government to extend the railway network to the North Eastern Region and this was his vision in 1977–78. He also emphasized self-sufficiency in matters relating to food grains and urged upon the farmers that those commodities which could be produced in the state be produced by them.

Sangma adopted the Gandhian approach to development especially on matters relating to industrialization and economic development of the state. As a pragmatic administrator who knew the geographical terrain and natural resources of his state and the level of employment of his people, his emphasis was not on large-scale capital-intensive industries but small cottage and medium industries based on local resources and labour. Rural electrification was one area which Sangma believed could bring development at the micro level.

Sangma played an instrumental role in the setting up of the Shillong Development Authority and in the beautification of this popular hill station. He also set up a 100-bed hospital in Tura and made the Jawaharlal Nehru Sports Complex functional. He knew that the terrain of Meghalaya could not be developed without the farmers cultivating a scientific temper in agriculture and horticulture and proper implementation of the policies and projects in the right direction. He set up two soil-testing laboratories at Nongstoin and Williamnagar so that farmers could have access to the latest soil-testing technology. He believed that honest effort on the part of the government and motivation on the part of the farmers could lead to development of the state. Farmers, according to him, should not be left at the mercy of financial institutions. Public investments in agriculture should rise at the national level to reduce the dependency of farmers on private moneylenders and financial institutions. He tried to help the farmers to the extent possible. Many areas were declared *anawari* as a result of which short-term loans were converted into long-term loans and the farmers became eligible for fresh loans. A Land Commission was also set up for the whole state to ensure that the land-use pattern and forest policy went together. The measures taken by him in strengthening the public distribution system were unprecedented in the history of the state. He believed that the first and the foremost duty of the government was to ensure adequate and regular availability of essential commodities of good quality to the people. Therefore, Sangma took effective measures to strengthen the public distribution system in the state. The policy measures taken by him were non-discriminatory and gave equal importance to strengthening the PDS system in both the rural and urban areas in the state. He has always worked towards developing Meghalaya as an economically viable state and he believed that this viability could be achieved through internal resource mobilization rather that 100 per cent dependence on Central grants. In his words: 'As tribals, we must try to stand on our own feet because we always feel proud standing on our own feet. So, we must also try to mobilize our own resources. Our policy must be to reduce our dependence on grants so that we can be self-sufficient on our own.' As a step further in this direction, he constituted the Meghalaya Resource Mobilization Commission under the chairmanship of P.R. Kyndiah to find out ways and means to mobilize internal resources for the development of the state.

Sangma was a people's chief minister. In his residence, 'Rock Side', he used to meet 200 to 300 people every morning. He realized that most of the people came to meet him from far-off villages like the Dawki area, Khliehriat area, Garo Hills and West Khasi Hills, etc., except the young ones who visited him for jobs. Given the geographical terrain of the state and other practical reasons, it was not possible for the chief minister to visit each and every village to meet the people. Therefore, Sangma took the innovative measure of setting up centres for the people at the district levels so that they could forward their grievances to the chief minister which needed to be addressed by him. This established a link between the people, district administration and the chief minister's office; thereby, he could bring the administration and the chief minister's office closer to the people.

Development of education in the tribal state of Meghalaya or for that matter in other tribal areas also is a subject close to the heart of Sangma. His firm stand was that maintenance of administration of primary schools must remain with the state government and there should be no ad-hocism on this issue. Therefore, the Meghalaya Board of Primary School Bill, 1988, was passed when his government was in power in the state. With the passing of the Bill, the district administration of the education department was restructured and the administration of primary schools was taken over by the government from the District Councils, as functioning of primary schools was seriously jeopardized by the District Council managements. For example, teachers were not receiving their salary for three to four months which had led to great resentment among them and adversely affected the quality and level of teaching in primary schools; a dissatisfied and hungry teacher could not be expected to do justice to his pupils. Given this scenario, the takeover of the maintenance of primary schools by the government from the hands of the District Councils was a step in the right direction by the then government of the state. His government also introduced 10+2 system in the state which could help solve the unemployment problem in the state to a great extent because the whole concept of the 10+2 system of education is job-oriented.

Sangma believes that it is the duty of the tribal leaders to ensure that tribal culture, tribal identity, tribal institutions and tribal values are protected and preserved. He strengthened the tribal institutions like the Nokmas in Garo Hills, the Syiemship in Khasi Hills and the Dalois in Jaintia Hills. He believes that tribal institutions, if best used, can serve as good substitutes for the Panchayati Raj system in these areas. The popularity of Sangma was so phenomenal that the members of the Opposition have frankly admitted in the state legislature that they had never doubted his leadership. Atal Bihari Vajpayee, the former prime minister, has described him as the brand ambassador of the North East in the capital. He is certainly the brightest star of the North East.

AWARDS CONFERRED

Sangma was recognized both at the national and international levels for his work and contribution to public life. He was conferred the Michael John Roll of Honour of the Tata Workers' Union for distinguished contribution to the cause of labour and to the parliamentary system in 1997. He was also awarded the Golden Jubilee Award of the Indian National Trade Union Congress (INTUC) for outstanding contribution to the cause of the working class by Dr Shankar Dayal Sharma, the then President of India in 1997. Hardly does it happen that a labour minister is awarded by a labour union but it was Sangma's vision and his untiring work for the welfare of the labour class that brought him this award from a labour union. Sangma was also nominated Man of the Year by *Competition Success Review* (*CSR*, 1998) and he also received the Saraswati National Eminence Award in the category of Public Leadership from the South Indian Education Society, Mumbai, in January 2003. Further, Sangma received the Mother Teresa Beatification Honour, 2003, for outstanding services, achievement and contribution to society. Besides these institutional awards, the real award that he has got is the appreciation of the people whom he had served and represented. Sangma has been admired cutting across political divisions and ideologies and even respected by his opponents.

Sangma is a multifaceted personality. A man of letters, he has been closely associated with various social organizations and educational institutions. The people of Meghalaya will fondly remember him for his editorial skills during his stint as the editor of the Meghalaya daily *Chandambeni Kalrang.* He has also edited two volumes of the book *India in ILO* and another parliamentary publication, 'Into the Third Millennium: A Speaker's Perspective'. Few people know that Sangma is a polyglot who can speak Garo, English, Hindi, Assamese and Bengali with remarkable ease. He is a voracious reader too. Besides reading and writing, he also has a special liking for tribal, Western and Indian music.

His concern for larger social welfare and upliftment of the downtrodden led him to be associated with various social organizations like the Red Cross Society, Youth Hostels Association of India and educational institutions. He was instrumental in setting up night schools for poor and needy children in his constituency in Tura, Meghalaya. Social service and tribal welfare have always been his special areas of concern and attention. Sangma is also a very spiritual person. He clearly understands the world of difference between being spiritual and being religious and believes that spirituality is above any religion. He believes that the clear force of spiritualism can save us from moral degradation. Prayer, according to Sangma, can remove all doubts. Sangma says: 'We should not talk about religion of individuals. Instead, we should talk more about spiritualism of individuals. The emphasis should be on spiritualism and it is necessary to stop moral degradation in the country.' As a Christian, he is both religious and rational. For him, clear conscience is the best friend and guilty conscience is the greatest enemy. He had declared in Parliament that the tribals, whether they were Christians or not, were true citizens of this country and the impression that when a tribal became a Christian, he became a foreigner and ceased to be an Indian was a misconception.

To conclude, P.A. Sangma is a suave but simple, educated and secular person with a reputation for unwavering honesty – a personality who does not conform to the conventional image of the politician. Despite his liberal outlook and his wholehearted espousal of democratic and secular values, Sangma has never forgotten his roots. He is inextricably linked with the people of the North East, particularly Meghalaya, and the constituency which he has nurtured for more than three decades, Tura. Sangma believes that more than the laws it is the change of heart in those administering the country which is needed to improve the social and economic status of the poor, the tribals and the downtrodden. Re-education of administrative personnel can bring change in their outlook and this is essential for the restructuring of our social set-up to make it equitable and just. To the world at large, he is a successful parliamentarian, an efficient and popular minister and a non-partisan Speaker, but at heart he remains a simple family man, a son whom every parent would be proud to call their own, a loving husband and a caring father. The way he has brought up all his children to maturity and particularly the way he has groomed his daughters is admirable. He has never allowed his political stature to define his personality. He goes out of his way to help virtual strangers, and nobody is ever allowed to go away from his house feeling neglected, belittled or undermined. He is truly a man of the masses who professes and practises politics as a mission and not as a profession.

PART II

Articles

P.A. SANGMA: A GREAT LEADER WITH GREATER POTENTIAL

*S.C. Jamir**

As one who has been in public life for almost five decades, I have watched the rise of my esteemed friend, Mr P.A. Sangma, right from his early years in politics from close quarters. My admiration for him has, if anything, grown steadily with his meteoric rise in public life and I am really proud that he has attained the stature of a national leader within a short period.

I see a number of similarities between my own life and that of Mr Sangma's. Both of us came from humble tribal backgrounds. Both of us were law graduates. At the age of thirty, we were elected to Parliament from our respective states. Likewise, both of us served as Union ministers and then both had the privilege of becoming chief ministers of our respective states.

Mr Sangma is a man of many seasons. He was an outstanding student, lecturer, lawyer and journalist before joining politics. As things unfolded, he turned out to be one of the most popular leaders from the North East having been elected to Parliament nine times.

Sangma comes from the easternmost part of the country bordering Bangladesh. In spite of his modest background, he rose to his present stature by dint of his affable nature, brilliance, relentless struggle and work for the masses.

Mr Sangma was a disciplined and dedicated follower of the first chief minister of Meghalaya, Capt. Williamson A. Sangma.

My interactions with Mr Sangma increased when I was chief minister of Nagaland and he became a Union minister. Mr Sangma's return to state politics and becoming the chief minister of Meghalaya in 1988 provided us with an opportunity to work closely, both for the North Eastern Region as well as for the Congress party.

---

*The author was previously the governor of Maharashtra.

I found him to be extremely intelligent, having a grasp of the problems dealt by him. He is also a gifted orator. Few people know that Mr Sangma is a polyglot, who can speak Garo, English, Hindi, Assamese and Bengali with remarkable ease.

Mr Sangma's election as Speaker of the eleventh Lok Sabha brought to the fore his best innate qualities. The fact that he was elected as Speaker unanimously despite being a member of the Opposition is a testimony to his popularity across the political spectrum. By virtue of his vast experience as a parliamentarian, knowledge of rules of parliamentary business and practices, and his knack of handling tricky situations using wit and commonsense, he has left an indelible imprint of his work as the Speaker of the Lok Sabha. No wonder, Mr Sangma is reckoned among the best Speakers we have had in the history of Indian Parliament.

At the personal level, Mr Sangma comes across as a lovable and transparent person. Sporting a mischievous smile on his face, he can mix with anybody without any hassles. In fact, he has got all the good attributes required to become a great leader. Having worked with him closely for several years for the North Eastern Region and for the country, I know the tremendous capacity and potential Mr Sangma possesses as a national leader.

His decision to leave the Congress party hurt me. I was really sad and felt as if my right hand had been chopped off. Nevertheless, we continue to remain best friends.

As a much elderly person than he is, I have always felt that a leader of his calibre requires to be encouraged in all positive ways. I only wish and hope that together we shall be able to work jointly once again for the betterment of the country in general, and for the North Eastern Region in particular.

P.A. SANGMA: A UNIFIER

*Jaswant Singh**

My association with this outstanding Indian, a great representative of his people, a unifier, began in Parliament some decades back. A person of

*The author is a member of Parliament and former Union minister for external affairs and finance.

happy disposition, Shri Purno Sangma brought to his parliamentary duties a remarkably balanced and positive approach.

His tenure as a Speaker of the House will always be remembered as that of a wise steward, leading the House adroitly and far-sightedly. He is a unifier. It was under his speakership that the Parliament adopted a resolution, through a joint sitting of both the Houses, a truly historical document about how the members of Parliament ought to conduct themselves in Parliament and what their responsibilities were in regard to the House, as also the country.

I am glad that a book is to be published about his achievements. I commend this effort and wish it great success.

P.A. SANGMA: AS I KNOW HIM

*Nitish Kumar**

Sangma Saheb, I can say with confidence, is one of the most popular personalities in the Indian political scenario. Among a few faces who do not need any introduction, one is that of Shri P.A. Sangma. His smiling face welcomes each and everyone and the man in front of him does not need his introduction but has to introduce himself. I still remember the warmth of our first meeting. His simple and smiling face also reflects the three Ds, the character of determination, discipline and dedication, which are deeply rooted in his personality.

From a humble beginning in a small tribal village of the West Garo Hills district of the state of Meghalaya, what he has achieved is the result of the above-mentioned three Ds. It is not that he appeared like a shooting star in Indian politics; rather he began his political career as a Congress worker and gradually rose step by step.

Sangma Saheb is a man of many attributes, having been, in the course of his career, a lecturer, a lawyer and a journalist before he joined politics. In politics, his rise has been phenomenal. After spending a few years in state politics, his career in national politics began in 1977 when he was elected to the Lok Sabha in the sixth General Election. As a deputy minister, minister of state and Cabinet minister in the Union

*The author is the present chief minister of Bihar.

government, his performance in various portfolios is a matter of envy. He is well known for his meticulous homework, complete mastery of the subject in hand and a sharp and long memory. He was a minister who could reply to debates without any help from the official gallery. He is particularly sensitive towards labour and the working class. During his stint as labour minister, there was a sharp decline in industrial strikes and lockouts.

His performance as Speaker of the Lok Sabha was commendable. He maintained decorum, dignity and authority of the House with meticulous impartiality. He ensured that rules were observed by the members. He was successful in ensuring free debates, objective deliberations and healthy criticism.

His impartial handling of heated debates won the admiration of both the ruling coalition and the Opposition. His wit and sense of humour made long debates interesting and enjoyable. In order to maintain high tradition in political life, his principle was to maintain a standard of conduct both inside the House and outside. He expected the same from others.

Admiration is not a rule to be enforced, it comes directly from the heart. I admire Sangma Saheb and wish him all the best for the future.

~

P.A. SANGMA: WORKERS' OWN LEADER

*M.K. Pandhe**

I had occasions to interact with Shri P.A. Sangma when he was the minister of labour and later minister of coal in the Union Cabinet. The special feature in his official position was that he was always accessible to visitors. I remember meeting him on several occasions without even taking any prior appointment. Whenever he had official meetings during office hours he would give time at his residence.

He would always tell us that as a minister in the Central government he had to go by the official policies of the government. However, within that framework, whatever maximum he could do for the labour, he would be prepared to do. 'If you are not satisfied with my steps you are free to criticize and I will not object to that,' he used to tell us.

---

*The author is the serving president of CITU.

Smiling was a weapon in his armoury to meet the criticism of the trade unions. He would never get agitated even when the trade unions criticized the policies of his ministry. He would only smile and often it became his reply to the criticism. 'If I show any annoyance to criticism it would only encourage the critics,' he used to comment when we used to ask him why he always smiled.

He disliked the formality that generally marks the demeanour of ministers in this country. He was reluctant to read out written speeches and would speak extempore even in official meetings. Even if the written speech was circulated to the participants in the official meetings, he would make off-the-cuff comments from time to time to enliven the debate.

I remember once a seminar organized by the PHD Chamber of Commerce in Delhi on labour laws, which was inaugurated by Shri P.A. Sangma. The president of the organization in his introductory remarks proposed to change the Industrial Disputes Act by deleting Section 20A which provided taking clearance from the government before closing down any unit. In his speech, Shri Sangma sarcastically remarked whether the employers currently faced any difficulty to close any unit due to this provision in the law. He noted that so many units had been closed down when employers did not pay electricity bills and the supply of power was cut. The union raised disputes but the unit got closed down anyhow.

I was also one of the speakers in the seminar. When I met him during teatime he told me in the presence of the employers' representatives, 'I did not know that you are here in the seminar. Otherwise, I would not have made the observations in your presence. I thought it was only an employers' gathering.' The representatives of the employers also laughed at these comments.

The initiative taken by Shri P.A. Sangma on the question of the linking of trade policy with a social clause relating to the ratification of the ILO conventions was noteworthy. During the Indian Labour Conference under his presidentship, it decided to oppose linking of trade relations with ratification of the ILO conventions, a policy insisted by WTO provisions. Sangma thought of holding a conference of developing countries to evolve a common understanding among all developing countries. Accordingly, an international tripartite conference was held in Delhi under his presidentship which evolved a common understanding among a large number of developing countries to oppose linking of trade with a social clause.

All the trade unions in India took a common stand that they were for the Government of India accepting the core ILO conventions in a phased manner. However, they were not prepared to link up trade policies with ratification of these conventions, since it would adversely affect the trade of the developing countries. Already, at the global level, the share of the developing countries in world trade had been declining and such a step would further deteriorate the situation in the developing countries. The trade union movement in the developing countries would strive to get ratification of more ILO conventions through a national movement.

The successful tripartite meeting created a common understanding among the developing countries, and the WTO attempt to link trade relations with a social clause was not implemented. Shri P.A. Sangma's role in evolving this understanding among the developing countries is worth noting.

When he was the minister of coal, trade unions gave a strike notice for a higher bonus payment. Shri Sangma rushed to Kolkata and called a meeting of trade unions to discuss the matter. The management argued that due to the inadequate performance of Coal India Limited it was not possible to pay higher bonus to the workers, since the formula worked out for the coal industry did not provide it. The workers' representatives took the stand that workers were in no way responsible for the inadequate performance of the coal industry. They noted that if the management took effective steps, the trade unions were prepared to improve the performance of the coal industry. Shri P.A. Sangma found a solution to the problem. He told the management to grant higher bonus to the workers on the basis of the assurance given by the trade unions to ensure full cooperation in fulfilling the targets of production. The CIL management had to agree to the proposal and the strike was thus settled.

Once, in a tripartite meeting, some trade unions criticized the policy of the labour ministry in dealing with the problem of workers due to bureaucratic bungling. Shri P.A. Sangma retorted in the meeting, 'Unless our administration commits some mistakes how will you get the opportunity to speak?' Though the reply was addressed to the trade unions, it was actually meant for the officers whose functioning he wanted to criticize indirectly.

When the National Renewal Fund was established by the Government of India, it was not under the Ministry of Labour but was handed to the

Ministry of Industrial Development. We got the impression that Shri Sangma was not happy with this development but he could not officially say so.

The trade unions were always complaining that it was a National Retrenchment Fund. It was supposed to train the retrenched workers for new vocations but jobs were not available in that sector. At the insistence of the trade unions, Shri Sangma visited some of the education centres and stated in a joint meeting that he felt that such training could not lead to creation of new jobs. He agreed to take up the matter with the Ministry of Industrial Development, but not much progress was noticed. Ultimately, the fund ceased to operate. Shri Sangma commented, 'Such things happen in several government schemes. This is a part of our administration framework.'

It was a customary practice in the Ministry of Labour to call a meeting of the delegates for a dinner one day prior to a conference. Some informal discussion used to take place in which the labour ministers used to appeal for a cordial debate. However, Shri Sangma was of a different type. He used to say, 'Speak your views frankly in the meeting. Otherwise, the debate will be dull and there will be no fireworks. In the absence of this, the labour minister's concluding remarks will be a tame affair.'

Because of his frank remarks, he faced embarrassing moments with the officials at times. Somehow or the other, the officers also got used to this type of functioning. We in the trade unions, however, used to enjoy the situation.

One day I myself, along with some trade union representatives, visited his house and commented about the excessive security arrangements made for the ministers. He replied, 'I do not know why they are making so much security arrangements. I have done no harm to anyone; why would anyone be interested in attacking me.' He further laughed and said, 'If I am kidnapped no one would come forward to pay any ransom. Many people would think that it is a good riddance. The prospective kidnappers know this and hence nobody would be interested in kidnapping me.'

Many things can be written about him. Politically, we belong to different camps. However, memories of such personalities who come in contact with us, but have different political perceptions, do occupy some space in the hard disk of one's memory. I have just drafted some remembrances of Shri Sangma. They just play a role in highlighting the characteristics of his personality. There is no other purpose except this in writing these remembrances.

~

P.A. SANGMA: AS I SEE HIM

*B.B. Dutta**

This write-up is a humble attempt to sketch, against a political canvas, the profile of one of the most controversial North East politicians of our times. It is about a man I know and the political personality I have worked with so closely and intimately for more than three decades. So, as I pen down my thoughts and reflections on Shri P.A. Sangma, that diminutive political giant from the Garo Hills of Meghalaya, my mind and my thoughts fly back in time. It is a thrilling experience to relive those hectic days beginning from the 1960s when a new awakening, after centuries of slumber, seized upon the minds and hearts of the hill tribes of North East India. It is also a highly educative journey to revisit those tumultuous events, the conflicting aspirations and interests of different social groups, the role of their leaders and the excitement they created and to see them afresh against the deep calm of the still of a perspective made so clear by the passage of time.

Two historic events set the pace and determined the complex nature of that awakening known as the 'autonomy movement' which basically aimed at the protection of indigenous identities and cultures. First, the Naga rebellion close on the heels of India's freedom. It was a movement that aimed at total sovereignty and complete independence for the Naga people. Secondly, the reports of the States Reorganization Commission recommending reconstitution of the provinces of erstwhile British India into states of the Indian republic on the basis of the language in which they, as small ethnic communities, perceived a threat to their political, economic and cultural freedom.

I had joined St Anthony's College in the year 1962, the year of the Chinese aggression, as a lecturer in economics, and I could see how the college was playing a role in that awakening. St Anthony's was at that time probably the largest college in the region where students from more

*The author is a former member of the Rajya Sabha.

than eighty-five tribes and communities of the North East mixed and mingled. A large number of movement leaders operating from different platforms came out of this college. Its academic culture, charged with the inspired teaching of a batch of distinguished teachers, possibly created a space for freedom-loving youngsters to respond to challenges thrown by the sudden and rapid changes taking place in and around them. The atmosphere produced a bonanza of political activists, the likes of which are yet to be produced again in the region. Mr Hoover Hynewtta, a student who became a member of Parliament, made his mark as an eloquent parliamentarian. Mr G.G. Swell, a teacher, became not only a member of Parliament but rose to the position of deputy Speaker of the Lok Sabha. Mr Muivah, the rebel Naga leader who became a great political figure next only to Phizo, was an Anthonian. In an interview given at Bangkok and widely covered by the media, Muivah said that he drew a lot of inspiration in developing his political ideas from being a student of St Anthony's and particularly mentioned the name of Prof. Bibhuti Gupta, a brilliant teacher heading the Department of Political Science. A large number of North East MLAs, MPs, Speakers, ministers and chief ministers were ex-Anthonians. Once, over a dinner party hosted by the college in honour of a prominent minister, Rev. Father Joseph, the principal of the institution jokingly told his distinguished guest, 'Sir, I can, if I want to, preside over any Cabinet, overground or underground. I can make or unmake governments in any part of the North East simply because my boys are there.' But nobody at that time could imagine that the one who would surpass them all was indeed a national leader in the making and had left the college only a couple of years back.

I first met P.A. Sangma or Purno, as he is locally and popularly known, during his registration as an undergraduate student in St Anthony's College in the years 1966–69, and I remember him as a student who did make an impression. An impression that grew in richness over the years as he moved up in life from one phase to another. He was in my class, economics being his pass subject. In those days, very few good students would join the arts or humanities stream. Science was in vogue and engineering the goal of all promising students. Courses in arts honours were made up mostly of second divisioners with very few first divisioners – at times none could be found. So, whenever a bright student was found it became a source of joy for the teachers concerned. I remember we used to discuss in the college common room such students by name while discussing student profiles and impressions. P.A. Sangma's name cropped up frequently and prompted me to take a special interest in him in the class. He would sit silent and attentive. As I saw him more and more, I felt something I knew not what. But what impressed me most was not that he appeared to be a bright student but some other features that dwelt in this budding youngster. His diminutive physical frame, plainly and cleanly dressed, gave an indication of the very humble background he came from. But his two deep penetrating eyes radiating an inner intelligence and the mysterious smile he wore on his face not only overshadowed those externalities but rather blended so well that he looked a picture of simplicity and charm.

After securing a master's in political science along with a law degree, he started practising at Tura district court and joined the Indian Youth Congress. When I heard this, I was quite surprised by his choice. Regional parties were reigning supreme and in Meghalaya there was no hope for the Congress at that time, especially with regional stalwarts such as Capt. W.A. Sangma and B.B. Lyngdoh leading the APHLC government. No youth with any political aspirations then would ever look at a national political party. Sangma's first choice, therefore, at that early stage in life, in the midst of opposite currents sweeping the minds of the tribal masses, was a clear indication that he had from the very beginning a different vision of India in which he visualized a place of honour for his people. As a Youth Congress leader, he fought tooth and nail against Capt. W.A. Sangma and his APHLC, denouncing regionalism, an emotion that is the prime cause of inhibiting progress.

There was a sudden change in the political situation with the declaration of National Emergency in June 1975. In 1976, the regionalist chief ministers of the North East decided to join Congress at the Jawahar Nagar AICC Session in Guwahati. In March 1977 when Mrs Indira Gandhi ordered the Lok Sabha elections, Capt. Sangma of Meghalaya displayed statesman-like acumen when he decided to nominate Shri P.A. Sangma, his trenchant critic and a street fighter, for the Lok Sabha seat on a Congress ticket. As an intellectual member of the Meghalaya PCC, I was close to state Congress leaders but Capt. Sangma also received us with open arms and I found myself in the election committee which decided Shri P.A. Sangma's nomination. I remember how Capt. Sangma silenced growing criticism for not selecting any of the veterans from his erstwhile APHLC by citing appropriate reasons. He told the committee, 'In Parliament, we need people who can cope with the demands of national politics and protect our regional interests. I have a strong feeling that he has the intelligence and necessary courage to respond to both. Let us give this promising young man a chance.' It was a compliment and a prophetic statement. Capt. Sangma earned a lot of respect and admiration from the members of the original state Congress for choosing this young tribal from the Garo Hills whose first choice was a national political party like the Congress.

From then on there was no looking back for Purno. He continued to make his mark as he moved in life since his student days from one stage to another. At this juncture, it would be prudent and appropriate for me to narrate a few apparently small anecdotes which may otherwise go unrecorded and be easily forgotten. To my thinking, these stories reveal a lot about Purno Sangma, the hero of this narration. He won the 1977 election to the Lok Sabha hands down in the midst of the worst ever defeat the Congress party had suffered in history. The sixth Lok Sabha into which he made his first entry lasted for only thirty-two months. The fight for leadership to snatch the control of the party and the near-total rejection of whatever Mrs Indira Gandhi stood for resulted in attempts to throw her out from the political arena. The struggle for power rocked not only the Congress but all political parties, the Parliament and the nation.

Crises are an opportunity for true leaders to flourish and Mrs Gandhi played a flawless innings from an unimaginably difficult and hostile wicket of Indian politics. This was, therefore, also an ideal period for the probationers to have political schooling to train themselves in the political art of conducting the affairs of the republic. Shri P.A. Sangma again proved to be an adept and good student. Guided by Capt. Sangma, he remained for a while in the official Congress platform after Mrs Gandhi had split the party and formed her own party, namely the Indian National Congress (Indira). P.A. Sangma maintained for a while a silent neutrality between the INC and the INC(I) and the time was utilized by Capt. Sangma to organize all the small PCCs of the North East to take a common stand on national politics and join INC(I) together. This resulted in the formation of a platform in the name of North East Hill Leaders Conference, and through intense dialogues all the hill leaders who had joined the Congress in the Jawahar Nagar Session of 1976 arrived at a consensus, true to the political tradition of the tribes, to join INC(I) led by Mrs Gandhi just before the historic Chikmagalur by-election. P.A. Sangma with his feet firmly planted on the crease became more and more articulate, ingenious and active in Parliament as a follower of Mrs Gandhi.

The Janata Party which had wrested power from the Congress collapsed under the weight of its own inherent contradictions, and in the 1980 General Elections Mrs Gandhi once again came back to power with a two-thirds majority. Shri P.A. Sangma made his second triumphant entry into the seventh Lok Sabha (January 1980) on an INC(I) ticket. His capability in dealing with issues advancing sound arguments and his understanding of the subject attracted his leader's attention. He was taken into the AICC as a joint secretary and after a brief and highly successful spell there, he was inducted into the Union ministry as deputy minister for industries. This was the beginning of his climb up the national executive ladder.

As deputy minister, he found, to his dismay, that no files were coming to him. The Cabinet minister in charge of industries was ignoring his presence leaving him with no work. True to his courage to face challenges head on, he did something which others normally do not do. He told Mrs Gandhi, 'Madam, there is no work for me. I should better be working in the AICC where there is a lot of work.' Remedy followed quickly and files started coming in.

As an executive, he moved up quickly because of his good performance and began to appear in the national limelight as more and more responsibilities were entrusted to him. As a minister of state for commerce, he did very well and developed a very good relationship with the late Shri V.P. Singh, who was then heading the ministry and later became the prime minister of a non-Congress government. Members of Parliament and leaders from all political parties found in P.A. Sangma a very fair and understanding minister without any bias against any party and with an uncanny capacity to go into the heart of any problem brought before him, with the ability to take prompt decisions courageously. This quality of his became more evident when as minister of coal he turned the Coal India Limited from a company in the red to a profit-making enterprise. His appointment as labour minister, a position which normally politicians used to avoid for being infertile and ridden with insoluble problems caused primarily by politically guided labour unions, was taken by many as a kind of demotion. But within months, the labour ministry found itself so activated that it rose in status, and an increasing number of departments under various ministries found themselves answerable to its queries and had to become amenable to its suggestions. Sangma was being fondly mentioned by all as the best labour minister of India.

A small example may be given which will reveal a lot about his remarkable perception and understanding of human relations and the way he used to utilize this knowledge to influence work culture and productivity. I remember how he inspired the officers and engineers of Coal India to work beyond time by visiting the different units and personally going into the pits and working with them. And then one day he announced a dinner party to be hosted by him in honour of all the wives of the officers to felicitate them for the support they had given to the menfolk, for the time they should have got from their husbands which they did not get and for having to attend to all the duties of nurturing the children for which the husbands' contribution was missing, and to attend to assorted works they are not normally supposed to attend to. So in recognition of the time and energy they contributed, he presented each one of them with a beautiful wristwatch which I think they wore not so much on their wrists as in their hearts. No wonder that he attracted national attention by turning the ever-losing Coal India into a fertile profit-making enterprise. Indeed, an inspiring example of how to bond different categories of people with diverse backgrounds and direct their energies to accomplish tasks in the mission of nation building.

As labour and coal minister, he developed a close friendship with the trade union leaders and Opposition leaders, particularly from the Left parties, who controlled the union activities. He used to accommodate any genuine request for help and even went further by financially supporting their labour welfare projects. They also reciprocated by maintaining a reasonably peaceful stance on the labour front. But at the same time, he would never tolerate nonsense. He attacked the leftist union activities which had affected very seriously the work culture in West Bengal and Tripura in his characteristic style and with disarming good humour. He popularized a slogan in Bengali, and expressed it in his own inimitable style of speaking that language: '*Amra asle gale maina pabo, overtime dile kaam korbo*.' Which translated means: Our salary is for coming to office and going back home. But if we are expected to work, we must be paid overtime. I saw how the Left leaders including their members of Parliament took the barb laughingly, feeling guilty at the same time, because of the naked truth it revealed without doing anything to strain the relationship with Sangma whom they loved and considered a friend in need.

Once, while he was touring the North Eastern Region as commerce minister, he displayed a marvellous way of sending an unpalatable message across without antagonizing anybody. A press correspondent had drawn his attention to a case of cheating committed by tribal businessmen on their local non-tribal counterparts. Purno laughed and quipped, 'I am delighted to hear this. Our fellow tribals are coming of age. I shall be most happy when they will be able to cheat businessmen coming from Calcutta or Delhi.' The remark was widely covered by the media and enjoyed by the tribals and non-tribals alike. It had the effect of bringing two different social psyches to develop a better understanding.

On election campaign in Mizoram, he did a similar thing. He was then the Union minister of state for home affairs. A wave of hatred against non-Mizos was sweeping the hills. With Chief Minister Lalthanhawla by his side on the dais, he told the huge gathering, 'You call non-Mizos Vai which means foreigners. And you say, this is not their land and they must leave Mizoram. They must not have the right to vote or do business here. Now nobody dares to question your devotion to Lord Jesus. But may I ask you one thing, was Jesus a Mizo or a Vai?' The crowd listened to him with rapt attention without any protest from anyone. The speech did not erode the Congress vote base as was feared. It was a direct hit to puncture the cloud of communalism and regionalism that had enveloped the minds and hearts of the people arising from an exaggerated fear of losing their identity and culture. Here was a message to have self-confidence and stand up with courage. And he himself demonstrated that courage to say this in an election meeting which no other leader before or after him had ever uttered.

He repeated the same daring in the difficult and highly sensitive political territory of Nagaland. For a small assembly constituency with only several thousand voters, a candidate had to spend lakhs and lakhs of rupees to make a serious bid to win elections. Village people used to say, 'They come only in times of elections to win power and make money. We can get something only at that time. We want money.' The situation was such that it was sheer nonsense to abandon the policy of spending huge sums of money if a party had to make an impact in the elections. Sangma felt very bad about this ideology and kept on telling people in all the election rallies, 'Please remember that this flow of cash is dangerous. Cash is like fire. It spreads quickly and burns all our social and cultural values, destroys our bonding and makes our tribal societies bankrupt. If values are gone, what remains with us?' It was a message that sank deep into the minds of the brave Nagas living in the interiors. It worked silently and slowly. If today some changes in some areas are visible, the credit goes to leaders like Sangma.

In his capacity as the chairman of the North East Congress Coordination Committee of which all Pradesh Congress Committees of the region were members, he spoke with devastating frankness in his address at Pasighat, in Arunachal Pradesh, 'In a democracy, you have every right to make legitimate demands and agitate for realizing them. But have a look at what we have already got during the last couple of decades. For a few thousand voters we have one MLA. But in the rest of India one MLA is for about two lakh voters or so. We have a development block for about thirty thousand people which is less than one-fifteenth of the population entitled to have a block elsewhere in India. The size of our districts and our states is small, but we have the same administrative set-up with required number of officials. The same is true about the number of ministers. More and more examples can be given. My point is, are we utilizing these big advantages for the good of our people and of the state? Or are we trying only to improve our individual gains at the cost of our fellow tribals, blaming others for all the ills that afflict us? Will this blame game help us? Today we have a lot of power with us. We have to be confident and learn to take responsibility.' No hypocrisy, no flattery and no pampering, only an example of a fearless attempt to politically educate people to develop a healthy public opinion.

I can never forget that evening at Dimapur (Nagaland) before the commencement of the conference of the North East Congress Coordination Committee due next morning. As its general secretary, I had authored a couple of reports relating to the economic and infiltration problems of the region after a painstaking effort to collect some authentic facts and data. The second report contained a considerable number of pages on infiltration. I showed him the same which formed a part of the general secretary's report for his approval. He read every paragraph line by line, his face brightened and he said, 'Yes, we will pass it in the conference tomorrow.' He called at once for a closed-door meeting of the PCC presidents and chief ministers and explained in detail why they should agree to pass it unanimously. All were convinced. I was delighted to see his clear understanding of the menacing problem and the implications of changing demography in the geopolitics of the region and their possible impact on India and her true location in Asia. The report made a big impact on the nation and its neighbourhood.

His stand on the highly sensitive issue of reservation policy is yet another unique example of political courage. A member of the very scheduled tribe which is a direct beneficiary of that policy, he is unhappy about its adverse effects on the social psyche of his people. Promoting irresponsible demands backed by an increasingly fostered 'dependence psychology', the policy kills the power of initiative and the courage to take responsibility that are so crucial for all-round progress of the people. He did not like to wear the badge of 'Scheduled Tribe' and exhorted tribal students to use the opportunity given by reservation to come up to be at par with their advanced brothers and sisters without asking for lowering of qualifying marks either for admission or for jobs. None of his two daughters and two sons ever claimed any concession and their parents taught them to tap what is deep within them and grow shoulder to shoulder with others. His family is an example of how tribal children can compete and even surpass others, if groomed properly. From many a platform, he, without being bothered by his ministerial responsibilities and ever throwing caution to the wind, aired his views openly and boldly. He did stand for constitutional safeguards for rapid advancement of historically backward social groups like the ST, SC and OBC. But he wanted them in a way that would not divide the Indian society into 'we' and 'they', avoiding the strains it brought into inter-tribe and tribal–non-tribal relations that had developed into a phenomenon called ethnic conflict and caste war. He appreciated the plight of non-tribal students hard hit by the quota system and went forward to help them as generously as he did the tribal students. I know a large number of non-tribal students who got help in getting admissions in various private institutions. The poor among them were helped financially and even provided with jobs after completion of their studies. This is possible for a man with a vision whose heart is set on unity among all sections of Indians.

P.A. Sangma became Speaker of the eleventh Lok Sabha. His unanimous election as Speaker of the Lok Sabha with spontaneous support from all parties at a time when political instability rocked the republic is a record unbroken till now. It was the result of the goodwill he earned and the unique leadership qualities he displayed as a minister, spending every ounce of his energy to be just and fair to all without compromising in any way the interest of the nation.

These qualities further flourished when he demonstrated, while presiding over the sessions, many of them turbulent, that he respected difference of opinion 'which is the first element of democracy' and that he enjoyed dealing with such 'democratic' turbulence. He would appreciate the thinking part of anything said, and reject with tact and good humour what must be rejected without wasting time. The entire nation, particularly the youth, would get glued to the TV telecast to watch with avid interest P.A. Sangma presiding over sessions of Parliament. Shri Atal Bihari Vajpayee developed great love and admiration for Sangma, and Sangma reciprocated it so spontaneously that their relationship often crossed party lines even in dealing with highly contentious political issues. P.A. Sangma, with his Congress and secular background, and Shri Atal Bihari Vajpayee under the shadow of Hindutva added to the strength of the democracy, invigorating its roots with lively debates with values, the standards of which were in a steady state of decline.

P.A. Sangma also cast a positive influence in the administration of the Lok Sabha secretariat and its most prestigious component, the Parliament Library. Any member of the staff was free to meet him to air any grievance and offer suggestions for improvement, and if these were found correct and acceptable, prompt decisions were taken. This created a picture of happiness and efficiency in the functioning of the Speaker's secretariat. When I visit the Parliament Library, I come across a good number of officers who make eager enquiry about Sangma and would like to know when he is going to play a role again at the Centre. This is a measure of love Sangma enjoys from people of any strata of our social and political life.

Besides all these, the one more courageous decision he took will always linger in my memory. It was at the time of the Golden Jubilee celebration of India's freedom. The programme was under preparation. It was decided that after the opening songs selected speeches of Mahatma Gandhi and Jawaharlal Nehru would be played for two minutes each. Mrs Krishna Bose, who was then a member of the Lok Sabha and who hails from Netaji's family, came up with a suggestion to the Speaker that two minutes should also be allotted for playing a selected portion from one of the recorded speeches of Netaji Subhash Chandra Bose. Some of us belonging to different political parties formed an informal group and I was asked to fix an appointment with the Honourable Speaker. We were not very sure of a positive result as some serious efforts on the part of some MPs were required to get Netaji's portrait installed in the Central Hall of Parliament. And that too as late as on 23 January 1978, under a changed political climate. However, we met Sangma and put forward our proposal. He thought for a few seconds and then with his characteristic smile said, 'Why not? I think it is a very good suggestion.' He called the officials concerned and requested them to feed it into the draft programme for discussion and a final decision by the committee concerned. With his full and firm support, a decision was taken to allot two minutes to Netaji's speech.

In the inauguration ceremony of the Golden Jubilee, all the three speeches were played. It shall remain an abiding memory for those who witnessed the historic occasion. First, Mahatma Gandhi's speech in Hindi was played and then Nehru's famous 'Tryst with Destiny' speech in English. The Central Hall of Parliament packed with national and international dignitaries, including the Honourable Speaker of the House of Commons, UK, and MPs of both the Houses of Indian Parliament, heard the speeches with rapt attention and each speech was greeted with loud applause. Then came Netaji's speech. There was an electrifying change in the atmosphere. Almost the entire House stood up in thunderous applause. It just happened. Nobody planned it. It was so spontaneous that some high dignitaries sitting in the front were taken by surprise. Many of us remembered that moment when a free democratic India for which Subhash Bose sacrificed everything paid a tribute to this illustrious son of Mother India whose contributions are always sought to be played down by the rulers and the English-speaking intellectuals for some mysterious reasons. This tribute demonstrated how he had become a part of the collective consciousness of the people of this land, and it is from there that he continues to influence the course of our march with destiny. It also demonstrated the courage of one man P.A. Sangma who exercised his prerogative as the Speaker. Otherwise, it could have been cleverly stalled. Incidentally, Sangma never compromised on the question of protocol regarding the chair of Speaker and he displayed his unflinching loyalty to this institution, firmly rejecting any attempts that would even slightly affect its dignity irrespective of the direction they came from.

It is at this stage that his popularity reached an all-time high crossing all barriers of ethnicity, language and religion. Leaders from India's north, south, east and west took a great liking for him. His name and fame travelled to the countries of South and South-east Asia and Central Asia where people saw in him something of their own. The West took notice of him with expectations. He was being talked of as India's future prime minister.

Though he came from the small state of Meghalaya having only two Lok Sabha seats and one Rajya Sabha seat, from a Christian minority with a share of only about 2 per cent of India's population, and from a scheduled tribe numbering less than ten lakh, the heart of democratic India was broad and sound enough to give him space to rise to this height. But it was also handicapped in its functioning because of the inherent resistance coming from party mechanism preventing the fullest expression of the 'will' of the people.

Then came the clash and the eclipse. He walked out of the Congress to form with other kindred souls the Nationalist Congress Party (NCP), defending his action on issues of principles of nationality. The Congress, however, re-emerged stronger while the NCP failed to politically capitalize on the stand it took. A large number of people belonging to different social groups keep on harping that his political eclipse is a great loss to the country. It should not have been allowed to happen. His services must be reutilized. Again, there are many who think that he committed, for whatever reasons, a grave error in political judgement by going the way he did by damaging his own political career in the process. Be that as it may, the question continues to tantalize: whether his current fate was the by-product of misplaced ambition or whether it was the deliberate outcome of the political undercurrent within the Congress.

There is, however, truth in both contentions. But I, for one, have a different view of the man, knowing him so closely as I do. It was a clash of visions, between the true vision of India and the parasitic vision of the all-powerful party. He has always seemed to me to be one with the spirit of India, her cultural values and political ethos so strong in his own tribal system of governance. It is a quality which many of us lack in the more advanced parts of India, where under the influence of ideas and isms foreign to our philosophy, we have become forgetful of our own heritage.

The battle revealed the Achilles heel of the man who had never lost an election yet. He took politics as a mission, not as a profession, unlike so many of his creed. In a party based on parliamentary democracy, the party is all-powerful and not the people. A party member, however senior or powerful, who carries a vision for the people, must first convince his party of his vision. Failing to do so, despite the conviction of the wisdom, has only one route: create a new party whatever the pain and costs involved. This is the system we have and as the system is not going to change, it is better not to quarrel with it. The easy option is to fall in line, follow the leader and not ask questions. It is the best way to power within the party system. The phenomenon of dynastic rule or absence of strong opposition in our democracy is best explained by the fact that for stability and success, we need a leader who has the pedigree to lead in 'presidential style' in a party based on parliamentary democracy. There is no room for any visionary leader to be born from the common people of India. No room for such individuals to take momentous decisions required for implementing strategic policies. Incidentally, even charismatic leaders who risked taking strategic decisions could not carry them to their logical conclusions because of party considerations. The history of more than six decades of freedom bears testimony to this leadership failure in the first Republic of India.

Sangma failed for obvious reasons. After the last US presidential elections, there was a lot of discussion and talks among political experts and intellectuals on the scope of an 'Obama phenomenon' happening in India. The answer to my mind is 'No'. Obamas die in the labour rooms of political parties. As parties become more and more dependent on hypocrisy, flattery, money and muscle power, individuals with independent minds or visions of their own are either aborted or, worse, strangulated the moment they indicate the rigidity of their moral spine.

The other day Sangma told me he was writing his autobiography. No doubt it will enthrall its readers with anecdotes on the epic saga of a tribal boy's journey from a Garo village of Meghalaya to the Speaker's chair of the world's largest democracy. No doubt it will be an Indian version of the American 'Log Cabin to White House'. It will once again demonstrate to the world the power of the indomitable spirit of man irrespective of his origin or creed and how Indian democracy has the elasticity to accord space and dignity to such spirit. Sangma has seen how it all happened; he is the product of the Constitution of India, with all its merits and demerits, and if the man is to be believed, Indian democracy has a lot more to offer and give its people. Purno has often spoken of the need to revisit, review and restructure the Constitution. No doubt he will speak extensively on the subject in his autobiography. We shall wait with bated breath for what he has to say on the second Republic of India which lies in the womb of the future.

P.A. Sangma is sixty-four now, an age of mellow prudence and sagacity. He has already shown that tribal India pulsates with the heart of the nation and that tribal leaders can shine as the best jewels in the diadem of Mother India. The nation expects a lot more from him.

PART III

Select Speeches in Lok Sabha

POLITICAL AND ADMINISTRATIVE ISSUES

Need for Administrative Reforms in India*

On the recommendations of the Kothari Commission, the UPSC decided a year ago that the regional language under the Eighth Schedule of the Constitution should be a compulsory paper. I have been listening to friends on both sides and they have been very vehemently advocating that English should be done away with, that the regional languages should be encouraged more, that Hindi should be encouraged more. As far as encouragement of Hindi and the regional languages is concerned, I do not dispute it at all, but there is a problem in many parts of the country, especially in my region, that is the North Eastern region. There are thousands of languages, dialects which are spoken in our country. Even in my Garo tribes, we have got seven languages. If you talk of Nagaland, the Nagas have got seventeen languages. If you talk of Arunachal Pradesh, they have also as many as seventeen tribes and seventeen languages. If you look at the Eighth Schedule of the Constitution, you will find that there are only fourteen languages which have been recognized as the regional languages. Now the people in those parts of the country, whose languages have not so far been recognized as the regional languages under the Eighth Schedule of the Constitution, if they do not have the medium of instruction in any of the regional languages included in the Eighth Schedule, how do you expect the people of that area to compete in this examination? Janata Party Government was very firm on insisting on this recommendation of having a compulsory paper on the regional language. Honourable Members of the Sixth Lok Sabha will remember that I took up this

---

**L.S. Deb.*, 12 June 1980 (Spoke while participating in the Motion on Twenty Eighth Report of the Union Public Service Commission).

particular issue on the floor of the august House and the House had to be adjourned on this issue. As far as our region is concerned, we cannot accept it, we are helpless. We have been saying that there may be a compulsory paper on the regional language for the rest of the country, but at least people from our part of the country should be exempted and an alternative paper in lieu of the compulsory regional language paper should be allowed for our people in the North Eastern region. This has been done for one year. Last year because every one of us demanded and because there was a lot of agitation, it was extended for one year. I would like to know from the honourable Minister, what is the policy of the Government of India on this particular point? For future, is the Government considering to extend this relaxation so that the people in the North Eastern region will be exempted from appearing for the compulsory regional language paper? I would again appeal to the Government that as far as our region is concerned, there should be an alternative paper in lieu of the compulsory regional language paper.

There has been a lot of discussion in UPSC Report, not only now, but for so many years. Regarding the representation of the Scheduled Castes and the Scheduled Tribes in the All-India Services, today, the Government of India is very keen that the Scheduled Castes and the Scheduled Tribes should come up. But if this recommendation of the Kothari Commission is accepted, then the people living in the North East will be at a disadvantage and it will be a conflict of policy. Therefore, I would again submit that the people in the North East, whose languages have not been included in the Eighth Schedule, should be allowed to take an alternative paper.

Now, as far as the representation of the Scheduled Castes and the Scheduled Tribes is concerned – I belong to a Scheduled Tribe – I think, here the question is not the representation of the Scheduled Castes, Scheduled Tribes and the rest; the conflict is between the poor and the rich, it is between the rural and the urban people. Whatever steps the Government of India have taken, to bring up the rural people, to bring up the Scheduled Castes and the Scheduled Tribes, have not worked very much till today. There are so many coaching centres that have been started by the Government of India. That is very good. I welcome it and it should continue. Still, we have not been able to solve the problem because the root cause lies in the foundation of education one receives. As some honourable Members who preceded me pointed out, how can we expect a student, whether he is a Scheduled Caste or a Scheduled Tribe or even a Brahmin or a high caste, living in a village having no facility of any schooling, having no facility of any good education, to compete in an examination of this type which is the highest in the country?

What is, therefore, required is to take necessary measures to bring up the standard of education in the rural areas. If we go to the rural areas and find out the condition of schools there, we will find that the conditions are appalling. Majority of us have come from the rural areas and we know the conditions under which the people are living in the rural areas. I want to give you an example of my own constituency, the most backward constituency. After the last session, I had gone to my constituency. I had been going from village to village for about one-and-a-half months. You will be shocked to know that I have in my possession hundreds of memoranda in which they have demanded for a map of their district. In the LP schools, the lower primary schools, they do not have a map of their district. Therefore, they want a Member of Parliament should take it up with the Government to provide them with a map of their district. I have received memoranda in which they have stated that they do not have a blackboard in the school, therefore, they have demanded that they should be given a blackboard in the school. If the conditions of our schools are such, how can we expect these boys and girls to compete with others?

* * *

I did not assure them before election to provide blackboards. But I had occasions to raise these matters on the floor of the House in the Sixth Lok Sabha regarding the conditions of our schools in the Garo Hills. There were a lot of strikes by teachers who were without pay for seven to eight or nine months. I had raised these matters on many occasions on the floor of the august House. Even this time, I have given notice of questions. But I get this kind of a reply, 'We regret to inform you that your question cannot be admitted because it falls under the Sixth Schedule of the Constitution of India, under the Autonomous provision.' This is the position.

I say, it is not the question of Scheduled Castes and Scheduled Tribes and the rest. In the case of Scheduled Castes and Scheduled Tribes, people who have the facility of educating their children in good schools, their children will certainly come up. Even in the case of a Brahmin or a high-caste person who has no means of educating his children in good schools, his children will never come up. Therefore, what is required is to improve the quality of our education and improve the facilities of our educational institutions in the rural areas. It may not fall under the Ministry of Home Affairs, but I think, the Ministry of Home Affairs should bring out this specific point to the Ministry of Education. This I sincerely feel is the real point.

I know many of our boys and girls who have appeared in the IAS examination and who have seen the face of a train only when they were coming to appear in the IAS examination. Our area is completely isolated. Out of seven states in the North Eastern region, Assam is the only state having a railway connection. Other states do not have any railway connection. Even graduate boys who are appearing in the IAS examination have not seen a train, except perhaps in the picture. How can we expect them to compete in the examination, appear in the interview, talk of international issues, philosophy and all that? It is completely impracticable. Therefore, my appeal is that necessary steps should be taken to improve the standard of education in the rural and backward areas. Good schools should be opened and finance should be given for the purpose. We have many good schools in the cities. But we do not have schools at all in the rural areas. This imbalance has to be looked into and necessary steps have to be taken as far as our region is concerned. I have pointed out the real problem.

I would once again appeal to the Government of India that the compulsory paper of regional language should be done away with as far as our region is concerned.

~

Atrocities on Minorities: Theoretical and Ideological Framework*

Mr Chairman, Sir, 10 December 1998 was the occasion of the Golden Jubilee of the adoption of the UN Charter on Human Rights. The rights of the minorities have a special place in the Bills of Human Rights.

**L.S. Deb.*, 15 December 1998 (Spoke while participating in the discussion under Rule 193 regarding atrocities committed on minorities in various parts of the country).

Sir, I would have expected this Government to take an initiative either to pass a unanimous resolution on that day to celebrate the Golden Jubilee of the adoption of the UN Charter on Human Rights or at least during today's debate, as has been contemplated earlier. I would still urge the Government to find out some ways and means to see whether we can celebrate the Golden Jubilee of the adoption of the UN Charter on Human Rights. It can still be debated in Parliament.

As far as the atrocities on minorities are concerned, I would not like to go through the incidents or the specific incidents which have already been mentioned by many honourable Members who have participated in this debate. I would only like to point out one fact, that is, ever since this Government came to power, there has been an increase in atrocities on the minorities. Secondly, what I am more worried about is the response of the Central Government. I am not going to attack anybody. In response to the question of Prof. P.J. Kurien, the honourable Minister of Home Affairs dismissed it as a state subject and that it is a law and order problem.

* * *

What I want to say is that these are not mere incidents that are taking place and that they can dismiss it as a law and order situation. It has something to do with their ideology. It has something to do with the ideology of Sangh Parivar.

Since there is no time, I want to come to that aspect straightaway. I want to deal with the situation from two aspects of ideological framework of the BJP and the Sangh Parivar and the theoretical framework of the BJP and the Sangh Parivar. What is the ideological aspect of this? The BJP manifesto is very very clear. What does the BJP manifesto say? You talk about cultural nationalism. What is cultural nationalism? The cultural nationalism is that you are committed to the concept of one nation, one people and one culture. It is very much there in their manifesto of 1998. I quote the manifesto:

> The BJP is committed to the concept of one nation, one people and one culture. Our nationalist vision is not merely bound by the geographical and political identity of Bharat but is referred by our timeless and cultural heritage. The cultural heritage, which is central to all regions, religions and languages and civilizational identity, constitutes a cultural nationalism in India which is the core of 'Hindutva'. That is the ideology of one nation, one people and one culture.

Another example that I would like to give is an attempt to saffronize our education system. I have a great respect for the honourable Minister of Human Resource Development, Dr Murli Manohar Joshi. But the way the agenda of the Government was sought to be pushed through in the recently convened Conference of the Education Ministers is something which I personally could not believe that a respected person like Dr Joshi could do. We are aware how an RSS activist, Shri P.D. Chitlangia was asked to preserve the theory of this saffronization of education.

We are all aware of the attempt that was made to introduce '*Saraswati Vandana*' and '*Vande Mataram*' and the attempt to introduce Sanskrit as a compulsory subject. We are all aware of that. Now the question is this: Has it come just like that? Is it a new idea? No, it is not. It is very much in the ideological framework of the BJP and is being carried out by its constituents, the RSS, the VHP and the Bajrang Dal. That is the danger. The RSS and the Bajrang Dal were very old organizations but they have not been that active in the past. Why have they suddenly become so active? Why have they suddenly become so much anti-Christian, anti-Muslim and anti-Minorities. It is because they know that they have the backing of the Government of the day. They know that it is being very much in tune with the ideological framework of one nation, one culture and one people, Hindutva.

I was surprised to read a report on the idea of the honourable Home Minister, Shri Advani, on Buddhism. On 6 November 1998 when the honourable Home Minister was inaugurating the World Unity on Buddha's Trinity at Saranath, he Hinduized and Aryanized Buddhism. What did he say? Sir, he said, I quote: 'Buddha only reinstated the ancient ideals of Hindu Aryan civilization.' The honorable Home Minister went on to say: 'Gautam Buddha was an incarnation of Vishnu and his philosophy flowed from the Bhagavad Gita.'

We all know the reaction of the Buddhist scholars on this reported interpretation of the honourable Home Minister about Buddhism. What is happening today? It is because of the patronage in thinking, in philosophy and in ideology which are emanating from the leaders of the Government of the day.

The second aspect is the theoretical framework. What is the theoretical framework of the ruling party? We know about several statements made by the leaders of the VHP, the RSS and the Bajrang Dal. I do not like to name them because somebody will object that: I cannot take their names because they will not be able to defend themselves. But everyone of us knows that the most prominent leaders of those organizations are saying that Christians are anti-national. There should be second Quit India Movement. The churches should be closed because they serve liquor in the church.

* * *

All right, I will modify my statement. It could be wrong. I will be happy if it is wrong. But it is reported that the former Minister of Delhi, Shri Rajindra Gupta, has made this statement. I think, it is because of the ignorance of Christian religion. I do not blame him. He alleged that the liquors are being served in the Church. Therefore, under the Excise Rules, it should not be allowed and it should be closed. I have read it. I do not know how you did not read it. No, because you are challenging my statement, I am just saying it.

* * *

I know that the honourable Home Minister was the product of St Patrick's School, Karachi. I know that many people who matter in this country, whether they are politicians, bureaucrats, diplomats or media journalists or whether they are industrialists, many of them have been educated in Christian institutions; and we are proud of that because that is our contribution to this country. If you accept that, why is that thousands of Bibles are being burnt today? Why? Why are churches being attacked today? This is my question. Why are dead bodies being exhumed from the graveyards? This is the question that I want to ask.

* * *

I think it is becoming very uncomfortable for the ruling party. I do not want to proceed further. Let me caution. Shri Ram Vilas Paswan made a very significant statement on this debate. Look at our borders. It is the minorities who are defending our borders. I want to go one step further that if India is projected in the whole world being a country which is anti-Muslim and anti-Christian, we have to remember that we will get further isolated. We are already isolated because of many things that had happened in our country. You talk of Babri Masjid. You talk of nuclear tests. We already stand isolated. If we continue like that, I do not think it will be good for our country. After all, basically the world is divided into two blocs. Let me be very frank and blunt about it. India, in the process of globalization, cannot afford to be isolated by the world. Please remember that. I am happy that the honourable Home Minister today is very assertive. I am very happy that of late the honourable Prime Minister has also started saying that he is very assertive because he has got three of his most trusted people in the Ministry. But the only comment that I would like to make about the honourable home minister is that your assertiveness or the honourable prime minister's assertiveness is, perhaps, belated. It is already late. I am told and I know that every morning the Hindus do a puja called Surya Namaskar. That is to prevent blindness. I read it somewhere that it is to prevent blindness. But unfortunately, Shri Advani and also the honourable Prime Minister are doing Surya Namaskar after they have become blind. But I can tell you that the people of India and the country are not blind. That has been proved in the recent elections of Delhi, Rajasthan and Madhya Pradesh. Thank you, Mr Speaker.

Role of Parliament of India*

Mr Deputy Speaker, Sir, on 20 March 1998 when the honourable Prime Minister sought the confidence of this august House, I had reminded the House and I quote:

> This is the fifth Motion of Confidence during the last 22 months. I do not know how many more Motions of Confidence would be coming up before this House in the near future but I am quite sure that there could be at least one more in less than one year.

Well, I was wrong. I expected a Confidence Motion in less than one year but here we have today another Confidence Motion in slightly more than one year.

This morning while participating in the debate, the honourable Prime Minister referred to Article 67 of the Constitution of Germany wherein

**L.S. Deb.*, 15 April 1999 (Spoke while participating in the Motion of Confidence in the Council of Ministers led by the then honourable Prime Minister, Shri Atal Bihari Vajpayee).

he pointed out that the Motion of No-Confidence has to be accompanied by a proposal for an alternative Government. I do not think today this House is discussing a No-Confidence Motion. We are today discussing a Confidence Motion moved by the honourable Prime Minister himself. So, where is the question of the Opposition presenting before this august House an alternative? I had expected the honourable Prime Minister to have told this august House as to how this Confidence Motion has come about. What are the reasons for it? Why did the honourable President of India directed the honourable Prime Minister to seek the confidence of the House? I think the whole country was expecting that honourable Prime Minister in his initial observations, after moving the Motion, would tell this august House the reasons for seeking the Vote of Confidence. The honourable Prime Minister said that instead of speaking first, he would prefer to listen. I think there is a confusion between the Confidence Motion and the No-Confidence Motion. Today we are not discussing the No-Confidence Motion but the Confidence Motion.

During the General Elections of 1998, the slogan of the BJP was 'an able Prime Minister and a stable Government'. This Government assumed office on the basis of a National Agenda for Governance. In the last thirteen months of this Government, I have neither seen the stability nor the governance. I think these thirteen months have been a period in our country where the country has witnessed a rule of non-governance. While participating in the debate on the Confidence Motion last time, though I elaborately dealt with the prevailing political instability in this country, I emphasized that as far as our nation is concerned, more than stability, it is the governance which is more important. I would like to quote:

> Is it enough for our country to have a stable Government if that Government does not govern? I think the important thing today is not merely stability. It is the good governance which is the issue today.

I further said:

> I am not worried about the stability of Mr Vajpayee's Government. I am only worried about the governance by this eighteen party Government.

I would have liked to go into the matters relating to finance. But then I do not have much experience of finance. Whatever the honourable Finance Minister has claimed just now about the economy, I think tomorrow somebody will reply to all those things. I have something with me. I do not want to waste my time by contradicting the honourable Finance Minister. But who does not know what is the state of affairs in this country today? You talk of economy or you talk of foreign policy. Of course, again, I am not going to deal with the foreign policy. Though the honourable Home Minister made a reference to this in the morning, my colleague Shri Natwar Singh will be dealing exclusively with the foreign policy tomorrow or may be late this evening.

Look at the law and order situation in the country. And look at the morale of the nation as a whole. I do not think anybody need to explain all this with the type of electronic media and print media that we have and with the information technology that is available today in this country? It does not matter what Sangma is speaking on the floor of the august House. People already know; people can judge whether Sangma is speaking truth or not. It does not matter. I am not going into all this and make a reply to these points.

Today, I thought, I will deal exclusively with one area of concern. That area of concern is the denigration of institutions that is taking place in our country. The way our institutions are being weakened, the way our institutions are being destabilized, this is the cause of worry for us. If we are able to preserve, promote and strengthen our institutions and if we are able to strengthen and preserve our systems, the country will move even with instability of the Governments. I am told Italy had fifty-one Governments in fifty years. But it is moving. So is the case in many parts of the world. Therefore, what is important in our country to remember is that how do we preserve, protect and strengthen our institutions. I am sorry to say that in the last thirteen months, a lot of damage has been done to our institutions and I have no courage to blame the honourable Prime Minister for this. I have faith on him. But how has it happened? Is it deliberate or accidental or conscious or unconscious? Perhaps, it is due to lack of experience in governance. Look at the institution of the office of the honourable President himself. The honourable President's name was being dragged on the floor of the august House to facilitate a debate so much so that the next day, the honourable Minister for Parliamentary Affairs had to intervene saying that the honourable Speaker will go through the records and will expunge all those remarks. It was in a very bad taste. The honourable President of India and the Government communicate with each other. Secret correspondences are there; confidential correspondences are there, but today, we find that even the secret communications between the Government and the honourable President are being leaked to the Press. Are we not denigrating the office of the honourable President?

Look at the manner in which Admiral Vishnu Bhagwat had been dismissed. The honourable President of India is the supreme commander of the Armed Forces but we are told through the Press that the honourable President of India was not even consulted on this matter.

* * *

It was not the question of approving or signing it. What did the Government do? This is what we read in the papers. Mr Prime Minister, if it is not true and even then we are deliberating it, it is because you never told the Parliament about it. This is another charge I want to level against you. You never tell the Parliament as to what is happening and we come to know about it through the electronic and print media. But the allegation is that the honourable President did not sign it. The honourable President was simply informed. I am worried about it. Again, Mr Prime Minister, I want to say that I have no allegations against you because you would not have done it deliberately and it cannot be so. You may come to the Parliament itself.

What is happening in Parliament? I am sorry to say that today Parliament has become non-functional. In the last session, 17.29 per cent of the time had been lost because of disorder. I know that you will ask as to who created the disorder. Is it not the Opposition? You can ask me this legitimate question. If the Opposition was creating this problem, was it not your failure of floor management? Do you ever think as to how the floor has to be managed? If the Treasury Bench has no patience to hear the Opposition, if the honourable Minister for Parliamentary Affairs provokes the Opposition, does not even talk to the Opposition leaders and wants to impose decisions on his will, then how do you manage the floor of the Parliament? The management of Parliament is the sole responsibility of the Treasury Benches. Today, if the whole country is witnessing slogans, if the whole country is witnessing the honourable Members coming to the well of the august House and if the country is witnessing disruptions in the proceedings of the House, then I hold the Ruling party responsible for this. It is the failure of the Government's floor management.

Then, what is the Parliament of India? The Parliament of India consists of the President and the two Houses.

* * *

I am raising serious issues. I am not blaming you fully. Perhaps, we are also partly responsible. But I am holding you more responsible. These are the serious issues of the country. We must apply our mind. I am sure, the honourable Prime Minister is with me a hundred per cent.

I said, right at the beginning, that what has happened has not happened deliberately because Shri Vajpayee would not have consciously allowed all these things. That is why, I attributed it to lack of governance and lack of experience in governing the country. That is what I am attributing to you. Therefore, you should learn this.

* * *

What happened to the Prasar Bharati (Amendment) Bill? It was passed in the Lok Sabha. The Government decided not to send it to the Rajya Sabha. Is it not a violation of the constitutional obligation and constitutional requirement? Can the Government just take the Parliament for a ride? It thinks that the Upper House of Parliament is just nothing. Did the same thing not happen with regard to the imposition of Article 356 in regard to Bihar? Was it not the duty of the Government to see that after having passed it in this House, it should automatically have gone to the Rajya Sabha. But the Government decided not to send it to the Rajya Sabha because technically the Government can withdraw its decision. Are we going only by the technicalities? Is the imposition of President's rule in any state a matter of mere debate in the Lok Sabha or Rajya Sabha? Do we not have a Constitution of India? Why are you doing it?

What happened in the last thirteen months? I do not want to hurt my friend Shri Pramod Mahajan. What is happening in the Information and Broadcasting Ministry is because of him only. Shrimati Sushma Swaraj is here. She was a very good Minister of Information and Broadcasting after me.

* * *

I am not touching Commerce. I am not touching exports and imports. Today, there is no CEO. There is no Director General, Doordarshan. The employees are on strike. Only Shri Pramod Mahajan is there. So, I was asking somebody this question: What is happening in Doordarshan? He said that there is no more Doordarshan. I asked why is it so. He said that it is the Sarkar Darshan now. It is no more Doordarshan but it is giving the Sarkar Darshan.

* * *

I am talking about Parliament. Shri Yashwant Sinha, you remember that when you presented the 1998-1999 Budget, for the first time in the history of the Parliament, the Demands for Grants of all the Ministries had to be guillotined. The Demands of only one Ministry, the Ministry of Agriculture, were discussed for exactly fifteen minutes. Shri Balram Jakhar spoke for fifteen minutes. If the Parliament of India has to deny the people of this country a debate on the Budget proposals and we have to just guillotine everything, are we doing justice? Is the Government functioning? Is the Parliament functioning? I am asking these very serious questions.

From the day one you took over, till today, this Government have promulgated thirty-five Ordinances. They have not been ratified by the Parliament of India. Is it a Government by Ordinance only? Where is the relevance of the Parliament of India? I am talking of the weakening of our institutions and Parliament is the most sacred institution in the country. If the laws of this country have to be only promulgated and in thirteen months you have promulgated thirty-five Ordinances that could not be ratified by the Parliament of India, are we doing justice to the Parliamentary democracy?

Come to the institution of Governorship. Come to any other institution. I do not want to name them. Today, anybody can become a Governor. You only have to be a loyal party man and after having occupied the post, you continue to be a party man and declare yourself to be a party man. Where is the impartiality of the office or of an institution? It is all right. One can have an ideology. I have an ideology. Tomorrow, I can become a Governor. But the moment I become a Governor, I think, I am a Governor and that is all and nothing else, if I have to do justice to my job. Therefore, anybody can become anybody in this country today. I think we are not doing justice to the institutions. Institutions are suffering.

* * *

Come to bureaucracy. I do not want to go into the details. What happened to the Enforcement Director, Shri Bezbaruah? What happened to the Secretary, Urban Development Ministry?

* * *

Whatever it may be, Mr 'a' or Mr 'b' is appointed Secretary to the Government of India and the Minister says, 'She will not exercise the power of a Secretary and I will not give her any work.' It is not correct to do so. We are denigrating the established system, the established institutions. I can go on and on to many other things. But I do not think I need to because I promised my party that I would take only half an hour.

In the last debate, I also spoke about a hidden agenda, a hidden agenda for saffronization of the educational system. My apprehension was, how RSS is going to work in every school of India? Dr Murli Manohar Joshi promptly stood up and said, 'You are wrong, Shri Sangma, we do not have any hidden agenda.' I told this august House, well, I am only expressing my suspicion. I used the word 'suspicion'. Have we not seen this in the thirteen months? Are we not seeing in thirteen months what is happening to the HRD Ministry? Was this country not stunned when in the Conference of the Education Ministers of this country, Dr Murli Manohar Joshi introduced an RSS man saying that here is a person who will formulate our education policy and here is a person who will brief what will be the future policy of education where '*Saraswati Vandana*' is going to be compulsory. We only remember that. I do not think anybody has forgotten it.

* * *

That expert's name is Shri Chitlangia. It is a very difficult name to pronounce. Sir, I have information as to how people are being selected for institutions in the Ministry of Human Resource Development, how people are being posted, how the syllabi are going to be changed, how the history is going to be refined, etc. We know how the Indian Council of Historical Research (ICHR) was reconstituted. They may deny all these things. But I strongly feel that we are heading towards a situation where there will be a danger for our democracy as such.

Then, there is the example of handling the issue of Admiral Vishnu

Bhagwat's dismissal. We read in the Press that he was a threat to national security. The official statement issued on 30 December 1998 said that the Admiral Bhagwat's conduct threatened national security. It went on to say that Vishnu Bhagwat has taken a series of actions in defiance of the established system of Cabinet control over the Armed Forces.

Sir, I have already referred as to how the honourable President was ignored. I have also read about Shri Brajesh Mishra claiming that the Opposition people were consulted, Shri Sharad Pawar was consulted, Shri I.K. Gujral was consulted, etc. I know that Shri Sharad Pawar has described it as a total falsehood. We read everyday statements and counter statements being issued by Admiral Bhagwat and Shri George Fernandes. Yesterday, I received a big booklet explaining as to why he was sacked. I want to ask how a courageous person and a person with a clear conscience like Shri George Fernandes, who is very close to me – I have a lot of admiration for him; he helped me so much when I was the Labour Minister and he was a trade union leader – is frightened today. He is going to the Press everyday to defend himself and he has now come out with a booklet to defend himself. If the Defence Minister has become so defensive, what will happen? Instead of defending the country, he is now defending himself. How will the country run?

Sir, I am not going into this matter further because we are expecting a debate on this issue and I will be participating in that debate. Therefore, I am not going into the whole issue of the dismissal of Admiral Bhagwat. But I only want to ask this question that when the matter is before this august House, when the honourable Speaker has admitted a Motion and it has to be discussed on the floor of the House, why has the Government been going to the media everyday? Why did the Government not come to the Parliament earlier and tell us what had happened? We came to know everything from the Press. The Parliament has not been told anything about it. Why is the Government trying to justify his action through the media and not through the Parliament of India? I take a strong objection that when a matter is lying before the august House and when the honourable Speaker has admitted the Motion, I think, the Government should stop going to the media. Whatever the Government has to say, let them say it on the floor of the august House. Otherwise, the whole thing is going to be prejudiced.

I never talk that I have some element of being a prophet. But on 28 March 1998, here is what I have said. I was reading my speech and I found that whatever I had said on that day is happening. I spoke so much about non-governance. Another thing I spoke about on that day was very interesting. I referred to the National Agenda for Governance where it had a reference to the National Water Policy. I attributed that this National Water Policy has been included there to please somebody in the south. I wished the honourable Prime Minister all the best and success. I would like to quote that:

> I wish you well in your effort to please somebody in matters of Cauvery water. I wish you success in solving this problem. But having known the South Indian river, which is as mighty and as sacred as the Ganga, I am only afraid that the Cauvery and the riparian water issues may wash away your Government.

That is how, I think, you are here today. And that is precisely the reason why we are discussing this Motion. I cannot wish you all the best second time. I have to oppose the Motion moved by the honourable Prime Minister. Thank you.

~

Political Stability and Economic Development*

Mr Deputy Speaker, Sir, first of all, I would like to join all the honourable Members who have spoken before me in extending my heart-felt thanks to the honourable President of India for having taken pains to address both the Houses of Parliament assembled together. The honourable President in his address to the Parliament has described the thirteenth Lok Sabha as the first Lok Sabha of the next century. He has asked us to look at the country's past with pride and her future with hope and confidence. The honourable President has reminded us to look at our many missed opportunities in the past.

Finally, he has urged that our collective strength should be pressed into service to meet a great future. By reminding all this, the honourable President was actually expressing his concern about – the seniormost

---

*_L.S. Deb._, 29 October 1999 (Spoke while participating in the Motion of Thanks on the President's address to both Houses of Parliament).

Member of the House has already pointed out – the stability of the Government, the governance itself and the stability of the polity itself. Shri Indrajit Gupta has expressed his doubt as to whether, in spite of the fact that there is a feeling in the ruling group that they have a mandate to rule, the coalition will work.

I would like to share his feelings, whether they really have the mandate and whether there will still be stability.

If you look at the results of the last election to the thirteenth Lok Sabha, there has been much of change visible, as Shri Mulayam Singh Yadav also had pointed out. But I feel that two things should be taken note of. One is that the people of India seem to be very much dissatisfied with the national parties and the people of India are going towards the regional parties.

What was the position of the BJP in the last elections? The strength of the BJP in the twelfth Lok Sabha was 182 and their strength in the thirteenth Lok Sabha is 182. It is same. Not even an increase of one seat. What was the strength of the Congress party in the twelfth Lok Sabha? It was 140 and now it is 112. Let us concede 112. What was the strength of the CPM in the twelfth Lok Sabha? It was 32 and in the thirteenth Lok Sabha it is still 32. What was the strength of the CPI? I do not want to go into all the details. But it has come down. So, the seven recognized national parties, with the exception of the Bahujan Samaj Party, have either maintained their figure of the twelfth Lok Sabha or they have come down. There is not a single national party who could improve its position even by one more Member. That is the position of the national parties in our country today.

When you look at the regional parties on the other hand, you find that they have improved. Let us take TDP. In the last Lok Sabha, they were 17 and today they have 29 Members. The seats of the Samajwadi Party in the last Lok Sabha were 20 and today they have 26. The Siva Sena in the last Lok Sabha had 6 seats and today they are 15. The BJD had 9 seats in the last Lok Sabha, today they are 10. The Trinamool Congress had 7 seats in the last Lok Sabha and now they are 8. The PMK had 4 seats and today they are 5. The MDMK led by Sri Vaiko had 3 seats in the last Lok Sabha and today they are 4. I have many more figures but I do not want to quote all those figures.

* * *

I think, we have to now think whether it is a healthy trend or not for the country. I am not talking from any other angle. I am talking from the angle of the stability of the Central Government. In the last Lok Sabha, we had a Government of 18 political parties. Today, we are having a Government of about 24–25 political parties. The 18-party Government survived for thirteen months. I do not know whether the 25-party Government will survive for how many months.

It is from this angle of giving a stable Government at the Centre, of having stability at the Centre, I am talking about the trend that is emerging in our country today.

The irrelevance of the national parties, as we have seen from the results of the last General Election, is certainly a disturbing trend. The role of the national parties has to be recognized and today the first point that I would like to make is to call upon the national parties to examine why the people are rejecting the national parties. Of course, the reasons are obvious. If the national parties have failed to respond to the aspirations, the regional aspirations of the people in different parts of the country would develop. This is a point which I thought that we should ponder about.

Now, coming to the stability aspect of the present Government, I find that this is a minority Government. This is not a majority Government. The NDA's figure of 304 looks to be a very interesting figure, perhaps a 'feel-good' figure as far as you are concerned and you must be feeling very good but whether it is a 'feel-secure' figure. I am trying to bifurcate the NDA and the coalition. I will not accept that the NDA and the coalition are the same.

The people have given the mandate to the NDA. I accept it but my question is as to why the entire NDA is not in the Government today. Had the entire NDA been in the Government today, perhaps there could have been more hope – I am using the word 'hope' – of stability. But it is not the case. Out of 304 Members, 29 Members of the TDP are outside the coalition. That makes the strength as 275. If you take out five more Members – there is another party, that is Chautala's party – of the All-India Lok Dal, who are outside the coalition, then the strength of the Government comes down to 270. If you take out two more Members of the Shiromani Akali Dal, then the strength of the coalition Government comes down to 268. Will this coalition Government with the strength of 268 be able to give stability to the country and fulfil all the promises that have been given in the honourable

President's address? That is a question which I would like to leave to this august House, particularly to the coalition partners to think about.

You have a very big responsibility to give us a stable Government. We, on behalf of the NCP, are not for destabilization. I join with Shri Indrajit Gupta in wishing you all the best because in the interest of the nation, stability is a must. We want to have a stable Government but please do not be complacent because your position, as I said, may be a 'feel-good' position but not a 'feel-secure' position.

As Shri Somnath Chatterjee has mentioned, there are many points on which one would like to touch upon but because of the constraint of time I do not like to go into all the details.

The second point that I would like to make here is to draw the attention of the Government to paragraph 28 of the agenda of the National Democratic Alliance. I want to read out the relevant sentence from paragraph 28, which says:

> We will enact a legislation to provide eligibility criteria that the high offices of State legislative, executive and judiciary are held only by natural born citizen of India.

This is what your agenda for the National Democratic Alliance has stated. It does not get reflected in the honourable President's address. I would like to know the stand of the Government on this issue. Are you going to bring in a legislation before this House? If so, when? You have to bring an amendment, either to the Constitution of India or to the Citizenship Act or to the People's Representation Act or altogether a new Act. Let it be in whatever form, but I would like to know your stand on this particular issue.

The third point that I would like to make is on the question which has already been raised by Shri Indrajit Gupta, that is on population. The honourable Home Minister pointed out that there was a reference in the honourable President's address about population. But I am sorry to say that it is just a passing reference. It just simply says you will stabilize the population. It is stabilization of the population. I really do not understand what is the meaning of stabilization of population. I do not want to go into all the aspects of the population problem because we all know about it. But may I point out two aspects of the population problem in our country? The first aspect is the rate of growth itself. The second aspect is the pattern of growth of population.

As far as the rate of growth of population is concerned, we all know that it is, at the moment, growing at a rate of 2.1 per cent and by this rate, the population of India is going to be 1,264 million by 2016. If you are talking about arresting this present growth rate by stabilization of the population, then you are not correcting the trend. You just want to maintain the same. Is it the meaning of stabilization? If you say 'yes', then what you mean is that you just want to maintain the present rate of growth by not increasing it. Even then, our problem is not solved.

What is more important is the pattern of growth. The pattern of growth is really disturbing. More than 50 per cent of the population growth is unfortunately contributed by the four states of India. We call it 'BIMARU' states – Bihar, Madhya Pradesh, Rajasthan and Uttar Pradesh. I can produce this paper to the honourable Home Minister or even to the Prime Minister of India because – I can claim that this is a pet subject of mine – I have made a lot of studies and research on population growth. I would like to share one thing today. The second part of my worry is regarding the pattern of growth, the distorted way of growth. Our study shows that between 1996 and 2016, in 20 years, at the rate of 2.1 per cent, the growth of additional population that we will be adding to our country will be 350 million. More than 50 per cent of the 350 million population will be contributed by the 'BIMARU' states. This is one scenario.

The second thing that I would like to say is how it will have a political implication. In 1977, by an amendment of the Constitution of India, the delimitation of the Parliament of India has been frozen at 1971 census. So, at the moment, the delimitation of the Parliament is on the basis of 1971 census because we have frozen it by an amendment of the Constitution.

Now, this freeze will continue up to AD 2000. What is your stand now? I think, the Government has to explain. Are you going to remove that freeze? Are you going to go for a new delimitation of parliamentary constituencies? If you are doing so, to how many years you are going to extend this freeze of the limitation of the Parliament? Why I am saying so is that if you remove this freeze and if you delimit the parliamentary constituencies which is on the basis of population, then the net result would be Bihar will get two more parliamentary seats; Uttar Pradesh will get fourteen more parliamentary seats; Madhya Pradesh will get five more parliamentary seats; Rajasthan will get four more parliamentary seats and on the other hand, Tamil Nadu will lose eight parliamentary constituencies.

* * *

I am not going to every state. We have taken a lot of pain in studying the situation. Tamil Nadu is going to lose eight parliamentary seats; Kerala – a small state – is going to lose four parliamentary seats; Andhra Pradesh three; and Karnataka one at the present growth rate of population and present pattern of growth of population in our country. I feel that besides this problem on the economy of the country and everything, it is going to create a political problem for us and we have to collectively tackle this problem.

I would urge upon the Government that we have an all-party conference on population growth. We have a special sitting of Parliament to discuss about this and reach a consensus on the New Population Policy in our country; otherwise, we are going to face a lot of problems in future.

I will quickly cover the points. The fourth point I want to mention here is economy. Of course, I am not going to deal with economy as of today because we will have an opportunity to discuss the Budget. The honourable Minister of Finance is here. We will do it at that time. But I only want to point out that in the honourable President's address, on the one hand, the honourable President mentions about the fiscal rectitude through improved expenditure management, and the President also promises setting up of an Expenditure Commission. It is your idea. The Expenditure Commission would inter alia lay down the road map for downsizing the Government. It is very good and I must welcome the repeated statements of the honourable Minister of Finance who says that his topmost priority is to bring about a financial discipline and containment of Government Expenditure. This is what the honourable Minister of Finance has been repeatedly telling the nation and the honourable President has promised us that soon there will be fiscal rectitude through improved expenditure management as well as Expenditure Commission to downsize the Government. If that is your policy, why this Government had to create so many new departments? You have created a new Department of Primary Education and Literacy. Where is the need for the Government of India to have a Department of Primary Education? Primary education under the Constitution of

India is under the domain of the Panchayati Raj. Instead of decentralizing the power, instead of decentralizing the process and the system, why do you want to concentrate more and more at the Central level?

I have some suspicion on this. Why the Government of India or the Government of the BJP, with so much of strength coming from the RSS and the VHP, should take over direct administration of the primary schools in the country is a big question mark. I have my suspicion and I would like the Government to answer this. If their policy is to downsize the Government structure, why have they gone on to create new Departments of Drinking Water and Supply, Road Transport and Highways, Shipping, Telecom Services, and so on? Of course, I welcome the creation of the Department of Information Technology because that is the need of the hour. That is a new Ministry they have created. But my question is why did they have to create so many new departments and bring such a huge financial burden on the exchequer?

* * *

I have always taken a position, it is known also, that instead of creating new Ministries and Departments, I have advocated for abolition of certain Ministries at the Centre. The Ministry of Rural Development is not required, the Ministry of Youth Affairs and Sports is not required. These are all state subjects. People sitting in New Delhi cannot understand what is happening 3,000 kilometres away from here in the villages. What is the point in Central Government having a huge establishment of rural development, sports, and what not? I am in favour of dismantling some of them. Take agriculture, for example. I can understand your keeping the ICAR as far as the research part is concerned, but why agriculture? It is just to keep control over the states. It is just to delay the delivery of the finances. I am speaking from my own experience as a Union Minister as well as a Chief Minister. We will have to downsize the Union Ministries. They are thinking about downsizing the Government. I quite agree to that. They should please go ahead and do that. But, in the meantime, they should not create many new departments.

Having said so, I must deviate from my stand and welcome the creation of a new Ministry for Tribal Welfare. I congratulate the Government and thank the Government for that. I must also thank the Government and both the Houses of Parliament – the Upper House and the Lower House – for having passed the Constitution Amendment

Bill for extending the reservation for the Scheduled Castes and the Scheduled Tribes for another ten years. But the honourable Members who have participated in the debate – I did not participate because I wanted to give chance to others – have expressed so many things. They have said that in spite of all this, nothing much has happened in these fifty years. I would say that nothing is going to happen also until and unless the Governments at the Centre and in the States are really serious about the welfare of the Scheduled Castes and the Scheduled Tribes. I am not going into all the details but I shall give one example and that is for the attention of the honourable Finance Minister. The Ninth Plan document says – please check it up – that over Rs 200,000 crore of outlay earmarked under the Special Component Plan for Scheduled Castes was not actually used for their benefit during the Eighth Plan. I am reading from your Ninth Plan Document. Similarly, about Rs 220,000 crore earmarked under the Tribal Sub-plan during the Eighth Plan period were not utilized for the benefit of the Scheduled Tribes. We have spent fifty years with slogans and slogans. I do not want to proceed further. I think the Ninth Five Year Plan Document itself gives a lot of messages. If Rs 200,000 crore had been spent for the Scheduled Castes.

* * *

It was about the Eighth Five Year Plan. For your information, we were not in the Government during the Eighth Five Year Plan. We were not there. I am not saying we did not make a mistake. If you look at the Seventh Five Year Plan, perhaps the situation is the same. If you look at the Sixth Five Year Plan, perhaps the situation is the same.

* * *

Sir, much has been said about Kargil. I know that the time allotted to me is very limited. I will complete in five minutes. Much has been said about Kargil. I am not going to speak about it. I endorse what Shri Indrajit Gupta has said. I understand that a committee – Subramanyam Committee – has been formed to go into all aspects of the Kargil war, our failures here and there. I request the Government to make available the Subramanyam Committee report to us and it can be discussed. During the debate on Pokhran II, I advocated for a nuclear doctrine. At that time, the ruling party Members were smiling at me and laughing at me. I am happy that the Government has now come out with a draft nuclear doctrine. The Nationalist Congress Party has, in our manifesto, gone a step further to say that why only a nuclear doctrine, we should have a National Security Doctrine itself. I would like the Government to place the draft nuclear doctrine on the table of the House and, perhaps, we can have time to discuss about it.

Shri Somnath Chatterjee has made a reference to the CTBT. Shri Indrajit Gupta has made a reference to tomorrow's WTO meeting. I am not going to say all sorts of things. On CTBT, I think, we should take note of two happenings. The President of the United States, Mr Bill Clinton was the first to sign the CTBT. But then he could not get his proposal ratified by the Congress there. That is one aspect. The second aspect that we have to keep in mind is the termination of the democratic Government in our neighbourhood, Pakistan. Keeping these two developments, I would urge upon the Government to be extra cautious regarding our stand on CTBT.

Mr Deputy Speaker, Sir, I would like to make two more points. They are very important. One is on the North East. I am very disappointed to note that the honourable President's address simply says that: 'We are going to restructure the North Eastern Council.' That is all the honourable President's address has said and nothing more or nothing less. I do not want to emphasize what we have been doing in the past. But I think the North East certainly requires much more attention from the Government than simply making a statement that they are going to restructure the North Eastern Council.

The last point: I would like to make a reference to the honourable President's address to the writings of the Father of the Nation, Mahatma Gandhi in 1931. He described the India of his dreams as India in which all communities shall live in a perfect harmony. I am pointing out this because in these days we find a lot of news coming about the reservation from certain sections of the people on the visit of the Pope to India.

I do not see any reason for why we should have any objection to the Holy Father visiting India. I want to point out that this is not going to be the first visit of the Holy Father here. It is going to be the second visit. The first visit was a much more longer visit. He travelled throughout India and visited all the important towns and cities of India. At that time, nobody raised any finger. There was no demonstration. There was no Press statement. There was no yatra held. Why is all this happening at the time of his second visit? It is because, I think, they are getting some strength from somewhere to take up such activity. Please ensure that the visit is a success and peaceful.

I belong to Christian community and I can tell you that we are a very timid community. We are just two per cent of the population after 2000 years of Christianity in this great country. Where is the room for apprehension? I do not understand. We have made our contribution to this country in every possible way, especially in the field of education and in the field of medical care. I think a large number of honourable Members here, I am sure, are products of Christian institutions. We have done our bit.

I also want to point out that this is not a religious affair only. The Holy Father is not only the head of a religious organization, but also the head of a Government, head of a sovereign State. So, he is coming here not merely as the head of the Church but also as the head of a State. I think, if anything that is unpleasant happens, it will have an impact on our diplomatic relations, our external affairs and our foreign policy. I urge upon the Government to ensure that everything goes off peacefully. I am speaking this on behalf of the Christian community of this country because I must confess that we are not only hurt but also really distressed about this. Thank you very much.

Jammu and Kashmir Autonomy—Article 370 and Beyond*

Mr Deputy Speaker, Sir, I consider that this debate is a very important debate because we are dealing with an area which is very sensitive, especially after the resolution which has been adopted by the Jammu and Kashmir Assembly on the question of autonomy.

Unfortunately, there has been an obvious ambivalence in the utterances of the Central leadership about the resolution itself. Initially, the honourable Minister of Home Affairs is reported to have said that this

**L.S. Deb.*, 26 July 2000 (Spoke while participating in the discussion under Rule 193 regarding the resolution passed by the Jammu and Kashmir Legislative Assembly for autonomy).

matter would be discussed in Parliament and perhaps decided by the Parliament. The honourable Prime Minister seems to have initially defended the Chief Minister of Jammu and Kashmir saying, 'Well, there is nothing wrong if it is within the framework of the Constitution of India.' After having made these two important statements, the Cabinet rushed for a decision on the matter and outrightly rejected the resolution. I do not know whether each demand by the Assembly of the Jammu and Kashmir, which was on the basis of the Report of the State Autonomy Committee, has been really analysed and discussed by the Cabinet one by one because of the time frame that was available to the Government. I have some doubt whether every issue that has been raised in the resolution has been discussed totally by the Cabinet or not.

I have gone through the Report of the State Autonomy Committee and basically the demands can be summarized under ten headings. It covers at least ten areas of importance and in those areas there are issues, which were discussed in 1952 itself and where an agreement could not be reached. The matters were put off. That is alright, we shall see later on whether we can do something about it or not. There are at least two items which were deferred in 1952.

Now, my point is when the honourable Minister of Home Affairs had agreed and made a public statement that the matter would be discussed in Parliament, then what was the necessity for the Government to finally decide and reject it? After the Government has taken a decision to reject it outrightly, I really do not know whether this discussion in Parliament will now really be meaningful or not unless the honourable Minister of Home Affairs comes out and says, 'Yes, we still have an open mind; and on the basis of what has been discussed in Parliament, perhaps the matter can be again looked into.'

* * *

I do not think there is any meaning in discussing it here. However, having decided to discuss the matter in Parliament, I thought I will make a few points. I am not going to make a long speech.

Sir, as the august House is aware, though I do not want to go into the whole history of it, I just want to refresh the memory of the House that in October 1947, Maharaja Hari Singh executed an Instrument of Accession which was executed in 1947, perhaps some people have the impression that the Instrument of Accession by Maharaja Hari

Singh was unique or different from other Instruments of Accession. It was not.

The same form or paper of accession used for other rulers was used for Jammu and Kashmir. There was no separate form or paper especially meant for Jammu and Kashmir. It was a common form of accession to the Government of India. This is a very important thing to note. Therefore, in 1947 itself, by this very Instrument of Accession, Jammu and Kashmir became legally and irrevocably a part of the territory of India. There is no doubt about it.

Then, in 1950, when we adopted our Constitution, Jammu and Kashmir was included as a Part-B State in the First Schedule to the Constitution of India, and in 1957, when the Constitution of Jammu and Kashmir was adopted, the Constitution of the State declared Jammu and Kashmir to be an integral part of the Union of India. Therefore, on this count, we have made this point several times, nationally, internationally, in all forums that Jammu and Kashmir is an integral part of India. I just thought that there should not be any doubt on this.

Having accepted the situation that was obtaining at that time in Jammu and Kashmir, the Government of India then thought that the case of Jammu and Kashmir was something different from the rest of India and, therefore, they had to be given special safeguards, special protection, and therefore, Article 370 was incorporated. Everything now depends on Article 370. By the incorporation of Article 370, Jammu and Kashmir already enjoys autonomy. They have a separate Constitution, they have a separate flag and the Parliament of India has limited jurisdiction over Jammu and Kashmir. All these autonomies were given by Article 370. Subsequently, by different Presidential Orders, a lot of modification and perhaps innovation was made. I was wondering why this issue was now being raised and what was at the back of the mind of the people of Jammu and Kashmir. I think we are aware of the position of the BJP or the constituents of the NDA on the question of Article 370. There have been demands that Article 370 should be deleted from the Constitution of India. It certainly gives a lot of apprehension into the minds of the people of the Jammu and Kashmir. I think this point has to be understood very clearly by the Central Government, by the ruling party and its constituents. I would like to know from the honourable Home Minister, when he replies, what is the stand of the BJP and what is the stand of the NDA Government on the status of Article 370. If you make that position clear, I think much of the apprehensions of the people of Jammu and Kashmir can be contained. After all, the people of Jammu and Kashmir, by and large, have accepted that they are part of India. We have already had democratic process in the last election to the Jammu and Kashmir Assembly. Every political party participated in that election, which is a tremendous sense of satisfaction for all of us. Today, we have a popularly elected Government in Jammu and Kashmir to whom we can talk, with whom we can have a dialogue.

The National Conference is a part of the NDA Government here. The grandson of Sheikh Abdullah himself is a member of the Council of Ministers here. The grandson of Maharaja Hari Singh is a member in the Council of Ministers of Jammu and Kashmir. Dr Farooq Abdullah is an out and out Indian, a true patriotic person. Nobody can doubt about this. When we have all this before us – a patriot as a Chief Minister of the State, popular election having been conducted, the National Conference being a part of the NDA Government – we can have a free and frank exchange of views.

There are allegations from the leaders of Jammu and Kashmir that the report of the State Autonomy Committee, the report which was submitted to the Jammu and Kashmir Assembly in April 1999, had been immediately forwarded to the Government of India for their comments, for the opinion of the Union Government. I do not know, perhaps, they did not get much of a response from the Union Government. That is one version. I would like clarification on that.

On the other hand, we get an impression from the media that the Chief Minister of Jammu and Kashmir has assured not only the honourable Home Minister but also the honourable Prime Minister of India to the effect that this report was going to be discussed in the Assembly and only a discussion will take place and no resolution would be adopted. We had gathered from the media that this assurance was given by Dr Farooq Abdullah to the honourable Prime Minister and the honourable Home Minister; and yet they have passed the resolution in the Assembly. Why? Where is the misunderstanding?

When the Cabinet ultimately decided that 'No, this report has to be rejected outright,' without Dr Farooq Abdullah's reactions having come out – I do not know whether it is true but media reports say – 'Well, Dr Farooq Abdullah can decide whether he would like to continue with the NDA Government or not; he is free either to remain or to leave,'

I think somewhere there has been a communication gap between the leadership in the Jammu and Kashmir and the leadership at the Centre.

I must thank the Chief Minister of Jammu and Kashmir that in spite of all these provocations, he is still cool; he has not withdrawn from the Government of the NDA. He still says, 'Well, I am agreeable to a discussion; I am agreeable to a dialogue.' I think these are very positive signs which the august House should appreciate. There is no point in jumping to a conclusion that whatever they have done is hundred per cent wrong. I think it will be appropriate for the Parliament, perhaps, it will be appropriate for the Government, to look into as to how Article 370 of the Constitution has functioned and how did it work. After all, whatever autonomy we had to give, we had given to them.

May be that there could be a special kind of a study by a team of experts from outside – not from Jammu and Kashmir – an independent body who will objectively make a study of the working of Article 370 of the Constitution of India and see whether any changes are required.

Though I pointed out that there are certain matters which were discussed in 1952 but a careful reading of all these demands thus give a feeling to me that the Jammu and Kashmir Assembly had demanded to go to the pre-1952 position. Of course, I am not agreeable to that personally. I do not know why we are talking about autonomy and why this word 'autonomy' is so attractive. I think, what the people of Jammu and Kashmir would like to achieve can be achieved without even using the word 'autonomy'. I think, the Cabinet certainly took note of that and very cleverly, while rejecting the resolution, has also kept an option if there is any route to avoid certain problems.

Shri Santosh Mohan Dev: When you are speaking, you keep in mind that you are also a member of the Constitution Review Commission. You have expressed many things and views.

P.A. Sangma: I know that. That is why I am talking about it. I am thinking not only about Article 370 but also Article 371 which is applicable to the North Eastern States. I am also thinking about the future of Assam as a member of the Commission, for your kind information. I only want that the Government should also take an initiative whereby these matters of special importance can be assigned to some people who are impartial and go into the working of a particular article. The Commission is for looking into the working of the entire Constitution. My emphasis is on Article 370. The Cabinet talked about devolution of power by quoting NDA manifesto that it is not a matter of autonomy as such: it is a matter of devolution of power. That is what the Cabinet decision rejecting the resolution has said.

The Minister of Home Affairs (Shri L.K. Advani): We have not used the word 'reject'.

P.A. Sangma: Yes, they did not use the word 'reject', but the sum and substance of it is rejection.

Shri L.K. Advani: We have said, we cannot accept it.

P.A. Sangma: That is why, I am saying that they have very calculatedly and very wisely spoken about the devolution of power.

* * *

Yes, it has appeared in the newspapers saying that it is a matter of devolution of power and not merely of autonomy. That is the sum and substance of the decision.

I think, therefore, what is important is to emphasize on the devolution of power and the basis, as I have always been saying, should be the Sarkaria Commission Report. The Sarkaria Commission Report speaks of cooperative federalism. It is a new word, but it has become a very popular word. May be, there could be a way. The cooperative federalism as per the Sarkaria Commission Report may be made applicable to the rest of India, but as far as Jammu and Kashmir and the North Eastern States are concerned, I think that Article 370 and Article 371 are very important and we will have to see how these articles can be made more effective and more workable.

I come from an area where there has been a lot of insurgency. So, we have a similar experience of the situation the people of Jammu and Kashmir are subjected to. On the one side, there are militants and terrorists, and on the other, the security forces. We know how security forces behave in the North Eastern region.

I think, the people of Jammu and Kashmir are really fed up of what is happening there. They have been sandwiched between the militants and the terrorists on the one side, and the security forces on the other side. I had a lot of interaction with the people of Jammu and Kashmir. People are looking for a solution. This is the time when we can really, perhaps, get a solution because people are wanting it. After 52 years of suffering and bitter experience, I think, they are wanting it now. Therefore, I do not think that we should close everything. I am not, I want to make it very, very clear, agreeable to any autonomy position which is pre-1952. But within the framework of the Constitution, within Article 370 of the Constitution of India, whether we can do something more for the people is the point.

I was reading some articles in a magazine which says, 'Eight to ten thousand students, boys and girls, of Jammu and Kashmir are studying in various colleges of Karnataka, after paying Rs 5 lakh to 7 lakh of capitation fees. Four to six thousand students from Jammu and Kashmir are studying in Maharashtra; they are studying in Gujarat, and in other parts of India.' Just imagine their plight; just imagine the kind of suffering they are undergoing. Therefore, I think, the economic development is a very important issue; job creation is a very important issue; people are not getting jobs there.

I would like to support Shri Madhavrao Scindia's point that when we talk about Jammu and Kashmir, our whole attention goes to the Kashmir Valley. In the process, we forget the people of Jammu; in the process, we forget the people of Ladakh. I think, it is a big injustice to them. When I visited Jammu, a few months back, they straightaway asked me, 'Should we also become terrorists? Should we also take to arms because unless we do it, we are not getting any attention from the Government? People who are taking to arms, those who are going underground, are the people who get every help, all the resources are poured there, and all the facilities are given there. Just because we are simple and peace-loving people, we are being neglected.' I think, this is a very important point to be noted down. Shri Madhavrao Scindia has made this point very effectively.

After all, Ladakh has resisted the resolution for autonomy, and they said 'no'; people of Jammu said 'no'. What does it mean? The people of Ladakh and the people of Jammu have rejected the demand for autonomy which was passed by the Jammu and Kashmir Assembly. I think, we must recognize that and do something special for them.

Sir, I plead with you that let this matter be taken very seriously and cautiously. Let us not condemn everybody. It has to be solved through a dialogue. I am very happy that the Government of India is going to open a dialogue with the Hurriyat leaders and there has been a ceasefire. This is a very, very positive development. I must congratulate the Government for that. The only question mark is, somewhere I read, whether this move has anything to do with the Prime Minister Vajpayee's visit to USA in September 2000 when he meets President Bill Clinton. We do not know what transpired between President Bill Clinton and Prime Minister Vajpayee during the American President's visit last time. They are due to meet in September 2000 and we know what America thinks about all this. So, there are some apprehensions. I set it aside, but the initiative to talk to them and the ceasefire is a welcome thing. I congratulate the Government for that.

I think, when we are talking about a dialogue, we will have to have a dialogue in a democratic way. People are really representing the people, and therefore, this is very important. Thank you.

The Uttar Pradesh Reorganization Bill, 2000*

Mr Chairman, Sir, I rise to support the Bill and I support it wholeheartedly. In fact, according to me, the creation of Uttarakhand or Uttaranchal – whatever it may be – the creation of Chhattisgarh and Jharkhand have been long overdue. Today, I am very happy that this session of Parliament is responding positively to the aspirations of people of Uttarakhand, aspirations of the people of Chhattisgarh and aspirations of the people of Jharkhand. In fact, I beg to differ from honourable Member, Shri Basudeb Acharia, who says that creation of more states will be dangerous to the unity and integrity of the country. In fact, it is the other way round. If the country today fails to respond to the aspirations of the people in different parts of the country on time, then, there is a danger.

Today, why are national parties declining? Today, why is there a mushroom growth of regional parties? It is because we have failed as far as the regional aspirations of the people are concerned. Today, why are people taking arms? Today, why is the country facing the problem of terrorism? It is because we have failed to respond to the aspirations of

L.S. Deb., 1 August 2000 (Spoke while participating in the Uttar Pradesh Reorganization Bill, 2000). The Bill provided for creation of a separate State of Uttarakhand by reorganization of Uttar Pradesh.

the people on time. You may differ, but this is my perception. Everybody has got his own perception. Today, why are people demanding more autonomy? It is because we have failed to respond to the aspirations of the people on time. According to me, responding to the aspirations of the people is very important. Today, why are there so many regional disparities? Because of the regional disparities across the country, today, you can yourselves see what is happening in this august House. The composition of this House is a reflection of those regional disparities. From one-party Government, today, we have twenty-four-party Government. Why is it so? Therefore, I am in support of creation of more States. I am for it. According to my humble and personal view, Uttar Pradesh needs to be further bifurcated. I am very clear about it. I extend my full support to Shri Ajit Singh who is spearheading a movement for a separate Western Uttar Pradesh State. I think he is justified. I support him. I do not want to discuss everything here today. When the country like the United States of America, which is smaller than our country, can have fifty States, what is wrong in India having thirty States?

* * *

I am talking about population. Our democracy is based on people. I am talking about the people of India. That is what democracy means. It is not land which is democracy. Today, I think, we are going to have twenty-eight now, with three more addition. Therefore, Mr Chairman, Sir, I fully support this bill. I fully support the creation of the three States. I am grateful to the Government and to most political parties who had supported this Bill.

I know, why Shri Basudeb Acharia and my respected senior friend Shri Mulayam Singh Yadav are opposing it. They have some reservations. I think, there are some political considerations. We cannot even ignore that. They have some political considerations. But on principle, I do not want to speak much on this having supported it wholeheartedly. I do not have much to say. I only want to suggest a few things. I fully support the amendment of Shri Jitendra Prasad that in this Bill, there should have been a clear provision for reservation of seats for the Scheduled Castes and the Scheduled Tribes.

* * *

Yes, Kumari Mayawati also raised this. I think, my respected leader Shri N.D. Tiwari also raised this.

Out of five parliamentary seats, there is one seat reserved for the Scheduled Castes. I would plead with the Government that one more seat for the Parliament could be reserved for the Scheduled Tribes of Uttarakhand. This is one request that I would like to make. Out of ninety Assembly seats, that would be created, as Shri Jitendra Prasad has already given an amendment – of course, I would differ on number, he has asked for four, I would certainly ask for more – I would suggest that it could be eight seats for the Scheduled Tribes.

* * *

With this, modification, I fully support it.

Another point that I want to bring to the notice of the august House is that though the Scheduled Tribe population in the undivided Uttar Pradesh was about 0.2 per cent and yet as far as access to Government services in the State was concerned, the Scheduled Tribes were given two per cent jobs. Two per cent jobs were reserved for them. Now that their population percentage-wise will be much higher within Uttarakhand, I would request the honourable Home Minister, of course it is not in his jurisdiction but when the Government is formed there, to impress upon that Government, if it could be impressed, that some reservation with a higher percentage in the State service be reserved for the Scheduled Castes and the Scheduled Tribes.

I will not dispute the fact of Shri Mulayam Singh whether Uttarakhand will be economically viable or not. But that is a point which Shri Singh has raised. When you are talking about the unity and integrity of the country, when you are talking about strengthening our nationhood, I do not think, we can every time on all occasions go by economic considerations.

Why Shrimati Indira Gandhi, the then Prime Minister of India decided to create seven States out of one in the North East? Was it on economic considerations? No, it was a political consideration. She knew that the North Eastern States would not be economically viable at that time and yet a decision was taken. We cannot go everywhere on economic considerations. What is important from the point of view of unity and integrity of the nation is the political consideration, the social consideration, besides the economic considerations.

Uttarakhand is going to be a very rich State because it has got so many natural resources. I think, Gen. Khanduri has spoken very confidently about how it is going to be economically viable. I wish him all the best. But till it becomes economically viable, perhaps, Uttarakhand could be considered to be included in the list of special category States at par with the North Eastern States.

One more point I want to make for the protection of the tribals in the Uttarakhand area. I am suggesting this for the new Government which will come in. For them, I am suggesting firstly to create a separate district in the areas which are predominantly dominated by the tribals, and then at a later stage, if these areas could be brought under the Sixth Schedule of the Constitution of India, then, I think, the economic progress and the social progress of the tribal people in Uttarakhand will grow very fast.

On behalf of my party and on behalf of myself, through you, Sir, I would like to covey my congratulations to the people of Uttarakhand, the people of Chhattisgarh and to the people of Jharkhand, and wish them all the best, all success, progress and prosperity.

Minorities and Secular India*

Mr Chairman, Sir, we, in our country, have the heritage of one of the oldest civilizations in the world. As has already been stated, our country is known for its tolerance, our country and our people are known for our commitment to secularism. Unfortunately, our life at the threshold of the third millennium has been marked by atrocities against minorities, particularly, the Christians and the Muslims.

It is a fact that the atrocities against minorities, particularly, the Christians since 1998, have been much more than the attacks cumulatively from 1947 to 1998. Therefore, there is a question mark. How is it that after the BJP-led Government came into being in our country, the atrocities on Christians have gone up? It is not merely the atrocities that are worrying us.

*_L.S. Deb._, 17 August 2000 (Spoke while participating in the discussion under Rule 193 regarding Atrocities on Linguistic and Religious Minorities in the Country).

As far as I am concerned, there are five areas of concerns which I would like to point out to the honourable Home Minister. First is a geographical spread that a systematic attack on Christian community is not confined to any particular area or region, it is spread all over the country. Some reference has already been made to the meeting of our honourable Prime Minister with the Holy Father, Pope John Paul II. We do not have any official information as to what transpired between the two leaders. But I did read in the newspaper that on 24 June 2000, when our Prime Minister came out after meeting the Pope and when he was asked by the media, he replied, 'Attacks on the members of the Indian Christians are only isolated acts and there is no organized campaign against them.'

But the facts are otherwise. I was going through the reported incidents that took place since 1998, and I found that there are as many as 13 States, in the North, in the South, in the West, in the East and in the North East where there have been attacks on the minorities. Now, if the attacks are taking place in the North East and they are taking place in the North, in the South, in the West, in the East and in the Central part of our country, how can we say that the attacks are isolated? They are not. It is taking place all over the country.

The second area of concern is the severity of violence. Each type of crime that is described as grievous crime has been committed—housebreaking, theft, robbery, illegal detention, murder, arson, rape of nuns, desecration of places of worship, burning of the Bible, etc. Therefore, the severity of the violence is such that today the minorities of our country are certainly losing their faith in the Government. There is no doubt about this.

You may defend it in any manner you like; you may speak in any manner you like; you may quote from anywhere. You may quote here any type of statistics but what is important is the feeling of the minorities. What do the minorities feel about it? You cannot overcome the feeling of the people by mere statistics. The feeling today is, as Shri Suresh Kurup has said, that we are being treated as second-class citizens in this great country of ours. Therefore, as you may try to do whatever you want to do – as the popular saying goes, 'justice not only has to be done but also seem to be done' – you have to bring confidence in the minds of the minority people of this country. Merely giving a good speech is not going to assuage the feelings of the minorities. Therefore, the matter is very serious.

The third area of concern is the connivance of the political parties and the connivance of political elements. Whether it is the Bajrang Dal, the VHP or the RSS, these organizations have been in existence for years and years. How is it that they did not operate in that scale before 1998? How is it that after 1998 these organizations are openly coming out and making all inflammatory statements. This would not have been possible had there not been a support behind the political parties, by groups that are part of the political parties. Therefore, I think, the Government of India has a very important role to play.

The fourth area of concern is the complicity of the state machinery. Whenever an accident takes place, some enquiry is made outwardly. The state machinery is not serious to find out the real culprits. Shri Santosh Mohan Dev has asked if it is not the Bajrang Dal, the RSS, the VHP or the BJP, who has been doing it? Is it the ISI? I will come to the subject of ISI later on, but it is very important that we find the truth, and the machinery is geared up for that.

The fifth and the most important point that I would like to make is about the casual, technical and routine attitude in the replies of the honourable Minister of Home Affairs. The matter was raised in the last session of Parliament. The matter was discussed during the twelfth Lok Sabha. During the twelfth Lok Sabha and the thirteenth Lok Sabha, a number of Starred and Unstarred Questions have been asked. If you look at the replies by the honourable Minister of Home Affairs, there is no difference. The same replies given during the twelfth Lok Sabha have been given again.

The same reply has come for that I have the latest reply. On 25 July 2000, honourable Home Minister, replying to Shri J.S. Brar and Shri Kamal Nath, had said that the incidence of violence against the Christians has increased to some extent. I do not know what does this 'to some extent' mean. He further said that the law and order is under the domain of State Government and therefore, we have nothing much to say. I do not think that is enough.

If you really take a serious note of what I had said about the geographical spread, the severity of the crime and the way the State machineries are functioning, I think, the honourable Home Minister has to take it as much more than a routine matter. The Home Minister cannot escape from the responsibility, simply by saying that law and order is a State subject. It is something more than the State subject. I was wondering as to why such a thing is happening. What is the fault?

What is the crime that the Christian community in India has committed? I have not been able to find out any reason.

I can tell the honourable Home Minister and I can declare it on the floor of the august House that the Christian community in this country is a very very timid community. In fact, I have been blaming the Church leadership. I have myself been blaming the Church hierarchy as to why they made us very timid. I told them that they have never taught us to fight for our rights. I told them that they always told us that if somebody gives a slap on the right cheek, we must turn the left cheek and say, 'Give me one more.' They said that this is how we should do and we have been trying to do that. We have not harmed anybody in this country. If that is the case, why should anybody be against us? I do not know.

As a single community, we have contributed so much to this country. We have thousands and thousands of educational institutions. We have more than ten million students studying in Christian institutions and ninety-five per cent of them are non-Christians.

During the twelfth Lok Sabha when the matter was being debated, I remember, the honourable Home Minister, Shri Advani stood up promptly and said, 'Do you know, Shri Sangma, I am also a product of St Patrick School.' Kumari Uma Bharati also stood up and said, 'Do you know, Shri Sangma, in my house, I have the picture of Christ.' 'Come and see that I have a picture of Christ in my house,' is what Kumari Uma Bharati said. If that is the attitude, why do these atrocities happen?

Dr Malhotra has given us some hints. He said that the Pope had come here and spoke about harvesting of souls. He asked what is the meaning of harvesting of souls. I do not know whether Dr Malhotra has read the Bible or not. He feels that harvesting of souls means conversion. What is conversion after all? They are afraid of mass conversions. Where are mass conversions going on?

I do not know from where did Dr Malhotra get the figures about the Muslims, increasing from eight per cent to twelve per cent.

* * *

No, I am sorry. It is not. I think, you have not been given the correct picture. I have got the correct picture with me, which I have taken from the Census of India, 1991. You do not have to come to my rescue. I will do it myself. This is the Census Report. According to 1961 Census, the percentage of Muslim community in India was 10.7; in 1971, it was 11.2; in 1981, it was 11.4 and in 1991, it was 11.7. This is what the Census figure is.

* * *

Come to Christianity. What is the population of Christians in India? In 1961, it was 2.4 per cent; in 1971, it was 2.6 per cent; in 1981, it was 2.4 per cent – from 2.6 per cent it has come down to 2.4 per cent; and in 1991, it was 2.3 per cent. Population of Christians are coming down and not going up. But you say mass conversion is going on. Because of this mass conversion in India to Christianity, our population has come down by 0.1 per cent.

* * *

We had hundreds of years of British rule in India. We had Portuguese rule in Goa. We had French rule in Pondicherry. Still we are only 2.3 per cent. How is it? Where is the fear?

Let's take up the North East. They say the whole North East has been captured and that the people of North East have been converted into Christianity and that they have become anti-nationals. What is the picture in the North East? North East has got seven States. According to the Census figures, the Christian population in Arunachal Pradesh is 10.29 per cent; in Assam, it is 3.31 per cent – remember in Assam, the Christian population is 3.31 per cent – in Manipur, it is 34.1 per cent; in Meghalaya, it is 64 per cent; in Mizoram, it is 85 per cent; in Nagaland, it is 87 per cent; and in Tripura, it is 1.6 per cent. Out of the seven States, only in three States, the Christians are in a majority and in the remaining four States, Christians are in minority. Then, how do you say that the entire North East has been converted into Christianity? These are all unfounded fears. I do not know whether I should speak so much. Dr Vijay Kumar Malhotra mentioned about protection to minorities. I am very happy that he mentioned about it. Of course, Shri Santosh Mohan Dev has said who has started this protection to minorities. What does the Constitution of India say?

When I was the Speaker of Lok Sabha, that year happened to be the fiftieth year of our independence. The august House would remember that we had a special session to commemorate the fiftieth year of independence. At that time, a lot of foreign visitors and research scholars came to me to find out how India could preserve parliamentary democracy for fifty years without any interruption, whereas many developing countries could not preserve their democracy. How could India preserve its democracy for fifty years without any interruption? A lot of research work is still going on. Whoever had met me told me that they are impressed with one thing, namely, they were convinced that democracy in India could survive for fifty years without any interruption because the Constitution of India has given enough protection and safeguards to the minorities and weaker sections of people. Do not destroy it. Do not try to distort it. Protection to minorities is the secret of our success. Protection and safeguards to minorities is the secret of preservation of democracy of our country.

Prof. Malhotra talked about what you call the 15-Point Programme and the Minorities Commission. The whole House knows how the 15-Point Programme is working and how much benefit the minorities are getting out of the 15-Point Programme. I do not think I need to repeat it. I only want to say one thing. The National Commission for Minorities Act was passed in 1992. It replaced a Commission which was established in 1973. I have ascertained from the Government sources as well as from the library that so far twelve reports of the Commission have been tabled in both the Houses of Parliament. But unfortunately, none of these twelve reports has ever been discussed. Not even one report has been discussed. Now, who is at fault? I do not blame the Government alone. I think the Opposition is also needed to be blamed. We only talk about the minorities. I do not know how many of us have got the copies of those twelve reports. Twelve reports have been tabled and not even one report has been discussed. I would like to get an assurance from the honourable Home Minister that if not in this session, in the next session of Parliament, the reports of the Minorities Commission would be discussed.

I would like to make one more point. I am not very much worried about the atrocities. Prof. Malhotra, if you read the history of the Church all over the world, you will find that the history of the Church is nothing but the history of persecution. I am not worried about it. What I am worried about is that it is tarnishing the name of secular India outside. The honourable Prime Minister was trying to justify what is happening in India when he met the Pope in Rome. I may inform you, the honourable Home Minister and my friends in the Treasury Benches, that when I go abroad – I do go abroad quite often – questions are asked to me about the atrocities committed in this country. I feel sad about it. I can inform you that as far as possible, I have been trying to defend our actions here. I have been saying that India is a secular country. What is happening is just a temporary affair perhaps and India will return to secularism. I have been saying so. Therefore, what kind of image we are creating for India in the rest of the world? What kind of impact is it going to have on our foreign policy? Do you want to make all the Christians of the world our enemy? Do you think India can live in isolation in this global era? It has so many other implications. It is not merely a question of burning a church here. Do we have the statistics how many temples are there in Europe? How many Gurudwaras are there in Europe? How many temples have been constructed in Africa? How many Hindus live outside India? Do you know that it can have some impact on them? Have we thought about our brothers and sisters who are outside India? A couple of years ago, I went to a country called Croatia. In Croatia, there is a small town called Split. I stayed there for a day's holiday to see the rural area. The honourable Deputy Speaker accompanied me. When I was walking the street of Split town in Croatia, I found a lot of people gathering and watching something.

Out of curiosity, since I had gone there for walking, I thought let me see what is happening there. I went there. You know what was happening there; '*Hare Rama Hare Krishna*' was going on in that remote place of Croatia. It was so nice and so beautiful. I felt so happy and proud. Therefore, I think, we should think of all these implications. If somebody feels that India can be ruled and India can survive just like that, I am afraid.

I would like to remind one more point for the benefit of the august House. I would like to remind the speech of our former Prime Minister, Shri P. V. Narasimha Rao during the debate in the special session on fifty years of freedom of India. He spoke about a future Cold War on the basis of what is popularly known as Huttington's Thesis. It is written on a book called *Clash of Civilisations* where he said that the future Cold War is not going to be between two sovereign nations. The future Cold War is going to be between two Blocs – the Islamic Bloc on the one side and the Christian Bloc on the other side. God forbid that it does not happen. Suppose it happens and the world is moving towards that, then where do we stand? Where will India stand? If India is compelled by circumstances that either we have to identify with one of the Blocs, either Islamic Bloc or Christian Bloc, then what is going to be our choice? It is good to keep that in our mind. It is good to keep that in mind as responsible leaders of the country.

I do not want to take much time of the House. There are many honourable Members who want to speak on this subject. I had a lot of things to say. But may I, once again, request the Treasury Benches, the leadership there, to ensure that we uphold secularism in this country. It is secularism and secularism alone which will strengthen the unity and integrity of this country.

Thank you.

~

The Prevention of Terrorism Bill, 2002*

Mr Chairman, Sir, much has already been said about POTO today. The Lok Sabha and the Rajya Sabha have debated separately. I do not want to take much of the time of the august House. I would basically make 3–4 points.

There are different dimensions of terrorism. The first dimension is to deal with the export of terrorism into our country, which we call 'cross-border terrorism'. The second dimension is domestic insurgency. I come from an area and region where we experience every day as to what domestic insurgency means. The third dimension of terrorism is the combination of the first and the second one, that is the exported terrorism and domestic insurgency. The fourth dimension is narco terrorism, which includes terrorism across the borders and the related crimes. Then, of course, the fifth dimension of terrorism, that is, the organized crimes and terrorism operating in tandem.

Another one, which sometimes we forget to think about, is the way terrorism is growing technologically. Terrorism growing technologically with highly destructive weaponry and the use of communication system. Last but not the least is globalization of terrorism. It is no more the crime confined to a particular country or any particular area. It has become global.

**L.S. Deb.*, 26 March 2002 (Spoke while participating in the discussion on the Prevention of Terrorism Bill, 2002, moved by Shri L.K. Advani). The Bill provided for the measures for the prevention of and for dealing with terrorist activities and for matters connected therewith.

Sir, Al-Qaeda is reported to have their operation centres in twenty-one countries including India. Now, given these dimensions of terrorism, how do we deal with that is a very pertinent question. The question arises whether the present type of terrorism that is existing here and everywhere, particularly in India, can be dealt with by the existing legal systems, the Indian Penal Code or the Criminal Procedure Code – TADA has been repealed. Can this problem be dealt with the existing law is a question before the nation. My humble opinion is that the dimensions of terrorism has taken such a shape – I have given some examples – that this problem cannot be tackled by the existing legal system, within the framework of the existing laws.

What is terrorism? What does our law say about terrorism? Is terrorism a crime under the Indian Penal Code? Has terrorism been defined in the Indian Penal Code? To my knowledge, 'no'; terrorism has not been defined. Therefore, we feel that there is a need for a separate legislation to tackle terrorism in our country. We are the country which has suffered maximum due to cross-border terrorism and India has been pleading with the whole world at every international forum, impressing upon the world community on the dangers of terrorism, the dangers of cross-border terrorism.

I had the privilege of leading Indian delegations many times to many countries. In every international forum we had impressed upon them to recognize how dangerous it was, how India was facing cross-border terrorism. We did not get much of a response, to be very frank. Even recently, the Government of India was very kind to send parliamentary delegations to many countries. I had the privilege of leading one of the delegations to the European Parliament. We went there to tell the European community what cross-border terrorism means, what terrorism means. Smt. Margaret Alva is just back from the IPU Conference at Marrakesh and Smt. Najma Heptulla is the Chairperson of the IPU. I know that there was an India-sponsored resolution in the IPU Conference, because when I went abroad, to European countries, I got a lot of fax messages saying that I must campaign for getting support to the resolution to be tabled by India on terrorism. When we have been doing all this and when we have been trying to mobilize the world opinion against terrorism, how can we say that we should not have a law to curb terrorism? I do not think we can sell this idea now. A law is required. We will have to have a law and terrorism has to be dealt with very seriously.

When this Ordinance was promulgated, we had reservations. We had a party meeting chaired by our President Shri Sharad Pawar. We asked our legal cell to advise us. We had a lot of reservations about the Ordinance, but when the honourable Prime Minister called the All-Party Meeting, my leader Shri Sharad Pawar attended it and he proposed eight specific amendments to be carried out in the revised Bill.

I must thank the Government. The Government has accepted most of the amendments that we suggested in that meeting. We are grateful for that.

The apprehension that is being expressed is very genuine. There might be a misuse of this law as TADA had been misused. Particularly, the minority communities in this country are very apprehensive. We must recognize that and accept it. We must ensure that this law is not misused.

But the point is that it will be misused. I do not think there is any law in our country that is not misused. Every law is being misused. In my view, that apprehension for misuse of the law should not be a reason for not enacting a law. How can this be a reason not to enact a law?

Now, who will do the misuse? That authority which is implementing it will do the misuse. It is the State Government that will invoke POTA. It is the State Government that will implement this law. As Shri Somnath Chatterjee has rightly pointed out, most of the States in this country are being run by the Opposition parties. So, I do not know why they are thinking of misusing it. They should not. I appeal to them not to misuse this law.

With these words, I extend our support to the Bill.

~

Strengthening India's Security Management System*

Madam, at the outset, I would like to say that cross-border terrorism by Pakistan, visits by the Ministers, by the leaders of the political parties to the places of terrorist attack, statements by the leaders of India, diplomatic responses by the international community, the so-called high level

---

**LS Deb.*, 17 May 2002 (Spoke while participating in the discussion under Rule 193 regarding the terrorist attack on the Passengers and the Army Camp at Kaluchak in Jammu).

meetings, and, of course, the discussion on the floor of Parliament, chat shows on the electronic media, stories in the print media and life as usual thereafter have become all too routine.

Please look at the latest situation arising out of the terrorist attack in Jammu, the issue which the august House is discussing now. The honourable Defence Minister is very prompt in visiting the places of attack. So also, so many other leaders visited those places. Statements have come right from His Excellency Mr Kofi Annan, the Secretary General of the United Nations down to Prof. Vijay Kumar Malhotra, the spokesperson of the ruling BJP Parliamentary Party.

What kind of statements have come? I would like to remind this august House about the immediate reaction of the honourable Prime Minister of India. I quote: 'The incident is outrageous.'

What is the immediate reaction of the honourable Defence Minister of India? I quote: 'Nothing better can be expected from President Musharraf. Pakistan will be punished. Appropriate action will be taken at the appropriate time.'

Now, this Parliament and one billion people of India will have to wait when that appropriate time will come. Prof. Vijay Kumar Malhotra is very bold. I quote: 'America cannot be depended upon to help us. We have to fight our battle ourselves.'

Congratulations. What was the reaction of the official spokesperson of the Ministry of External Affairs Ms Nirupama Rao? I quote: 'The United States understands our concern.'

We are talking so much about the United States of America, my elder brother Shri Dasmunshi has extensively quoted from Ms Christina Rocca. But what did the official spokesperson of the White House say? I quote: 'Kashmir is a difficult situation with occasional violence.'

That is what the White House spokesperson has said.

My friend His Excellency Mr Blackwell, the Ambassador of the United States of America, said this. I was seeing it on the Star Television. After meeting the honourable Home Minister, he comes out and says: 'Terrorism is terrorism is terrorism.'

But the Chief of our Armed Forces, General Padmanabhan, is, of course, very forthright. He said: 'Time for statements is over. Now, it is time for action.'

He is very bold. Though the time for statements is over, in addition to all the statements that I have read out, I am compelled to make one more statement. I am constrained to say that we have become a nation of empty statements and statements of the obvious. How long are we going to make statements? How long are we going to have the so-called high-level meetings? How much benefit has been brought by the visits of the different Ministers and the leaders of the political parties? Have we found any solution? Under the present circumstances, what are the options available to us? Have we really explored the possibilities? Did this Parliament today try to find out what are the possibilities that are available to us? I am afraid, we are lacking in application of mind. The so-called experts on defence, the so-called experts on security policy are giving a number of options open to us which everyone of us is reading in the newspapers.

What is the first option? We must go for limited war. I really do not understand as to what is the meaning of limited war. Can there be a limited war? If there is a limited war, what kind of limited war we are talking about? After the nuclear tests, Pokhran-II, when the Parliament debated about our nuclear policy, I said on the floor of the House that till today the whole world had recognized us as a military superior than Pakistan. But we did the tests. Followed by Pakistan, all that we did is that we had equated ourselves with Pakistan. We have become equals. India is a nuclear power and Pakistan has become a nuclear power. So, from the military superiority, we rendered ourselves in equality.

After that till today or till before yesterday, I am afraid, I may have to make amendment in my previous statement. I am not sure as to whether we are still continuing to be equals. I am not very sure about it. Today, we are in such a receiving end, absolutely. You talk on diplomatic channels that you are talking about. You talk of cross-border terrorism: the number of people being killed in this side. The way we were stuck in Agra, are we still equals? I do not know. We have to think over it very carefully.

We have become a nuclear power and the Government of India has vowed before the whole world that we will not use it first: there is 'No First Use Policy'. We have to wait till Pakistan attacks us. We go on waiting till Pakistan attacks us and go on tolerating and tolerating and say that lets have a diplomatic offensive. The honourable Defence Minister goes to Jammu and Kashmir; let the Parliamentary delegation go to Jammu and Kashmir, we will not use this nuclear weapon. We have adopted before the whole world 'No First Use Policy'. I do not know, I hope the people of India are listening.

What is the other option? They say that we must go for economic sanctions. What kind of economic sanctions? Is Pakistan dependent on trade with India for their survival? Are they dependent on us? We declare economic sanction, America and the West, for their own selfish interest, will pour in millions and millions of dollars in Pakistan. What are your economic sanctions going to do? Is it practicable? It is not a practicable option.

We must wind up the office of the High Commission. We must expel the High Commissioner of Pakistan from India. What is the result? I do not know. I do not know as to what result abrogation of the Indus Water Treaty would bring in? These are the options that are before us. We do not know as to whether they are the real options and as to whether we can openly discuss here. If the country had been very serious about this, I would have perhaps preferred Parliament sitting in camera.

I would have preferred that, if we were really serious about our future. Then, what should we do? Where is the solution? The solution actually lies here, in the Kargil Review Committee Report. Here is the solution; fifty per cent solution lies here in this book and fifty per cent solution lies with the will of the Government of the day. If the Government has the will and if they follow what is written here, we can find a solution. The Kargil Review Committee Report was submitted almost three years ago. The House had an occasion to discuss it and when it was placed before the august House, the Government stated:

> The Kargil Review Committee has made as many as 25 recommendations which seek to bring out mainly the deficiencies in India's security management system . . . After due consideration of these recommendations, a thorough review, through an appropriate body, of the national security system in its entirety, including the area covered by the above recommendations of the Committee is being ordered by the Government.

Madam, almost three years have gone. What action has been taken in this respect? I would like to remind this nation – maybe we have forgotten, even I almost forgot about it; I woke up only when I was asked to speak by my leader on the floor of the House, I tried to bring out this book from my library – what is written in the Kargil Review Committee Report. I think it is good for the country to know. I may be permitted to read only three paragraphs from Chapter XIV of this Report which contains recommendations. It says:

> The findings bring out many grave deficiencies in India's security management system. The framework Lord Ismay formulated and Lord Mountbatten recommended was accepted by a national leadership unfamiliar with the intricacies of national security management. There has been very little change over the past 52 years despite the 1962 debacle, the 1965 stalemate and the 1971 victory, the growing nuclear threat, end of cold war, continuance of proxy war in Kashmir for over a decade and the revolution in military affairs. The political, bureaucratic, military and intelligence establishments appear to have developed a vested interest in the *status quo*. National security management recedes into the background in time of peace and is considered too delicate to be tampered with in time of war and proxy war. The Committee strongly feels that the Kargil experience; the continuing proxy war and the prevailing nuclearised security environment justify a thorough review of the national security system in its entirety. Such a review cannot be undertaken by an over burdened bureaucracy. An independent body of credible experts, whether a national commission or one or more task forces or otherwise as expedient, is required to conduct such studies which must be undertaken expeditiously. The specific issues that required to be looked into are set out below.

The next paragraph is very important.

* * *

I do not know and I would like to know from the Government. With all my due respect to you and every individual – no aspersions – please listen to the next paragraph. It says:

> The National Security Council (NSC) formally constituted in April 1999 is still evolving and its procedures will take time to mature.
>
> Whatever its merits, having a National Security Advisor, who also happens to be Principal Secretary to the Prime Minister, can only be an interim arrangement. The Committee believes that there must be a full time National Security Advisor and it would suggest that a second line of personnel be inducted into the system as early as possible and groomed for higher responsibility.

May I know from the Government whether recommendations of the Kargil Review Committee has been implemented? Do we have a full-time National Security Advisor of the country or are we still continuing with a part-time Advisor? This is a very important question. This

Government owes an explanation to this country. This Report speaks so much about the Military Intelligence. We read and saw in the electronic media that those Pakistanis who had gone to Afghanistan to help the Taliban regime had been sent back to Pakistan. Do we know what they are doing now? Do we know where they are? Do we know how many of them are there?

The newspapers and the electronic media has predicted that the cross-border terrorism is bound to increase because those people, who were in Afghanistan, are back in Pakistan. Could we not anticipate that? It was because we did not perhaps have any agency to anticipate that.

I have only one question today. I would like to get an answer from the Government of India to each and every recommendation, numbering 25. What action has been taken on all those 25 recommendations? This nation should know about it.

Thank you.

~

Cross-Border Terrorism: What Should Be India's Response*

Mr Chairman, Sir, I join this House in condemning the Kasimpura massacre of the innocent people by the terrorists obviously from across the border. On 17 May 2002, this House had debated on the massacres in Kaluchak. In that debate, the House explored the possible options against Pakistan – whether we should go for a full-fledged war, whether we should go for a limited war, whether we should go for economic sanctions, whether we should go for coercive diplomacy, etc. The House was unanimous that certain actions have to be taken against Pakistan and we left entirely to the Government to decide what kind of action should be taken. We gave the Government a blank cheque saying do whatever you want to do, we are completely with the Government, behind the Government, and that you can go ahead with whatever you

---

**L.S Deb.*, 16 July 2002 (Spoke while participating in the Motion for Adjournment on the massacres in Kasimpura, Jammu, on 13 July 2002 and the failure of the Union Government to combat cross-border terrorism, initiated by Shri Shivraj V. Patil).

want to do. The Government in its own wisdom decided to go for, what you call, the coercive diplomacy.

After having opted for coercive diplomacy, the Government has claimed that their policy has been successful. Now, as part of that diplomacy, what did the Government do? I would like to trace the history of our policy and our actions on Kashmir issue since this Government has taken over. The honourable Defence Minister, Shri George Fernandes mobilized the forces along the LoC. He also mobilized the Navy on the Arabian Sea strategically. The Government expelled the Pakistan High Commissioner from India. The Government of India prohibited the Pakistani flights over our air space. The Government withdrew our High Commissioner from Islamabad. My good friend, Shri Jaswant Singh, the then Foreign Minister did his diplomatic work. This is what has been done from the side of the Government. Internationally, there was subtle diplomacy on the part of the American authorities right up to the Defence Secretary, Mr Rumsfeld, the European Union authorities, and Mr Jack Straw from the United Kingdom also joined the bandwagon. They kept on visiting New Delhi and Islamabad. I do not know how many times they came. I have to remember it. Every time they came to India, whether it was Mr Jack Straw or whether it was Mr Rumsfeld or whether it was anybody else, they deeply appreciated the restraint on the part of India. They also claimed that General Musharraf of Pakistan had promised to end infiltration and cross-border terrorism into India permanently. That is what they claimed and the Government of India was very happy. Our Defence Minister, our Foreign Minister, our Prime Minister and our Home Minister were very appreciative with the kind of help that the United States, the United Kingdom and the European Union were giving.

They believed them so much that the Government and the Defence Minister decided to call back the Navy. The Navy was withdrawn. The Government decided to restore the Pakistani flights over the Indian space. The Government also decided to restore the diplomatic relations with Islamabad. The Indian High Commissioner to Pakistan has already been named though he has not yet joined there. Having done that, what is the atmosphere in Pakistan? What is the reaction of General Musharraf? General Musharraf is laughing. He has ridiculed India.

The *Times of India* in its report on 25 June 2002 quoted General Musharraf as saying that the so-called de-escalation by India and withdrawing the Navy from the Arabian Sea is a measure which is cosmetic. That is what he has said; that it is nothing but a cosmetic measure. General Musharraf said:

> By the so-called de-escalation, India is easing its own problems. The Defence Minister of India, by mobilizing the Forces in the LoC and also mobilizing their Navy in the Arabian Sea, created problem for themselves and therefore they wanted to ease that problem and they have withdrawn the Navy. It is only easing their own problems.

This is what General Musharraf is talking about our honourable Defence Minister and our honourable Prime Minister. In spite of the fact that, the Defence Secretary of USA saying that General Musharraf has promised to end infiltration and cross-border terrorism into India permanently, he said that he had not given any assurance to anybody about these things. I myself saw and heard what General Musharraf said on the electronic media. He has said that he has not given any assurance to anybody regarding infiltration and that he cannot assure that nothing will happen for years to come. This is what General Musharraf said. He said, 'I have not given any assurance to anybody. I cannot guarantee that there will be no more cross-border terrorism, that there will be no more infiltration in India. I cannot guarantee that.' This is what General Musharraf says. But because Americans were saying, 'No, General Musharraf has told us and has promised that he will stop infiltration and cross-border terrorism permanently,' the good Indian Prime Minister and the good Indian Defence Minister believed the Americans so much. I remember Shri Fernandes appearing before the Star TV and saying that there was downscaling of cross-border terrorism. He has claimed that. How do you justify your statement that there is downscaling of terrorism and cross-border terrorism after what has happened in Kasimpura? Does it justify the statement of the honourable Defence Minister?

I really respect and appreciate our Minister of State for Home Affairs, Shri I.D. Swamy because he is really an articulate and very confident person. Whenever he appears on Television, I find him so confident and articulate that I really admire him. I heard him on TV saying about the Kasimpura incident. He said it on TV that an incident of this kind cannot be prevented. What a state of helplessness on the part of the Government and what a state of surrender on the part of the Government of India? It is a Government for one billion human beings and the honourable Minister of State for Home Affairs speaks like this. I have also been the Minister of State for Home Affairs at one point of time, may be 15 years ago. I never dared to make a surrendering statement like that. Why should a Minister of State for Home Affairs of the country say that an incident of this kind cannot be prevented? All right, if it is not practically preventable, you are not supposed to say like that. It demoralizes the whole nation. It demoralizes the country. I think the honourable Minister should be a little more careful in his own statements.

What is the net scenario today? It is a very difficult situation. We have the ruler in Pakistan who speaks in multiple voices. He enjoys ridiculing India. I have seen him so hundreds of times. He enjoys ridiculing India. And we are a very silent society and a silent country absorbing everything. We have the so-called international community, the United States, the United Kingdom and the whole European Union who are not able to hold General Musharraf, who are not able to make General Musharraf do what he had promised to do.

When it comes to the United States and when it comes attack to the twin towers of New York, Americans are very sensitive. They feel that it has hurt their ego and they declared a war against terror. They are very concerned and committed to implement the United Nations Resolution No.1373. But when it comes to India and when it comes to Jammu and Kashmir, it is all right. What to do? It has been happening for the last fifty years. It will continue to happen. They are not at all concerned. What about us?

On 17 May in this august House I delivered a much lengthier speech on the attack at Kaluchak. Every time something happens, Opposition demands that there should be a debate in the House. The Government says that it is ready for discussion on any matter. Everybody speaks out, everybody criticizes the Government and everybody gives his ideas. Once Parliament Session is over, everything is forgotten. Every time in Parliament we say, 'We authorize you to do whatever you want to do, we are with the Government and the nation is united.' After all this, innocent people die. What are we doing? What is the benefit of the debate of 17 May? I have not seen any effect of Parliament of 17 May, two months back. I read out chapter after chapter of the Kargil Report. There were about 25 recommendations of the Kargil Commission. Let me know whether any of those 25 recommendations of the Kargil Commission has been implemented by the Government. I shouted on the floor of this House. Till today, has any one of them been implemented? No. Then, what is the point of debating here? I think the

Opposition should apply its mind very carefully while demanding for a debate. If the Opposition demands for a debate and when the Government immediately concedes it, then we are helping the Government only. It may think, okay, let it be laid over, let them shout and let the discussion take place. We have nothing to do. Let the Opposition shout, let them speak whatever they like. We will sit quietly. The debate that takes place in Parliament is a regular feature but what happens after the session is over. Everything is forgotten by the Government.

I feel the so-called coercive diplomacy of the Government of India has been a disaster, absolutely a disaster. The Government claims that its diplomacy has been a big success. If it has been a success, then to whom the credit goes? The credit goes to Shri Jaswant Singh, the then External Affairs Minister. Then, why has the Government transferred him to Finance Ministry? What is the logic? A successful External Affairs Minister, who successfully carried out the Government's policy of coercive diplomacy has suddenly been shifted to the Finance Ministry. And who has gone to External Affairs Ministry? It is Shri Yashwant Sinha. I was in the Government of India for seventeen years as Union Minister. I have dealt with the bureaucracy. I know the ego of the IAS officers. I also know very well the ego of the IFS officers. From my past experience, I have my own doubts about an IAS officer presiding over the kingdom of the IFS officers. Mr Minister, please do not do such things for the sake of doing it. you must apply your mind. Shri Yashwant Sinha, who was a bureaucrat, who was an IAS officer, cannot possibly preside over the kingdom of the IFS officers. I have my own doubts about it. I would request you to think over about it. I do not understand the interchange of the Foreign Minister becoming the Finance Minister and the Finance Minister becoming the Foreign Minister.

The BJP has a lot of good qualities. You are very capable. I think the BJP is the only party which has a very solid kind of think tank which applies its mind. This has been demonstrated in such a manner that the BJP think tank has been able to conduct a coup against the honourable Prime Minister, Shri Atal Bihari Vajpayee so smoothly, so successfully and so democratically. When you can conduct a coup against the Prime Minister Shri Vajpayee, I do not understand why you cannot plan and do a similar coup against Mr Musharraf. Why you cannot do it? If you want to do it, I know you can do it. You have done it. A coup against the Prime Minister is a big thing. Why you cannot do it against

Pakistan? Please do it, Mr Deputy Prime Minister, I think it is time you act. At the same time, I am not at all advocating a war. But if the USA can go to Afghanistan and destroy the training camps, the terrorist camps in Afghanistan, if the USA has a right to do it, why should India not have the right to do it? You are depending so much on what the USA is doing. You should also do what the USA is doing. Please do not depend on what they say. You should also do what the USA is doing. Please act.

With these words, I thank you for having given me this opportunity to speak.

Gujarat Incident: An Erosion of the Secular Credential of the Country*

Mr Chairman, Sir, thank you very much for giving me this opportunity to speak on this Motion. I rise to support the Adjournment Motion.

Sir, I was trying to go through the proceedings of the House for the last few years and I found that this Parliament, rather this tenure of the NDA Government is a period where this House has discussed the communal situation in the country for the maximum number of times. Never before has this House discussed the communal situation in the country, on the floor of the House, as frequently as we are doing now. I think, the House will remember as to how many times we have discussed the situation in Gujarat. We discussed this during the last Budget Session as well as during the Monsoon Session. We should apply our mind to the fact as to why this is happening. The honourable Home Minister, in particular, should find out, why is it that the august House has to spend so much time on discussing the communal situation in the country again and again without any results?

Sir, in fact, I was reluctant to participate in this debate because I find that we are wasting time by accusing each other and things are going on unabated in Gujarat. I think, the honourable Prime Minister and the honourable Home Minister should take a serious note of this.

---

*_L.S. Deb._, 18 November 2002 (Spoke while participating in the Motion for Adjournment on the issue of failure of the Government in curbing the communal elements in the country, especially Gujarat).

It is not a fact that there has not been any communal riot situation or a communal problem before. Of course, there has been. But what happened in Gujarat has no parallel in the history. That is the most worrying factor. In the words of Justice Verma, Chairman of the National Human Rights Commission, 'The communal carnage in Gujarat is nothing short of a war in terms of suffering and misery undergone by the affected.' So, it is a very serious situation. Therefore, what I am personally worried is the manner in which it all happened. The shape the communal riots had taken in Gujarat is really a very worrying factor.

I do not want to waste time of the august House. I am concerned in three areas. Watching what is happening in Gujarat, I find that a communal divide appears to be the sole strategy to return to power by the BJP. That is a very dangerous thing. It is true that in spite of so many solemn assurance by various political parties on communal harmony that communalism will never be used during the time of elections – we all make promises – every political party does indulge in some sort of a religious sentiment. That we cannot deny. But what is happening in Gujarat today is that the election strategy of the BJP itself seems to be completely hinged on the communal divide. I think this is not good. Not only for Gujarat, this is very very dangerous for the future of India, for the unity and integrity of India, and more so for secularism in this country.

The second point that I would like to make is with regard to the kind of disrespect being shown for the institutions. The manner in which the Chief Minister of Gujarat is defying and castigating a constitutional authority like the Election Commission is a very dangerous sign. Even the Supreme Court is being challenged by some Chief Ministers. I am not blaming A, B or C, but the tendency to attack, to defy and to denigrate the constitutional institutions is a very dangerous trend. After all, if a nation has to survive – I have spoken on the floor of this House on this issue once elaborately – we have to ensure that we uphold the systems that we have created in this country. Once you try to dilute a system, the question of good governance does not arise. So, for the purpose of good governance, we have to preserve, we have to strengthen our system and follow the systems that we have set. We cannot afford to deviate from that. We do have to uphold, respect and strengthen our institutions. So, I would appeal to all constitutional authorities—whether it is Governors, whether it is Chief Ministers, whether it is

Members of Parliament, whether it is bureaucracy—that the first duty of a responsible citizen of this country should be to respect our institutions.

The way Mr Modi has gone out of the way to attack the Chief Election Commissioner pains me very much. Mr Lyngdoh comes from my State. I know him very well. It is very difficult to get an upright person like Mr Lyngdoh who believes in sincerity and commitment. We the people from Meghalaya feel very very proud of this gentleman. He is so impartial; he is so committed to the Constitution and to his duties. To say that Mr Lyngdoh is having a nexus with the Opposition leaders and with the Congress Party – I am sorry – is nothing but making wild, wild, wild allegations against this gentleman.

This is unfair. This is very very unfair. In fact, I personally feel and the people of Meghalaya feel that it is an insult to us, it is an insult to the tribal people, it is an insult to the people of Meghalaya; and it is an insult to the people of the North Eastern region. Please for God's sake, do not do like that. It is not good, and I do not like it. I want to make it very very clear.

Besides upholding the institutions, to attack an individual who is a responsible citizen of this country is unfortunate. Please stop it.

After all, who is Mr Modi? Constitutionally, he has no moral right to continue there. He has no moral right to continue as the Chief Minister. I do not know why the honourable Home Minister has not imposed President's Rule; and why Article 356 has not been invoked?

Again, I come to my first point that the communal divide is the main election strategy of the BJP in Gujarat, and to do that they find that Mr Modi is the right person. Therefore, he is not being removed, and he is being allowed to continue.

Sir, with all my due respect, please do not think about winning one election. You may win five elections; you may lose two elections. Winning and getting defeated in elections does not matter. It does not matter at all. What is important is the future of India; what is important is the future of generations; what is important is the Constitution of India; what is important is the systems that we have established; what is more important is the constitutional institutions that we have developed. We have the right and duty to preserve all this. I appeal to the Government to keep all this in mind.

With these few words, I conclude. Thank you.

Successful Democracy: Fulfilling the Aspirations of People*

Mr Deputy Speaker, Sir, yesterday the honourable Defence Minister quoted a paragraph from the book written by one of the Ambassadors of America to India. Today, I would like to quote some other Ambassador. Mr John Kenneth Galbraith, once upon a time an Ambassador to India, has described India as a functioning anarchy. He described India as a functioning anarchy. I was wondering if Mr Galbraith would have witnessed the proceedings of this august House, perhaps he would have described it as dis-functioning anarchy. I think, we need to do something to have a meaningful debate. It is not necessary to have the debate always in tension. We should relax sometimes, listen to each other and have some tolerance.

This is the 26th No-Confidence Motion in the history of Indian Parliament. With my due respect to Shri Yerrannaidu, I would say that it is the right of the Opposition Party to table a No-Confidence Motion. It is a question of judgement for the Opposition about the timing, purpose and issue of the No-Confidence Motion. Yesterday some people had come to see me. They were telling us:

> After listening to the speeches of Chandrashekharji and Mamataji, I am feeling that what was the necessity of No-Confidence Motion.

I think Shri Chandrashekhar had referred to the way the Congress has been cooperating with the Government in passing the Bills without any discussion. One of them was a little desperate. I think, he is a very strong supporter of the Congress. He said, 'I do not know who has advised Madam to bring this No-Confidence Motion'. The other person said, 'Do you not know who has advised her?' The first one said, 'No,' to which the second one said, 'Arre, it must be Atalji himself. It must be the Prime Minister himself who has advised the Leader of the Opposition to bring this No-Confidence Motion.' There is an impression that there is a perfect understanding between the ruling party and the main Opposition party, at least between the two heads.

Whenever we listen to Shri Jaipal Reddy, some of us have the

**L.S. Deb.*, 19 August 2003 (Spoke while participating in the discussion on the Motion of No-Confidence in the Council of Ministers).

opportunity of enriching our English vocabulary and some people like me, of course, get nervous. There was a point of order raised by an honourable Member that he was not able to understand what Shri Jaipal Reddy was speaking and the Chair upheld the point of order saying, 'Even I do not understand.' Shri Jaipal Reddy said yesterday why this No-Confidence Motion was brought and I quote: 'To win the hearts and minds of the people.' This No-Confidence Motion has been brought for winning the hearts and minds of the people. Who has coined this phrase 'winning the hearts and minds of the people'? Incidentally or accidentally, it happened to be coined by Donald Rumsfeld, the Defence Secretary of the Bush Administration to justify its war on Iraq. I do not know why Shri Jaipal Reddy has particularly chosen this expression from Donald Rumsfeld.

The immediate reason for bringing this No-Confidence Motion, as we all understand, has been the PAC report vis-à-vis the CVC. I do not go into the details of that. I think, it is proper for me to quote Shri K. Subrahmanyam who was quoted yesterday by the honourable Leader of the Opposition. Shri K. Subrahmanyam, in his recent article, 'How Safe We Are Is a Secret' – that is the title of the article – writes and I quote:

> Post World War II, defence management and budgeting have been thoroughly overhauled and modernised in the UK and USA but in India this crucial sphere remains an arena for political grandstanding. For example, our so-called scams regarding weapon's acquisition deals almost invariably focus on the procedural aspects of such negotiations losing sight of the fact that it is not the procedure which calls for scrutiny but the clandestine payoffs that take place outside the loop. The result is that often the purchase of urgently required material is chronically delayed because those entrusted with the task are too wary to take a decision for fear of being subsequently pilloried for corruption. Once again, in the name of national security, the same security is jeopardised.

I think that is good enough.

I would like to make one point. Many other honourable Members of the Opposition have pointed out regarding the boycott of the Defence Minister. As a humble parliamentarian – I have been in this Parliament for more than 25 years now – I feel that it is not correct for the Parliament or for any party to boycott a Minister. It amounts to a challenge to the constitutional authority of the honourable Prime Minister. Therefore, if anybody has to be boycotted, I think, it should have been the Prime Minister and not the Defence Minister. I am, therefore, happy that yesterday the Congress party was good enough to hear his speech.

The honourable Deputy Prime Minister and Minister of Home Affairs yesterday, while opening his speech, said, 'I welcome this Motion because it has given an opportunity for the Government to highlight their achievements.' I think for more than two hours this morning the honourable Minister of Parliamentary Affairs, Smt. Sushma Swaraj has also tried it. I have prepared a very small progress report of this Government. I will be very brief and I will just go through a small progress report that I have prepared about the NDA Government.

In the first paragraph of the NDA manifesto of 1999, it says: 'Time-bound programmes for administrative reforms including police and other civil services'. This is stated in the first paragraph. I do not know what action has been taken. In my knowledge, no action has been taken. Para 2 of the manifesto says: 'Bring GDP growth to seven to eight per cent level and control the fiscal and revenue deficits'. I think we all know what the GDP growth is. The GDP growth rates have been 6.25 per cent in 1999-2000, 4.3 per cent in 2000-2001 and 6.00 per cent in 2001-2002 and it is estimated to be 4.2 per cent in 2002-2003. That is the performance of the NDA Government. In the same paragraph they said: 'Achieve foreign direct investment of at least 10 billion US dollars per year'. That is stated in paragraph 2 of the manifesto. Honourable Minister Shri Arun Shourie is very much here and he will tell us. But my information, according to your Economic Survey, the actual inflow of foreign direct investment has been 2.2 billion US dollars in 1999-2000, 2.3 billion US dollars in 2000-2001 and 3.9 billion US dollars in 2001-2002. This is against ten billion US dollars per year as stated in the manifesto. Paragraph 6 of the manifesto says: 'Increase national savings to 30 per cent of the GDP'. This is what your manifesto says. But the total domestic savings as per the Economic Survey is only of the order of 23 per cent. Paragraph 7 of the manifesto says: 'We will constitute a development bank to promote the requirements of the self-employment and unincorporated sectors.' I have not heard of such a development bank which wants to promote self-employment to our young people. Paragraph 11 of the manifesto says: 'Make labour in the organized and the unorganized sectors equal partners in production'. I know that the second National Labour Commission has been appointed and its report has been submitted on 1 June 2002. I take a lot of interest in this matter because I happened to be Labour Minister for nine years. I am not sure whether this report of the National Commission is being implemented or not.

On unemployment, they have said in paragraph 12 of their manifesto, 'thrust on berozgari hatao.' Now, according to your own report, unemployment level is seven to eight per cent on current daily basis as far as unorganized, uneducated labour is concerned. When you come up to educated youth, unemployment ranges from 17 to 20 per cent. I would like to know from this Government where is the slogan of berozgari hatao?

In para 13 of the manifesto, it is said, 'We will embark on a strategic pro-poor policy for the upliftment of people living below poverty line.' Now, all the various activities under poverty alleviation programmes, which have been in existence for long, started by the Congress party are being continued. May be, people say that the number of people living below the poverty line has come down to 26 per cent, but I do not know the actual position.

In para 14, the manifesto says, 'We will ensure food security for all to create a hunger-free India and improve public distribution system.' We know what is happening in Orissa. We have starvation death reports and as against the requirement of 17 million tonnes as buffer stock, we do have a stock of 48 million tonnes of foodgrains, yet our public distribution system has thoroughly failed.

On drinking water, para 15 of your manifesto says, 'Provision of drinking water to all villages within five years'. Now, my information says that there are still 127,000 habitations in the country which are only partly covered or fully uncovered as far as supply of safe drinking water is concerned. Where is the slogan of safe drinking water in five years?

Education for all is what para 16 of your manifesto says. It says, 'Education for all and investment on education at six per cent of GDP'. In fact, investment of six per cent of GDP for education was decided by the Narasimha Rao Government, but what is the position of its implementation today? If you scrutinize the budget, you will find that the country as of today is spending only 3.7 per cent of the GDP for education though we made a policy that six per cent of GDP shall be spent on education.

This morning, there was a heated debate on empowerment of women, political empowerment of women. I am not going into that. My name was also dragged by Smt. Sushma Swaraj, but I do not want to make any comment on that.

NDA manifesto in para 18 says that you shall establish a development bank for women entrepreneurs. I do not know where is that development bank for women entrepreneurs. I am yet to see it and I am yet to hear about it. Then, para 20 of your manifesto says, 'Establishment of national charter for children to relieve them from hunger and illiteracy and give them health care'. I do not know where is the national charter.

In para 21, you have mentioned to stabilize population by 2010 by improving access to primary education, health services and universalization of primary education. I think, we all know that it is a big goal.

Now, on Scheduled Castes and Scheduled Tribes, your manifesto on para 37 says that you will present a national charter for social justice for Scheduled Castes and Scheduled Tribes. I do not know whether this has been done, but on this particular issue, I would like to make one more point. I had spoken about this particular issue on a number of occasions on the floor of the august House. I have met the honourable Home Minister also a number of times. The reservation of jobs for Scheduled Tribes in the jobs of Delhi Government has been kept in abeyance. Thousands and thousands of jobs, which were meant for the Scheduled Tribes in the Delhi Administration, are not being given to the Scheduled Tribes. They are just being kept in abeyance. We have made a lot of moves. The Commission for Scheduled Castes and Scheduled Tribes have taken a decision; the honourable Home Minister has assured me so many times, but till today it has not been done. I am sorry to state but the Scheduled Tribe boys and girls have no access to the Government jobs in the capital of India, and then you talk about bringing the tribals into the national stream or mainstream. It is absolutely contradictory of what you are doing.

I am sorry and I find that the honourable Home Minister is not here. I have decided that if this matter is not decided in the next one week, I will go on an indefinite hunger strike in front of the honourable Home Minister's residence.

Next, I come to the point on secularism. I just do not want to talk much on secularism. Last time, in the debate, I talked about Professor Huttington's book on clash of civilizations. I do not want to talk about it and repeat it. But, what I want to point out is the manner in which the minorities – particularly the Muslims and the Christians – are being subjected to so much of atrocities. I think you forget that millions and millions of our people have gone to those countries where they belong to that particular religion. You talk of West, you talk of America, you talk of Middle East; millions and millions of Indians have gone there and are earning their livelihood, and here we have treated them in such a manner. I think, it is very very unfair. I think, your outlook has to be broadened and this has to be done.

As far as this debate is concerned, I do not want to prolong more, but in the beginning I started by saying that had Mr John Kenneth Galbraith witnessed our session, then he would have described it as a dis-functioning anarchy.

* * *

Sir, today in the *Times of India*, there is a very interesting cartoon by Shri R.K. Laxman, and it shows two MPs entering the Parliament and they are shown as saying: 'Pandemonium at eleven, stalling the proceedings at eleven thirty, walkout at twelve o' clock. After that we can meet and plan our election strategy.' This is the impression of people about us; about the Parliament; and about our behaviour. Let us correct ourselves. Please, as a former Speaker of this august House, I would once again plead with all the honourable Members that let us listen to each other. Why do we have to make too much provocative speeches? I think the ruling party is still suffering from Opposition syndrome. I remember, Atalji proudly saying in many occasions that: 'I have been in Opposition for forty years.' With pride he speaks, the honourable Prime Minister, I think, this forty years in Opposition is not going out of his mind, and out of the mind of many of you. Therefore, I still see the Opposition syndrome in the Treasury Benches. Why do you have to make such provocative speeches?

I do not think you need to worry about this No-Confidence Motion. The honourable Defence Minister has come here and he knows much more about defence. Of course, my leader was also a Defence Minister, once upon a time.

I am told there is something called UXO. It means Un-exploded Ordnance. I think this No-Confidence Motion is nothing but UXO. It will not explode.

~

Need for Amendment of the Citizenship Act*

Mr Speaker, Sir, the IMDT Act has been one of the most controversial piece of legislation since its enactment in 1983. This Act has dominated the politics of Assam for more than two decades. This Act was also the election issue for more than two decades.

I had an opportunity of being a Member of the Standing Committee for the Ministry of Home Affairs and the Leader of the House was its Chairperson. I have heard all the representations; all the evidences; and gone through a lot of documentation, but I do not want to go into all those details. The fact remains that infiltration is a problem in the North East and nobody can deny it. the fact remains that demographic changes are taking place in the North East and nobody can deny it. The fact remains that it is a genuine concern of not only the people of Assam but of the entire North Eastern region.

We have heard the speech made by the honourable Member from Arunachal Pradesh, and we will hear from a representative from Assam on this issue. I also feel that this problem has to be tackled.

I am not blaming anybody and, perhaps, it requires a bigger debate. Today, we are debating on the Supreme Court's verdict of scrapping the IMDT Act. While you can see, on one side, that the people are rejoicing on the verdict of the Supreme Court, on the other hand, you can see the fear psychosis in the minds of the minorities. I agree with Mr Kapil Sibal who says that we should not do anything that will divide the country. But I can tell you that this one piece of legislation which really divided the people of Assam between the majority and the minority. You cannot deny that fact. But now that we are in a stage where the Supreme Court scrapped this law, and we must recognize the genuine fears of the minorities, something has to be done. I will only deal with that point.

I fully agree with the honourable Leader of the House who in his speech has said that it was our duty to protect the genuine rights of the genuine citizens. I fully subscribe to that. My only difference is that in order to achieve this objective of protecting the genuine rights of the

---

**L.S. Deb.*, 26 July 2005 (Spoke while participating in the Motion for Adjournment on Massive Immigration from Bangladesh).

genuine citizens of India residing in Assam, who belong to religious minorities and also, maybe linguistic minorities, I suggest that instead of going for an amendment of the Foreigners Act, the Government should examine the possibility of amending the Citizenship Act. This is the difference I have got with the Leader of the House. You think that the Foreigners Act needs to be amended. I do not subscribe to that. To my mind, we must go for an amendment of the Citizenship Act. That will overcome the problem which Shri Kapil Sibal has also pointed out – the amendment to Section 3. That will also be worked out, once you come out with a proposal for amendment.

The point that I am trying to drive is that we have wasted more than two decades in trying to identify the foreigners. I have the figures which have already been quoted. I have the same figures because we have the same source which the Leader of the House has. The only thing that the Leader of the House forgot to mention is that the number of illegal migrants who were detected was 11,306, but the number of people who were deported was 1,500. It means that not all of them were deported. We have wasted our time in trying to detect the foreigners. My suggestion to the Government is why not look the other way round. Let us try to identify the genuine Indian citizens first. Please identify the Indian citizens, give them, as suggested by the honourable Member from Arunachal Pradesh, a National Citizenship Identity Card. For example, I would like to quote from the same figures. Under the IMDT Act, enquiries were made against 368,609; enquiries were completed against 361,162, and the number of illegal migrants detected was 11,306. It reveals that out of 368,609 enquiries, 349,658 are Indian citizens. Why cannot we straightaway give these 349,658 people Citizenship Identity Cards so that the police will not harass them? What the minorities really want today is only protection and they should not be harassed.

Under the Foreigners Act, out of 517,955, only 28,000 were detected as foreigners. That means 517,531 were genuine Indian citizens. Why do you not give them identity cards so that they will have no fear psychosis and policemen would not go and question them? I want the process to be reversed. Instead of going after foreigners, you identify Indians, give them certificates and give them identity cards. But, that has to be done within a time frame of six months. After that, those who are registered as Indian citizens can be given identity cards. To the remaining, you can give work permits.

Millions of Indians are working in Gulf countries. Millions of Indians are working in other parts of the world. Why cannot Bangladeshis come and work in India? You give them work permits. Let them work here and let them earn their living, but they will not have any political rights. That is the thing. Leaving aside those who have been issued identity cards and those who have been issued work permits, the rest of the population should automatically be deported. That is the formula I would like to suggest to the Group of Ministers constituted by the honourable Prime Minister.

Thank you.

MATTERS RELATING TO COMMERCE, INDUSTRY AND ECONOMIC DEVELOPMENT

Developing the Handloom and Handicrafts Sector in India*

Mr Deputy Speaker, Sir, I will be very very brief in my intervention. Honourable Members are aware that the Export–Import policy has been announced on the fifth of this month and some of the honourable members have now just referred to it. I feel it has become the latest fashion with the Opposition to take the name of IMF and what not. I need hardly point out to the honourable Members that our policy has been not only welcomed by the trade and industry including the Press, but I must say it has been hailed as bold and a gift to the small-scale sector, etc.

Sir, I am only confining myself to a very limited issue. I will be referring to the two important sectors – handloom and handicraft. Handlooms have been given a pride of place in our new textile policy which has been announced last year and also it has been given a very important place in the revised 20-point economic programme announced by the honourable Prime Minister.

In terms of employment, the handloom industry which provides employment to nearly ten million people is next only to agriculture.

The Sixth Five Year Plan envisages a total production of 4,100 million metres in this handloom sector. This represents an increase of nearly 40 per cent over the base level as against 8 per cent in the mill sector. The importance that the Government attaches to this sector, the priority that the Government have given and the commitment that we give to the development of handloom industry will be evident from the fact that

*_L.S. Deb._, 8 April 1982 (Spoke while participating in the General Discussion on the Demands for Grants for the Ministry of Commerce, 1982-1983).

under the Sixth Five Year Plan, the outlay stands at Rs 120 crore as against the Fifth Five Year Plan outlay of Rs 37.70 crore only. In addition to this, a further provision of Rs 190.93 crore has been made under the State sector.

Many a times questions have been raised in this House during the Question Hour regarding the availability of yarn to the weavers. In order to ensure the availability of hank yarn to the handloom weavers, the Government has taken a number of steps and some of these are the following:

There is obligation on all the spinning mills and composite mills to pack not less than 50 per cent of their total marketable yarn in the form of hanks. Further, 85 per cent of the hank yarn should be in count 40s and below.

Number two: Setting up of 25 handloom weavers' cooperative spinning mills each with 25,000 spindles for which a provision of Rs 32 crore has been made in the Sixth Five Year Plan. So far, 36 mills with 84 lakh spindles have come up in the handloom weavers' cooperative sector. During 1981-1982, Rs 650 lakh has been given as assistance and a provision of Rs 800 lakh has been kept in the year 1982-1983.

Regarding the availability of working capital to the handloom weavers, I want to inform the honourable Members of the august House that there has been a considerable improvement in this respect also.

As far as the credits in the cooperative sector is concerned, the Reserve Bank of India has considerably liberalized the terms of credit on the recommendations of the Committee set up to study the RBI scheme for handloom finance. The credit limit sanctioned under the scheme has increased from Rs 26.43 crore in 1976-1977 to over Rs 60 crore in 1979-1980 and Rs 90 crore in 1980-1981 in the current financial year, the figure is likely to exceed Rs 100 crore.

As far as weavers outside the cooperative fold are concerned, the Government are considering the recommendations of the study group set up to study the commercial bank lending to handloom sector. Already the handloom weavers are eligible for composite loans to the extent of Rs 25,000 with interest rates varying from nine per cent to 11.5 per cent and carrying an initial moratorium.

Some honourable Members also have mentioned about Janata Cloth Scheme. This scheme for production of control cloth in the handloom sector was started in October 1976, with the twin objectives of providing cheap cloth to the weaker sections of population and sustained work to the handloom weavers. The scheme is currently being implemented in 14 States and one Union Territory. The total production of Janata Cloth went up from level of about 10 million metres in 1976-1977 to an impressive figure of 290 million metres in 1980-1981. The provisional figure for the first nine months of 1981-1982 is about 258 million metres and our target for 1982-1983 is 325 million metres.

The august House is aware of the various measures taken by the Government to protect the handloom sector. One of the important policy support measures for tackling the marketing problems in the handloom sector is the scheme of reservation of certain lines of production exclusively for the handloom sector. As the honourable Members have pointed out, I must admit that there are a number of practical difficulties which limit the usefulness of the reservation orders as they exist today. The notifications have been repeatedly challenged in courts. In order to study the various problems about the reservation of handloom sector, a Study Group under the Chairmanship of erstwhile Textile Commissioner was set up by the Ministry of Commerce. The Study Group was expected to study the whole gamut of the reservation orders including the necessity for bringing in a fresh legislation instead of putting the reservation under the Essential Commodities Act. The report of the Study Group has already been submitted and is under consideration of the Government. We have also announced earlier that the Government has decided to set up National Handloom Development Corporation and we hope to launch it within this financial year. We also hope that the Institute of Handloom Technology for North East will start functioning soon. The handloom export has registered a phenomenal increase from Rs 25.61 crore in 1970-1971 to Rs 330 crore in 1980-1981.

Now, coming to the Handicrafts sector, I must say that this is an equally important segment of the decentralized sector of our economy. For the year 1982-1983, an outlay of Rs 10 crore has been provided.

The major developmental activities to be undertaken during 1982-1983 pertain to massive training in carpet weaving, art metal wares, hand-printed textiles, cane and bamboos, designing and technical development, preservation of heritage of craft skills and marketing. A provision of Rs 6.90 crore has been made for this purpose. In hand carpet weaving alone, 463 training centres are running and over one lakh persons have been trained. The trust now is being shifted to advanced training in weaving carpets of higher knot and quality. In other crafts also, training centres are being run, and there are 41 in art metal wares and 39 in cane centres and bamboo. It is proposed to set up a National Carpet Institute and an Institute of Hand-printed Textiles so that technical and design improvements can be made in both these items.

* * *

We will take a decision regarding location of these institutes. Sir, it is also proposed to set up 100 advanced training centres in Jammu and Kashmir. In order to benefit the craftsmen, who generally belong to weaker sections, it is proposed to set up common facilities centres with the cooperation of the State Governments, State Corporations and cooperative societies. If you read the annual reports, you will find that it is also mentioned there. These common facilities centres will be set up in the craft concentration areas of various crafts including handloom-printed textiles, carpets, wood, and metal ware and will provide facilities such as dying, wood seasoning, electro-printing, etc. It is also proposed to take up a scheme of assisting the craftsmen in building housing-cum-work sheds with the cooperation of the State Governments and banking institutions. As a result of the measures that we have taken, especially in the field of training, our export of handicrafts, excluding gems and jewellery, has risen from Rs 37.54 crore in 1970-1971 to Rs 314.26 crore in 1979-1980. Shri Patil has mentioned that the exports in handicrafts mainly pertain to gems and jewellery, but the figures that I have given exclude the export of gems and jewellery.

According to the provisional data, the exports have risen to Rs 357.10 crore in 1980-1981 and Rs 313.60 crore in the first ten months of 1981-1982. In order to further improve our export performance, a new Export Promotion Council for carpets has been registered in February 1982 and is expected to function shortly.

I had also thought that I would deal and say something about the silk industry, but very recently, this House had the opportunity of discussing about the silk industry in detail, when we moved the Amendment Bill to the Central Silk Board Act. I do not, therefore, propose to deal further with the subject of silk industry. I can, however, assure the august House that as far as the handlooms, handicrafts and silk industries are concerned, we are taking all possible steps to see that there is an all round development in these fields.

With these words, I conclude. Thank you.

The Handloom (Reservation of Articles for Production) Bill, 1985*

Mr Deputy Speaker, Sir, I beg to move:

> That the Bill to provide for reservation of certain articles for exclusive production by handlooms and for matters connected therewith, as passed by Rajya Sabha, be taken into consideration.

This is a very important Bill. Handloom is a very important sector of the textile industry. We have about 3.5 million looms spread all over the country and it gives employment to about ten million people. It is from this point of view that Government has been taking a special care to see that the handloom industry is protected and that the weavers of our country are also protected. During the First Five Year Plan, the Central Allocation for the development of handloom was only Rs 11.10 crore and by the Sixth Five Year Plan, it has gone up to Rs 120 crore. An equal amount has also been earmarked in the State Plans. Now our handloom sector produces about 3,252 million metres of cloth which is roughly 30 per cent of the total production of cloth in the country. If we look at the export front also, the handloom industry has been doing very well and in 1983-1984, the total foreign exchange earned from this sector is to the tune of Rs 310 crore. Now, because the handloom sector is spread all over the country, it is very difficult for the sector to compete with the other two sectors of the industry, namely, the mill and the powerlooms because the mill and the powerlooms have superior technology and they have also higher productivity and they are better located. Therefore, from the very beginning, the Government of India had been reserving certain items for exclusive production by the handloom sector. This was done for the first time in 1950 by the Textile Commissioner under the powers conferred on him in Clause 20 of the Cotton Textile Control Order, 1948. Then in 1955, it was brought under the provisions of Section 3 of the Essential Commodities Act, 1955. But of late, we have been facing some problems because some people have gone to the court challenging this very order of the Government of India. Therefore, from

---

**L.S. Deb.*, 28 March 1985 (Spoke while moving the Bill in the Lok Sabha). The Bill provided for reservation of certain items for exclusive production by handlooms and for matters connected therewith.

various forum there has been a demand that there should be a legislation which should give protection to handloom, and to achieve this object, we have brought forward this Bill which has already been passed by the Rajya Sabha.

In the present textile policy, handloom occupies a very important place. Now, you are aware that we are on the formulation of a New Textile Policy and I can assure the House that the handloom sector will continue to occupy an important place in our new policy also.

* * *

I am sure, the whole House will support this Bill unanimously. With these few comments, I commend this Bill to the House.

* * *

Mr Chairman, I am grateful to all the honourable Members for having welcomed and wholeheartedly supported this Bill. I must admit that every honourable Member of this august House, who has participated in this debate, has made very relevant and important points. They have also made lot of valuable suggestions and I can only assure this august House that all the suggestions that have been made will be kept in mind, when we frame our rules under this Act and when we go ahead with the implementation of various projects towards the development of handlooms.

One thing has to be kept in mind as a background and that is that handloom is a State subject. It is primarily the responsibility of the State Governments to develop the handloom industry. In fact, till 1976, the Central Government had practically nothing to do with the handlooms. But the Central Government felt the importance of the handloom sector in this country and, therefore, a committee was constituted under the Chairmanship of Shri Sivaraman to go into those areas where the Central Government could be involved towards the development of handloom sector and on the basis of the recommendations of that Committee a separate Department was created in the Government of India and a post of Development Commissioner, Handlooms, was created. Since then, the Government of India has been trying to help the various State Governments in various ways.

Many honourable Members have raised the question whether it will be possible for the Government of India to set up a separate Ministry or a Department to look after the handlooms. I am afraid that this proposal may not be acceptable to the State Governments.

Practically all the honourable Members have mentioned that this particular Bill will not solve all the problems of the handloom industry. I agree with them on this point. But I am sure that this Bill will go a long way in solving many of the problems of the handloom industry.

When we talk about the handloom industry, it is not a question of merely reserving certain items for production in the handloom sector. The honourable Members have rightly pointed out that the Government should give attention towards supplying essential inputs to the weavers, modernization of the looms and also providing them marketing network. All these things are very important. Unless and until we can provide them marketing network, help them to modernize their looms and make the inputs readily available to them within the reasonable price, the lot of these people will remain the same. We are fully aware of that fact. I am sure the House remembers that 1984 was declared as the year of the handlooms. We have taken a number of steps towards helping the State Governments to help the weavers. I myself had gone round the country and met corporations, apex societies, weavers, Directors of Handlooms and also the Ministers in charge of Handlooms. I had separate meetings with them. As a result of that, Government of India had, in fact, brought out a number of schemes for the development of the handloom sector. I can only assure the honourable Members once again that we have made an in-depth exercise as to what more should be done for the handloom sector during the Seventh Five Year Plan. We are committed to do that.

If we discuss about the various aspects of development of handloom industry, I think, it will take a lot of time. What is more important is supply of inputs, particularly yarn to the handloom sector, which has always been a controversial subject, because sometimes the prices go up very high and even if the prices are low, weavers do not get the benefit. The Government of India has taken a number of steps to overcome this problem. For example, the Government of India has made it compulsory for the spinning and composite mills to prepare not less than 50 per cent of their total marketable yarn in the form of hank yarn. Out of that 50 per cent, it is also made compulsory for them that 85 per cent should be below forty counts which is primarily required for the handloom sector. This is one step the Government has taken and already enforced.

Also as a long-term policy, we had decided initially to set up 25 weavers' cooperative spinning mills with a capacity of 25 lakh spindles, during the Sixth Five Year Plan. We had also decided to expand six spinning mills under the weavers' cooperative sector so that the weavers themselves can look after their requirements. A sum of Rs 32 crore was earmarked for this purpose. Later on, when we found that the money we had earmarked was not enough and the number of units that were to come up could not come up – in fact, instead of 25, the number came down to 13 – we went to the Planning Commission and got about Rs 10 crore as additional allocation for that purpose and ultimately we could raise the number from 13 to 20 spread all over with an additional capacity of 5.84 lakh spindles. I am sure that now all these new units are under various stages of implementation, once they come up into operation, most of the problems of yarn scarcity will be solved.

In order to meet the minimum requirements of yarn for the weavers, we have also thought of setting up yarn banks. Shri Priya Ranjan Dasmunshi made a strong plea for that. In fact, the National Handlooms Development Corporation which we have set up recently, has been working on that and so far we have been able to establish one such bank at Gauhati for the entire North Eastern region, two have already been opened in the State of Kerala and very soon we are going to open one in Bihar.

* * *

Well, in the meantime, the policy of the Government in regard to the spinning mills has changed because we have already achieved the full capacity of spindles in our country. We have the highest installed capacity of spindles in the world. Therefore, we have removed it from the delicensed list to the licensed list. It is not banned but I think in future the spinning mills will have to be located on merits and we are trying to confine it to a category of districts.

As far as the other States are concerned, we have said that the State Governments are free to set up their yarn banks and whatever assistance we can give, we are ready to give. In fact, the State Government of Kerala has taken an initiative at their own. I have been impressing upon the State Governments that they should immediately go in for these. Our Commerce Minister has actually decided that the yarn which we produce in our National Textiles Corporation will be made available to the Yarn Banks which would be set up by the respective State Governments, at mill rate. We are not going to charge anything more.

* * *

In fact, we give very liberal bank credits to the apex cooperative societies and I may inform this august House that in 1976-1977, the credit limit for the apex societies was Rs 24 crore, in 1982-1983, it was raised to Rs 153 crore and now in 1983-1984, we have further raised it to Rs 198 crore. We are also giving interest subsidy to the respective State Governments. Therefore, it is not a fact that the handloom sector is not getting credit. Credit is available. It all depends upon how active the respective cooperative or apex societies are.

Some of the honourable Members have very rightly raised the question of the middlemen making money. It was also suggested that the handloom sector should be brought under the cooperative societies. This has been the deliberate policy of the Government of India. In fact, during the Sixth Plan, our target is to bring 60 per cent of the handloom sector into the cooperative fold. I am happy to inform the august House that we will be able to achieve the target of 60 per cent under the cooperative fold.

Processing is another area which the honourable Members have not mentioned. But I want to mention it. Pre-loom and post-loom are very important parts of the handloom. We have been advancing a lot of money for this also. I do not want to quote the figures about the money we have given to the various State Governments for the establishment of dye houses at various levels. I can assure the House that if, in future, the State Governments come for assistance, we are ready to give it. I am not boasting, but it is a true fact that I have gone to some States and insisted that they should take some money, instead of allowing it to lapse.

Marketing is a very important sector, which was very rightly and very ably stressed and honourable Members expressed concerns about it. Unless we give a marketing network to the handloom weavers, it is very difficult for them even to survive, what to speak of progress. I do not know how we will be able to solve this problem. At the moment, we have a system of organizing national handloom depots at different cities, or at different places in the country, where we give 20 per cent rebate on the handloom cloth. Apparently, it looks as if it is working very well.

I do not know whether it is really working well, because some honourable Members have made some complaints. The honourable Member from Tamil Nadu was saying that we are not paying enough money for reimbursement. I may inform him that recently we have released about Rs 5 crore as rebate to the Government of Tamil Nadu. So, we have been trying to help them.

I have been personally thinking – I am not expressing this as the decision of the Government – what is important in the handloom sector firstly is to make the inputs, particularly the yarn, available to the weaver regularly and at reasonable prices. I have been personally trying to see how best it can be done. During the Seventh Plan, we should be able to come out with some formula about this.

Shri Reddy raised a very valid point as to why we did not have a Schedule where we could have mentioned a number of items which we are thinking of reserving for the handloom sector. We did not deliberately do it for two reasons. As I said in the beginning, while introducing the Bill, Government is at the moment formulating a new textile policy, where we are looking at the very structure of the textile industry. Therefore, we thought it better that we do it later on.

Secondly, if we have a Schedule and put it as an appendix then, if we have to revise any item at any time, Government have to come to Parliament for amendment of the Act, which may be a time-consuming process. That is why we have deliberately kept it open so that, if and when we think it necessary to revise the list, we can immediately do it. I can assure Shri Reddy and the House that we really mean business and I will ensure that no delay is there in implementing this Bill. We will certainly implement this Bill as early as possible.

* * *

Well, Mr Daga has raised a very interesting point. I was forgetting you Mr Daga – Mr Daga, of course, is a very interesting Member of the august House. I have been observing him for the last five years and now for the last three months. Every time a Bill is discussed in the House, he says that this Bill is not necessary, there is no point in bringing such Bills, these laws are not implemented and therefore, this Bill should not have been introduced and that this Bill should not have been brought at all. I think Mr Daga is by mistake in this august House.

* * *

You cannot rule out the relevance of laws and enactments in the country. That is what you have been advocating against. After all, what is the function of the Parliament? It is a legislative body of the Government.

* * *

Another point which Mr Daga again, and I think, an honourable Member from Karnataka, have raised is about Khadi.

* * *

Mr Daga forgets that he comes from a desert area and I come from a Himalayan area. If Mr Daga were to come to my place with his Khadi shirt, he will not survive there for two hours; and if I were to go with my Himalayan dress to the desert area, I will not survive there for two hours. So, I think the dress of a person should be left to the taste and requirements of the person and the area to which he belongs.

If we talk of Khadi, in my personal view, I would say we should think about the concept of Khadi when Khadi was propagated during the Independence movement. Gandhiji had given a call for every one of us to wear Khadi, to spin Khadi for ourselves only because at that particular time the textile industry under control of the British Government was not acceptable to us. Therefore, there was an incident of bonfire and Gandhiji gave a call that we should not wear clothes produced by the British textile mills. And what was the alternative? The alternative was that we should go in for Khadi and weave our own clothes.

Now, is it relevant today? Now, if today we have to say that everybody has to wear Khadi, I think the textile industry which has grown in the last thirty-five years may not survive.

* * *

Sir, I must respectfully submit that I am not against Khadi. Khadi has to be there. Khadi is a national dress. It has been accepted, but I am only saying that at this stage it may not be good for us to say that everybody should wear Khadi. That is not possible. I for one, if I do not like to wear it, I am giving my personal opinion.

* * *

I must humbly submit, I mean no disrespect to Khadi. Khadi has to be there; I am not disputing it at all, in fact when I say that I am not used to it, I must tell you that I do wear Khadi sometimes, but I do not wear it every time. I am giving my personal explanation, that is all.

* * *

The other points which have been raised by the honourable Members include constitution of the Advisory Committee. And on the other points I can only assure you that while constituting this Committee the Government will certainly keep all the suggestions which have been made in this august House in mind.

There was one particular point of penalty which, I think, a few honourable Members have raised and that is that the penalty of six months and Rs 5,000 is very small. I think you have read it partially. It is Rs 5,000 per loom. The penalty prescribed is Rs 5,000 per loom.

Another honourable Member has raised the question that there is no provision for making rules. Actually Section 19 empowered the Government to make rules.

With these few words, I request that the Bill be taken into consideration.

* * *

I should like to point out that Clause 19 of the Bill empowers the Government to frame rules, as to in what manner the Advisory Committee will be constituted. Clause 19 also clearly provides that all these rules, after these have been framed, will be laid on the Table of both the Houses of Parliament and, if the Parliament so desires it can discuss the rules and make recommendations for change in the rules. I can add that while constituting the Advisory Committee, we shall certainly keep the interests of the weavers in view, as I have promised.

* * *

Sir, I beg to move:

> That the Bill be passed.

The Coffee (Amendment) Bill, 1985*

On behalf of Shri Vishwanath Pratap Singh, I beg to move for leave to introduce a Bill further to amend the Coffee Act, 1942.

* * *

On behalf of Shri Vishwanath Pratap Singh, I beg to move that the Bill further to amend the Coffee Act, 1942, be taken into consideration.

As the august House is aware, the Coffee Board has been functioning with the prime objective of development of coffee plantations and regulation of sale and export of the produce from such coffee plantations. The Plan and non-Plan expenditure of the Board is met from the proceeds of the duties of customs and excise levied under the Coffee Act, 1942. The present rate of duty of customs and duty of excise on coffee have reached the upper ceiling of Rs 11.80 per quintal each fixed under the Act. These rates have been in vogue since 16 December 1977.

The Plan and non-Plan expenditure of the Board, excluding loans and subsidies, has increased from Rs 1.78 crore in 1978-1979 to Rs 3.90 crore in 1984-1985. The Budget Estimates for 1985-1986 are of the order of Rs 6.45 crore. The expenditure is, however, shot up tremendously over the years whereas the rate of duties of customs and excise are at the same level as they were fixed on 16 December 1977.

Under non-Plan, there has been increase in expenditure mainly due to increase in DA, ADA, Interim Relief, etc., in the establishment side and due to increase in research activities and marketing activities. Under Plan side also, a number of new schemes, viz., manpower development, opening of coffee demonstration farms, setting up of chemical laboratories, storage and warehousing capacity, etc., have been taken up and eight new schemes are proposed to be taken up during 1985-1986. The proceeds of the two duties would not be sufficient, and therefore, the Central Government had to resort to grant-in-aid to meet the expenditure of the Board during the financial year 1985-1986. Finding that the proceeds of the two duties levied under the Act are not commensurate

---

**L.S. Deb.*, 29 July and 19 August 1985 (Spoke while moving the Bill in the Lok Sabha). The Bill provided for further amendments of the Coffee Act, 1942 to inter alia make the provisions of Customs Act, 1962, applicable for the purpose of, and exemption from, the payment of duty of customs under the Coffee Act, 1942, w.r.t. export of coffee.

with the increasing expenditure of the Board, it has been found inevitable to amend Sections 11 and 12 of the Coffee Act to provide for a higher ceiling of levy of duty of customs and duty of excise at a rate not exceeding Rs 50 per quintal for each. The actual operative rates of the two duties will, however, be fixed at such levels as may be sufficient to generate funds to meet substantial part of the Budget expenditure of the Board in future.

In the interest of uniformity and administrative convenience, it is also proposed to make the provisions of the Customs Act, 1962, applicable for purposes of refund of, and exemption from, the payment of duty of customs under the Coffee Act, 1942, with regard to exports of coffee.

Opportunity is also being availed of to substitute for the provision relating to laying of rules contained in Subsection (3) of Section 48, a new provision on the lines recommended by the Committees on Subordinate Legislation.

With these few words, I take leave of the House for consideration of the Bill.

* * *

Mr Chairman, Sir, I thank the honourable Members who have participated the debate and have given very valuable suggestions.

Sir, the purpose of this Bill has been explained by me at the time of introducing the Bill for discussion in this House. So, I would not like to go into that once again.

As the organization grows, as the activity of an organization increases, naturally the expenditure also increases and therefore, it becomes necessary that in order to keep up the activity of the organization, the promotional activity of the organization, they should also have some sources of revenue. In 1984-1985, the total availability of revenue by way of cess collection was only Rs 143.29 lakh. The opening balance as on 1 April 1985 stood at Rs 67.22 lakh. And our budget estimates for this year, for Plan and non-Plan expenditure excluding loans and subsidies which I have mentioned earlier, is to the tune of Rs 6.45 crore. Therefore, it has become necessary for us that we look for some funds so that we can carry on the normal activity of promoting coffee production.

Coffee is a very important crop. It contributes substantially to the economy of our country, particularly in the southern part of the country. It gives employment to about 3.5 lakh people and its contribution to the foreign exchange earning is quite substantial – to the tune of Rs 400 crore. I am not going into details. One important aspect of the coffee industry is that unlike tea industry, 97 per cent of the coffee growers are small growers. Therefore, it becomes all the more important that Government takes proper care of them. an allegation has been made that the Government has been giving too much of importance to the tea industry and not to the coffee industry. Well, I think we differ in this and I would certainly not agree that there has been some sort of stepmotherly treatment to this industry, as somebody called it. On the other hand, I would submit that as far as coffee growers are concerned, they have been fortunate in the sense that there has been a stable policy as far as coffee is concerned. Whether it is in the field of production, whether it is in the field of auctioning in the domestic market, or for the export market, there has been some stability which stability has not been formed in the case of tea industry. The tea industry's fate has been fluctuating. This problem has not been faced by the coffee growers, only because the Government has all along been following a very stable policy as far as the coffee industry is concerned.

Somebody has pointed out that this Bill has come at a time when it should not have come. For a long time probably the honourable Member has this in mind that the price of coffee has fallen down in the international market. I agree that the price of coffee has fallen down in the international market, and it is because of this reason that recently, as soon as the price of coffee fell down in the international market, the export duty has been reduced and the honourable Members are aware of that.

Somebody made a point about the minimum release price. Though the minimum release prices are determined every three years, I think, it should have been done every year. But I am told that the price determination is so cumbersome that there is some difficulty in that. But I am trying to impress upon the Members that as far as possible we should have price determination every three years. I hope I will succeed in this. But one point which should be remembered is that though the minimum release price has been fixed at the rate of Rs 654 per bag, the ruling price is to the tune of Rs 911 per bag. Therefore, the ruling price is much higher than the minimum release price. Therefore, it would not be correct to say that the growers are not getting remunerative prices. On the other hand, as I have mentioned, the coffee growers have been getting remunerative prices and their prices have always been stable.

One more point I want to make on the export duty. Export duties are not charged when the international prices of the cheapest variety of coffee fall below the base remunerative price. It is only when it is above the base remunerative level, the export duty is levied. Therefore, I think, as far as the Government is concerned, we will make all efforts to see that there is stable policy so far as the coffee is concerned.

Only one more point I want to make to which Mr Rath has referred. It is regarding the growing of coffee in non-traditional areas. Coffee is not grown in all parts of the country. It is only grown, so far, in some of the States. We are contemplating a comprehensive plan for the cultivation of coffee in the non-traditional areas, particularly in Andhra Pradesh, Orissa and Nagaland.

I once again thank all the honourable Members who have participated in the debate.

* * *

I beg to move:

That the Bill be passed.

The Tobacco Board (Amendment) Bill, 1985*

Sir, on behalf Shri Vishwanath Pratap Singh I beg to move for leave to introduce a Bill further to amend the Tobacco Board Act, 1975.

* * *

Sir, I introduce the Bill.

* * *

**L.S. Deb.*, 9, 20 and 22 August 1985 (Spoke while moving the Bill in the Lok Sabha). The Bill provided for further amendments of the Tobacco Board Act, 1975, to inter alia increase the representation of growers on the Tobacco Board and matters connected with production, processing and licensing of Virginia tobacco.

Sir, I beg to move:

> That the Bill further to amend the Tobacco Board Act, 1975, be taken into consideration.

The Tobacco Board set up in 1976 under the Tobacco Board Act, 1975, has been functioning with the prime objective of development of the tobacco industry and regulation of the production and curing of Virginia tobacco having regard to the demand therefor in India and abroad and promotion of exports of tobacco and tobacco production. The working of the Tobacco Board, the efficacy of various provisions of the Act and their shortcomings, the problem of growers, curers, traders, exporters and others connected with unmanufactured tobacco and tobacco products have been in continuous examination of the Government. With a view to enable the Board to play a more effective role in production, development, marketing and export of tobacco, it has been found necessary to amend suitably the provisions of the Tobacco Act, 1975. It is accordingly proposed to bring about amendments to the Act to achieve the following objectives:

(i) To increase representation to the growers on the Board for more effective participation.

(ii) To empower the Tobacco Board to regulate production of Virginia tobacco inter alia on the basis of differences in soil characteristics and agro-climatic factors in different regions of the country where this type of tobacco is grown, and the effect thereof on the quality and quantity of tobacco produced in these regions.

(iii) To require the processors of Virginia tobacco and the manufacturers of products made therefrom to register themselves with the Tobacco Board. This will help the Board in having control over cigarette manufacturers who are the major buyers of Virginia tobacco and in monitoring the regular offtake of this tobacco by the manufacturers from the growers.

(iv) To provide licensing of graders to take up commercial grading. This will help the farmers to bring properly graded Virginia tobacco to the auction platforms which will help in their securing better prices in the auctions.

(v) To provide for licensing of construction and operation of barns which would regulate barn capacity, thereby effecting production control indirectly.

(vi) To prohibit certain unfair practices in the tobacco trade.

(vii) To provide for prosecution for contravention of not only the provisions of the Act or rules made thereunder, but also regulations made under the Act and to provide for enhanced penalties for contravention thereof.

Opportunity is being availed of to include, in accordance with the recommendations of the Committee on Subordinate Legislation in the Act, provision relating to power of the Tobacco Board for writing off losses. Opportunity is also being availed of to provide for laying of the regulations under the Tobacco Board Act before the Parliament.

With these few words I beg to move:

> That the Bill further to amend the Tobacco Board Act, 1975, be taken into consideration.

* * *

Mr Deputy Speaker, Sir, I thank the honourable Members for having participated in this debate and also for having expressed their interest in the tobacco crop, particularly for the welfare of the growers for which the Tobacco Board exists.

One honourable Member has said that the Government should bring forward a more comprehensive amendment Bill. Prof. Ranga, Mr V.S. Rao and many other honourable Members referred to the recommendations and observations of the Estimates Committee and the Committee on Public Undertakings. After having gone into all these recommendations of the Estimates Committee as well as the reports of the Committee on Public Undertakings, the Government of India in 1981 constituted an expert group to go into the whole aspect of the tobacco industry and tobacco growers. This Bill is the result of this exercise. In my view, the present Amendment Bill is very very comprehensive and I have no doubt in my mind that this Bill, when passed, will go a long way to help the farmers in our country.

Tobacco Board has been entrusted primarily with three functions. First is to regulate production, second is to ensure remunerative prices to the growers and the third is to maximize the export of tobacco from our country. Many honourable Members have expressed their concern as to why the production of tobacco in our country should be regulated.

It is a fact that in the last few years we have been resorting to the regulation of production. In 1981, I think, it was 1.9 lakh hectares – the area which was under tobacco production; in 1982, we had brought it down to 1.3 lakh hectares, in 1983, to one lakh hectares and the latest thinking is that we will bring it down to 90,000 hectares. The reason for regulating the tobacco production in our country is very simple. We do not want to put our farmers in distress. Unless the Government can give them remunerative prices, unless we give them market at home and abroad, there is no point in growing more tobacco. If we look at the situation in the country and the world as such, we find that almost in all the countries, the production of tobacco is going down and the world production of tobacco is also quickly coming down. I do not know whether I should go into all the details why the production has been reduced and all these things, but I can only say one thing, because Shri Amar Roy Pradhan has vehemently made a point that tobacco should be banned as it is very very injurious to health. The campaign against smoking in the world is really gaining ground. Now, in the United States of America, there are certain places where smoking is totally banned. If we take the United Kingdom, the latest reports show that the Government of the United Kingdom has decided to ban smoking in the London underground trains for a period of twelve months as a trial. The insurance companies in the United Kingdom have also, of late, been refusing to bring the smokers under insurance cover or they are insuring for only some reduced amounts. They are allowed a minimal amount.

One of the studies has shown that, from a record annual rate of 137 billion cigarettes in 1984, the consumption has come down to 100 billion cigarettes; and with all this campaign, the consumption may go down further. I do not know whether the number of persons smoking is going down or not but the number of cigarettes smoked has certainly been coming down. And, therefore, the Government has to take a very conscious view and take a decision as to whether we should encourage our farmers to grow more or whether we should tell them frankly that they should not grow more tobacco, and try to find out some other means of livelihood.

In our view, we feel that it is better that under the special circumstances obtaining today, it is not conducive for us to grow more tobacco. We feel that it is the duty of the Government to tell the farmers that the situation as it stands today, is not conducive for us to go in for more production of tobacco in our country. Therefore, we have been telling our farmers very frankly that they should try to find out some other means of livelihood. And, therefore, we have to resort to regulations in terms of production.

In fact, on two or three occasions, as Prof. Ranga has rightly pointed out, our farmers did really have problems because there were no buyers of tobacco. In 1978, 1979 and 1983, the Government had to give the direction to the STC to enter into the market in order to help the farmers. In 1978, the STC purchased 14,131 million kgs, in 1979, 5,660 million kgs, and in 1983, 18,000 million kgs. In this the expenditure incurred by the Government in 1979-1980 was Rs 13 crore and in 1983 Rs 21.40 crore. And I myself had to go to Guntur to supervise the tobacco purchase.

Our concern is to help the farmers. The fact is that farmers were in distress. The fact is that they were not getting a chance to dispose of their product. At the request of Prof. Ranga and many other leaders of the Government had intervened to rescue the farmers and in the process Government lost Rs 21 crore. But we are proud of that.

Many honourable Members have rightly expressed that the farmers should get remunerative prices for their produce. I quite agree with the feelings of the honourable Members. It has always been the consistent effort of the Government of India to see that the tobacco growers do get remunerative prices for their produce.

Mr Rao has said that as there is a minimum export price and there should be a minimum support price also. Minimum support prices do exist.

* * *

The Agricultural Prices Commission takes into consideration the cost of production and all that. This is not my assessment, this is the assessment of the APC. They come out with the fixation of prices. But I can only tell from our experiences that the price of tobacco that has been ruling in the last many years, has always been above the minimum support price fixed by the Government of India. It was particularly so last year when the Government of India had introduced the auction system. After having introduced the auction system, I can only say that the prices have gone up. In fact, before the auction started, we had made it a compulsory regulation that the first bid in the auction would be 15 paise more than the minimum support price. So the lowest auction price cannot come below the minimum support price. In fact, in Karnataka in 1984, the highest price that we got through auction was Rs 25 per kg and in Andhra Pradesh it was Rs 21 per kg and the average support price was Rs 12 per kg. This is not so in all cases but in some cases. But the average auction price was not below Rs 13 per kg when the average minimum support price was Rs 9 per kg.

Another point I would like to emphasize is, as many honourable Members have pointed out, that so long the farmers were being exploited by the trade in the sense that the farmers were not getting their price continuously for two years.

If they sold their tobacco this year, they would get their money after two years or even after three years. That was the condition of farmers. In Karnataka, we have introduced the auction system whereby the farmers can get their payment, hundred per cent payment, within ten days by cheque on the spot. Before that they had to wait for two to three years to get the payment. In Andhra Pradesh, we have made it a point that the farmers get 50 per cent of their payment within the first ten days and the remaining 50 per cent in the next 45 days. So, I think the Government is very much conscious of the problems of the farmers and this effort of the Government of India has certainly gone a very long way to help them.

Some honourable Members have expressed their views that there are dues which are still pending since before the introduction of the auction system. I would not be able to exactly say what is the position but I will certainly have a look at it and see what can be done about this. So, we have tried our best to help the farmers, and in the process of introducing this auction system, Government of India have spent, in fact, to the tune of eight crore of rupees.

* * *

Construction of warehouses and all that is being done. A point which Prof. Ranga and others have made is about the affair of shifting the headquarters from Guntur to Hyderabad. I can assure the House that the headquarters of the Tobacco Board shall not be shifted from Guntur. It will remain at Guntur, and we have already released Rs 85 lakh for the construction of an administrative building and the work has already been allotted to the CPWD.

Another point I would like to make is about increasing our exports. But as I have pointed out in the beginning, we are finding difficulties in the matter of exports, and, in fact, in the last two or three years our exports have been coming down. This is precisely because of lot of campaign against cigarette smoking and all that. In 1982-1983, our export value was Rs 192 crore ; in 1983-1984, it came down to Rs 161.8 crore; and in 1984-1985, it further came down to Rs 139.6 crore. We have to be conscious about it.

Mr Rawat has made a point that we should not only depend on the traditional markets that we have but we should also try to explore non-traditional markets and other markets. These have been our efforts and, in fact, in the last few months we have been able to get some other new markets. I have myself been to Morocco. For the first time, Morocco has agreed to buy tobacco from us and a trial shipment has already been done. In fact, we have already tried our best to see that we export more and more.

There are few individual points. Credit requirement is another point which has been vehemently made by the honourable Members. We are aware of this. In fact, when we tried to introduce the auction system, one of the points raised was that though the farmers were getting their payments two or three years after selling their goods to the traders or the exporters, but they also used to help the farmers by giving them advance money. They used to give them credit. This is what I was told. There are some people who told me that the farmers may be in trouble now. After the auction system is introduced, they may not get the credit which they used to get from the traders. I said, I will take the responsibility of even giving credit to the farmers but the auction system had to be introduced, and against many odds we have introduced the system.

* * *

There was a demand that other types of tobacco like Beedi and Shrink tobacco could be brought under the Tobacco Board. Well, we are concerned with the exportable commodities. Because we are Commerce Ministry, we are looking after the commodities which are exportable, and 90 per cent of export of this commodity is of Virginia tobacco. Therefore, Commerce Ministry's jurisdiction is only Virginia tobacco. The other varieties of tobacco come under the administrative control of the Agriculture Ministry.

I think you have made a point very vehemently that we have been trying to help the exporters and traders and you wanted to know whether the Tobacco Board exists for the protection of the growers. I have explained what we have done for the growers, but I must also emphasize that it will not be enough only to encourage and help the growers. We must also create conditions for the exporters, because unless your tobacco gets exported, growers have no place. Therefore, it is the duty of the Government to see that we also help and create congenial conditions for our exporters so that they can export the product. Therefore, we cannot completely wipe out the exporters.

The last point which has been made is about the representation of the growers that it should be not less than rather than not more than. Well, we have at the moment 20 members on the Board – of which eight are non-officials and twelve are officials. Officials mean representation of various State Governments, various Departments – Agriculture Department, ICAR, Commerce Ministry, Finance Ministry and so on. Out of eight non-official members at the moment, we have 50:50 – four growers and four manufacturers and exporters. Now, we are going to raise it to six. So, from four, it will be raised to six. Therefore, out of ten total non-official members, we are going to have six representations from the growers. If you make it not less than, then all ten could go to the growers and we cannot exclude the exporters and manufacturers also. They have to be given representation. But I think it is a very fair representation. And if you take effective membership of the growers, I think easily three more members who are representing the growers are there. Under the official category, there are three Members of Parliament, two from the Lok Sabha and one from the Rajya Sabha, who are representing on the Tobacco Board and I think I should take it for granted that they would be representatives of the growers.

* * *

The entire purpose of the Bill is to bring all the stages, as rightly pointed out by Prof. Ranga, about the processing, grading and curing, into the purview of the Tobacco Board. Therefore, all other aspects will naturally follow.

* * *

Sir, I beg to move:

> That the Bill, as amended, be passed.

Role of Institutional Factors in Water Management in India*

Mr Chairman, Sir, at the very outset, I would like to thank our senior honourable Member Shri Somnath Chatterjee for facilitating this debate. This debate was possible because he and his colleagues from West Bengal had raised the issue of floods in West Bengal during Zero Hour.

I would like to say that the whole House is with the people of West Bengal. The floods in West Bengal have really been unprecedented. People have suffered and are still suffering. I would request the Government of India to extend the maximum possible assistance to the Government of West Bengal so that the sufferings of the people can be mitigated.

It is more than fifty years since we have achieved Independence. We have completed eight Five Year Plans. Today we are at the end of the Ninth Five Year Plan and very soon we will be going to the Tenth Five Year Plan. We have the National Water Policy of 1987. The latest National Agriculture Policy of July 2000 also has a chapter on risk management which deals with flood situations. In our country, both at the national and at the State levels, there are a number of institutions for water resource management, including flood control. We have a National Water Development Agency functioning from 1982.

And yet, we are still grappling with the problems of frequent floods, its fury and the toll that it takes on human lives, livestock resources, infrastructure, soil erosion and so on and so forth.

Why has it happened? We have a policy. We have a plan and yet, we are not able to tackle this problem. Perhaps, one of the reasons is that we have been for the last more than fifty years tackling this problem on a year-to-year basis. We are just indulging ourselves in a crisis management exercise. The Parliament debates this issue every year and we can see, when this serious issue is being discussed, the attendance in the House. This issue is always tackled by the Minister for Agriculture. I do not know what Agriculture Minister can do to stop floods and other national calamities. The relevant Ministers are not present here. The

**L.S. Deb.*, 30 November 2000 (Spoke while participating in the discussion regarding loss of lives and property due to floods, droughts and other natural calamities in various parts of the country).

relevant Ministers do not listen to the debate. I am so happy that Shri Arjun Sethi has come at the last moment because my speech has nothing much to do with your Ministry.

The relevant Ministry is the Ministry of Finance but the Finance Minister will never be present when such discussions do take place. Therefore, not only at the level of the Government I think, but even at the level of Parliament itself, we will have to debate this issue in such a manner so that all the Ministers concerned are present here and Government comes out with a long-term policy and plan.

The second reason as to why this problem is not being tackled effectively perhaps has something to do with the Constitution itself. Under the Seventh Schedule of the Constitution of India, inter-state rivers fall under the Union List. Water, irrigation, canals, drainage and embankments fall under the State List. Water Development as such falls under the Concurrent List. Ultimately, water management becomes nobody's baby. I think, we will have to think over it as to whether there is something wrong in the method of handling water resources itself. Every year, flood takes place as it has taken place this year in many parts of India. This has been very effectively articulated by honourable Members from different parts of the country. Shri Somnath Chatterjee has given us a detailed account of it. But what do we see when we discuss it? When we discuss this, the honourable Members from the states affected will usually blame the Central Government saying that the states have been neglected and that the Central Government has not given them any assistance. And what does the Central Government say? They say that the states have to mange it properly. Shri Sudip Bandopadhyay says that Bengal flood was man-made flood. That is his defence. That is the defence of the Central Government. And then, the Central Government says that though it was your failure, we are sending a Central team. The Central team goes there, makes an assessment of the losses, comes back and gives a report to Shri Nitish Kumar.

Shri Nitish Kumar, in turn, goes to the Finance Minister. The Finance Minister says: 'Thank you very much. Let me keep your report here. I cannot do anything.' Every year, the matter ends like this. I know about it. I had been a Chief Minister myself. The North Eastern region is very badly affected. Every year, we have natural calamities. I had been coming to the Centre when I was the Chief Minister there. I know how it functions and how the money comes. It is a very sad state of affairs. Therefore, I think, we will have even to go into the real policy of water management. The real policy of water management has to be gone into very deeply.

Sir, I do not want to take much of the time of the House. But I have to speak something about the North Eastern region. As the House is aware, there are seven States in the North East. We have six river basins. One is the Brahmaputra basin; the second is the Barak basin; the third is the sub-basin of Tripura; the fourth is the Imphal-Manipuri basin; the fifth is the Kolodyne basin in Mizoram and the sixth one is the Teza basin in Nagaland. All the States of the North East are very severely affected by floods and natural calamities. But the State which suffers most out of these floods is Assam because of the Brahmaputra River.

As the House is aware, the Brahmaputra River is one of the largest rivers in the world. It is the principal arm of Ganga-Meghna-Brahmaputra system. Its length is 1,629 km in Tibet; 278 km in Arunachal Pradesh; 640 km in Assam and 363 km in Bangladesh. The total annual flow of the Brahmaputra River is 500 billion cubic metres which is 30 per cent of the total surface flow of all the rivers in the country. If somebody has to understand the problem that is being faced by the people in Assam due to the Brahmaputra River, one has to go and see it for himself. Otherwise, it cannot be believed. The miseries of the people are so much that unless you go and see the spot for yourself, see the conditions of the people and talk to them, it is very difficult to appreciate the problem that is being faced. In the last few months, I have been touring in the state of Assam, sometimes extensively. I have been to Dibrugarh and I also worked in Dibrugarh. The original Dibrugarh town is no more there. It has already been submerged by the river. A new town has come up. Even the new town of Dibrugarh is so much in danger that thousands of hectares of land under tea cultivation are affected. The medical college and the airport are so much in danger of being eroded. I went to Jorhat. I went to a place called Neamatighat. I could see hundreds of refugees being kept in a camp because their whole village had been swept away by the Brahmaputra River. I was there. This had happened. I was in Marigaon district. I went to the place called Moirabari, Lahorighat Ulubari, Chutiagaon, Tengaguri, Balidunga, Buragaon, Niz-Saharia, Baralimori-Moyong, etc.

It is very sad. In the last two or three years, 356 villages have been washed away. They were not visible anymore. But when I met the people and had discussion with them, they told me a very interesting thing. They said: 'Sir, you do not worry about floods. We have learnt how to live with water.' So, flood is no more a problem. But the problem is erosion. How to protect the villages? That is the problem which needs to be tackled. Giving relief to the flood-affected people, whether it comes or not, whether we get shelter or not, we are used to be, for ages, not worried about our shelter and our food; we are worried about our villages. Please save our villages.

I went to Motichar in Dhubri town, I went to Saliswar, Balijora, Sonari, Goalpara town of Golapara district and the conditions are the same. I know that the Government of India has been taking a lot of interest in that. The Brahmaputra Board has been constituted by an Act of Parliament in 1980. Today we are in 2000. Twenty years have gone. What has happened in 20 years? I have the report: Water Vision for the North East-2050. Here, the Chairman of the Brahmaputra Board says that the Master Plan for 48 important river basins, identification of 33 drainage condition areas, the investigation of 17 multipurpose projects have been carried out. Construction of multipurpose projects can also be taken up by the Board in consultation with the State Government, which means nothing has been done so far. So, they are still discussing as to who will execute those projects.

Master Plan-I is very interesting. Master Plan-I is for the implementation of multipurpose projects and schemes – the main stream of Brahmaputra. The project outlay is Rs 91,000 crore. I do not know whether the Finance Minister of this country would ever have the courage even to look at this figure.

Master Plan-II relates to Barak River and its boundaries. The proposed outlay is Rs 4,000 crore. Master Plan-III relates to 39 important tributaries of the Brahmaputra and eight rivers of Tripura, and so on and so forth. Most of the proposals – I do not want to waste the time of the august House, I have everything – are lying with the CCEA, the Cabinet Committee on Economic Affairs. I think, I will pass on those papers. I will have a discussion with the Minister concerned perhaps.

Sir, in the meanwhile – I will take just two minutes more because it is important for the House to know – I was saying that if one has to understand and appreciate your problem, then, you have to pay a visit. I just give a glimpse of what is happening. I would take the figures of 1988 because that is the only latest figures available with the Ministry. This is your document, Mr Minister. Fortunately, I talked to some of your officers and they had sent me these documents. These documents have been supplied by the Ministry itself. Population affected in 1988 alone is 10.49 million; damage to the crops, Rs 334.10 crore; damage to the houses, Rs 225 crore; loss of lives, 232. This is one-year figure. What has been done? Well, I do not want to quote. If I quote this figure as to how much money has been spent to control the Brahmaputra River by the Centre and by the States, I am sure, it will demoralize the people of Assam so much that I do not really have the courage to quote those figures.

Sir, I think it is time that we wake up and it is time that we have short-term plan, medium-term plan and long-term plan. Of course, there is no dearth of plans; plans are being made, but what is required is the resource. What is required is the will of the Government to do it. I know there is a constraint of resource. I have been in the Government for long. I appreciate it. But, if there is a will there is a way. I hope this Government will have that will.

Thank you.

A Road Map for Management of Public Sector Undertakings*

Madam Chairperson, this is a very important debate for the sake of the country and I think this debate should be taken with all seriousness.

After we became independent, we established what is generally understood as command economy, viz., an economy in which public sector would be at the commanding heights. The main objectives of this policy were building infrastructure for development, creation of employment opportunities, creation of a self-reliant economy, generation of investible resources and prevention and reduction of private economic power. In pursuance of these objectives, we have Industrial Policy Resolution of 1948 and the Industrial Policy Statement of 1956. But over the years, the public sector generally came to be afflicted by the several problems and the result is that by 1998, we have 240 public sector enterprises, of course, we have 235 working enterprises, with a capital employment of Rs 274,000 crore. In the year 1998-99, the

---

***L.S. Deb.*, 20 December 2000 (Spoke while participating in the discussion under Rule 193 regarding Disinvestment of Public Sector Undertakings raised by Shri Basudeb Acharia on 19 December 2000).

number of loss-making public sector enterprises was 106 and the loss in that year alone was of the order of Rs 10,000 crore.

Now, why have all this happened? Madam, I had the privilege of being in the Ministry of Industry for two years as a Deputy Minister. I was in the Ministry of Textile looking after NTC for four years as a Deputy Minister. I had been the Minister of Labour in this country for seven years plus two years in my State. I was the Coal Minister for two years. So, a major portion of my career as a Minister was devoted to dealing with the public sector.

Several factors have contributed to the poor performance of public sector. They are: low technological upgradation, low productivity, poor management, excess manpower, low research and development and low human resource development. I would like to deal, out of all these factors, in a little detail on the poor management of the public sector.

Unfortunately, most of the time I have found that the top position in a public sector undertaking remains vacant. The process of selection of the Chief Executive Officer of a public sector undertaking takes such a long time that most of the time most of the public sector undertakings are without a CEO. Something ought to be done for this.

Secondly, in the absence of a CEO in a public sector undertaking, the Ministry partially runs that PSU from Delhi. The interference of the Ministry is so much that even if a PSU has its CEO at the helm, that gentleman has to come to Delhi perhaps twenty times a month to attend meetings convened by a Director one day, a Joint Secretary the next day, then again meetings convened by an Additional Secretary, the Secretary of the Ministry, the Cabinet Secretary and finally by the PMO. The officers of PSUs do not have enough time to attend to their work. They have no time either to apply their minds properly because they are so much subjected to the interference by the administrative Ministries.

The third important point I think is poor industrial relations. Unfortunately, all the major trade union leaders have concentrated their activities in the public sector enterprises. On top of that, every political leader of all political parties tries to have a union in the public sector. I am sorry to say that some of the honourable Members sitting here are no exception to it. With the multiplicity of the trade unions you will find that there are now more than one hundred trade unions in certain public sector undertakings. Therefore, it is impossible for the management to deal with that kind of trade unionism. When I was the Labour Minister, I tried to bring some reforms in the Industrial Disputes Act.

Anyway, this is certainly one of the reasons for the poor performance of the PSUs.

Another area where I am unhappy is the unnecessary vigilance and unnecessary inquiries against the public sector executives. Since the public sector executives are dealing with a large number of people including politicians and trade unionists, it is impossible for them to deal with all these people satisfactorily. So, somebody files a complaint against them with the CBI, I do not want to go into the functioning of the CBI at this stage. When the Bill on the Chief Vigilance Commissioner is discussed here I will be coming out with more details. But the number of CBI cases against officers of public sector enterprises is such that they do not have mental peace to attend to their duties. They have to give reply to the Vigilance Officer of the Ministry, the Police and the CBI Officers. Now, under the circumstances, how do we expect our public sector units to perform? I am speaking from my own experiences. Even if I would have been put as the Chief Executive of a public sector undertaking, perhaps, I would not have been able to perform. But in some cases, I did try to assume the role. For example, when I became the Minister for Coal, the first thing I did was to keep all the investigations against the officers in abeyance and not to entertain any new investigations. I told them just not to worry about investigations and cases and to go on with their work and work. The day I assumed office, Coal India was losing Rs 2,800 crore and in six months' time, we landed up with Rs 164 crore of profit. It was because the officers were allowed to work. We do not allow them to work.

By 1991, the situation had become so difficult for the public sector that the then Government headed by Mr P.V. Narasimha Rao as the Prime Minister – and I was also a member of the same – had to review the policy towards the public sector. A new policy statement was issued on focusing of public sector on strategic, hi-tech and essential infrastructure, review of public sector portfolio investments, referral of sick industries/enterprises to BIFR offering a part of the public sector shareholding, including for general public, to raise resources, and secure wider public participation which is being discussed just now, professionalism of the boards of the enterprises, performance improvement, signing of the Memorandum of Understanding, grant of autonomy for enterprises and ensuring their accountability. Therefore, the policy of disinvestment was actually first introduced by the Congress Government when Shri P.V. Narasimha Rao was the Prime Minister.

In 1996, the then United Front Government, through its Common Minimum Programme, further carried on this policy and it is they who appointed the Disinvestment Commission. The present Government is headed by the BJP which is the major party. What is the stand of the BJP? So, the policy adopted by the Congress Government in 1991 was again carried on by the United Front Government. The BJP in its Chennai declaration, said, 'A specific goal of the investment programme should be achieved and drastic and speedy reduction in our national debt so that the resultant savings in loan and interest payments can be channelized for production and development in the much neglected social sector.' To continue with it, then a year ago, the NDA Government of 25 political parties, constituted the Department of Disinvestment. The Department of Disinvestment was headed by Shri Arun Jaitley and now headed by Shri Arun Shourie.

I want to make a small comment on that. My plea to the honourable Prime Minister would be not to change the honourable Minister for Disinvestment too many times. When you are inducted to a Ministry, it takes three to four months' time to really understand the Ministry and by the time you understand the Ministry, if you are shifted to another Ministry, then you need another four to five months of time to understand it. And time is so precious and I do not think that the country can afford to lose it. Now, in spite of all these, we are still facing so many problems. We are still discussing it.

I have many points to make. The process of disinvestment is getting slow. I think the first reason is political instability. From 1989 to 1999, in ten years' time, where we had to have two elections, we had five elections; where we had to have two Governments, we had eight Governments and eight Prime Ministers. From a single-party Government, we have now come to not a coalition Government – I do not call this Government a coalition Government – but a multiparty Government. A multiparty Government with pulls and strings here and there cannot function properly. I do not know whether it can deliver goods. We may have stability. I think, I have spoken about stability and governance on the floor of this august House. Today, the Vajpayee Government may be stable with 25 political parties. But where is the Governance?

The third important reason why we are not able to take off is, I think, we have not been able to really achieve a national consensus though we all talk about a national consensus. I am saying that this debate has to be treated on a different footing. Today's debate has to be a non-partisan debate because on this particular issue we really need to have a national consensus. I do not think the present Government has been able to achieve that national consensus. Before they are able to have a national consensus, they will have to have a consensus within the BJP first. The BJP Government talks about disinvestment, and the Swadeshi Jagran Manch talks about socialism. Where is the consensus in the BJP on this policy. Where is the consensus among the 25 NDA partners on this policy? Where is the consensus in this House? Where is the time for this House even to discuss about a consensus on economic issues? We are seeing and we are experiencing ourselves how this Parliament is functioning. I am sorry to say it. We are more concerned about the ancient issues rather than the present issues and the future issues.

* * *

Coming to the point, I would submit that the Disinvestment Commission has submitted its report. It has made a lot of recommendations. Most of the important recommendations are there. What is the position of those recommendations? I have gone through all the three volumes of the report of the Disinvestment Commission. I think they have done fairly a very good job. Altogether, 72 PSUs were referred to this Commission. The Government withdrew eight of them subsequently. So, effectively, they went into the functioning of 64 PSUs. Recommendations in respect of 52 PSUs were made. What is the position? The Government has yet to take a decision on 30 recommendations of this Commission. Specific recommendations on PSUs were made. Out of the 14 general recommendations, the Government has yet to take decision on 11 of them. They have decision only on three of them. Those recommendations are very important and require urgent decision of the Government. For example, there is the establishment of a separate Disinvestment Fund. I will not read all these things because of paucity of time. Having been the Speaker myself, I do not like to defy the Chair. But I thought that this is an important debate and I should not stop at that. So, the establishment of a Disinvestment Fund is there. The Government has established a Disinvestment Fund in 1968. But the details regarding the scope and the purpose of the Fund are not available.

We have not decided about delinking the investment process from the budgetary exercise of the Government. This was a very important point I wanted to make, but I will not make it now. What is the action of the Government on this? The decision is, decision awaited. Transfer of management – decision awaited; reduction of Government equity – decision awaited; disinvestment packet – decision awaited; voluntary retirement scheme, which is so important from the workers' point of view, having been a Labour Minister for many years I would like to speak on it, but I cannot speak now – decision awaited; monitoring and supervision power – decision awaited; and setting up of implementation machinery – decision awaited.

I would like the Minister to see that these decisions are taken expeditiously in whatever way he wants. I would like to conclude by giving humble suggestions from my side. Firstly, we need to take a comprehensive package view of all general and specific recommendations of the Disinvestment Commission and have transparent policy of disinvestment and its implementation. Secondly, cutting across political spectrum, a broad national consensus has to be created to make disinvestment a success. Thirdly, initiative for the consensus has to be necessarily taken by the Government of the day. Fourthly, the process of disinvestment should be depoliticized. It is very important that the matter is left to the professionals and the Government is confining itself to the rim of the policy. but on this, when we are talking about individual cases, I think, a lot of voice has been raised about Air India, Indian Airlines, MTNL, Gas Authority of India, etc. I think, we have to be very careful in those areas. I have some suggestions to make, but I do not think I have time to.

I repeat what I said earlier. Disinvestment process should be funded. Disinvestment should be delinked from the Budget. Last and the very important point is, manpower issue should not be treated as a matter of nuisance value. Workers' interest will have to be protected and their future should invariably be safeguarded with provisions against loss of income.

Thank you.

~

Fiscal Management System in India*

Thank you, Mr Chairman, Sir, Shri Ram Manohar Reddy in his article in the *Hindu* on 17 July 2004 has observed and I would like to quote:

> The Central Budgets have long ceased to be the major policy documents. They are now prepared for the TV studios and headlines in the morning newspapers.

I could not agree more. Our Finance Minister, Shri Chidambaram is a very eminent lawyer. He is very articulate and has amply demonstrated his skill in presenting the Budget.

The first Budget which Mr Chidambaram had presented before the august House – I was presiding over the august House – was described as a dream Budget. That dream Budget had a very rough weather as to whether it would be passed or not. I had to find out a lot of ways and means to get that Budget passed. This Budget has been described by your well-wishers as a dream Budget come true. I really do not know whether it is really a dream Budget. I do not find any new grounds, any new direction and any new approach in the present Budget.

I can understand the constraints of the Finance Minister. I have been following you very closely for a long time. I have been reading your articles in various newspapers and magazines. I do not find any reflection of what you have been writing and saying in the present Budget that you have presented. I was particularly impressed by an article which was published on 21 January 2002 in the India Today. The title of your article was 'Poverty Eradication – Spending is not investment', I quote:

> Our approach to poverty alleviation is illogical and perverse. We attack poverty through subsidies and through too many anti-poverty schemes.

This is what the honourable Finance Minister had to write and today in this Budget what do we find? It is all schemes. We find schemes after schemes. I have gone through at least 23 schemes. The Finance Minister has just followed the ongoing schemes which the previous Governments have introduced. There are schemes after schemes and what did the Finance Minister do in those schemes? I have tried to analyse each

---

**L.S. Deb.*, 20 July 2004 (Spoke while participating in the General Budget 2004-2005 and General Discussion on the Demands for Grants on Account [General] 2004-2005).

scheme. The Antyodaya Anna Yojana and the Accelerated Irrigation Benefit Programme, these are two schemes where there has been no enhancement at all. In your Budget speech, you were very proud to announce the kind of importance the UPA Government is giving to the Accelerated Irrigation Benefit Programme. But what is the allocation? The allocation is just the same as it was before. It was Rs 2,800 crore in 2003-04 Budget and it is exactly Rs 2,800 crore in the present Budget. Where is the pride in that?

Now I have identified six ongoing schemes where, in fact, the Finance Minister has reduced the budgetary support. As regards Food-for-Work Programme, the food component of this Programme has been drastically reduced. The allocation has been reduced for Farm Income Insurance Project. As regards upgradation of the Industrial Training Institutes. I had been the Labour Minister of this country for nine long years and I had tried my best to see that the schemes for rural boys and girls are upgraded. The condition of our ITIs is very bad. I had an occasion to visit one of the States in the North East. In their Automobile Section, I found a vehicle and when I asked them where did they get this vehicle from, they replied that it was left by the Britishers during the Second World War. I tried to upgrade ITIs. I am sorry to say that the Finance Minister did not give a single naya paisa more for upgradation of Industrial Training Institutes.

How is the Finance Minister going to complete the schemes? Take the examples of the schemes like the Universal Health Insurance Scheme, the Seed Production Programme, the National Oilseeds and Vegetable Oil Development Board. I do not find any increase in allocation for these schemes. Therefore, the Finance Minister has certainly not been allowed to present his Budget. It is certainly not his Budget. It is certainly not according to his thinking; according to his perception and according to the policies. It is because I am a regular reader of his articles and his articles are politically correct and therefore, I find a different Chidambaram in this particular Budget.

Sir, a lot of things have been said in regard to emphasis having been laid on agriculture in this Budget. Where is the emphasis on agriculture in the Budget? What has the Finance Minister said about agriculture in the Budget? He has only said that credit availability to farmers will be doubled in the next three years. The Finance Minister has put the farmers at the mercy of the financial institutions. Where is the investment? I do not find any significant investment in the agriculture sector, though he has been advocating for it. I have already quoted from his articles. Public investment in agriculture has been stagnant at constant rate of 1.5 per cent of the GDP. That is what the honourable Finance Minister had stated in his articles. Where is the investment here? Except that, he has said that the credit availability will be doubled in the next three years. I come from a village, I know how the financial institutions behave and who are the creditworthy farmers. It is they who have not been able to pay their loans that they took earlier and when they go to the financial institutions, they say, 'You are not eligible. Please get out. You cannot get any loan.' Where is the investment in agriculture?

Sir, I wish to raise a particular point since my availability of time is very less. It is about Brahmaputra flood control. What is the allocation for this? Today the honourable Prime Minister is in Assam. A lot of people have already died. A lot of erosion have already taken place. Millions of people have got stranded and have got uprooted from their homes but he honourable Finance Minister speaks so much about the North Eastern region. How much has he allocated for Brahmaputra flood control? This is an ongoing programme. Last year, the allocation was Rs 10 crore and this year, the Finance Minister has allocated another Rs 10 crore for this project. It is just Rs 20 crore in all. How would this sum help in the control of floods in the Brahmaputra?

Mr Chairman, Sir, in the last Government you were the honourable Minister for Water Resources. Once when I had spoken on this subject on the floor of the House and approached you through the honourable Prime Minister, the then Prime Minster instructed you to release a sum of Rs 50 crore immediately and you were kind enough to do so. I am grateful to you for what you did at that time. But today what has been allocated in the Budget? A Government that has so much of a soft corner for the North Eastern region has allocated a sum of Rs 10 crore more than what it was last year for the Brahmaputra flood control programme. I am sorry this is not acceptable.

Sir, for the State of Bihar a sum of Rs 3,500 crore has been allocated for this purpose. I have a point on that also. How much has been the allocation in this Budget for flood control in the Ganga basin? A sum of Rs 5.5 crore more than what was allocated last year. What is the position in Bihar today? Shri Nitish Kumar was telling me about the kind of sufferings people are undergoing owing to floods in the State. Today it has not been possible for him to be present here. But in the Budget it has been very proudly mentioned that the Government has allocated a sum of Rs 5.5 crore more than what it was last year.

Sir, it has been mentioned that the Government is committed to speedy development of the North Eastern region and all Ministries and Departments have been mandated to allocate at least ten per cent of their planned Budget for the schemes and programmes of the North Eastern region. Is it a new thing? We have been hearing this from the days of Mr Deve Gowda. As the Prime Minister, Mr Deve Gowda went to the North Eastern region, and as I was the Presiding Officer at that time, I did have some influence on him. He came out with a suggestion that every Ministry will earmark ten per cent of their budget for the development of the North East and if that money cannot be spent, it will go to the non-lapsable pool of resources. The Finance Minister has exactly said what Mr Deve Gowda had said many years ago. What did you give us? Please tell us, Mr Chidambaram. What did you give to the North Eastern region? Did you provide a single paisa more for the North Eastern region? You are just following what Mr Deve Gowda has done. I am sorry that this is not the way to mislead the people of the North Eastern region.

I have watched the honourable Finance Minister on the television. He has been repeatedly saying that they will carry on with reforms and he has also said recently that they are the original reformers. What is that 'original reformer'? And how are you going to carry on with your reforms? I really do not understand. I was a member of the Council of Ministers when the reforms started in 1991. I was a member of the Cabinet and we were discussing about it in the Cabinet. The then Finance Minister, Dr Manmohan Singh, had been repeatedly saying that we have to see that the money is being spent for the public sector undertakings and if the public sector undertaking is not able to cope up or come up with any improvement, then the money that we saved from the investment towards the public sector undertaking should be given to the social sector. That was the idea.

I had the most difficult task those days of being the Labour Minister because labour unrest was there. Out of 224 public sector undertakings, 58 of them were chronically sick. The then Finance Minister told the Labour Minister that he cannot give the money and that it had to be closed down. I have been fighting for it. The argument was, 'No, we have to close down because the money which we are wasting has to be given to the social sector.' And what did your Budget say today? You have gone back from that.

Coming to State Electricity Boards, the then Finance Minster, who is the Prime Minster today, has been repeatedly telling in the Cabinet meetings and in the meetings of the Group of Ministers as, 'Today, the biggest burden on the country's economy is the Electricity Boards of the country. The loss is Rs 25,000 crore every year and we have to do something in that regard.' I do not find a word about the public sector in your Budget speech. What is your plan about the power sector? Not a word is found in the Budget speech. Now, when talking about the power sector, I do not know how you are going to carry with your reforms. It is not possible. I do not find any answer on those points.

As regards FDI, I have no quarrel about FDI with you. The reform process has to go on and you carry on with that. But the problem is whether you will be able to carry it through. The NDA has said that they will oppose the enhancement of your FDI cap. The Samajwadi Party has said that they are going to oppose it. Your allies, the Left Front, have said that they are going to oppose it come what may.

* * *

You say, 'We do not normally bark. We only bite.' And when you bite, you bite very bitterly. Let us see how do you bite on this proposition. I have a strong feeling that as far as FDI and other major economic policies are concerned, we must have a national consensus. We should not take it on political lines. I would appeal to the Left parties in this regard.

* * *

I would appeal to the whole House on this issue. Why cannot we have a serious debate on this? Why cannot we have a national consensus on this major policy decision?

For my Left friends, I would like to point out the policy of China. What is the policy of Chinese Communist Government? I will tell you that. Generally, the Chinese policy is that the capital from foreign parties should not be less than 25 per cent. So, they have set the minimum limit and not the maximum limit. Here, you are saying that the Government cannot go from 29 per cent to 49 per cent. The honourable Finance Minster himself has asked as to what is the difference between 29 per cent and 49 per cent. It is only a question of control, that is, control by the Indian company of Indian Government of private investor or foreign investor. The honourable Finance Minster himself has repeatedly said that there is no difference between 29 per cent and 49 per cent. I do not know how the Left sees so much of difference in that.

I think it is better if the Left Front friends learn something more from the Chinese experience. Let them see what the Chinese are doing. I have some figures about China. In FDI, they have surpassed everybody. They have even surpassed, I think, the United States of America. In 2003-04, Foreign Direct Investment in China is 52 billion US dollars, whereas for the United States of America it is only 40 billion dollars. Why? It is because they have set the minimum limit, a minimum limit of 25 per cent, you can invest anything. But it cannot be below 25 per cent. Here we are making so much of noise. I do not know what we are talking about.

I would like to point out one more thing about fiscal consolidation that the honourable Minister talked about. He has projected that he would bring down the revenue deficit to 2.5 per cent of the GDP. I really do not know how he is going to achieve it. I am not going into the monsoon factor, I am not going into the issue of Left and the Right opposing his FDI proposals and all that. The fact is that the projections that the Finance Minster has given to the country are highly optimistic. I have my own doubts. What does he say? He hopes to get across tax revenue to the tune of Rs 62,810 crore. That is his expectation. This is 25 per cent more than what has been realized last year. Mr Minister, do you agree? He hopes to collect service tax to the tune of Rs 14,150 crore. It is 70 per cent higher than what has been realized in the preceding year. Now, he is getting into the problem of transaction tax or turnover tax. You have projected a revenue of Rs 14,170 crore, which is 70 per cent higher than what the Government got last year. He hopes to collect corporate tax to the tune of Rs 88,436 crore, which is 40 per cent higher than the realization of 2003-04. As regards income tax, he hopes to get Rs 50,929 crore, which is a hike of 26 per cent over the realization of last year. I think it is overestimation. I have gravest doubts on the projections that he has made to bring down the revenue deficit to 2.5 per cent.

Mr Chairman, Sir, I know about the limitation of time. You are not interrupting me. You have been very kind to me.

I am worried about one thing. Budget will come and Budget will go and we will keep on debating about it. There are certain things which are happening in this country. I had an occasion to speak about how our institutions are decaying. We have not been able to keep up our institutions. We have our systems and our systems are not working. As I said earlier, our institutions are completely decaying – I do not know. I am very sorry to say that. Look at the kind of Governors. What has happened in Arunachal Pradesh? MLAs were going and gheraoing the Governor. They were asking him, by force, to sign. Where is the institution of Governorship? Our honourable Speaker in this House is repeatedly saying every day that the whole world is watching us, the whole country is watching us and we should behave properly. Where are the parliamentary institutions going? Now, the latest victim is the institution of the Prime Minister himself. The office of the Prime Minister has become the latest victim in this country. I do not understand what is the meaning of this National Advisory Council? What for is it required? It is a dangerous thing that you are doing. I am not going to elaborate much. I want only to warn this Government that it is going to be a dangerous precedent. Somebody is going to Chennai and saying: 'I will give rupees one crore?' From where will it be given? Who is the authorized person for that?

* * *

You have every right to say what you feel. I have every right to say what I feel.

* * *

Mr Chairman, Sir, I fully agree with the Finance Minister when he said that as the Finance Minister of this country, he can announce this on behalf of the Prime Minister. But who has announced it? With what locus standi was it announced? If it is a Minister announcing it, I have no objection. We used to do that. Do not take it lightly.

* * *

I am talking of a very serious issue. You do not know that I am a responsible man.

* * *

Sir, I am not boasting. I have been in this House for more than 25 years. I have presided over this august House. I have been a Union Minister for more than 15 years. I have been the Chief Minister of my State. I have been the Leader of the Opposition. Whatever I am saying, I am saying it with full responsibility as a citizen of this country. What is being done is not good for the country.

* * *

Sir, I am not opposing the money which has been given. It should have been more than one crore rupees, I am only saying that the manner in which and the person by whom it was announced was not correct. That is all I am saying.

They have provoked me so much. Let me put it very bluntly. Tomorrow, if they come back to power and they have a National Advisory Council chaired by the RSS President or VHP President, how will the Congress oppose it?

Thank you.

LABOUR ISSUES

The Contract Labour (Regulation and Abolition Amendment Bill 1986)*

Sir, I beg to move:

> That the Bill to amend the Contract Labour (Regulation and Abolition) Act, 1970, as passed by Rajya Sabha, be taken into consideration.

The honourable Members are aware that the honourable President had promulgated an Ordinance on 28 January 1986 to amend the Contract Labour (Regulation and Abolition) Act 1970. The present Bill has been introduced to replace the Ordinance.

The purpose of the Bill is that the same Government should be the appropriate Government in respect of an establishment under the Contract Labour (Regulation and Abolition) Act, 1970, as also the Industrial Disputes Act, 1947. This will help us in reducing in the multiplicity of inspection agencies which is not administratively desirable.

The Bill has already been passed by the Rajya Sabha on 11 March 1986.

With these few words, I commend the Bill for the consideration of the House.

* * *

Mr Chairman, Sir, I am grateful to the honourable Members who have participated in this debate, more so for having given an overwhelming support and approval to this Bill.

* * *

**L.S. Deb.*, 18 March 1986 (Spoke while moving the Bill in the Lok Sabha). The Bill was moved to replace the Ordinance promulgated by the then Honourable President on 28 January 1986 to amend the Contract Labour (Regulation and Abolition) Act, 1970.

Approval of the other side is so conspicuous by the absence of these honourable Members who have sponsored this statutory resolution but have failed to come to the House. They have chosen not to move the resolution. It speaks volumes of how the Opposition has supported this Bill and I am grateful to them.

* * *

I am not casting aspersion. I am thanking the Opposition from the core of my heart for giving so much of support.

* * *

The only point which the honourable Members have stressed is what has been brought forward is not enough, though it is a good move towards evolving uniform policy of industrial relationship in this country. All the honourable Members have felt that it is not enough and something more should have been done. I am inclined to agree with all the honourable Members. I have gone through the Act and I find that there are loopholes in the provisions of the Act and it has to be looked into very carefully. Many honourable Members have narrated their own experiences of how the workers are being exploited, how the provisions of the Act are not being adhered to.

* * *

I have also come across many complaints to that effect and one of the reasons I have discovered myself is, I think, the penal provision that is provided in the Act appears to be an incentive for the violation of the provisions of this Act because the penal provision is, if somebody violates any provisions of this Act, of this law, then the punishment is for three months imprisonment or Rs 500 fine. I think certainly it is easier to pay Rs 500 fine than to adhere to the provisions of this law.

* * *

Another point which has been made is about lodging of the complaints. We have to look into all these and I agree with the suggestions that we have to come up with another comprehensive amendment in this august House.

* * *

One more allegation is made and it is about an attempt to take away the powers of the State Governments. I would admit that nobody would like to take away the powers of somebody to have more headache. Some people have given the example of the Food Corporation of India. I will explain that. Now the Supreme Court has given a judgment saying that as far as the Food Corporation of India is concerned, the appropriate Government is the State Government and it had directed that by 31 December 1985 the State Governments should take a final decision whether they are going to abolish contract labour or not.

* * *

Government of Haryana has taken a decision to abolish. Bihar Government has taken a decision to abolish. Uttar Pradesh, Jammu and Kashmir, Orissa and Rajasthan Governments have said, 'No, we will not abolish contract labour.' Well, honourable Members from West Bengal spoke very much that 'We are trying to take away their power,' but for my information, West Bengal Government has not taken a decision in spite of the direction of the Supreme Court to take a decision. If the Government of India is not for the welfare of the workers, is was very convenient for us – the Supreme Court judgment was very convenient for us to say, 'I cannot do anything. State Government is the appropriate Government.' I could have easily shirked my responsibility. But we do not want it. We want uniformity of laws in this country, uniformity of policy in this country and if the workers of one State get the benefit, we do not want that the same benefits are denied in another State. That is the reason why we want that the appropriate Government, under the Contract Labour Regulation and Abolition Act and the Industrial Disputes Act should be the same. This is the reason why we have come with this proposal.

Mr Reddy raised the point about Supreme Court ruling about CPWD. Of course, it is absolutely correct. The Supreme Court ruling about CPWD is on the casual workers of the Department and here we are talking about the contract labour. You know what is engaged by the contractor. So it does not go. You have to implicate some motive that maybe we try to get rid of Supreme Court ruling of the CPWD. It is absolutely different. It has nothing to do with that.

Shri Somnath Rath has raised a specific question about the corruption of construction companies. I will certainly look into it. I will certainly enquire into it. I will certainly look into some of the specific cases which the honourable Member has mentioned . . .

* * *

With these few words, I once again thank all the honourable Members and I commend the Bill to the House.

* * *

Sir, I beg to move:

That the Bill be passed.

On Accident in Singareni Collieries*

A mining accident occurred at 8.20 p.m. on 27 March 1986 during the second shift in Godavari Khani No. 9 Incline of the Singareni Collieries Company Limited, located at Ramagundam, Karimnagar district, in the State of Andhra Pradesh. This accident was caused due to influx of noxious gases into the working panel No. 7 of No. 4 seam through fire seals of panel No. 8, from the same seam. Out of the persons working in the area, 12 persons were affected and rescued and out of which six died before reaching the Company's hospital. During the rescue operations, eight officials (including the General Manager, the Manager and two Undermanagers) were also affected by noxious gases and one mining Sardar died later on. Thus, in all seven persons got killed and thirteen were affected. Of the latter, who received treatment in the hospital, twelve have been discharged and one person is under observation.

Immediate measures were taken for rescue of the affected persons

**L.S. Deb.*, 3 April 1986 (Spoke while participating in the Calling Attention to Matters of Urgent Public Importance regarding the Accident in Singareni Collieries).

working in the mine. All workers working in the other parts of the mine were also immediately withdrawn. Two Deputy Directors of Mines Safety, Hyderabad Region, reached the site of the accident on 28 March 1986. Subsequently, the Director of Mines Safety, Hyderabad Region and the Director General of Mines Safety also visited the accident site to assess the situation and to render appropriate advice. Director of Mines Safety, Hyderabad Region, is conducting the enquiry under the Mines Act, 1952.

The Mines Act, 1952, rules and regulations framed thereunder, contained provisions for the safety of the workers in the mines. The Director General of Mines Safety and his officers enforce the statutory provisions in respect of mines. The Director General of Mines Safety has been directed to intensify inspections of mines and take other actions under the Mines Act, including issue of improvement notices, prohibitory orders, launching of prosecutions, etc. to ensure that mines managements take appropriate preventive measures. Steps are also being taken to strengthen the inspecting machinery of the Director General of Mines Safety.

* * *

Mr Chairman, Sir, I am grateful to the honourable Members of Parliament who have, in the course of putting their searching questions, have also given very valuable suggestions for the future action. Mr Bhoopathy has mentioned that there was a threat earlier, a threat was noticed in this particular panel. This was brought to the notice of the Management. This is a fact. It was because the threat was noticed and it was brought to the notice of the Management, the panel No. 8 where the accident had occurred was abandoned. That was in March 1986, just a month back. They were sealed. First seals were put. People working there were shifted to some other panel. So, the accident occurred in panel No. 8 which was abandoned. The gas leaked and it affected another panel No. 7 where the accident did not take place. The sufferings has occurred because the accident has taken place in one panel and it has affected another panel. This is the correct situation.

Another question arose whether there were enough safety precautions and safety measures available in the mines. I would not like to claim that enough safety measures are available. I do not know what is enough safety measure and what is not. So, I would not be right in claiming that. But I must say that some arrangements existed and perhaps the management thought they were adequate. But accidents are accidents. Sometimes even with adequate protective measures and preventive measures accidents take place. Accidents cannot be avoided. I am told that safety measures were available in the mines like Sensitive Gas Detectors. These Sensitive Gas Detectors were being used and I am also told that every one hour or so, the gas was being checked. And safety lamps which the honourable Member has refereed to were also available and I will not go into lot of things. Active rescue-trained persons with apparatus are also kept near the places.

* * *

As far as equipment are concerned, the honourable Member has asked as to whether sophisticated equipment are available in our mines. I am told that in many places sophisticated equipment are not available, the reason being that these sophisticated equipment are not manufactured in our country and these equipment have to be imported.

Now, the Coal India has constituted a committee and these Singareni Collieries have also requested that their colliery also should be included in it in order to study the requirements of those safety equipment necessary in all the coalfields of India and how much risk would be caused and how much it would cost. Because it is not available within the country we have to get it imported. So, all these exercises are going on and are being done by the Coal India.

As far as the occurrence of the accident of this type is concerned, in this particular mine, in the last five years that I had the figure, only one accident occurred in 1985 where one person was killed, and in the last five years this is the second accident that has taken place. But if we take Singareni colliery as a whole, of course, the figure is different – I am talking about this particular thing, but if we look at the figures of the accidents that are taking place in mines in our country and if we compare them with the figures of accidents taking place in other parts of the world, well, the figures are comparable. But that does not mean that we are satisfied with them. We must prevent accidents and we should go to the extent of not having any accident at all.

To just give you a comparative statement, the death rate per thousand persons in Indian mines in the year 1984 is 0.32, in Belgium, it is 0.97, in Czechoslovakia, it is 0.49, in Japan, it is 3.87, in USA, it is 0.63 and in West Germany it is 0.40. That is the overall picture all over the country and we, in our country, have been able to contain it. At least the number of deaths due to accidents is not going up. It has been contained for the last many years but I think there is certainly a need to make serious effort to check and to prevent those accidents that take place in our country.

A number of steps have been suggested for this in my statement itself. I have said that the inspections should be intensified and more prohibitory orders should be issued and prosecutions should be launched. All these actions under the Mines Act have been taken and I directed that they should be intensified. Besides this, I think what Shri Reddy has suggested is a very correct point. Shri Reddy has said that we should go in for more rescue stations and rescue rooms in the mines. I do agree with the suggestions of Shri Reddy and I do feel the necessity of going in for more rescue stations and rescue rooms. In fact, a high-powered committee has been constituted by the Government to make an assessment of how many rescue stations and rescue rooms should be set up and our intention is that rescue stations should be available at least within a kilometre's range. This is the intention of the Government of India and we are working towards that.

As far as this particular mine is concerned, we have a plan or scheme which we call Survey of Accident-prone Mines and Identification of Corrective Measures. This scheme was actually formulated for Dhanbad coal mines, but the Government of India has decided that this scheme should also be extended to Singareni collieries. We are going to do this also in Singareni.

Then, there was a question whether some people have been prosecuted or no person has been prosecuted at all. We have been launching prosecutions. As far as Singareni collieries is concerned, in the last five years . . . we have launched prosecution in eight cases. As far as the present incident is concerned, I have stated that the Directorate of Mines has been asked to go into it. He is investigating the matter. What further steps can be taken would be thought of only when we receive the report from the Director of Mines. He is at the moment going into all this.

One last point has been made about the compensation paid to them. Those who died, funeral expenses of Rs 500 each were paid and another interim compensation of Rs 10,000 for deceased person has been paid. This will be the part of entire compensation that their heirs will be entitled to under the Compensation Act. This is what has been done.

But I want to place on record my appreciation about the officers who have been on the site. As I have stated in my statement, out of twelve persons who had been affected, six persons were the people who were working there. The seventh person who died was a person who had gone to rescue them. So, the rescue operation immediately started. The eight persons who had been affected include the General Manager, the Manager and two Undermanagers. They have gone into such a risk of rescuing people that they themselves were affected. So, I would place my deep appreciation for the prompt action taken by them.

With these few words, I conclude. Thank you.

The Apprentices (Amendment) Bill 1986*

I beg to move for leave to introduce a Bill further to amend the Apprentices Act, 1961.

* * *

I introduce the Bill.

* * *

Sir, I beg to move:

> That the Bill further to amend the apprentices Act, 1961, be taken into consideration.

As honourable Members are aware, the Apprentices Act was enacted in 1961 with the objectives of regulating programme of training of apprentices in industry for imparting training. The Act was amended in 1973 to bring within its purview the training of graduates and diploma

**L.S. Deb.*, 5 May and 30 and 31 July 1986 (Spoke while moving the Bill in the Lok Sabha). The Bill provided for amendment of the Apprentices Act, 1961, to create a separate category of apprentices and also to amend sections 3(a), 6(b) and 6(aa) of the Act.

holders in engineering/technology as graduates/technician apprentices in addition to the trade apprentices.

The vocationalization of higher secondary education has been attempted in this country as part of the efforts to provide meaningful education leading to suitable employment opportunities at the appropriate levels. It is also hoped that this would relieve the pressure on our higher education system. Vocationalization implies education through work experience and hence adequate facilities are to be provided for the vocational stream to learn the practical aspects of the subject through field studies and to supplement the institutional learning. Providing apprenticeship facilities to the products of vocational stream assumes relevance in this context.

A pilot scheme called Special Vocational Education Training Scheme to provide 'on the job training' to the product of the vocational stream was launched in 1983-84 under the supervision of the Regional Boards of Apprenticeship Training under the control of the then Ministry of Education. The scheme also provided for training of weaker sections, specially the Scheduled Castes and the Scheduled Tribes, minorities, physically handicapped and women.

In the light of the experience gained during the two years which indicates that the scheme has been welcomed by the States, training agencies and the products of the vocational stream, if it proposed to amend the Apprentice Act, 1961, to provide training for the products of vocational stream by creating a separate category of apprentices called 'the technician (vocational) apprentices' and administer the scheme through the Regional Boards of Apprenticeship Training who are implementing the apprenticeship training scheme for graduates and technician apprentices.

The object of the Apprentices (Amendment) Bill, 1986, which is before you for your kind consideration, is to create a separate category of apprentices, viz., technician (vocational) apprentices for providing on the job training to the products of the 10+2 vocational stream under the Apprentices Act. This will help to ensure that adequate competence and skills required for various occupations are acquired by the products of the 10+2 vocational stream which would lead to suitable employment or self-employment opportunity in organized industries, agriculture and other service sector of economic activity including agro- and rural-based industries.

The scheme envisages payment of a minimum rate of stipend prescribed under the rules, 50 per cent of which will be reimbursed by the Central Government to the training establishments as in the case of the graduate and technician apprentices. It is estimated that about 4,000 trainees will be benefiting from the scheme in the first year of its operation. This opportunity will progressively increase to around 12,000 by the end of the Seventh Five Year Plan. The amount that is likely to be reimbursed by the Central Government during the Seventh Five Year Plan period would be in the order of Rs 744 lakh.

The opportunity is also being availed to amend Section 3 (a) and 6 (b) and 6 (aa) of the Act. The present proposal to amend Section 3 (a) of the Act is aimed to remove the difficulties in the working of the scheme of reservation of training places for the Scheduled Castes and Scheduled Tribes. Since the word 'Trade Test' used in the Section 6(a) and 6 (aa) is not commonly used by all examining bodies, the proposed amendment suggests the inclusion of the word 'Examination' in addition to Trade Test.

Sir, with these few words, I commend this Bill for the consideration of this House.

* * *

Sir, I am grateful to the honourable Members for having given full support to this Bill though some of my friends on the other side have some reservations. My friend Dr Datta Samant gave limited support.

* * *

I am also grateful to the honourable Members for having given very valuable suggestions. In fact the House was unanimous that this amendment is not enough and that Government may have to think about more and comprehensive amendment to this Act. I agree to the suggestions of the House and we shall be coming with a comprehensive amendment to the Act. In fact, the Central Apprenticeship Council has already appointed a Working Group in October last year to go into the functioning of the scheme itself as to how these are being implemented. It has also been entrusted to go into the implementation of this Act. After having gone through all these they will suggest whether amendments were required to be done. So, this Working Group is already going into all these aspects. Hopefully, when the Central Apprenticeship Council will meet in October this year, they will be able to submit a final report. I am given to understand that this Working Group has already had four regional seminars all over the country and we hope to get the report by October. After we get the report, we will examine these things and the suggestions which have been given today and yesterday by the honourable Members. We will certainly keep them in mind while we come with a comprehensive amendment to this Act.

Sir, we have come here with a limited issue of introducing a new course and also to remove some loopholes in the reservation policy for Scheduled Caste and Scheduled Tribes. Perhaps we could have come, let us say, after October. 'But the idea of coming with this was also to know the mood of the House, to be frank; so that when we come with comprehensive amendment, then we can give due consideration to the advices and suggestions given by the honourable Members.

The New Education Policy emphasizes on the vocationalization of the education, or we may call it job-oriented education. This amendment is in line with the New Education Policy . At present under the Apprentices Act, we have three categories of apprentices contemplated. One is, trade apprentice course including ITI students which is meant for standard 5th to 10th those who have completed standard 5th to standard 10th. Second is Technician Apprentice for the diploma holders and third is graduate apprentices for graduates in engineering technology, Now we want to add the fourth category for the Plus-2 students.

This is how we have come with this amendment to add a new category of apprentices for 10+2 students. We are calling it Technician Vocational Apprenticeship. We hope that the amendment will result in at least three things. That is, in pursuance of the new education policy, it will be an attempt to vocationalize the education. Secondly, we hope that it may give an opportunity for those who have finished this training for self-employment. Thirdly, it will certainly relieve pressure on the general higher education system.

The points that have been raised and emphasized by the honourable Members are that the number of trainees that we have projected and the amount of money that we have provided are too little. Well, it may be too little. I am not certainly satisfied with what has been provided with, I wish something more could have been given. But when we talk about the new category of apprentices that we are trying to introduce, it has to be seen from the context of the whole vocational training that we are giving and the apprenticeship training that is going on in the country.

As I have said, there are three categories which are already existing and this is the fourth one. I think we have to look in totality. If we look at different courses that are already going on, now we may find that under the first category of apprenticeship training we have the capacity of 181,935 seats all over this country. Then, for the graduate and diploma courses the total seats available are 26,240. Over and above, we have the seats, it is all over the country with a capacity of 260,000. That makes, in fact, the existing seats available in all the three courses to 488,175. After the introduction of the fourth course we will have 12,000 additional seats, and the total seats available in the country for apprenticeship training in all the four categories will be a little over five lakh. So, it is not that bad. I am saying that it is not that bad because the next question comes whether the existing seats which are available are being properly utilized. That is another question.

I tried to look at those figures and I am sorry to say that the existing seats which are available in these courses are not being utilized fully. For example, in apprenticeship training out of 191,935 seats available the total utilized seats are 136,345. These figures are for the year 1985-86. Therefore, we still have unutilized seats to the tune of 55,590. If you look at the graduate and the diploma courses the total seats available in the country are 26,240 and out of these seats only 13,746 are utilized. So we have 12,494 seats unutilized . . . I hope that whatever seats we are making available now under the fourth category will be fully utilized.

I once again make a statement here that we shall see how it takes off. The projected figures can be flexible. I think the amount which is projected here can also be flexible. But, of course, this is going to be administered by the Ministry of Human Resources. I believe if the programme takes off well, I think, the Government can certainly be flexible and, if necessary, we may even come up with higher seats or higher allocations at a later stage depending on how it works.

Sir, some honourable Members pointed out about the 25 trades that we are going to introduce under this new category and also the list having not been given. I will read out the list of these 25 trades. Shri Tombi Singh wanted to know whether the new course will have relevance to the North Eastern region. I am happy to say that the new trades which we are going to introduce have a lot of relevance for the North Eastern region. I will read it out: Accountancy and Auditing; Banking; Marketing and Salesmanship; Office Secretaryship/Stenography; Food Preservation; Bakery and Confectionery; Poultry farming; Fisheries/

Fish Processing; Dairying; Medical Laboratory Technology/Assistants; Health workers/Nursing; Childcare and Nutrition; Health care and Beauty Culture; Ophthalmic technique; Crop cultivation/production; Sericulture; Horticulture/Floriculture; Plant Protection; Dress design and making; Textile and designing; Civil construction/maintenance; Mechanical servicing; Electrical servicing; Electronics servicing and Automobile servicing. These are the 25 trades.

* * *

We have already got 135 trades for trade apprentices. The 25 trades which I have just now mentioned are the new trades which we propose to introduce. We do not want to conflict with the ITI and trade apprentices courses which are already there. These are the new trades which we propose to introduce keeping in view the requirements in various areas including North Eastern region as has been mentioned by Shri Tombi Singh.

Some honourable Members have voiced their concern about the functioning of it and that the equipment that they are using are outdated, and modernization is required, etc. I quite agree with them, the facilities available are not up to date. The standards of the facilities that are in the country need to be upgraded and modernized. For the first time in the Seventh Plan, for the modernization of these facilities in the country, we have made a Plan allocation of Rs 17 crore and to start with we are going to choose those which are fifteen years or more old, because we thought that those who have done quite a bit of work should be modernized first.

* * *

Perhaps we will have to look at the entire policy of how to run and how to maintain that. I propose to take a meeting to review the whole thing. The training centres are not only run by the State Governments, but these are run by the private people also and they have to be affiliated to NCVT; they have to get affiliation and recognition. We have a large number of it; there is a mushroom growth of them in the country and they are coming for affiliation. Mr Thomas is here. In States like Kerala, number of it is coming up and they are asking for affiliation. Mr Anthony has also written a number of letters. We have to look at the whole thing, whether we should modernize or update the present ones or allow the people to go on starting more such centres. All these aspects are to be seen. I hope we will take a decision on that also very soon.

* * *

Then, of course, one very important and pertinent question that has been raised in the House is that out of those people who have already been trained in ITIs and those who have obtained their diploma or degree, how many of them have been employed and whether it is easy for them to get employment. Sir, I have no figure at all in this regard. But I have instructed that we should make a sample survey because it is very difficult to have an entire survey on that aspect. Through this sample survey, we will try to find out as to how these trainees who have completed their training are living, whether they have got a job, if so, whether it is in the Government or whether it is self-employment or it is in the public sector or private sector.

* * *

The sample survey will certainly help us in knowing the position and condition of these people who have already been trained. And unless we know the position, we cannot formulate any policy and we cannot find any solution for that. When the survey report comes, I will certainly be glad to place that report on the Table of the House.

Then Sir, a point has been raised about the reservation for Scheduled Castes and Scheduled Tribes that there has been a very poor intake of these Scheduled Castes and Scheduled Tribe candidates. The Act provided for trade-wise reservation of seats based on the percentage of population. Therefore, they did not qualify. Now we are going to take the availability of the seats in totality rather than having it trade-wise. So, after this amendment, I hope the intake of tribal and Scheduled Caste students will certainly go up.

These are the few points that I wanted to mention. As I said in the beginning, the valuable suggestions that the honourable members have made will certainly be noted and they will certainly be taken into consideration when we come to Parliament again for a comprehensive amendment as desired by the House.

* * *

I beg to move:

That the Bill, as amended, be passed.

Beedi and Cigar Workers (Conditions of Employment) Amendment Bill, 1985*

Sir, I am grateful to Mr Saha for having brought this Private Member's Bill, for the reason that it has given an opportunity for the House to discuss the problems of beedi workers all over the country. I am grateful to the honourable Members for having pointed out many problems, and I can assure the House that all the points that have been made by the honourable Members have been noted, and we shall see what can be done about them.

There are about 32.75 lakh beedi workers all over the country, spread over mainly 12 states. It is a fact that beedi workers are in an unorganized sector. Therefore, in 1966, in order to bring some relief to these beedi workers, Government of India enacted a law called the Beedi and Cigar Workers (Employment and Conditions of Service) Bill, to improve their conditions of work and for measures connected therewith. But this Act was to be implemented by the State Governments, and there were many complaints that the provisions of this Act were not being implemented or enforced effectively. Even on the floor of this House, many honourable Members in the previous Lok Sabha were voicing the problems of the beedi workers, and therefore, Government of India, in 1981, i.e., on 21 January that year, convened a tripartite meeting to look into the problems of these beedi workers. This tripartite committee decided to constitute a compact Standing Committee to monitor the implementations of the various provisions of this Act; and the Standing Committee had several meetings on 2 Febraury1982, and December 1982, 27 September 1984, and the last meeting on 3 January this year. One of the recommendations of this Standing Committee itself is that the existing law has some loopholes, and therefore, some

---

**L.S. Deb.*, 18 July and 14 August 1986 (Spoke while replying to the Bill in the Lok Sabha). A Private Member's Bill moved by Shri Ajit Kumar Saha regarding the problems of the beedi workers in country.

amendments should be brought in, in order to plug those loopholes. We have examined those proposals, and we in the Ministry of Labour are convinced that an amendment to this Act is necessary. We shall be coming up with a proposal for amendments to this Bill.

There are various issues on which we may require amendments, e.g., we may have to enlarge the definition of 'employee' in order to include those people who are working in godowns and others. We may have to enhance the power of the Inspectors. We may have to take the assistance of Inspectors of the Central Government and, therefore, we may have to empower the State Governments to notify the Central Government officers as Inspectors. These workers are not entitled to holidays. Even legally, they are not entitled to holiday on 15 August, and maybe on 26 January, which are national holidays. All this have to be examined, and we are examining them. I hope that if not during this session, by the next session of Parliament, we should be able to bring in amendments to this Act.

One most important point to understand about the conditions of the beedi workers is that because work is confined to families, because work is done at the respective homes, sometimes it becomes difficult to establish the relationship between the employer and the employee. I had taken a meeting of the employers, and there, they themselves admitted that they did not know who were the employees. Then you can imagine the extent of the difficulty. Therefore, what is more important is that we have to first identify who are these beedi workers, and then to establish the relationship with their employers. This is a very important thing. Therefore, when I took over in January, I had instructed our Welfare Commissioners and requested the State Governments and trade union leaders to help us in identifying the beedi workers. I am glad to inform the House that out of 32.75 lakh beedi workers we have been able to identify, by the end of last month, 20 lakh workers and issue identity cards to them.

This will go a long way in trying to help the beedi workers. The other provisions of the law could not be applied to them because they were not known. That is why I am emphasizing on the identity cards and the identification and the establishment of relationship.

Now, under the Act, we also have Beedi Workers Welfare Fund and we try to do some welfare activities. I am not going to elaborate on them. We give them medical facilities. In fact, throughout the country, at the moment, we have 113 static-cum-mobile dispensaries. We have nine in Andhra Pradesh; we have seven in Bihar; we have five in Gujarat; we have fifteen in Karnataka; we have seven in Kerala; we have eleven in Madhya Pradesh; we have six in Maharashtra; we have eleven in Orissa; we have ten in Rajasthan, nine in Tamil Nadu and eight in UP; and we have nine in West Bengal. I am happy to inform the House that another eighteen static-cum-mobile dispensaries will be established all over the country. Sanction orders have already been issued and these will be located one in Assam, one in Karnataka, five in Madhya Pradesh, seven in Maharashtra, two in Orissa, one in Tamil Nadu and one in West Bengal.

* * *

There are many activities on which I would not like to elaborate. For example, we also look after the children of the beedi workers. We try to give them medical facilities.

* * *

Well, I will not claim that these dispensaries and hospitals are running well; I only said that these are in existence. I would not certify that they are good because I have not gone there and seen them. All these are being done by the Welfare Organization of the Ministry of Labour.

* * *

Well, in Hyderabad, we would not have done so much. As far as educational facilities are concerned, the information that I have on the file is that in 1984-85, Rs 51.5 lakh were spent; we spent to the tune of Rs 51.5 lakh only for awarding scholarships to the children of the beedi workers; in 1985-86, Rs 61.7 lakh have been spent.

* * *

I will certainly visit those places. In fact, I have visited West Bengal; I have also visited some portion of Karnataka along with the Labour Minister of Karnataka. I have not been able to go to Maharashtra. You know for how many months I have been here. So, I have already visited those States. I will certainly do that and I will try to go to as many places as possible. These are the few points I would like to state and I would request the honourable Member to withdraw this Bill because I have myself said that we ourselves are coming up with a comprehensive amendment to the Bill.

* * *

During the debate on Private Member's Bill of Shri Ajit Kumar Sabha, the Beedi and Cigar Workers (Conditions of Employment) Amendment Bill, 1985, I had stated on 18 July 1986 that the dispensaries and hospitals were being run by State Governments. The correct position is that these dispensaries and hospitals are being run by the Welfare Organization of the Ministry of Labour.

On page 0779, the figure of 16.7 lakh appears to be a typographical error and should be read as 61.7 lakh.

Improving the Conditions of Tea Garden Workers*

First of all, though the Plantation Labour Act, the Central Act, was passed by this very House, the appropriate Government for the implementation of the Plantation Labour Act is not the Central Government as contended by the honourable Member, it is the State Government. Though the Act is of the Centre, the implementation is to be done by the State Government.

Mr Tirkey has alleged that they are the lowest-paid people. He has quoted some figures. I want to correct them slightly. I confine the figures to the tea-growing states only. In Assam, the minimum wage fixed for agricultural sector is Rs 12.50. For the non-agricultural sector it is from Rs 8 to Rs 12. The present rate of wage of the tea-garden workers is Rs 10.30.

* * *

**L.S. Deb.*, 26 November 1986 (Spoke while participating in the half-an-hour discussion on low wages for tea plantation workers).

As far as Kerala is concerned, for the agricultural sector the minimum wage is Rs 15, for the non-agricultural sector it is from Rs 5.75 to Rs 20, and for the tea-garden people, at the moment it is Rs 14.45.

In West Bengal, for agricultural sector it is Rs 11.70, for non-agricultural sector it is from Rs 15.58 to Rs 23.35 and for tea-garden people, the present rate of wage is Rs 11.28.

In Tamil Nadu, your own State, Sir, for the agricultural sector it is Rs 8, for the non-agricultural sector it is from Rs 15 to Rs 23 and at the moment the tea-garden workers are getting Rs 15.02.

This is the position of the minimum wages and the wages being earned by the tea-garden workers. While it looks slightly lower than the agricultural sector and the non-agricultural sector, the one aspect that has to be kept in mind is that as far as tea-garden workers are concerned they get not only the wages in cash but also to certain extent they get it in kind in the sense that they are given – as you have yourself rightly pointed out – subsidized rate of foodgrains. They get free firewood, of course.

I am just placing these before the august House. Though in monetary terms, it looks slightly lower than the other sectors, if you take into account the wages, that they get in terms of kind, in the reduced subsidized rate, the position of the tea-garden workers are comparable, I may just say it is comparable. This is the precise position of the industry. As far as the contention of the honourable Member that since they are earning huge foreign exchange, therefore, the real wages should go up. I do not know how far this argument can be accepted. If we accept this then we may have to accept the other way round also that is, whenever the export earnings go down the wages of the workers will also go down. So, this is not a correct argument. The export earnings keep on fluctuating. It is not that every year export earnings keep on rising. In 1983, the export earnings were Rs 557 crore. In 1984, the export earnings were Rs 740 crore whereas in 1985, it came down to Rs 711 crore. The present concept of sharing profit is the bonus concept. That is the real concept of sharing the profit of the industry and this is being done.

Sir, fortunately the tea Industry is an industry where the trade union movement is very very strong. Therefore, the wages are normally determined not on the basis of minimum wages fixed by the respective State Governments but it is always on the basis of bilateral negotiations. As far as West Bengal and Assam are concerned the bilateral negotiations took place in August 1983 and has expired in August 1986. As far as Tamil Nadu is concerned the wage negotiations took place in January 1984 and the present settlement expires in December 1986. Therefore, both in the south and in the east, the fresh wage negotiations are due. I have no definite information whether wage negotiations have been resumed, but wage negotiations are due.

Sir, as I said earlier, the trade union movement in this area is so strong that the wages are determined through bilateral negotiations.

Sir, the implementation of the Plantation Labour Act is not satisfactory. We in the Labour Ministry have made a study on the implementation of the Plantation Labour Act throughout the country. It was commissioned in 1983 and was over in 1985. This study report reveals that the implementation of Plantation Labour Act is not at all satisfactory. We have an industrial committee for tea plantation industry and this matter was put before industrial committee on 6 August this year. This committee appointed a subcommittee to go into the report as well as the working of the implementation of the law and the working of the industry. The subcommittee has, in fact, in a short time been able to submit its final report and has given its recommendations. On the basis of the recommendations of the subcommittee appointed by the industrial committee on plantation industry we are now considering a number of proposals to bring changes into the Plantation Labour Act which will mainly deal, of course, with the welfare part of it, particularly, health, housing, and we are going to add a new chapter which would exclusively deal with the safety of the workers.

These are the few initiatives which the Ministry has taken and hopefully by the next session of Parliament I am confident that I would be able to come to the august House with the proposed amendment and the House will be in a position to discuss.

* * *

The basic questions on which the discussion has centred are the minimum wages and welfare measures. It is where myself personally and my Ministry are concerned. From time to time, we write to the State Governments and we also lay down certain guidelines for the revision of minimum wages, not only in the tea industry but in many other industries as well. I can only assure the august House that after what has been discussed here, I will take the matter up with the respective State

Governments to see whether they would be in a position to revise the minimum wages or not. It is for the State Governments to do it but I will certainly take it up with them.

As far as welfare measures are concerned, Mr Acharia has raised a number of questions. I have already admitted earlier that the implementation of the Plantation Labour Act is not satisfactory. The welfare measures contemplated under the Act are not being implemented. That is why we have set up a committee, and it has gone into all these aspects. We are trying to rectify the situation to some extent.

As far as enforcement of the law is concerned, perhaps the enforcement machinery available now is not adequate enough. Under the proposed amendment Bill, we are trying to strengthen the enforcement machinery also.

So, this is one aspect I would like to say, though I will not be able to spell out everything what we are thinking of. For example, they are supposed to cater to medical facilities to the workers and all that. I have myself reviewed the situation of how the hospitals and dispensaries in the tea industry are being run; whether they are adequate; whether medicines are available; whether doctors are available; whether nurses are available. It is not a happy state of thing. I myself have found it out. One of the reasons they say is that the doctors are not available but they have infrastructure; they have hospitals; they have the equipment, but doctors are not willing to serve there. So, I ventured to offer to them. I mean gave a suggestion to them that if the workers' children are to be educated and if they want to go to medical profession with an agreement, when they have their MBBS degrees or whatever it is, if they are willing to come back and serve these, whether you will be willing to sponsor these candidates and finance them. I am happy to inform the august House that there is a spontaneous response from the tea industry and I propose to take up the matter with the Ministry of Health to give us some seats so that we can sponsor some medical students for the tea industry. So, all these aspects, we have been going into.

* * *

There is no bar on creation of fund; creation of fund can be done. In fact, in Assam, they have already created a Tea Welfare Development Fund out of the cess which is being collected from tea. So, that already there. The only question is whether this cess development fund should be run by the Central Government as a whole or it should be run by the respective State Governments. This is a question which I have certainly talk to the State Governments. But at the moment, Assam Government has gone into that and they have already formed what is called a Tea Welfare Development Fund; and I do not see any reasons why the West Bengal Government cannot do it when the Assam Government has already done it.

* * *

About the Tripartite Committee that you had referred to, it is an Industrial Committee; it is a Tripartite Committee represented by the trade unions and the industry and the government where the Labour Secretaries of the tea-growing States are the members. So the State Governments are certainly taken into confidence whenever we discuss these problems.

Regarding setting up of provident fund offices, we have talked about it. We have sanctioned their offices in Siliguri and it has started functioning, not much. If I tell you the problem you will be an unhappy man because the Calcutta office union is not willing to part with the files relating to Siliguri, Jalpaiguri and Darjeeling. So, there is some problem of shifting the files, I have talked to your Labour Minister and told him to sort it out. But an office is not only sanctioned in Siliguri but also in Darjeeling. The only thing remaining is about Jalpaiguri. I have made a condition that first the files pertaining to Jalpaiguri and Darjeeling should be transferred to them; then only I will consider the question of setting up an office in Jalpaiguri. Otherwise, I will not. This is what I have told your government. So, if you can kindly influence your union leaders it would help us to make this office function in a proper manner.

As far as nationalization is concerned, I think the position of the government has been made absolutely known. It is not the policy of the government now to go on taking over every sick industry or every sick mill; government cannot afford to become a hospital of the sick and the dead mills or dead industries. Therefore, our position is very clear here. With these words, I have made my position clear and I thank the honourable Members for having initiated the discussion. I can only assure you that while formulating our amendment, we will keep the suggestions made in this behalf.

Thank you.

The Child Labour (Prohibition and Regulation) Bill, 1986*

Sir, I beg to move:

> That the Bill to Prohibit the engagement of children in certain employments and to regulate the conditions of work of children in certain other employments, as passed by Rajya Sabha, be taken into consideration.

According to the Planning Commission's estimates made in March 1985, the number of child workers is approximately 17.58 million. Most of these children moreover work in the unorganized sector where few labour laws are applicable. This has been causing the Government a great deal of concern. In India, as in many other developing countries, children belonging to the poorest families contribute in substantial measure to the income of their families. In these circumstances, it would neither be desirable nor possible to impose a total ban on all child labour. On the other hand, there can be no two opinions on the point that in certain employments/industries, the employment of children is hazardous in the extreme and should, on no account, be allowed.

As of today, the employment of children in certain industries/occupations is prohibited under the law. The Constitution of India stipulates that children below the age of 14 years should not be employed in any factory, mine or hazardous employment. Labour laws, like the Factories Act and the Mines Act, prohibit the employment of children below a certain age in factories and mines. The Employment of Children Act prohibits the employment of children in certain industrial occupations and processes. In other Acts also, like the Plantation Labour Act, the Merchant Shipping Act, the Motor Transport Workers Act, and the State Shops and Establishments Act, the employment of children below a certain age is prohibited. However, there is no uniformity in these Acts, nor is there any procedure laid down for deciding the employment from which child labour should be banned.

**L.S. Deb.*, 3 and 9 December 1986 (Spoke while moving the Bill in the Lok Sabha). The Bill provided for prohibiting the engagement of children in certain employments and to regulate the conditions of work of children in certain other employments.

In most of the areas where child labour today is not banned by law, children work without the benefit of law, children work without the benefit of protection of labour laws. There are no maximum working hours, no periods of rest, and no holidays prescribed for these children. Consequently, many children work under conditions of exploitation.

One of the reasons for the existing restrictions on child labour not being effective is that the penalties prescribed in the different Acts are not stringent enough. They are also not uniform. Several employers who have been found guilty of employing children in violation of the provisions of different Acts, have, therefore, got off with light sentences. To ensure that the penalties have a more deterrent effect on employers, the Employment of Children Act, 1938, was amended in December 1985, enhancing both the fine and the imprisonment prescribed. It is felt, however, that the offence of employing and exploiting child labour is an extremely serious one and therefore, the penalties should be further enhanced.

It is to take care of these aspects that the present Bill has been introduced. The Bill seeks to do primarily three things: (a) ban the employment of children below 14 years from employment in certain specified occupations and processes considered hazardous and set up a procedure for identification of employment/occupations which are hazardous for children and where their employment needs to be banned; (b) regulate the working conditions of children in areas which are not hazardous and where there employment is not banned by law, in such a manner that child workers cannot be exploited; (c) enhance the penalties for violations of the provisions relating to child labour to make them sufficiently deterrent. The penalty for the first offence, now proposed is imprisonment from 3 months to one year or fine from Rs 10,000 to Rs 20,000 or both, and for a second offence mandatory imprisonment for a term of not less than 6 months and up to a period of two years.

Central and State Governments will be empowered to frame rules pertaining to the safety and health of children working in any establishment. The rules would pertain to matters like drinking water, safety of buildings and machinery, dust and fumes, lighting, etc.

We are aware that the existence of a law prohibiting and regulating child labour will not in itself solve the problem of child labour. Child workers are among the most deprived sections of our society, and are often unable to get access to facilities like education, health care, vocational training, etc. For this purpose a concerted action plan pooling the resources of all concerned Ministries in the Central and State Governments is being drawn up in consultation with the concerned Ministries. This plan is expected to be finalized soon.

I request that the Bill as passed by the Rajya Sabha be taken up for consideration.

* * *

Sir, I am grateful to the honourable Members who have participated in this debate and ventilated their concern, feelings and anguish over the problem of child labour in our country. All of us in this august House very much know the problem of child labour. I think some of us not only know this but understand it because some of us have experienced it also. At least, I have experienced.

Mr Choubey said that I had come to this House with a good intention. Sir, I have come with this Bill not only with a good intention, but I have come with a conviction. We cannot take this problem lightly. The fact that there are 17 million children working in our country means that it is something very grave. Therefore, we must try to understand why they are working.

More or less, the House has come to a conclusion that in most of the cases among these children, it is an economic necessity. I do not think everybody understand what is an economic necessity. I do not think everybody understand what is meant by poverty. Those who are talking against this Bill, would not have talked so, had they undergone poverty. We know what is poverty in this country. We know what starvation means in this world. These millions of children are forced to work for their livelihood.

An honourable Member has said that he supports this Bill with disappointment. Do you think that I am not disappointed? It would have been my wish if child labour could have been abolished with a stroke of pen. If I come to this House and say that the child labour is hereby abolished and the whole House welcomes it and claps, do you mean that the child labour would be over in this country? It will not be. Therefore, we have given a lot of thought to this. There were three ways open to us. One, let it remain as it is; two let us abolish it, ban it, but as I said: Is it possible? When, it is not possible, when we cannot abolish it, and at the same time, we cannot just let the things happen as now, we thought, something must be done. Keeping the whole situation in view, we thought, wherever possible, we should ban it and wherever it is not possible, we should regulate it.

Some honourable Members have raised the question of constitutionality of the Bill. Article 24 of the Constitution prohibits employment of children below the age of 14 years in mines, in factories and in other hazardous occupations. It does not ban everywhere, otherwise the framers of the Constitution would not have mentioned specifically these three things. Therefore, according to the provisions of Article 24 of the Constitution, we have come here to ban the employment of children below the age of 14 years in those areas which are contemplated under Article 24 of the Constitution. But in the other areas, non-mining, non-industry and non-hazardous areas, we thought that under the present circumstances, the best way for us is to regulate it and then we should also come forward with some welfare measures. All the honourable Members were very right in expressing their disappointment that this Bill does not contain anything about the welfare measures. I must take the House into confidence that we really thought over this and we decided to deal with the problem of child labour in three ways. First, we should ban it where it can be banned and where it cannot be banned, we should regulate it, and then rehabilitate them and draw up a welfare programme for their education, health and nutrition. Everything should be provided for them.

When we discussed this, there was a suggestion that we should go, as some honourable Members suggested, for imposition for a cess and create a welfare fund in order to undertake the welfare measures. Somehow, after a lot of deliberations, we came to the conclusion that we should not impose any more cess for the creation of welfare activities and we must go with a budgetary support and since we did not opt for cess, it did not find a place in the Bill. But I want to make the intention of the Government very clear that we want to deal with the problem for child labour in three ways. First, ban it or prohibit it in mines factories and hazardous areas; two, regulate it in non-mining, non-industry and non-hazardous areas and three, which is the most important, come out with welfare measures which will include the education of children, health of the children, nutrition programme for the children, etc. We are working on these welfare programmes.

I have had occasions of taking a couple of meetings at the highest level in the Government of India and hopefully, not hopefully but definitely, in the next session of Parliament, I will come back to you and I will announce the National Child Labour Policy which will contain a concrete action plan for the welfare of the working children. I shall be announcing it in the next session of Parliament.

These are the few remarks that I thought I will make it.

I do agree that this Act will become meaningless unless it is strictly implemented. Implementation is the most important thing. This problem, I must say, is a national problem and this has got to be tackled by the whole nation. This is what I would like to submit. Therefore in the Act itself, we have contemplated one aspect. In Section 16 of the Act, in order to prosecute, in order to launch either a prosecution or a complaint, power has been given to every citizen of this country.

I must also mention about welfare measures too. We will also involve voluntary organizations in doing the welfare work in this regard and in the next session I will be coming with an announcement about this aspect. Therefore, the whole nation has to address itself to this problem and we must all put in a concerted effort to solve this problem.

The other day, a delegation comprising a number of women came and met me. They are from all over India, almost from every part of the country. They came to my office and abused me saying that I was inhuman and what not, because I was going to legalize child labour. They abused me like anything. Fortunately for me, I knew only a lady member in that group because I know her husband who happens to be a big exporter and I was in touch with him when I was in the Ministry of Commerce. I told her, 'Madam you do not know that I know your husband very well. Now you are a very rich woman. Your husband is a very rich man. You have two children but you have the capacity to look after more than 100 children. You have got that much of wealth. If you are so concerned about children's welfare and child labour, will you please adopt one more child at least? If you do not do it, this is the last time you are meeting me in your life. You have no right to see me again until and unless you adopt one more child.' I am telling you all this because unfortunately we do not practise what we preach. People come with delegations because they want to see their names in the newspapers or they want to see themselves on the television.

Therefore my appeal to the nation is this. So far as children's welfare is concerned, those who preach about their welfare in this country should also do it in actual practice. If that is done, I am sure that the problem of child labour in this country can be solved to a great extent.

With these words, I once again thank the honorable Members for having supported this Bill and I earnestly appeal to Shri Piyus Tirkey that instead of graciously opposing this Bill, he can graciously agree to it.

* * *

I beg to move:

> That the Bill, as passed by Rajya Sabha, be passed.

The Factories (Amendment) Bill 1987*

I beg to move:

> That the Bill further to amend the Factories Act, 1948, be taken into consideration.

The Factories Act, 1948, provides for safety, health and welfare aspects of the workers employed in factories. The Act extends to the whole of India and is enforced by the State Governments and Union Territory Administrations through their Factory Inspectors. The Act also empowers the State Governments/Union Territory Administrations to frame rules, so that the local conditions prevailing in the States are appropriately reflected in the enforcement. Uniformity in the administration of the Act in various States is sought to be achieved through Model Rules framed by the Directorate General, Factory Advice Service and Labour Institutes, Bombay. The Act was last reviewed and amended in 1976.

As honourable Members are aware, since the last amendment of the Act in 1976, there has been considerable changes in the industrial and technological situation in the country on account of setting up of several chemical industries dealing with hazardous and toxic substances and introduction of new technologies. The developments have necessitated a review of the existing provisions in the Factories Act, 1948.

**L.S. Deb.*, 19 and 20 March 1987 (Spoke while moving the Bill in the Lok Sabha). The Bill provided for further amendment of the Factories Act, 1948, to provide for safeguards to be adopted during use and handling of hazardous substances and for laying down of emergency standards and measures.

Government has received a number of suggestions from the State Governments who enforce the provisions of the Act, Central Ministries/ Departments which are concerned with Departmental and Public Sector Undertakings, Central Workers' and Employers' organizations, trade unionists and others. These suggestions were examined particularly in the context of the December 1984 gas leak disaster at Bhopal and other recent industrial accidents elsewhere.

It is now proposed to amend the Factories Act, 1948, to provide, among other things, for safeguards to be adopted during use and handling of hazardous substances by the occupiers of factories, laying down of emergency standards and measures; procedures for setting up of hazardous industries and workers' participation in safety management.

With the amendments proposed in the Bill, there would be greater check on dangerous substances, major hazards and pollution, working and general environments. The building up of the concept of product safety and measures for fixing responsibility on manufacturers, suppliers and importers, besides the occupiers and owners of factories, would result in safe working operations. The policy of siting of hazardous industries would check adverse effects of industrial pollution as well as reduce the potential risk to the general public. Proper monitoring of threshold limit values through adoption of techniques on industrial hygiene will make working environment healthier. Workers' participation in safety management will promote measures for greater involvement of workers in safety processes. Measures taken by State Governments and Union Territory Administrations for strengthening factory inspectorates and streamlining procedures would result in better enforcement of safety laws and in turn, minimize occupational accidents and diseases. Stringent and deterrent punishments for violation of the provisions of the Act will have a salutary effect on the management of hazardous industries and will compel them to be more safety conscious. I am sure that these provisions will definitely help in improving the safety, health and welfare aspects of the workers.

With these words, I commend that the Factories Amendment Bill, 1987, be taken into consideration.

* * *

I once again take opportunity of thanking all the honourable Members for having supported this important piece of legislation.

While the Bill has an overwhelming support of the august House, the House in the course of the debate has expressed its concern about the implementation of the existing laws and also the apprehensions as to whether the law which is going to be passed today will be effectively implemented. Sir, since the Bill has got an overwhelming support, I will not go into the merits of the Bill. I would only try to submit a few things. The major point which has been raised by the honourable Members is about the implementation of the laws. Sir, it is true that the number of inspectors required for inspection of the factories and the number of inspections done by them in all the States are not adequate. According to the law, an inspector is supposed to inspect 150 factories twice a year. But Sir, the number of inspectors are not adequate in many States. These inspectors are required to inspect more than 150 factories, that is, more than the number required to be inspected under the law. There are States where an inspector may have to inspect about 600 units or even 700 units. Therefore, I will not agree with the onion expressed by the honourable Members that the inspectors are not doing their job and they have a collusion with the management and all that. I think, they are doing their work with the best of their ability. They are required to inspect 150 factories and if they are to inspect more than this number, I think there is no use in blaming our inspectors. I think they deserve our encouragement. As far as the inspectors are concerned, it was expressed by some honourable Members that the inspectors are not able to inspect all the factories. Honourable Member Shri Ajoy Biswas was very emphatic on this point. But for your information, Sir, even in your own State, the State of Tripura, the inspection done last year was just 40 per cent against 90 per cent in some States, 60 per cent in some other States. But in Tripura and West Bengal, 40 per cent inspection was done. I am not blaming them. I am only saying that the inspection is not adequate.

* * *

What is required is strengthening the inspection machinery and I believe the State Governments have their own problems and the normal complaint they make to me was that the Department of Labour was giving such a low priority when they go for plan allocation to the Planning Commission. They normally cannot put across their viewpoints. The State Governments, on a number of occasions, told me about the fund allocation. I have myself taken up the matter with the Planning Commission last year and I am happy to say that the Planning Commission was very kind to enhance the plan allocation for the Department of Labour, particularly in respect of the safety measures and hence with more plan allocation. I am confident that the State Governments will be able to strengthen their machinery and their performance will certainly improve.

As far as we are concerned, in the Central Government, we have a very limited role to play, but then we have been trying to associate ourselves very actively with the State Governments. Now, one point which is very important here is, even if the Inspectorate is strong, even if we have adequate number of inspectors, now still there is another question whether these inspectors are properly trained and whether they are properly qualified. We feel the necessity of upgrading the knowledge of the inspectors, they should be given proper training and we have taken lot of steps to improve the performance of the inspectors in terms of giving training, both at home and abroad. Sir, in the last two years we have been able to send about 27 factory inspectors for a specialist type of training in Australia. As far as the domestic training facilities are concerned, we have also tried to strengthen our institutions so that they will be able to give more and more training to our inspectors. Our training facilities at the Central Labour Institute and the Regional Labour Institutes have been considerably strengthened. The training not only involves training of factory inspectors but also training of management's representatives in the field of safety because we believe that it will not be enough to train the inspectors only. We need to train the management and we need to bring safety consciousness among the workers themselves. Workers themselves should be able to know what is the danger before them and they should be able to point out to the inspector and the management that such precautionary measures need to be taken and this they can do only when they are properly trained. Under the present amendment, we have given that power to every worker to bring it to the notice of the inspectors and to the management that such dangers exist and such rectifications need to be done. So, all these powers have been contemplated under this Act, but giving power alone is not enough, they need to be trained. Therefore, we are giving training not only to the inspectors, but also to the workers and the management in that process we have also included a scheme as a subject of safety in the training of education officers conducted by the Central

Board of Workers' Education and also we have strengthened the faculty of the DG.

* * *

In fact, the Central Board of Workers' Education is having 47 regional centres all over the country and so far they have been conducting educational programmes only about their rights and duties.

* * *

But the safety was not included in the syllabus. We have included safety also now in the syllabus just to say that we are aware of the requirements in the country as far as safety is concerned.

We also tried to formulate some guidelines which we give to the State Governments and we have formulated a national programme for Safety and Health Accident Reduction Action Programme. In short, it is known as SAHARA, and this programme has been accepted by the State Governments where we are also actively involving the workers themselves. I am very happy to say that there has been a good response from all the State Governments in this regard. The Government also have formulated guidelines for on-the-spot and off-the-spot emergency plan and circulated the same for adoption to the State Governments and Union Territories. Even here also, we have a very good response. What was very important to start this programme of bringing about a consciousness in the safety affairs was, first of all to know in every State, how many industries are there which are hazardous to the health and safety of the workers. So, we have requested the State Governments to make a survey of their own States to identify the number of industrial units whom they consider to be hazardous according to the guidelines we have issued. This exercise has been done by all the States. They have identified all those units which are dangerous and we have already started taking remedial measures as to how to improve it, so that even the inspectors know to which units they have to go to because they have the list of identified industries.

We also have a centrally sponsored scheme for strengthening the industrial hygiene laboratories and this has also commenced operation. This scheme envisages supply of equipment, books and chemicals to the industrial hygiene laboratories. A total outlay of this scheme is Rs 106 lakh in the Seventh Plan. It is not a very big amount but we have just started it and this scheme will be 100 per cent centrally assisted scheme. The State Governments have nothing to do here. It will be funded 100 per cent by us. Then, we have also concluded the UNDP project for strengthening the industrial hygiene laboratories in all the States and UTs where chemical industries are concentrated. This is also a special programme. Under this UNDP programme, we have 18 industrial hygiene laboratories in various States and we have been able to strengthen all this. Therefore, we have started taking a number of steps so far as safety is concerned.

Honourable Member Shri Ajoy Biswas mentioned that the rate of accidents and injuries in the country was going up. But I do not think it is going up but it is certainly fluctuating. The position is that there was a decreasing trend between 1971 and 1975. Then, there was a rise from 1976 to 1978. From 1979 onwards, it came down and there was a rise in 1981. But from 1982 onwards, it has considerably come down and I can give the figures of the last two years. The total number of injuries in 1984 was 302,726. In 1985, it came down to 279,126. The number of fatal injuries in 1984 was 824 and it came down to 807 in 1985. It is not a very small number. But the fact that it has started coming down. But there are a few specific points raised by the honourable Members and on one or two I would like to react. Some of the honourable Members have pointed out that the word 'occupier' has to be enlarged as it has a very limited definition. If you look at the definition of the 'occupier' from the original Act and the amendment that we have brought in, you will see that we have tried to enlarge the definition of 'occupier'. In page 2, line 35 you will see thus:

> Provided that –
>
> (i) In the case of a firm or other association of individuals, and any of the individual partners or members thereof shall be deemed to be the occupier.
> (ii) In the case of a company, any one of the director shall be deemed to be the occupier.

So, we have tried to enlarge the definition of 'occupier' in order to bring many people under the purview of the Act and that we are able to fix the responsibility on a particular person.

* * *

There was another suggestion for the Enquiry Committee. This Act is to be administered by the respective State Governments and, as I said, we have a very limited role from the Central Government. But we have under this Bill taken a power with us to deal with a situation in case there is an emergency like the Bhopal tragedy. We have also taken precaution to see that in case the State Governments do not act properly, in such emergency case, then Central Government will take up the problem and, in the process, we have provided for the constitution of an Enquiry Committee by the Central Government. The suggestions from the honourable Members were that we should give this Enquiry Committee full necessary power. It should not be an advisory body. I do not think it will be a sound proposition for the Government to give absolute power to any Enquiry Committee. Enquiry Committee is to enquire and submit the reports to the Government and it has to be left to the Government what action has to be taken. If we give that power to the Enquiry Committee to say that Government must do this as final authority, I do not think it will serve our purpose.

* * *

Honourable Member Shri Sriballabh Panigrahi raised a very pertinent question regarding Clause 23:

> No female child shall be required or allowed to work in any factory except between 8.00 AM and 7.00 PM.

The question is why this provision has come after the Child Labour Prohibition and Regulation Act has been passed. The difference is that under the Child Labour Prohibition and Regulation Act, we have defined a person who has not attained 14 years of age. Under the Factories Act, the child has been defined as a person who has not attained 15 years of age. So, there is a slight difference of one year. That is why, this is to be provided in this Act. But I wish that we could have a uniform thing. I tried to do it but somehow I do not know it has happened. There is a slight difference between 14 and 15 years. I do not think there has been any other pertinent point which has been raised. I hope I have answered all the points. I once again thank all the honourable Members.

* * *

ILO has commissioned a study after the Bhopal incident. Two members from ILO and one from India have made a study. They have submitted their recommendations and while we have finalized our thing, we have taken the recommendations into account. As I said yesterday, this is the result of two years of exercise of many studies and many seminars at regional level and at national level and many articles. We have gone through all these things. We have come with this and we have taken into account all the suggestions that have come from various quarters.

* * *

Occupational disease is certainly drawing our attention very much. So far, we did not have the facility of looking into this occupational disease. As the honourable Member, Shri Damodar Pandey, has pointed out, we have the ESI hospitals all over the country. Of course, they have nothing to do with the Factories Act. It is ESI. We are designating one particular hospital in each State of the ESI whose duty will be only to deal with occupational disease. It is a very difficult proposition. I cannot explain everything here. We need to have the cooperation from everybody.

* * *

We have formulated a model form which we have circulated to the State Governments for reporting back to the Central Government, as to how many inspections have been done; how many prosecutions have been launched and how many people have been penalized. So, we have drawn up a team. We have circulated it to the State Governments. This is a method of monitoring. We are doing that. I am sure that things are going very well. Let us hope for the better.

* * *

I beg to move:

> That the Bill, as amended, be passed.

The Cine Workers Welfare Fund (Amendment) Bill, 1987*

I beg to move:

> That the Bill to amend the Cine Workers Welfare Fund Act, 1981, be taken into consideration.

Sir, the administration of Cine Workers Welfare Fund Act, 1981, along with two other enactments relating to Cine Workers, was transferred from the Ministry of Information and Broadcasting to the Ministry of Labour with effect from 1 April 1986. It provides for the following facilities:

Financing of activities to promote the Welfare of certain Cine Workers and in particular –

(a) to defray the cost of such welfare measures or facilities for the benefit of Cine Workers as may be decided by the Central Government;
(b) to provide assistance in the form of grants or loans to indigent Cine Workers; and
(c) to sanction money in aid of any scheme for the welfare of the Cine Workers which is approved by the Central Government.

It is proposed to amend the provisions of this Act so as to make it more effective and also to enlarge its coverage. The proposed amendments are based on analogues provisions in other Welfare Fund Acts for Mica, Limestone and Dolomite, Iron Ore Miners, etc. The amendments proposed are as under:

(i) To amend Section 2(b)(ii) of the Cine Workers Welfare Fund Act, 1981, to raise the present ceiling from Rs 1,000 p.m. to Rs 1,600 p.m. and where such a remuneration is paid by way of a lump sum, to raise it from Rs 5,000 to Rs 8,000.
(ii) To amend Section 4(1)(c) of Cine Workers Welfare Fund Act, 1981, so as to include 'Family Welfare including family planning

---

**L.S. Deb.*, 20 March and 4 May 1987 (Spoke while moving the Bill in the Lok Sabha). The Bill provided for further amendment of the Cine Workers' Welfare Fund Act, 1981, to make it more effective and also to enlarge its coverage.

education and services' as one of the purpose for which the fund may be utilized; and

(iii) To amend Section 6(2) of the Cine Workers Welfare Fund Act, 1981, to remove the ceiling on the number of members of the Central Advisory Committee.

The ceiling on wages and benefits under the Cinema Theater Workers (Regulation of Employment) Act, 1981, as also under the welfare schemes for the other Welfare Fund Acts is Rs 1,600 per month. It is, therefore, desirable to substitute the present ceiling of Rs 1,000 per month by a ceiling of Rs 1,600 per month, and where the remuneration is paid by way of lump sum to raise the present ceiling of Rs 5,000 to Rs 8,000.

It is proposed to include the components of family welfare including family planning, education and services as one of the purpose enumerated in Section 4(1)(c) of the Act for which the Fund might be utilized. This is being done in pursuance of the recommendations of the International Labour Organization Tripartite Seminar on Compatibility of Labour Laws with National Policy on Population Moderation held in 1984.

Section 6(2) of the Act provides that 'the Central Advisory Committee shall consist of 11 members appointed by the Central Government and the members shall be chosen in such manner as may be prescribed'. In all the Advisory Committee constituted under the various Labour Welfare Acts, the principle of tripartism is observed and equal number of representatives of Government, Employers and Employees are included. It will not be feasible to adhere to the ceiling of 11 members and it is proposed the Section 6(2) of the Act may be amended to remove the ceiling on the number of members.

The amendments proposed in the Bill, I am sure, will help in improving the administration of the Act. With these words I commend the Bill for the consideration of the House.

* * *

I am grateful to the honourable Members who have participated in this debate. It is a very small Bill, the Cine Workers Welfare Fund (Amendment) Bill, 1987.

As the august House is aware, this Bill was also passed and intended to be administered by the Ministry of Information and Broadcasting, and it was recently only in April last year that it was transferred to us and since then we have tried to take some steps.

There are only two or three points which have been raised during the time of the debate. That the amount of money which is available for the welfare of the cine workers under the present Act is very small because the cess that we impose is very small. As it is, we impose a cess of Rs 1,000 for each film and the honourable Members have expressed that this needs to be increased.

I will have consultations with the Ministry of Information and Broadcasting and I also feel that the cess that we are imposing at the rate of Rs 1,000 is small and it needs to be increased.

Some honourable Members wanted to know the amount of money that is available at the moment from the collection of cess, we have only Rs 22.41 lakh at the moment but as the honourable Members are aware, from the profits of the Gandhi film we have about Rs 103 lakh. So, at the moment, the amount available is from the cess and also from the profits of the Gandhi film – Rs 125.41 lakh, and this money will be transferred to the Ministry of Labour after this Budget. But before the money was available with us, whatever facilities were available with the Government of India in the Ministry of Labour, all these different welfare funds, we have already started extending the same benefits to them; the hospitals and dispensaries which are available under the various welfare funds have also been notified and we have already issued and as the august House know all these facilities should be extended to the cine workers also.

We have also started taking other steps. We are in the process of appointing a Central Advisory Council for this.

About the question of identification, we have Labour Commissioners under different Welfare Acts. We have notified those Labour Commissioners as Welfare Commissioners for this purpose. It will be their duty to identify cinema workers and issue them identity cards by the Labour Commissioners is not an easy job, we have a tripartite advisory council. They have a confederation of cinema workers. This confederation has undertaken in that meeting to identify the workers and help the Welfare Commissioners for the purpose of issuing identity cards. Once the identity cards are issued then there will be no problem of giving benefits to the actual cinema workers.

* * *

It is true that the Act was passed in 1981 but this was transferred to us only on 1 April 1986. I come into the picture from that date. From that date onwards we have been trying to take a number of steps. Some cinema workers have already been identified. I do not have the exact number here with me at hand. But they have been identified. In fact, from the funds available with us we have given scholarships to children of the cinema worker worth about a lakh of rupees. So, the identification and the issue of cards is going on. But since it is only one year, nothing much has been achieved. We have had only two meetings but after the amendment of this Bill we propose to call another meeting, either in Southern Region or in Western Region. I do not know. We have not decided the venue. We want to discuss everything how it can be done.

Since the scope of the Bill is very limited, just to increase the level up to Rs 1,600 a month and since the honourable Members have raised only these two limited points. I would once again thank the honourable Members for supporting the Bill.

* * *

To declare film industry as an industry within the meaning of Industrial Disputes Act is not within my power. This Act applies to the cinema workers who are earning at the moment Rs 1,000 a month. We are extending it to Rs 1,600 per month. And for lump sum from Rs 5,000 to Rs 8,000 we are extending.

* * *

Sir, I beg to move:

That the Bill is passed.

Labour Welfare and Government Participation*

Mr Deputy Speaker, Sir, I am grateful to all the honourable Members who have taken part in the debate on the Demands of Grants of the Ministry of Labour for 1987-88. The keen interest which the honourable Members have shown during the debate really gives an indication of their commitment to the welfare of the working class in our country.

Many points were raised and most of the points were valid. I must concede that I do not think it would be possible for me to reply to each point which has been made by all the honourable Members but I can assure that each and every point would be replied subsequently, and here, I propose to deal with the main issues, not the specific cases.

I will try to briefly summarize what has been done in 1986-87 and what we propose to do in 1987-88.

If you look at the legislation aspect, the House will remember that in 1986, five Acts were passed. And those were Dock Workers Safety, Health and Welfare Act, 1986; Child Labour (Prohibition and Regulation) Act, 1986; and Contract Labour (Regulation and Abolition) Amendment Act, 1986. One honourable Member pointed out that this was promised but was not done. It has been done, maybe it escaped his memory. Then, the fifth Act was the Sales Promotion Employees (Condition of Service) Act, 1986. These five Acts were passed in 1986.

At the moment, we have four Bills under consideration of either this House or the other House. These Bills are the Cine Workers Welfare Fund Bill; Factories Amendment Bill, 1986; Labour Welfare Fund Law (Amendment) Bill 1986; and the Payment of Gratuity Act (Amendment) Bill, 1986. These are the major Bills pending for consideration either here or the other House.

On the top of that, we have on our agenda ten Bills which have yet to come before the House and out of that ten, seven will be amendments and three will be new legislations, The seven amendments that are proposed to be brought include Amendment to Employees Provident Fund Act. Some honorable Members have raised the question of raising the contribution by two per cent, up to ten per cent. In the last SLC

---

*_L.S. Deb._, 30 March 1987 (Spoke while replying to the debate in the Lok Sabha on the Demands for Grants, Ministry of Labour, 1987-1988).

meeting, it was agreed by the employers and the SLC that it should be raised. It is now under the active consideration of the Government and it will be coming in the form of amendment. I am saying all this because many honourable Members have raised what has happened to this and that is why amendments are not being brought by the Government. I am just saying how many Bills would be coming up. Then, the next is amendment to Employees State Insurance Act, Amendment to Contract Labour Act and amendment to Plantations Labour Act. This is going to be a very important Bill that would be coming. The honourable Members particularly from this side have not introduced amendments to Industrial Disputes Act and Tribunal Act. These would also be coming up.

* * *

The seventh Bill that would be coming is regarding the Equal Remuneration Act. On top of that, we have these three new proposals which will be coming in. Among these three new proposals there will be a Bill to set up a grievance-redressal machinery for hospitals, dispensaries, educational institutions, scientific research and training institutions which have been taken out of the purview of Industrial Disputes Act. So, we have to provide an alternative grievance-settlements machinery and that would be coming up before the august House very soon.

The second new Bill, which will be coming up before the august House is the Bill, which will be a simplification procedure, as far as adherence to various labour laws are concerned for the small scale industries. Today, the small scale industries have to fill up, as many as 60 forms to adhere to the various requirements under the various laws. We are trying to bring instead of 60 forms, by compressing them to only 3 forms. So this is an attempt to simplify the procedure and this will be quite an important Bill.

Then, we are also coming in with a Bill to provide safety for the workers in the building and construction industries. So, these are the few Bills that would be coming in. But while discussing about the Bills, honourable Members have made a very right point that mere passing of laws is not going to help the workers. What is more important is the implementation of laws. I agree hundred per cent with the honourable Members. In fact, I have myself been making lot of statements to this effect and I can assure the august House that except the Bills which are in the offing, which I have mentioned now, I have decided that, in 1987, we will not initiate any new Bill; 1987 will be devoted towards seeing that the existing laws are implemented.

* * *

Now, here the question is how most of the labour laws are to be implemented by the respective State Governments? We have very little role to play in the implementation of the existing laws, unless some of the laws, where the Central Government is the appropriate authority, we have to deal with directly. But I have no doubt that the respective State Governments will be in a position to implement these laws.

* * *

I will not blame the State Governments, saying that it is squarely the responsibility of the State Governments to implement it and Centre has nothing to do with it. I do not accept that proposition. The Central Government has a role to play. If Central Government is closely cooperating with the State Governments, it can be done. Now, Child Labour (Regulation and Abolition) Act was passed.

* * *

For the implementation of these laws, now the Consultative Committee of the Parliament itself were divided into two groups and tried to go to the States. One group went to see the conditions of the agricultural labourers and another group went to see the unorganized sectors, who are the non-agricultural labourers. Now, the non-agricultural labourers group decided to go to Firozabad first to see the conditions of the children who are working in that Glass and Bangles factory. I must tell you that the Uttar Pradesh Government fully cooperated and today, all their children, which have been working in the Glass factory are out.

* * *

The Parliament has passed the law that children shall not be employed in hazardous factories and mines. We have implemented this.

* * *

But there is another problem to this.

The honourable Member, Shri Kumaramangalam, has complained on the floor of the august House that all the 10,000 children have been rendered jobless. I am only trying to draw a point that if we are really interested in the implementation of the law it can be implemented. But, by implementation of the law what other problems will it lead to is a separate question. But we cannot say that this law cannot be implemented. Shri Choubey has raised a question of defaulters of the provident fund for jute industries.

* * *

Now, for the last 15 years or so, the jute industries have been evading the payment of provident fund arrears. I have taken a meeting with them, reached to certain agreement. We are getting the money though we have not got much of the money. We have started getting the money. Those who have not kept their promise adhered when we met. I sent my Provident Fund Commissioner to Calcutta. He had a meeting with your Home Minister, he had a meeting with IGP of West Bengal and they have started taking action and today 14 people have been arrested and put in jail. I must thank the Government of West Bengal for that. If the West Bengal Government wants to do it, they can do it.

* * *

The West Bengal Government has taken action. So far 15 years they thought, they could not be touched by anybody. But they have been touched. This is what I am saying. If the Central Government and the State Government move together laws can be implemented. But one thing we must understand, this cannot be done solely by the Central Government or solely by the State Government. Centre and State governments must cooperate. If we jointly move, I do not believe the laws cannot be implemented. And, therefore I can assure the august House that this year we are going to give importance to the implementation of the laws and I solicit the cooperation and active involvement of the honourable Members and more so the respective State Governments.

Sir, I do not want to deal elaborately. Next I come to the Industrial Relations.

* * *

Sir, among the important laws which need to be implemented, existing laws which should be implemented and the most important Act according to me is the Minimum Wages Act. If the Minimum Wages Act can be sincerely and effectively implemented, I agree with Dr Datta Samant that the conditions of our working class will change to a great extent. This is what we should try to do. As far as Choubeji's point of minimum wages versus the poverty line is concerned the minimum wages and the poverty line are two different things. Now, poverty line concept is based on the family income. When the Government calculates the poverty line concept, it takes into account the income salary. Now we have added clothing also but it is based on the income of the family and wage is only a component of that income. Therefore, the wage and the poverty line cannot be treated as same. But, I am only explaining the concept. I am explaining the concept not that what is happening is right.

But I do agree with the honourable Members that we must have a look at it. Whether we should continue with this concept. I do not know. I strongly feel myself that it requires re-examination and a relook. So, that much I can say. But as it stands today, these minimum wages and the poverty line are two different concepts.

Now let me come to the industrial relations situation in the country. I do not say that the industrial relation situation in this country is very good. Mr Choubey does not agree with me, because he has cited the figures of sickness and all that. I am not going into them.

* * *

I am coming to unemployment. I will answer all the major points, including that. But the fact, Mr Choubey, is that if you go by the calculation of man-days lost as a scale to know the industrial relations situation in this country. I am using the word 'if' . . . If you go by that standard, there is certainly an improvement in the industrial relations situation, because in 1984 the man-days lost were 56.03 million; in 1985 they were 27.37 million and in 1986 they have come down to 22.1 million man-days . . . The honourable Members from this side have asked: 'If we speak about the number of man-day lost due to strikes and lockouts, have we got the figures about man-day lost due to power failure, due to failure of the machinery, and due to shortage of raw materials?' We do not have them. I am admitting it. We must go into that aspect also . . . We have started it. That alone will give a clear picture; but according to the present norms, i.e., if we take the present norms into account, you cannot deny that there has been improvement.

* * *

As far as the Central sphere is concerned, the man-days lost here have been the lowest in ten years. They are only 1.04 million, and that figure is the lowest in the last ten years. If I give you all the figures, i.e., for the last ten years, Mr Choubey and other honourable Members may get disappointed with all these good figures. If you take the wage loss, it is the lowest ten years. It is Rs 21.42 crore . . . If you look at the figure for industrial disputes, the figures in 1985 was 2,095; for 1985 it is 1,755, and for 1986 it is 1,581.

So, there has been a progressive decline in the number of disputes also; it is not easy in the number of man-days lost but also in the number of disputes. Of course, one point must be made clear that while the number of man-days lost is coming down every year, if we analyse whether it is because of strikes or because of lockouts, the number of man-days lost because of strikes is coming down and the number of man-days lost because of lockouts is going up. That is also in your favour and I do not want to conceal it.

* * *

Now, I will come to social security because many honourable members have raised this question. I will be very brief. Now, I come to provident fund. I have already answered one part of the point which has been raised. Now, all the honourable Members have made a point that though in the last few years there has been a progressive increase in the rate of interest from 9.15 per cent in 1983-84 to 11 per cent in 1986-87. The honorable Members have felt that it is not adequate: it must be raised more. This has been the feeling of the august House. I assure the august House that this shall be examined and I hope to get a favourable decision on this.

There are so many other points which could be mentioned, but one more point that I would like to add is that there was a huge amount of money to the tune of Rs 14.68 crore which did not belong to anybody because nobody claimed that money; it is unclaimed money, somebody was having Rs 1,000, somebody was having 2,000 and odd: it was just kept like that. We have taken steps to identify the people to whom money belongs and I am happy to say that we have identified 3.77 lakh people to whom this money belongs and we will make every effort to see that the money which has been lying for many years and the workers did not know that money belonged to them, will not only be given that money to them but it will be given with interest.

Coming to ESI, it is a very difficult subject . . . There has been a lot of feeling among the Members of Parliament that ESI is not working properly. Well, there is a lot of improvement required in the working of the ESI; I admit that. But the main problem is that partly this is administered by Centre, partly by the Corporation and partly by the State . . . But if it is everybody's business, it is nobody's business. That is the situation today which I do not know whether we should continue like this . . . Some way has to be found out. We have constituted three committees to go into all this; and each committee is headed by an honourable Member of Parliament. I have deliberately chosen Members of Parliament to go into all this.

* * *

The Committees were constituted six months before. But the honourable Members have not been able to take a meeting because of the session. I think immediately after the session, they will go on tour. And we have deliberately requested the Parliamentary Affairs Minister to give a doctor by profession so that they know it better.

Sir, I will only mention about the expansion of the ESI Hospitals because that has been raised by many honourable Members in the House. Some of the new suggestions we will examine. But what has been decided I will just say. We propose to have ten more ESI Hospitals in 1987-88 and these hospitals will be as follows: One in Bihar in Ranchi (presently in Jharkhand), a fifty-bedded hospital; one in Delhi, a twenty-bedded hospital in Jhilmil; two in Kerala, one in Faruk and the other in Toda and one . . . We will have one in Madhya Pradesh in Bhopal, an eighty-four-bedded hospital and four in Uttar Pradesh. Four in Uttar Pradesh will be in Bareilly, Noida, Kidwai Nagar and Jag Mau in Kanpur.

* * *

Now, as far as safety is concerned, the House had an opportunity to discuss the Factories Act (Amendment) Bill where we have recently passed the amendments. This is one major step that the Government had taken after the Bhopal incident by introducing a comprehensive amendment to the Factories Act where we have added one more chapter to deal with the safety affairs. There are some more changes.

Recently, last year we have just passed the Dock Workers Safety and Labour Welfare Act. I have also to mention that as far as the construction workers are concerned and the building workers are concerned, we are now coming up with a new safety Act and we have also sent a lot of people for training which I had the occasion to mention on the floor of the House while discussing the Factories Amendment Bill earlier; but one major achievement is that we are going to establish a major accident hazard control system in our country with the assistance of the International Labour Organization (ILO) at an estimated cost of 1.6 million dollars. This will be a very god institute as far as safety is concerned. We are grateful to the ILO, our relations with the ILO are very good. The Director General of ILO was here in the month of January, I do not want to go into all the details.

* * *

Another important point that has been left out on safety is this, which I would like to state as Achariaji has made a point that the number of accidents and deaths has been going up in our country; which is not so, it is rather static.

If we compare the position of India with the rest of the world, ours is a comparable thing. It is not that we are happy with that. But the position is that it is not going up. It is, more or less, static and it is comparable with the rest of the world. For example, in core area in 1984 in India it was 0.32 per 1000 persons, Belgium 0.97, Czechoslovakia 0.54, Japan was the highest in the world, i.e., 3.77, USA 0.64, West Germany 0.40. So it is not that ours was the highest in the world and it is going to be very much comparable.

Coming to unemployment, most of the honourable Members have quoted the figures of employment exchange. I have, on more than one occasion, clarified this position on the floor of the august House that as far as unemployment figure is concerned, we do not depend on the figures of the employment exchanges, because employment exchanges do not reflect the real picture of unemployment. The reason being that once a person is registered with an employment exchange, his name continues to be there for three years. Only after three years, if he does not come for renewal, then his name is deleted on the presumption that he has got a job. But within these three years, it may so happen that some of them might have already got employment . . . A survey was conducted and in that survey it was found that 17 per cent of those whose names were registered in employment exchanges have already got their jobs and about 18 per cent or a slightly more are people who are still students in colleges and schools. Therefore, the employment exchanges do not give the correct picture of unemployment.

* * *

We depend on the figures of the Planning Commission, which Dr Datta Samant was quoting. According to the Planning Commission, the backlog of unemployment in the Sixth Five Year Plan was about 9 million. The net addition to the workforce during the Seventh Five Year Plan will be 39 million. Therefore, during the period of Seventh Five Year Plan, we have to generate employment for 48 million. The Planning Commission has projected employment for 40 million standard persons during the Seventh Plan period, thereby leaving 8 million people still to be unemployed by the end of the Seventh Plan. This is the correct picture, according to the Planning Commission. I am quoting this to show that we do not depend upon the figures of the employment exchange, but we depend on the plan document. That is why, I am saying that employment exchange figures cannot be taken as figures which really reflect the unemployment situation in the country.

* * *

I agree that unemployment is a very big problem for our country. We must pay our attention to unemployment problem. Dr Datta Samant may be right in saying that in the last few years there is a declining trend in the private sector. This is what I have also been told.

* * *

It will be absolutely wrong for us to expect that all these 48 million people can be provided jobs by the Government of India. It is just not possible. We must emphasize, according to me, on creating self-employment for these people, for which we will have to gear up our training centres all over the country, and, therefore, we are emphasizing on vocationalization of education, we are emphasizing on the modernization of the ITIs in the country and we are going towards that.

* * *

Even in the unemployment sector, if we compare our position with the rest of the world – I am quoting from the World Labour Report of the ILO – it is not that our position is absolutely bad. If you take the number of unemployed people as a percentage to the total population, ours is very much comparable – in fact, better than many countries – but if you take in absolute numbers, then there comes the problem because of the size of our population. I am quoting the figures of percentage of unemployment in 1985; I have got the figures for 1983 and 1984 also:

Canada	—	10.50 per cent
Hong Kong	—	03.90 per cent
USA	—	07.20 per cent
Japan	—	02.60 per cent
Republic of Korea	—	04.00 per cent
Philippines	—	06.10 per cent
Australia	—	04.80 per cent
Denmark	—	09.20 per cent
Spain	—	22.00 per cent
Italy	—	10.00 per cent
Germany	—	09.00 per cent
Sweden	—	02.00 per cent
India	—	03.04 per cent

It is very much comparable . . .

* * *

If we take that 3.04 per cent in absolute number, because of the size of our population it is a large number, but if you take it as a percentage to the total population, we are comparable. So, you cannot condemn everything that is happening in the country and say it is bad, and think that everything outside is good. We have done much better than many countries in the world and you must be proud of our achievement.

* * *

The last point that I would like to make is our emphasis is being given on unorganized sector. I wish I could have dealt with the unorganized sector elaborately – beedi workers, contract workers and what not – but I have had many occasions to speak in the past. Our policy is that we must pay more and more attention to the unorganized labour and that unorganized labour includes agricultural labour, child labour, construction workers, migrant workers and so on. So, all these people have to be looked after. We must do everything possible. I may remind the House that our Prime Minister Shri Rajiv Gandhi himself has announced in his Budget speech that there will be a National Commission constituted for them which will be announced on the floor of the august House very soon.

As far as child labour is concerned, we have taken some steps. I have had an occasion to refer to my visit to Ferozabad. With these few words, I once again thank the honourable Members. Thank you.

~

Payment of Gratuity (Amendment) Bill, 1987*

Sir, I beg to move:

> That the Bill further to amend the Payment of Gratuity Act, 1972, as passed by Rajya Sabha, be taken into consideration.

As the honourable Members are aware, the Payment of Gratuity Act, 1972, provides for a scheme for payment of gratuity to the employees employed in factories, mines, plantations, oil fields, ports, railway companies, shops and certain other establishments and for matters

---

**L.S. Deb.*, 30 July and 6 August 1987 (Spoke while moving the Bill in the Lok Sabha). The Bill provided for further amendment of the Payment of Gratuity Act, 1972 to inter alia provide for increasing the wage limit, timely payment of gratuity, compulsory insurance of employees' liability to pay gratuity, etc.

connected therewith. The payment of gratuity under the Act is, however, at present restricted to the employees drawing wages not exceeding Rs 1,600 per month.

Under the Act, the gratuity is payable in the event of superannuation, retirement or resignation from service subject to completion of five years' service. The condition of five years' service does not, however, apply in cases of termination of employment due to death or disablement. The employees in the non-seasonal establishments are entitled to gratuity at the rate of 15 days' wages for every completed year of service or part thereof in excess of six months, while the employees in seasonal establishments are entitled to 7 days' wages for each season. The payment of gratuity is further subject to ceiling of 20 months' wages.

The Labour Minister's Conference held in 1980 and 1982 had recommended inter alia that the time limit for payment of gratuity might be prescribed in the Act itself and that there should be a suitable provision for recovery of interest in cases where the payment of gratuity is delayed. The trade unions have been representing for suitable enhancement in the wage limit for coverage and the ceiling for payment of gratuity. The trade unions have also been demanding the setting up of a fund for payment of gratuity. The question of funding of gratuity was considered by a Group of Labour Ministers and the Indian Labour Conference held in November 1985, and they had recommended introduction of a suitable provision for compulsory insurance of employers' liability with the LIC or setting up of a Gratuity Trust Fund under the Income Tax Act for ensuring the payment of gratuity.

The various suggestions/recommendations have been considered and it is now proposed to carry out certain amendments in the Act. Some of the more important proposals for amendments are:

(i) The wage limit for coverage under the Act is being raised from Rs 1,600 to Rs 2,500 per month. An enabling provision is also being made for raising the wage limit for coverage by a notification, from time to time.

(ii) The existing ceiling of 20 months' wages for payment of gratuity is being replaced by a monetary ceiling of Rs 50,000.

(iii) Provision is being made for payment of gratuity within 30 days from the date it falls due. If the gratuity is not paid within the prescribed time limit, the employer shall be liable to pay simple interest at a specified rate.

(iv) Provision is also being made for compulsory insurance of employers' liability to pay gratuity under the Act or in the alternative for the setting up of a Gratuity Trust Fund under the Income Tax Act in relation to establishments employing 500 or more persons.

These are, in short, some of the more important amendments proposed through this Bill. I hope the honourable Members will welcome the proposed amendments which are of non-controversial nature. With these words, I commend the Bill for the consideration for the House.

* * *

Sir, I am grateful to the honourable Members who have participated in this debate and have fully supported this Amendment Bill though Dr Rajhans wanted this Bill to be a foolproof Bill. Honourable Member Dr Datta Samant has been a little uncharitable in saying that Labour Ministry has done nothing for the workers. Dr Datta Samant was a part and parcel of the Labour Ministry some time back in his career before I came in touch with the Labour Ministry. I thought Dr Datta Samant will at least claim during that time when he was a part and parcel of the Ministry, something good had been done. Anyway, we have tried to bring some improvement in the Gratuity Act. I certainly do not claim that it is a foolproof Act. No law can be so foolproof. I am afraid, it has brought some amendments. Wage limit has been increased from Rs 1,600 to Rs 2,500 which means now that it will cover more workers.

Shri Vyas and some other honourable Members – Shri Raj Mangal Pande has just now said that Rs 2,500 ceiling also is not enough and there should have been no ceiling at all and that I should come back to this august House and the ceiling should be increased. I want to submit that I need not come back to the august House to increase this ceiling because by raising this limit from Rs 1,600 to Rs 2,500 we have also provided an enabling provision for enhancing the limit. Whenever Government feels that it should be enhanced, the limit could be raised. So this enabling provision is available in this Amendment Bill. Whenever we feel that the ceiling of Rs 2,500 should be raised we can raise it.

Dr Datta Samant has, of course, made a point saying that there is no meaning of Rs 1,600 and Rs 2,500 because it will be calculated at Rs 1,600 which is not true. So, the law is that the gratuity will be payable on the basis of the last pay drawn. It can be Rs 1,700 or it can be Rs 1,800 . . . But upper limit is at the moment Rs 2,500. But Government can without coming for an amendment raise it. This is the law.

* * *

Now the second point which the honourable Members have unanimously raised was the qualifying years of service – five years of qualifying service. Why should it be five years? A person who has put in one year's service should also be entitled to gratuity fund, the benefit of gratuity. This what the honourable members have pleased. I wish we could have done that. But at the moment we are not in a position to do because even with five years of qualifying service under Section 4A of Payment of Gratuity Act as on somebody's petition, the Punjab High Court has struck down this particular Section 4(1). It says that in order to be entitled to gratuity benefit one should complete five years of service.

Now, it is observed like this and I quote the observation made by the Punjab High Court:

> The gratuity is essentially a retirement benefit payable to the workmen as a reward for good, efficient and faithful service rendered for a considerable period and as such it is essential that longer minimum period should be prescribed for earning gratuity in case of voluntary resignation.

That is what the Punjab High Court has said. I want to make it very clear that we respectfully differ from the judgment of the Punjab High Court and we have gone on appeal, the Government has gone on appeal against the decision of the Punjab High Court. The matter is now lying with the Supreme Court, and when the matter is sub judice before the Supreme Court, I cannot come and say that the qualifying year of service should be less than five years because five years' period has been struck down. This is the position which I want to clarify.

* * *

Sir, a point has been made that those who are not in regular service, the qualifying days of work are 240 days. It has been mentioned that this has not been made with leave, holidays and sickness and so many other things. It is very difficult for a casual and contract labour to fulfil 240 days of qualifying days of work. Now, in this amendment, we have come with a proposal that for the purpose of counting the 240 days work in a year, the leave and holidays shall also be counted. Even if a person has not worked on national holidays, these days will be counted as having worked for the purpose of calculating the payment of gratuity. So, that is a slight improvement. There has been a demand that it should be brought down to 120 days. That can be examined. But I must say that there is a slight improvement in this because holidays and other things have been taken into account.

The third point which was raised by the honourable Members was about the payment of interest that if the management does not pay the gratuity within a period of one month, they shall be liable to pay interest and that interest will be a simple interest. Now many honourable Members have said that instead of simple interest, it should be compound interest. Now, if a particular worker really feels that he should get compound interest because it has been delayed too much, he can go in for claim to the competent authority and the competent authority has the power of awarding to a worker the compound interest. So, that provision has also been made. Then, of course, the whole House has welcomed the proposal for creation of Gratuity Trust Fund and also compulsory insurance.

* * *

This was a point in regard to the Trust Fund. Well, people who are employing 500 or less should be exempted from going for the trust fund. For them, it is a compulsory insurance. They should also be allowed to go for trust fund, if they want. Now, the Act provides that this trust fund should be made from the date of the notification of the Act. If somebody has already created a trust fund, those establishments which are employing below 500 people, then they shall be allowed to continue with the fund. In fact, I had the delegation of some of the establishments. They wanted that they should be allowed to create fund. I said, before the Act is notified you go ahead. We will not disturb you and you shall be allowed. If any employers employing less than 500 employees want to go for creation of trust fund, they are welcome to do it and they shall not be disturbed. They will be disturbed only after the notification of this Act.

One honourable Member has raised the question of penalty, that the penalty is not stringent enough. The original Act provides for the contravention of any provisions of this Act as punishable and it may extend to one year imprisonment. That is the maximum limit that has been put. Of course, Mr Dighe, as a lawyer knows that it may extend to one year means, normally till the rising of the court or Rs 5 as fine. So, this is what we experience as lawyers.

The proposal which we have brought here is the minimum period of imprisonment as prescribed, on the other hand. Instead of saying, it may extend to one year, I have said that the punishment will be imprisonment of not less than three months. It can be more than three months to any extent but it shall not be less than three months. There is certainly an improvement in that. You cannot say that the quantum of punishment is not enough.

* * *

The point which Mr Dighe vehemently made, quoting from what you call the statement made by the then Labour Minster is that the payment of gratuity shall be made applicable to all establishments irrespective of how many number of people are employed. We did discuss this issue very thoroughly. Now the establishments which are employing less than 10 people are really a very tiny sector. They are not even a small scale sector. They are actually known in the industry as tiny sector and most of them are self-employed people. We are already having a lot of representations from the tiny sector that they are subjected to so many labour laws. I also feel that tiny sectors which are employing less than 10 people and most of them are self-employed people, they should not be subjected to so many burdens. That is why, we have deliberately, at this stage, kept them out. It is because we must also encourage people to have self-employment for themselves and then create some employment for others. If you put too much of pressure on them that they have to pay provident fund, ESI contribution, gratuity fund and all those things then, I don't think, we will be in a position to encourage self-employment for the people. That is why we have not gone for those people who have employed less than 10 people. Maybe in future, depending upon the economic growth, we can think of that.

Now for the purpose of giving gratuity, I have explained Dr Samant's point of 22 days or 23 days. The point was why only 15 days' salary, it should be one month's salary. This is absolutely in line with the gratuity payable to the Government servants. Even the Government servants under the Government of India Gratuity settlement also get gratuity equivalent to 15 days' or half a month's pay. So, we have also followed the same thing.

I do not think there has been any other important points raised. These are some of the points raised. But I can assure the honourable Members that as far as covering of more establishments is concerned, Government is competent.

* * *

It is precisely what the honourable Member, Shri Datta Samant, is saying that has been provided for in this Bill. We are saying that the gratuity must be paid within a period of one month. It was not there earlier. There was, therefore, a lot of delay in the payment being made to workers. Now we are saying that it must be paid within a period of one month and in case they fail, the workers must get interest. I have also said another thing. He has not read Clause 8. Clause 8 says that he controlling authority can also impose compound interest; only condition is that the interest imposed should not exceed the total amount of gratuity. It may be one paisa less or two paise less but should not exceed the total amount of gratuity. That is the only restriction we have put.

Sir, I beg to move:

> That the Bill be passed.

Strengthening Social Security Measures for Beedi Workers*

Sir, Mr Jain has been raising these points for a number of years. The very basic decision as to whether the Provident Fund Act should be made applicable to the beedi workers. The difficulty is that the manufacturers have been taking this beedi industry as an unorganized

---

**L.S. Deb.*, 12 August 1987 (Spoke while participating in the half-an-hour discussion on condition of beedi workers).

industry, registers are not available and what not, and their Provident Fund should not be made applicable to them. As we have always been saying that Government's policy has now been to give more benefit to the unorganized sector. The benefit of social security like ESI, Provident Fund, Gratuity and all these goes to the organized sector only. We want to extend this benefit more and more to the unorganized sector and beedi industry is one of those industries where the industry is unorganized, but we would like to extend social security to that kind of people.

Therefore, on 1 June 1977, a Notification was issued making the Provident Fund Act applicable to the beedi workers. Some of the manufacturers went to the Supreme Court pleading that it is an unorganized sector and it should not be made applicable. They got a Stay Order. On 1 October 1983, the Supreme Court gave a final judgment saying that the application of Provident Fund was absolutely legal and absolutely correct and it should be continued. Now the question was settled with the judgment of the Supreme Court that Provident Fund has to be made applicable to the beedi workers. The industry expressed their inability to give the money, the arrears, because it would be quite a large sum of money. I called a meeting of the industries, the State Governments and the workers. A tripartite meeting was convened on 20 June 1986. In that meeting, it was agreed that from the date of the judgment of the Supreme Court the industry must comply with the payment of their contribution and the workers' contribution to the Provident Fund.

As far as the pre-judgment period from the date of the Notification is concerned, that is, from 1 June 1977 to 30 September 1983 (just for that period) according to the judgment how this arrear has to be recovered should be discussed in a Tripartite Committee and accordingly a tripartite Committee was established to find out ways and means as to how to recover that money.

The Tripartite Committee has constituted a study group which has now submitted its reports. The final meeting of the Tripartite Committee is to be held soon and I hope to get the report of the Tripartite Committee very soon.

In the Starred Question out of which today's discussion has arisen, Mr Jain's contention was that since this is not being complied with in the State of Uttar Pradesh and in the State of West Bengal why other States should be made to comply with it? It is true that, according to the statement which I had made, there are 32.75 lakh beedi workers in our country and by the time the question was answered, we had just started implementing he Provident Fund Act. We have done much in West Bengal and in Uttar Pradesh by that time. But as the position stands now, that is, as on 31 March 1987 or a few months back, we have made certain progress and 3,568 establishments have been covered and have been made applicable; 9.18 lakh workers have been brought under the coverage of the Provident Fund and the total amount of money that we have realized comes to the tune of Rs 46.51 crore. So, we are making progress in colleting the Provident Fund and the total amount of money the benefit of which will go to the workers, I can assure the august House that beedi workers are not only the workers in the factory, it also includes home workers.

One of the points which was the contention of the manufacturers was that the home workers should not be treated as beedi workers because they have no connect with the factory and the manufacturers. The Supreme Court rejected their plea and said that the beedi workers also include home workers. We are also applying this Provident Fund to the home workers. It is not correct to say that the beedi workers in Madhya Pradesh have not welcomed it and they are not willing to come under the purview of the Provident Fund Act, as has been stated by Mr Jain just now. In fact, in Madhya Pradesh, we have covered 212 establishments and 31,679 workers have already been covered, as the study made on 31 March 1987 shows. Therefore, things have been settled and there is no question of withdrawing the government's Notification from the application of Provident Fund to the beedi workers. We are trying to implement it very sincerely and are trying to cover more and more workers.

* * *

Sir, the discussion actually should have confined to the application of the Provident Fund Act because the question was on that and I must admit that I do not have all the details about the welfare activities because the question relates only to the application of the Provident Fund Act, whether it is applied or not and if it is applied, to what extent it has been successful. But I must react to some of the points raised.

Dr Rajhans said that there is no improvement in the conditions of the beedi workers. But I beg to differ from the doctor. There are some improvements in the condition of beedi workers. The welfare activities under be Beedi Workers Welfare Fund are working quite well in a number of States. I should say that particularly the States in the south – Karnataka, Andhra Pradesh, Tamil Nadu and even Kerala – have been doing very well. Lot of work has been done.

* * *

I am sorry that in the eastern region it has not done very well. In the south, it has done very well because it is primarily the responsibility and the initiative of the State Governments which will bring some change. So, a lot depends on how much initiative the State Governments take. From our side we try to give as much help as possible.

An honourable Member spoke about education. For example, in the financial year 1986-87, from all welfare funds we spent about Rs 90 lakh for free education of the children of beedi workers and I am happy to say that today because of the free education that we have given, there are a number of doctors and engineers who have come up from among the children of the beedi workers. I was very happy to meet some of them. They are a very satisfying team. Therefore, it is not correct to say that nothing has been done for them. Well, we have not done enough. The desired goal that we would like to achieve has not been achieved. But something has been done and I am sure that if the State Governments take more initiative, we can do a lot.

Doctor, you also talked about the implementation of the Minimum Wages Act. What I can do is only to write to them and to remind them. You have also reminded me that my letters will not do anything because you knew that I was going to reply to you like that. I have been repeatedly reminding the State Governments. This, in fact, is in the priority list of my Ministry. Implementation of Minimum Wages Act is number one on the priority list because I believe that if this single Act, the Minimum Wages Act is implemented sincerely and effectively many problems of the unorganized labour will be solved. Therefore, we are giving so much importance to that.

* * *

Doctor, I am not a person who draws distinctions. I am saying that whichever government has done good, they have done good and the names of the State that I have given are all Opposition States. Why don't you understand my approach? No, Doctor, you are not interested in development.

* * *

You will feel shy to sit in front of me whenever I am in the House. I do not want to disclose about you in the House or on the floor of the House. Please mind that. I am a Labour Minister. I know the activities of all the trade union leaders. I know who are good and who are bad trade union leaders. Why you are talking about good governments and bad governments? There are also good trade union leaders and bad trade union leaders.

* * *

We have a number of special schemes in a number of hospitals under the Welfare Fund Scheme. We are also trying to expand our activity as far as health programme is concerned.

As the august House will remember, I have also made an announcement that we have to increase the excise rate on beedi and at the moment the position of workers was not found good. With increase in excise, we hope to get a substantial amount under the Welfare Fund and we hope to increase our activities.

Now, as far as the identity of the beedi workers is concerned, Dr Rajhans has said this is a very important point, I have been making it repeatedly: until and unless we know who are beedi workers, it is very difficult to extend any help to them. So, we are giving priority to the process of identification. We are issuing identity cards. The House will remember, in the last session, we passed amendment to the Act in response to the request of Shri Saha when we were discussing his Bill, and in that amendment I had brought in a provision that if any employer fails to identify and issue an identity card to his worker, he will be punished. It has been made a cognizable, punishable offence. Therefore, we have taken steps to solve the problem.

In regard to housing, Shri Rawat has raised very important question. At the moment we have two schemes.

1.We call it 'build your own house' scheme.

If any individual beedi worker wants to build a house, we give part as loan and part as subsidy. They can build their house.

2. Another scheme is taking off very well.

I must thank the respective State Governments. That scheme is housing for the economically weaker sections of the people. This scheme is really taking off very well. I must say that States like Maharashtra have done very well. There is a place called Sholapur. We have launched about 4,000 houses. Construction is very much in progress. Like that, Gujarat has taken this scheme. I can assure the august House that our priority is now the unorganized sector. Now within the unorganized sector we have identified certain sectors like child labour, women labour, construction workers and beedi workers where we propose to give special attention to them and that is why we are very keen that even in the implementation of social security schemes like Provident Fund, which today we have discussed, we are very keen that we should extend these Social Security Schemes to more and more people in the unorganized sector.

I thank the honourable Members for having given me this opportunity. Thank you.

The Equal Remuneration (Amendment) Bill, 1987*

I beg to move:

> That the Bill to amend the Equal Remuneration Act, 1976, as passed by Rajya Sabha, be taken into consideration.

Sir, one of the most important Acts relating to women's employment, the Equal Remuneration Act, was passed in 1976 replacing the Equal Remuneration Ordinance of 1975.

The Act provides for the payment of equal remuneration to men and women workers for the same work or work of similar nature and for prevention of discrimination against women in the matter of employment.

**L.S. Deb.*, 7 and 9 December 1987 (Spoke while moving the Bill in the Lok Sabha). The Bill provided for further amendment of the Equal Remuneration Act, 1976 inter alia for prohibiting discrimination against women during work, making the penalty clauses more stringent, etc.

The Act covers all categories of employments in the organized and unorganized sectors.

During the decade or so that the Act has been in force, certain lacunae and omissions have come to our notice which adversely affected the effectiveness of the Act more than we had wished.

To rectify these lacunae and omissions, therefore, we seek to make some amendments to the Act. The principal omission in the existing Act is that while the Act prohibits discrimination against women in recruitment, there is no specific clause prohibiting such discrimination during their employment. Under the existing Act, therefore, any discrimination against women in matters of promotion, increments, etc., does not amount to an offence under the Equal Remuneration Act. This is sought to be rectified in the present Bill.

One of the reasons the Act has not been as effective as it should have been is that the penalties provided in the Act are comparatively light. It is proposed to make these penalties far more stringent.

To make prosecution easier, it is also proposed to permit individuals and recognized welfare institutions or organizations to file complaints in the court. Section 15 of the existing Act is also being reworded so that it cannot be used to justify discriminatory practices against women workers.

It is felt that these amendments will go a long way towards removing the difficulties faced in the implementation of the Equal Remuneration Act and will prevent many of the discriminatory actions being practised against women in employment.

With these few words, I commend the Bill for the consideration of the House.

* * *

Madam, I am grateful to the honourable Members who have extended wholehearted support to this amending Bill and also gave so many useful suggestions. I must concede that the debate was very interesting and fruitful and by and large it really represents what is happening all over the country. Lot of discussion has taken place about discrimination against women but I must inform the august House that I come from a place and from a society where women reign supreme and if there is any discrimination it is discrimination against men. So if discrimination against women has to be solved the best way is to adopt our customs and our culture.

Sir, out of 292 million workforce in our country women account for 82 million which makes the percentage of women workers in our country to be 28 per cent. Out of this 82 million women workforce in our country 86 per cent of them work in the rural areas. I am saying particularly this aspect just to draw the attention of the House that 86 per cent of the women workers in our country belong to unorganized sector. Therefore, we are really concerned about the conditions of women labour in our country.

Sir, quite a number of legislations have been passed. We have Factories Act where there are special provisions for protection of women, Plantation Labour Act, Mines Act, Maternity Benefit Act, Employees State Insurance Act, the present Equal Remuneration Act, etc. After having so many legislations for the protection for women, I think, the august House has rightly questioned whether the women have really got protection. The august House has rightly questioned whether these laws have been really, strictly and effectively implemented. I must admit that much remains to be desired in the implementation of these laws, not to speak only of Equal Remuneration Act but I am talking about all other Acts which govern protection of women.

There are many reasons why these laws have not been effectively implemented. I think the august House has voiced it and so many reasons have been pointed out. I agree with that. The most important reason is that 86 per cent of the women workers are in the rural areas and they belong to the unorganized sector. They are not organized. They have no bargaining capacity. They cannot have nay bargaining capacity because they even do not know the provisions of law. How many women in our country today know that there exists as many as seven laws specifically enacted by the Parliament to protect them? Probably, there are many more in the various States. Few of them know about that. There is no awareness among the women workers in our country. This is the second important reason why their implementation is not being done effectively.

The third reason is that the State Governments as they told me – because of constraints of finance – are not able to have adequate enforcement machinery. I have reviewed the position of each and every State regarding the enforcement machinery available with them. I must say that it is very very inadequate. Whatever enforcement machinery is available with the State Governments, their mobility is very poor. They do not have transport with them. If they have to travel to a factory or a quarry for inspection, they normally travel in the employer's transport. You can understand if once they travel in the employer's transport, what will be the consequence. Therefore, their mobility is limited. The mobility has also to be strengthened while strengthening the enforcement machinery.

Besides, we have also found that whatever enforcement machinery is available, it is available mostly at the district headquarters and not beyond that. How many people in the rural areas can reach the district headquarters? They cannot. Even if some of the unorganized labourers are aware of the rights and privileges, they are not able to reach the place of justice because of long distance and lack of transportation. All these problems are there.

We had convened a Conference of the Labour Ministers on 28 May this year where we had only one topic for discussion. Normally such Conference had 10–15 items on the agenda. This time, I had said that we would have only one item and that was about the implementation of labour laws. We had a two-day session discussion about the implementation of the labour laws.

There are 140 labour laws in this country. I said I am not interested in all the 140 labour laws to be implemented. Let us shortlist and select only a few important laws. We will draw up a plan of action and see how it could be implemented. We have seven laws to lay an emphasis in their implementation. These are:

(i) Minimum Wages Act; I hold it the most important one;
(ii) Abolition of Bonded Labour Act;
(iii) Child Labour (Abolition and Regulation) Act;
(iv) Contract Labour (Abolition and Regulation) Act;
(v) Inter-State Migrant Labour Act;
(vi) Equal Remuneration Act; and
(vii) Beedi and Cigarette Workers Act.

So, out of these seven legislations which we have chosen out of the total of 140 laws. I am happy to inform the august House that the Equal Remuneration Act is also one them. We have drawn up a plan of action. I do not want to waste the time of the august House by mentioning all the Acts which have been published widely. One thing that I want to mention is that the plan of action which we have drawn up in the Labour Ministers Conference on 28 May 1987 shall be monitored. That monitoring will be at the regional level. We have decided to divide this country into six regions and have frequent regional meetings of the Ministers where we will review the decisions taken and how much progress they have made. We have already had a meeting at Madras (presently Chennai) of the southern region. We will also hold a meeting at Calcutta (presently Kolkata) of the eastern region on 12 December. We will have a meeting at Delhi of the northern region. On 17 December we will have a meeting at Bombay (presently Mumbai) of the western region. Like this, we have drawn up the programme and the entire exercise will be over by 15 January 1988. We are following each and every decision and I am happy to inform the august Hose that the State Governments have taken lot of interest in this. One of the decisions that we have taken is about the revision of minimum wages. We have also taken up that minimum wages should not be below the poverty line. This is a very important decision that has been taken. State Governments have been asked to revise the minimum wages above the poverty line and they have taken steps in this regard. Maharashtra has not yet done but on 17 December they will have to do so because I am going there on that day. I am proceeding in the way in which I want to proceed but I am thankful to the State Governments.

* * *

I am not only meeting the Ministers. I am also meting the Parliamentary Consultative Committee and the honourable Members of Parliament attached to the Labour Ministry, but I have divided them into two groups to go round the country. One is looking after the agricultural labour and another group is looking after the non-agricultural labour. I am happy that he honourable Members of Parliament have gone round the country. In fact, the Committee of Agricultural Labour is ready with the report and they are supposed to give it to me on the 11 December, i.e., day after tomorrow. Not only that, we have got two National Commissions to look after self-employed women. That Commission is also doing some work. We have also got a National Commission for rural workers which has a special reference to women workers. Honourable Members of the august House are also going round the country. I want to say that we trying to make the people aware that the Centre is really serious about the implementation for labour laws.

* * *

We have at the moment accepted the poverty line concept which has been evolved by the Planning Commission. I am also aware that this concept is not acceptable to the West Bengal Government. The West Bengal Government has given its own formula which is with me.

* * *

As I have always been telling the trade union leadership in our country, unfortunately the trade union movement in our country has remained confined to the cities, urban areas. In some cases, we have as many as 125 unions in one unit. We have 40 unions in one unit and I have given the example of DTC, where we have more than 40 unions. As I said, every trade union leader has been confining to the urban areas only. Ours is such a vast country, out of 290 million workforce in our country only 25 million are organized and 267 million people in our country are still unorganized. We do not have unions for them. May I appeal to the honourable Members of Parliament and the trade union leaders that they should go to the rural areas and organize the labour.

* * *

The question of making the workers aware of their rights has been raised several times and I have myself given a thought to it. We have decided in the Labour Ministers' Conference also to use media, particularly, the radio and the television to make the workers aware of their rights. We have not yet been able to finalize that scheme, but we are trying to do that.

* * *

I have said that the machinery available with the State Government is limited and inadequate and whatever machinery they have is not mobile. I have always stated that. This has been discussed also. The State Governments wanted certain Central assistance in order to strengthen their enforcement machinery. I have agreed to that and in fact, we have formed a small Subcommittee with one Joint Secretary from the Ministry of Labour and some other officers to formulate a scheme how the Central assistance can be given to the State Governments in these two points.

We have also stated in the Labour Ministers' Conference that the redressal mechanism or the claim authority must be taken as far as possible nearer to the people. At the moment, it is available at the district level. We have decided to take it to the block level in the beginning. For that we need to amend certain laws and it is under way and we are doing it. Therefore, whatever is possible form our side, we are trying. Now, the important provision which has been proposed in the amendment is that for the purpose of launching the prosecution, for the purpose of lodging complaints. We have by this amendment empowered any individual, voluntary organization and the trade unions. This has been a deliberate policy of the Government of India. It is not only here, this provision you will find in almost all the amendments that are coming in. We want to involve the voluntary organizations; we want to involve the individuals in this country to implement the labour laws because I know the limitations of the Government and the limitations of the inspectors. So far this power is available only with the inspector and now we want to give it to every individual. Any conscientious individual, who is in the social service, I think can take the initiative to implement these laws . . . I want to do it because every time people blame the Government. I think peoples' participation is required in it. We want to have peoples' participation in it.

As far as this Act is concerned, so many things like it has not been implemented have been said. I do not claim that it has been implemented.

* * *

I think Dr Samant and many other honourable Members have asked me as to how it is being implemented, whether I have got the facts with me or not. I am giving very reluctant figures and also not for many years but only for the year 1987. This year the number of inspections carried out was 1,037, the number of prosecution launched is 248 and the number of conviction is 138. Now, you may ask me what is the conviction. I will be very reluctant to tell you that the penal provisions provided in all the labour laws have an incentive for the violations. If somebody has to adhere to the laws, maybe he will have to spend Rs 50,000 but for not doing that when he is taken to the court he will be able to get out of it by just paying Rs 100 as fine. That is one of the reasons why these laws were not effective. Therefore, in all the labour laws including this particular one, we have brought in a provision where we have made the punishment more stringent. Therefore, Madam, I only want to submit that these amendments that we have brought in will go a long way to help us. The figures which I quoted are of the State Department and not from the Centre. The honourable Members have rightly pointed out that the remedy lies not in enacting these laws and amending them on the floor of the august House but in their actual implementation at the field level. I can assure the august House that we are trying our best to see that the implementation will be much better in future. With these words I once again thank all the honourable Members.

I beg to move:

That the Bill be passed.

The Agricultural Workers (Minimum Wages and Welfare) Bill, 1993*

Mr Chairman, Sir, I am grateful to the honourable Member Shri Chandubhai Deshmukh for having brought this Bill before this august House which has given an opportunity for this august House to discuss the problems relating the agricultural workers who constitute the largest working force in our country. I am also grateful to all the honourable Members who have participated in this debate. As many as 29 honourable Members of Parliament had participated in this debate.

Very valuable suggestions have been made and I am, quite grateful to all of them. But, if I unable to reply to each and every point raised by the 29 honourable Members, even if I allot myself minutes each, then the honourable Member, the mover of the Bill will have no time left for replying to the debate because we have to conclude it at 5.30 p.m. Therefore, I would not propose to reply point-wise to the honourable Members.

Sir, agricultural workers are the biggest workforce in our country. Out of total 315 million workforce in our country as many as 110 million are agricultural workers and agricultural labourers. If we take into

L.S. Deb., 30 July 1993 (Spoke while replying to the Private Member's Bill moved by Shri Chandubhai Deshmukh in the Lok Sabha).

account the small and marginal farmers, then the number of working class in agricultural sector will be around 180 million.

There are about half a dozen legislations available in our country which apply to agricultural works also and we do not have a comprehensive legislation to regulate the conditions of employment of the agricultural workers. Through the legislations like the Minimum Wages Act, the Inter-State Migrant Workers Regulation of Employment Act, the Workmen's Compensation Act, the Trade Union Act, the Equal Remuneration Act, etc., do apply to the agricultural labours. The conditions of Agricultural labours throughout the country are really in a very pitiable condition and the need, therefore, is to have comprehensive legislation which has been recognized. This question has been debated in the country for more than two decades.

I would just like to give a brief history of how a debate in this country has been going on regarding this legislation for agricultural workers in 1978. The Government appointed a Central Standing Committee on Rural Unorganized Labour to recommend legislative and administrative measures for improving the working condition of rural unorganized labour. This standing committee constituted a subcommittee which submitted its report in 1980 suggesting that there must be a legislation for agricultural labourers. This report was placed before the Labour Minister's Conference in August 1981. In the absence of any Chairman or even consensus for a Central legislation for agricultural labourers, it was decided in the Labour Ministers' Conference that the State Governments should enact legislation instead of Central Government. In this particular conference, the only legislation which was available in the country was the Kerala Agricultural Workers Act, 1975. Unfortunately, except the State of Tripura, no State Government till today had enacted that legislation.

Therefore, there was a fresh demand for Central Legislation and the Ministry of Labour did prepare a Cabinet Paper and went to the Cabinet in 1983 and Cabinet, in its wisdom, decided that in the absence of unanimity or even consensus among the State Governments, it would not be proper for the Central Government to enact a legislation more so because agriculture falls under the State List.

In 1986-87, there was a discussion in the Consultative Committee of the Parliament by the Ministry of Labour, I was the Labour Minister at that time also. On the demand of the honourable Members of the Consultative Committee, we constituted a subcommittee under the chairmanship of honourable Gurudas Das Gupta, a Member of the other House, and this committee went round all over the country and they submitted a report recommending a Central Legislation for agricultural workers. It was discussed in 1988 again in the Labour Ministers' Conference.

Actually, this piece of legislation for agricultural workers has been discussed as many as five items in the Labour Ministers' Conference, in 1981, 1990, 1992 and 1993.

But in that particular Labour Ministers' Conference of 1988, which was the 37th, the Ministers from the States said that there was no necessity for enacting Central legislation for agricultural workers. At that point of time, the Minister decided that it was important to see the implementation of the existing law available which govern the agricultural workers and while discussing about the existing law, stress was laid on the implementation of the Minimum Wages Act. Honourable Members who have participated in this debate have rightly pointed out that this is one piece of legislation, the Minimum Wages Act, which was not being implemented effectively, then many of the problems of the agricultural workers could be sorted out and, therefore, in the 37th Labour Ministers' Conference, it was resolved that the Central legislation which were already available governing agricultural labour like the Minimum Wages Act, Equal Remuneration Act, Workmen's Compensation Act should be implemented effectively. So, the matter stopped there.

In 1990, there was Indian Labour Conference which was the Apex Conference and this matter came up in this Indian Labour Conference, it was again represented by the respective Labour Ministers of the State Governments. Somehow, consensus emerged at the particular time that there could be a Central legislation.

Therefore, till 1990 Indian Labour conference, there has been no unanimity on the issue. The need to have a legislation was recognized. But the question as to whether this legislation should be enacted by the State Government or by the Central Government could not be resolved and it was only in 1990 in the Indian Labour Conference that somehow a consensus emerged that there could be a Central Legislation for agricultural workers.

Of course, in the meantime, we received the report of the National Commission on Rural Labour which also unanimously recommended that there should be a Central Legislation for the agricultural workers.

I do not want to go into the whole history but in 1992 Labour Ministers' Conference, we constituted a subcommittee of 13 Labour Ministers from the States with the Labour Minister of Maharashtra as its Chairman to go into the whole issue.

We are awaiting the report of the subcommittee of the State Labour Ministers which is under the chairmanship of the honourable Labour Minister of Maharashtra. In the meantime, on 7 July, we again have called the Labour Ministers' Conference in New Delhi. By that time, the Government of India had already had a draft Bill. A Bill had already been drafted. On 7 July, we had discussed this issue in the Labour Ministers' Conference and we had circulated a draft Central Bill to the Labour Ministers of the State Governments. On that day, the Labour Ministers of all the State Governments pleaded that they would like to go through the draft Bill and they would like to send their comments as soon as possible. We will wait for their comments. If there is any delay, I do not mind convening another meeting of the Labour Ministers to consider this issue.

Then, just a week ago, we had Consultative Committee meeting. In that Consultative Committee meeting also, we had distributed the draft Bill to the honourable Members. This morning, Shri Ajoy Mukhopadhyay was mentioning to me that the Members of the Consultative Committee among themselves met this morning and they are going through the draft Bill. I have narrated this history of how the country has been debating this particular issue, this very very important issue, just to say that we are, as a Government, aware of the conditions of the agricultural workers. We also feel that something has to be done not only in respect of regulation of their employment or giving them a mechanism for grievance redressal but more so, perhaps, there is a need to provide social security and welfare measures for the agricultural worker. So, we are quite convinced of that and that is why I have narrated it.

Sir, the Government of India is already seized of the matter. We went to a stage where we have already drafted the Bill. The draft Bill has already been circulated on 7 July to all the State Governments. Personally, I had handed it over to them in that meeting. I am awaiting the comments of the State Governments. As soon as I receive the comments of the respective State Governments, I will go to the Cabinet. Of course, I cannot say in what way the Government will decide. But I have proposed to go to the Cabinet. Since the Government has already come to this stage, recognizing the need for doing something for these agricultural workers, and while thanking the honourable Member Shri Chandubhai Deshmukh for having brought forward this Bill and given us an opportunity to discuss the problems, I would request the honourable Member to withdraw his Bill.

The Payment of Gratuity (Amendment) Bill, 1994*

Sir, I beg to move:

> That the Bill further to amend the Payment of Gratuity Act, 1972, as passed by Rajya Sabha, be taken into consideration.

As the honorable Members are aware, the Payment of Gratuity Act, 1972, provides for a scheme for a payment of gratuity to the employees employed in factories, mines, plantations, oil fields, ports, railway companies, shops and certain other establishments and for matters connected therewith. The payment of gratuity under the Act is, at present, restricted to the employees drawing wages not exceeding Rs 3,500 per month.

Under the Act, gratuity is payable in the event of superannuation, retirement or resignation from service subject to completion of five years' service. The completion of five years' service, however, does not apply in the case of termination of employment due to death or disablement. The employees in the non-seasonal establishments are entitled to gratuity at the rate of fifteen days' wages for every completed year of service or part thereof and in seasonal establishments are entitled to seven days' wages for each season. The payment of gratuity is further subject to a ceiling of Rs 50,000 total emoluments. The trade unions have also been representing for removal of the wage limit and also for suitable enhancement in the ceiling on the maximum amount of gratuity.

---

*_L.S. Deb._, 10 May 1994 (Spoke while moving the Bill in the Lok Sabha). The Bill provided for further amendment of the Payment of Gratuity Act, 1972, as passed by the Rajya Sabha. It inter alia provided for removal of the wage limit and raising the ceiling of Rs 50,000 on the maximum amount of gratuity to one lakh rupees.

The various suggestions/recommendations have been considered and it is now proposed to carry out the following amendments in the Act:

(i) The wage limit for coverage under the Act is being removed altogether. This will make all the employees legally eligible for gratuity, irrespective of their wages;
(ii) The existing ceiling of Rs 50,000 on the maximum amount of gratuity is being raised to Rs 1 lakh.

These are, in short, the important amendments proposed in this Bill. I hope the honourable Members will welcome the proposed amendments which are of non-controversial nature.

With these few words, I commend the Bill for consideration of the House.

* * *

Mr Deputy Speaker, Sir, at the very outset, I would like to mention that I fully understand the mood of the House and, therefore, I will be very very brief in my reply.

Sir, every debate enlightens us, gives us a lot of education because the honourable Members who participate in the debate come out with lot of new ideas and suggestions and it does help the Government in formulating its policies in future and also in taking proper actions for the welfare of the people. I assure this august House that every point that has been made on the floor of the House in today's debate has been noted by me and we will certainly keep them in mind for our future course of action. There are few important points that have been made and I would like to deal with them. The first point that I would like to deal with is regarding the Labour Ministers' Conference held at Delhi.

A point has been made that this proposal was mooted out as far back as 1983 in the Labour Minister's Conference and it is only this year that the amendments have been brought. It is true that it has been brought after a very long time. I quite admit that fact.

But then if you look at the history of this particular piece of legislation we find that this Act was passed in 1972. At that particular time this Act was applicable for the workers who were drawing a monthly salary of Rs 750. That was the beginning. Then it was raised to Rs 1,600 at a time when the Labour Minister's Conference took place. In 1987 the ceiling was raised to Rs 2,500. In 1992, it was raised to Rs 3,500. So, gradually the wage limit has been raised and today we are before this august House to remove the ceiling completely. So it is a progressive thing which the Government has done.

The second point which was raised was that the maximum limit which was kept as Rs 1 lakh is low and a suggestion was there that it should be raised to Rs 2 lakh. The fact remains that under other laws the Central Government employees and the State Government employees are also entitled to gratuity. They are governed by different Acts. This is governing only the industrial and other workers as I have mentioned. The highest limit for the Government employees is Rs 1 lakh. We thought that there must be uniformity in our policy, if we raise it to Rs 2 lakh now, then suddenly there will be a demand from the Government employees similarly to raise the ceiling up to Rs 2 lakh. The Government wants to maintain uniformity as far as practicable. That is why I have brought this ceiling of Rs 1 lakh as maximum.

* * *

We follow West Bengal. In fact it was West Bengal which first enacted the Gratuity Act in 1971. It was on the basis of the West Bengal Act, followed by Kerala Act, that the Labour Ministers in their Conference in 1971 decided for Central legislation and it was enacted in 1972. So we are following West Bengal. Mr Topdar has referred to the new amendments that West Bengal Legislative Assembly has brought in, which is lying for assent before the President of India. I do not recollect the provision of that Act; I will certainly go into it. I will see how much West Bengal has done and I will try to compare it. That was the second point made about the raising of the limit up to Rs 2 lakh. We are not able to accept this proposal because of its repercussions that I have just mentioned.

The third point that was made was about the late payment and non-payment. It is really a problem. I have tried to ascertain the position from all over the country. In fact we have written to all the State Governments to give us the information because I knew that this point would be raised in this debate. Unfortunately, I have not been able to get information except for the States of Delhi, Punjab, Tripura and Manipur. They have furnished some information. I am awaiting information from other States. As soon as I get the information, if any honourable Member is interested to know the figures, which will be very interesting for us to know, I will be willing to supply the information to the honourable Members.

Some honourable Members have made a suggestion that the gratuity should be paid within three months. I think Mr Topdar suggested this. In fact, Section 7 of the Act provides that the gratuity has to be paid within a period of 30 days. There is no question of three months. The Act provides for the payment of gratuity within 30 days from the date it becomes due. If an employer fails to pay it within 30 days or pays after 30 days, then he has to pay the gratuity with interest. That provision is also there. Some honourable Members made a demand that there should be a provision of interest; it is already there in the Act. In the event of the employer not paying, then, the worker certainly can go to the court. Of course, the punishment is prescribed in Section 9 of the Act to which I will not go. Even the penal provisions are available for non-payment of the gratuity; and the provisions are available for the recovery of the gratuity amount with interest, if it is not paid within the stipulated time.

Another point which has been made was about the Act being made applicable to contract workers and the badli (rotational) workers.

* * *

I am just pointing out the provisions. I think, it is a very important point which has been made during the course of the debate. Actually, the Act does not make any distinction about the permanent workers, contract workers and the badli workers. This Act applies to all establishments which have been listed out which I have read out in the beginning. The conditions necessary are that the worker should have worked for five years; and that the establishment where he works must employ ten people. These are the two criteria which have been laid down. Otherwise, it is applicable to the seasonal workers and you can very well say that it is applicable to the contract workers, provided they qualify these two conditions. Another question was asked as to why should it be for five years and why should it not be reduced to two years. Many honorable Members have made this suggestion. Kumari Mamata Banerjee, Shri Ramashray Prasad Singh and others have made this suggestion. In fact, as far as the Government servants are concerned, the required length of service is ten years to be entitled for payment of gratuity; as far as the industrial workers are concerned, we have made it five years. Therefore, we feel that five years of service, for the time being, is okay.

I think, Shri Dhananjaya Kumar made an important point about the exemption of income tax for the gratuity amount. It is already there. It is not taxable. Whatever gratuity amount is paid to the workers, it is exempted from the income tax.

Another honourable Member has made a point about unorganized labour, particularly the agricultural labourers, and asked what are we doing about them. I think, at least on one or two occasions on the floor of this august House, I have informed that the Government is exercising its mind to bring in a Central legislation for the agricultural workers and the contract workers in the construction industry. We have finished our consultations with the respective State Governments. I have received, by this time, the written comments of the State Governments proposed draft Bill which we have circulated to the State Governments. I hope that we will be in a position to finalize our views on these two very important proposed legislations because we talk about unorganized labour, the largest number of unorganized labour in the agricultural sector; and the number 110 million. Same is the case in the construction industry. I hope that we will be in a position to finalize those things very soon.

I think, these are the few points which have been made by the honourable Members here to which I thought I must react.

I once again thank all the honourable Members who have participated in the debate and who have the patience to be here now, so late in the evening; and I seek for the approval of the Bill.

* * *

You (Shri Mohan Rawale) have talked a lot about the private textile mills of Bombay. Your reaction was discernible in the august House on the other day also. With regard to the public sector, the NTC mills, a formula has been prepared after holding discussions in the Tripartite Committee and the remodernization proposal is to be sent to the Cabinet. With regard to the private mills, a meeting of the Tripartite Committee has been convened in Bombay on 30 May wherein this issue will be discussed.

* * *

Mr Deputy Speaker, Sir, I have no information about the individual mill. Sections 7, 8 and 9 provide for the mode of payment, mode of recovery in case of non-payment and punishment thereof and all that.

I beg to move:

That the Bill, as amended, be passed.

Need for Improvement of the Condition of Farms and Agricultural Labourers in the Country*

Mr Chairman, Sir, I am quite aware of the time factor. So, I will be very brief. I will make only three points.

Sir, agriculture is the backbone of our economy. Unfortunately, adequate attention is not being paid to this sector. The Economic Survey of the Government of India says that the growth of economy would be sustainable only if the average annual rate of growth in agriculture would be of the order of four per cent. What is the present scenario? If you look at the growth rate of agriculture in the last 15 years, you may find that it had stagnated at 3.6 per cent.

Whereas the Economic Survey says that it has at least to be four per cent from 1990 to 1997, the annual compound growth rate of foodgrains production has been 1.7 per cent whereas the growth rate of birth has been 2.1 per cent. I am making this point just to remind this august House that though we are very proud of our self-sufficiency in food production yet the fact remains today that the growth of population is higher than the growth rate of food production. Therefore, I think we will have to be very careful. There is a need, according to me, for a second Green Revolution in our country. That is what Dr Swaminathan has emphasized. He has suggested that the Green Revolution has to be the central emphasis of India. But in order to take the Green Revolution

---

**L.S. Deb.*, 22 November 2000 (Spoke while participating in the Motion for Adjournment on the severe crisis faced by the farming community due to the burden of the recent increased cost of production and crash in the agricultural commodity prices, moved by Smt. Sonia Gandhi).

to new areas, naturally, there is the question of investment. The Economic Survey itself has said:

> In order to ensure this growth, the Survey call for encouragement of high investment in rural assets and channeling of public expenditure towards supported infrastructure including rural roads, irrigation, agricultural research and extension services, soil conservation, irrigation and watershed management.

So, these are the areas where we will have to make adequate investments. As has been pointed out by the earlier speakers, unfortunately, adequate investments are not taking place in agricultural sector. Therefore, the management of agriculture in our country would need a lot of strategic thinking. It will need planning and monitoring.

The second point that I would like to make is that the current situation is an extraordinary situation, a crisis situation. The Economic Survey of 1999-2000 also says that the money that will be required to subsidize food will be to the tune of Rs 8,500 crore or something like that. So on the one hand, we are spending so much of money towards procurement for subsidized food, on the other hand, there are no takers today. The FCI godowns are overflowing with surplus stock. The oil depots are overflowing with surplus stock. The same is the case in the edible oil sector. There is a lot of surplus with the NAFED. On the other hand, we are spending and investing so much of money. Why? I think the reason is very obvious. It is a failure of the management. I reiterate that it is an absolute failure of the management. I do not know how today the market price of foodgrains and oil is cheaper than the subsidized food of the FCI or the NAFED or the Public Distribution System. On the one hand, we say that we are surplus in food production, on the other hand, we have millions and millions of people living below the poverty line. The reason, I think, is just mismanagement. We will have to improve our distribution system in the country. We will have to professionalize the functioning of the FCI and the other agencies.

The third point that I would like to make, keeping in view the time factor, as has already been pointed out, I think one of the main reasons for the crisis has been the import of foodgrains and oil.

Indiscriminate import of essential commodities, whether it be sugar, whether it be edible oil, in the last two years, we have been importing sugar from Pakistan, Brazil. Last year, I am told that the edible oil import is next to the import of petroleum products. Many honourable

Members have already pointed out the plight of our farmers. Be it in the area of sugar, wheat and rubber growers of Kerala and other places, we will have to be very careful.

I am aware of our commitments to the WTO but we did not have the framework of the WTO. I think the Government can and should take appropriate steps. One of the reasons, as Shri Madhavrao Scindia has already pointed out, is that we have the power to levy import duty. Why did we allow the oil to come without any import duty? Only yesterday the Government have decided to levy the import duty on the import of oil. It may be because the House would be discussing the issue today. Therefore, there are areas which can be utilized and Government can take corrective steps.

I would like to remind the Government that in Mexico – I think that we should draw our lessons from them – seven to eight lakh livelihoods were lost due to fall of maize prices consequent on the cheap import under the NIFTIER. That is what has happened to the economy of Moscow. In Philippines, the foodgrains sector underwent steady marginalization, which is happening in our country today. It happened in Philippines in 1998 and the result is that the situation came where the share of rice imports in Philippines rose up to 35 per cent of the total agricultural imports just a couple of years ago. Therefore, we should be very careful.

I am not at all in favour of indiscriminate imports which will lead to so many problems and sufferings to our farmers. But when we talk about farmers, when we are talking about the agricultural sector, I think, sometimes we forget to remember those who are agricultural labourers, those who are daily wagers. We have 315 million working force in our country, out of that, 110 million of them are the agricultural labourers. They earn their livelihood on daily wages. I think the Government should think about that.

I have been in the Ministry of Labour for some time. I know the conditions of the agricultural labourers. We had held a number of Conferences of Labour Ministers of the country as to what can be done for them. And a suggestion was, as Kerala has a legislation for the welfare activities of the farm workers, a similar thing for the agricultural labourers can be done by the Government of India. I think that it is at the final stage of drafting and the Government should expedite that particular Bill, which would regulate the welfare measures for the agricultural labourers.

We have done well since independence in the agricultural sector. Unfortunately, in the last few years, as I said, it has remained stagnant as far as growth rate is concerned. Much of the credit not only goes to our farmers, not only goes to our agricultural labourers, but I think the credit also goes to our scientists. Our scientists have done exceedingly well in their research. Unfortunately, today I am given to understand that our scientists are absolutely demoralized.

The manner in which Dr R.S. Paroda, the Director General of the Indian Council of Agricultural Research and Secretary to the Department of Agricultural Research and Education has been sacked form service is not correct. He is also the President of the Indian Science Congress Association for the current year. The Indian Science Congress is going to meet shortly and the Prime Minister is going to inaugurate it. I do not know how the Prime Minister is going to share the dais with the person who has been sacked by his own Government. I am really, very much concerned about the sacking of Dr R.S. Paroda, after the reported writing of Dr M.S. Swaminathan, Dr Abdul Kalam, Dr Khush, etc., expressing their shock. Many eminent scientists not only from India but also from abroad, including the Nobel laureate, Dr Norman E. Borlaug have expressed their shock and anguish over the way such an eminent scientists has been treated.

So, I would urge upon the Minister to please review his decision. We cannot afford to bring in demoralization among the scientists of our country, who have done so much service to this country. Therefore, I would personally plead with Shri Nitish Kumar to have a relook at his decision. If he can rectify his decision, it will be a great service not only to our scientists but also to Indian agriculture, which is the backbone of our economy.

Thank you.

SOCIAL ISSUES

Reforming Education Policy for the Scheduled Tribes*

Mr Deputy Speaker, Sir, the honourable Home Minister while addressing the Tribal Commissioners here at New Delhi on 15 July 1977 remarked that the tribal population in India had suffered the worst neglect. I would say that the tribals, the Scheduled Tribes, have not only suffered the worst neglect but have also suffered the worst exploitation and the worst blow. I say this because after 30 years of planning, after 30 years of independence and after 30 years of so-called protection and safeguards to the tribals, the conditions of the tribals in India have gone from bad to worse.

* * *

That is more so in the case of people who are living in the North Eastern region, and I would like to highlight some of the conditions that are prevailing there because the entire North Eastern region is a region which is inhabited by the Scheduled Tribes.

As I said, after 30 years of independence in the North Eastern region, as far as communications are concerned, except in the State of Assam and a few kilometres in the State of Nagaland, no other State in the North Eastern region has been connected with railways so far. There are places, a majority of the places, where for centuries past there are no road communications. In the State of Arunachal Pradesh, Nagaland and

---

**L.S. Deb.*, 3 August 1977 (Spoke while participating in the discussion on the Motion on the 20th, 21st and 22nd Reports of the Commission for the Scheduled Castes and Scheduled Tribes). This was the maiden speech of Shri P.A. Sangma in the Lok Sabha.

in my own State, Meghalaya, people have to walk days together to reach the market in order to get their essential commodities.

Not to speak of railways, there is not a single industry which has been established in my own State. Today, the honourable Minister of Industry has answered my USQ No. 6030. I had asked, 'Will the Minister of Industry be pleased to state: (a) the number of large and medium industries under public sector in Meghalaya and (b) whether Government are considering to set up any large/medium scale industries, under public sector in Meghalaya this year.' The answer to part (a) is 'none' and the answer to part (b) is 'there is no such proposal at present under consideration of the Central Government'. This is the state of affairs in our State.

The people who are living there are living under semi-starvation conditions. No serious attempt has been made to uplift those people and improve their conditions. I would like to lay stress more on education. They say that a lot of money has been spent on education, awarding pre-matriculate scholarship, post-matriculate scholarship, construction of hostels and what not. I would say that the money which has been claimed to have been spent is wasted in our State.

I would like to quote from the latest report of the Union Public Service Commission, the Twenty-Sixth Report where on page 28 it is said: 'The Commission were able to recommend candidates belonging to the Scheduled Castes against all the vacancies reserved for them at the examinations requiring general academic qualifications, like the Indian Administrative Service Examination, Indian Forest Service Examination, Indian Economic Service/Indian Statistical Service Examination (Indian Economic Service only) and Assistants' Grade Examination. Except for the Indian Forest Service Examination, the performance of candidates belonging to the Scheduled Tribes was, however, not up to the mark even after applying the relaxed standard sufficient number of Scheduled Castes and Scheduled Tribes candidates did not come up even by the relaxed standards prescribed for them for examinations like the Engineering Services Examination, and Stenographers Examination, which required technical and professional qualifications. The examination-wise details have been furnished in Appendix V-B.'

The reason is this: Government has not tried, first of all, to improve the standard of schools in our State. Unless Government establishes, or encourages establishment of good schools and good colleges, no student will come up to the standard. I would like to give my own example.

When I was studying in the lower primary school, I was taught by a schoolteacher whose educational qualification was only Class IV, he was running the school. When I studied in the middle school, there were three teachers and all of them were under-matriculates. I studied in a high school which was run for twelve years by one matriculate and one graduate. That is the condition of the schools in our State. This House can very well imagine as to what will be the state of affairs if an educational institution is run by unqualified and untrained teachers. How can the institution produce good citizens? Even today we have got about 2,000 lower primary schools in our district where the schools are run by under-matriculate – the qualification of some is Class IV, the qualification of some is Class V; some are even Class II. And they are not getting their pay for five or six months altogether. The same is the condition of high schools and middle schools.

Everybody who goes to the high school is entitled to a pre-matriculate scholarship. I was given a pre-matriculate scholarship. Everybody gets the scholarship, but there is no school worth the name. What is the use of spending that money on the student? It is a sheer wastage. Even with relaxed standards, our people, the Scheduled Tribes are not getting the reserved seats. That is because Government has not tried to establish good schools and colleges.

In the Report of the Home Ministry, so many things have been said – so many have been sent outside India, so many are given training, so many hostels have been constructed, so many this and that have been done. But we do not find anything in our State – no hostel for boys or girls or anything of that sort. We have schools run by ourselves. In the entire district of Garo Hills, there is only one government high school; in the entire district, there is only one college – which has been taken over by the Government a few years ago. Many institutions are run by the villages themselves, with their own contributions.

After so much of fight about three, four years ago, a Central School which we call 'Kendriya Vidyalaya' was established in my home town. But whoever goes to a good school is not entitled to scholarship but if he goes to a school where there are no good teachers, no building, no blackboard, no benches, etc., is entitled to scholarship. I do not know how we are running the country.

Therefore, I would earnestly appeal to the Government of today to give serious thought to the problem, review the whole situation and change the entire position. It is because there has been wrong planning and wrong policy has been followed that we are still backward. So, I would repeat that the first and foremost thing to be done is to establish good institutions so that our people – the backward people, the tribal people – come up. There is no meaning in giving reservations if we cannot fill up the vacancies even with relaxed standards. If reservation is given, it is all right, but if, instead of reservation, the Government tries to pull up these people and tries to raise their standards so that they can even compete with the other people, it would be better. We feel that, in the name of reservation, in the name of protection, in the name of this and in the name of that we people are being exploited. Therefore, Mr Deputy Speaker, I would urge upon the Government to look into the whole situation once again and take appropriate steps, especially in matters of educational policy which I have referred to.

Thank you.

Christianity, Secularism and Indianness*

At the very outset, I want to inform the honourable Home Minister that I am a tribal coming from North Eastern region and I am a Christian. Somehow, the people here have the impression that when a tribal becomes a Christian, he is a foreigner: he ceases to be an Indian.

* * *

We are tribals and whether we are Christians or not, we are the true citizens of this country. Unfortunately, the Christian community, especially belonging to the North Eastern region has been looked upon with suspicion by the Government. Just now the honourable Home Minister said, the Christian missionaries in the North Eastern region have been receiving crore of rupees. Why should the Home Minister feel jealous or suspicious about some money coming to our region? Today, if I am standing here in front of you . . . Please allow me to develop my point. I never interfered with anybody; I do not want anybody to

L.S. Deb., 27 March 1979 (Spoke while participating in the Calling Attention Motion regarding the demolition of churches, etc., in Arunachal Pradesh).

interrupt me. That is the tribal character. We do not interfere with anybody and we do not want anybody to interfere with us.

* * *

If today we have come to a certain stage, if today we can read and write, if we can go to schools, if we have some minimum medical facilities, etc., it is because of the missionaries. In the North Eastern region you go and see how many missionary schools and colleges are there and how many Government schools and colleges are there. You will find that there are more of missionary colleges and hospitals run by missionaries.

Merely because we are Christians, we do not lose our loyalty to the country. We are citizens of this country and we will ever be. The information given here in the statement is on the basis of the information received from the Arunachal Pradesh Government. I should remind you that Arunachal Pradesh is not a full-fledged State; it is a Union Territory; it is a Centrally-administered area. I am surprised how the honourable Home Minister could come here and say . . . Don't you have your own source of information?

* * *

Mr Deputy Speaker, Sir, so many circulars and official letters have been read out by my friends; I do not want to repeat the same. The honourable Home Minister has said that if some specific allegations are brought to his notice, he would look into them. I want to give you some specific allegations. I have with me here the memorandum which was submitted to the honourable Prime Minister of India (signed by the President of Subansiri Baptist Christian Convention) when he was in Itanagar, on 3 November 1978. I am sure, a copy of it had come to the file of the Home Minister. It is stated in para 4 of that Memorandum:

> 102 dwelling houses and 46 churches burnt down, one Christian member lost his life (Tana Ekha) by the persecutors. Recently, on 5 March 1978, five Christian students were expelled from the Government H.S. School, Yazali. They were told that the regular stipend of Rs 75,000 will not be provided to them. On 6 September 1978, Christians were tortured, tied in the post at Chulyu village. Animals were killed and burned at Chulyu Baptist Church . . .

These are the incidents which were brought to the notice of the honourable Prime Minister. Yet, the Home Minister is saying today in the month of March that they have not received specific allegations. I wonder how the Home Ministry is functioning. There was a reference to it in the *Amrita Bazar Patrika* yesterday, a portion of which has been read by my friend here.

Here it says:

> . . . he (Mr Wanglat Lowangcha) was a Christian and wanted to marry a Christian girl of his choice. The local Government officials insisted that he marry a girl of another faith instead. He cited another instance, where, he said, instigated by Government officials some people had stripped naked the wife of Mr Trainang who was on the platform with Mr Lowangcha because she would not change away from Christianity to another religion which the officials wanted her to. She was then hung upside down. Forty churches, Mr Lowangcha said, were burnt down at the instance of Government officials. He said that the church in Arunachal Pradesh had been established in 1830.

There are instances, these are the persecutions that are going on.

I understand that because of the latest Bill that has been passed by the Arunachal Pradesh Assembly and assented to by the President, conversion from one religion to another has been banned in Arunachal Pradesh.

* * *

What is the necessity of passing this Bill when forcible conversion is already a crime under the Indian Penal Code? When this Bill was passed and sent to the honourable President of India for his assent, the Christian community all over the country expressed the apprehension that it was primarily meant against the Christians and other minority religions. That has been proved now. Why a Bishop, who is an Indian citizen, who is a near relation of Mr A.C. George, was not allowed to conduct the Christmas service? Is conducting the Christmas service forcible conversion? When a boy wants to marry a Christian girl of his choice, is it a forcible conversion?

These are the things which are going on in the name of sensitive area and in the name of the tribals. The honourable Home Minister was proud to announce: we love the tribals. I say, you do not know the tribals. I am a tribal myself, and I say that in the name of the tribals, in the name of sensitive area, the people in the North Eastern area have been neglected, we have been suspected, and we have been kept isolated from the rest of the country.

* * *

It is because in the North Eastern area the majority of the people, tribals, are Christians. That is our crime.

The Home Minister said that nothing was going on, but we are asserting and telling the honourable Home Minister that persecutions are going. I would like to know from him whether he would consider sending a cosmopolitan parliamentary delegation, including Dr Subramaniam Swamy to go to Arunachal Pradesh and have an on the spot survey and give a report.

Ban on Cow Slaughter and Tribal Religion*

Mr Chairman, I rise to oppose the resolution. To me it appears that it is a very touchy, sentimental issue, though the mover and some other friends have tried to justify it from the economic point of view? I feel that the issue involved here is not economic but primarily a religious issue, because as it has been pointed out by so many friends from this side, if we are really thinking about the economy of the country, it is not only in the preservation of cows that lies the good of the economy of the country, it depends also in the preservation of many other things, other animals, forests, and other things. Why have we not thought of preserving other animals, minerals, etc., in this country? I am tempted to believe that this resolution is primarily a religious one.

Ours is a secular country and secularism is one of the basic structures of our Constitution. I was surprised when Mr Kamath, who is more or less like my grandfather, who was a member of the Constituent Assembly, said that the total ban on cow slaughter had nothing to do

**L.S. Deb.*, 30 March 1979 (Spoke while participating in the resolution regarding ban on cow slaughter).

with the Constitution and that it did not affect secularism in the country. I want to remind him that the Constitution of our country has given the right and freedom to 'freely profess, practise and propagate' any religion that one chooses. I lay stress on the word 'practise'. If my friend says killing is not a religion, I should say that my friend has not understood what is religion except perhaps the religion he professes. How many religions are there in this country? How many religions are being practised by the people of this country? Is it only Hindu religion? Is it only Buddhist religion? Is it Islamic religion only? There are many other religions in this country.

* * *

I am aware of the Supreme Court decision. Why I say that it is against the religion, because day before yesterday, the honourable friends will remember, the Home Minister was very proud of saying that we love tribals. He was saying that we love tribals. He was saying that we are very much for the protection of the tribal religion. How much do you know of tribal religious faith? What is the religion of the tribals? It is a part and parcel of some of the tribal religions to kill a cow. It is their (tribal's) religious function to sacrifice a cow. Does it not affect our religion? Is it not a practice among the Muslims? What is 'kurbani'? Then how can you say that it does not interfere with the religious sentiments of the people? It does.

I do not want to enter into many arguments given over here – economic and others. I only want to point out this particular point – if they are really religious, if we profess a particular religion as my friend has rightly pointed out – we must have respect for other religions. Ours is a secular country, where there is no State religion.

* * *

I am only trying to justify that it does interfere with some peoples' faith, i.e., the religious faith of the tribals. The Supreme Court may not be aware of tribals' religion.

I am talking of the Resolution moved by Dr Ramji Singh and also the Bill. It has connection with the Bill.

* * *

To have a total ban throughout the country is not proper. I am saying that our tribal areas are also part of this country and this cannot operate in our area.

In our religion, the indigenous faith, the tribal religion, sacrifice of the cow is a must. That is what I am trying to make you understand. In this context, it affects the secularism of our country because I have a right to practise my religion and anything that comes in the way of practising my religion is against the spirit of the Constitution. Therefore, I would appeal to Dr Ramji Singh to reconsider the matter, so that it does not affect the sentiments of a large section of the people. When I say I love my religion, I love God, I cannot love God unless I love others. The basic principle of the Christian religion is, love your neighbour as thyself. Do unto others as you would like others to do unto you. This is the basic principle of Christian religion. If killing a cow affects the Hindu religion, you must also understand the sentiment that banning cow slaughter also affects somebody's religion. That is why I appeal to Dr Ramji Singh to withdraw the resolution.

Thank you.

FOREIGN AFFAIRS AND INTERNATIONAL POLITICS

Foreign Policy of India: Past Consensus Vs Present Dilemma*

Mr Chairman, Sir, first of all I would like to congratulate Shri Jaswant Singh on his taking over the charge of the Ministry of External Affairs. Though it was very late, better late than never.

* * *

In a meeting of the Standing Committee on External Affairs, I voiced my concern about the absence of a Minister in the Ministry of External Affairs. When we discussed Pokhran-II, when we discussed here the foreign policy, I raised the question, 'Why at this crucial juncture India does not have a Foreign Minister?' Let me thank the honourable Prime Minister for ultimately giving us a very competent Foreign Minister.

After having said this, I want to make a very important point. The honourable Prime Minister of India had designated Shri Jaswant Singh, the Deputy Chairman of the Planning Commission, to negotiate with the United States. President Bill Clinton on his part designated Mr Talbott, Deputy Secretary of State, to negotiate with Shri Jaswant Singh. Today, Shri Jaswant Singh is no more Deputy Chairman of the Planning Commission alone. Shri Jaswant Singh is the Foreign Minister of this biggest democracy in the world. I would expect that India would urge upon the United States to upgrade the level of dialogue; I would not like Shri Jaswant Singh carrying on talking to Mr Talbott who is a

---

**L.S. Deb.*, 22 December 1998 (Spoke while participating in the discussion under Rule 193 regarding bilateral talks with the United States of America).

Deputy Secretary of State. I would expect that the future negotiations between India and the United States will be between Shri Jaswant Singh and Mrs Albright.

I have gone though the statement of the honourable Prime Minister. The statement says that what had happened in May 1998 at Pokhran was in continuation of the policy adopted by the Government of India 25 years ago. I respectfully disagree with this. In fact, in the previous debates, I had already pointed this out saying that the consistent policy of the Government of India after 1974 has been to reserve our options, to keep our options open whether to restrain ourselves or whether to go to a test. For 25 years, we have exercised our restraint. And, in May, the present Government decided to exercise that option to go for a Test. Therefore, it is not the same thing of the policy of the Congress Government and the successive other Governments to keep our options open. That is the difference.

The second difference, I had already pointed earlier, was that whenever there has been a new Test, it has been based on certain doctrines adopted by different countries. The 1974 option that we had exercised was very clearly on the doctrine of peaceful purposes, that we were doing it for peaceful purposes. But the present Government's option for a Test was not for peaceful purposes. It was for 'from the point of view of security threat from the neighbouring countries'. In fact, in the honourable Prime Minister's letter to Mr Bill Clinton, the countries were named, which is never in the area of diplomacy. And, therefore for the Prime Minister to come to the Parliament and say that what has been done is in continuation of the decision taken by the Government of India 24 years ago, I do not subscribe to this view.

What is the outcome of this? We all know that today India stand isolated in the community of nations. Whether we like it or not, our country has come to be projected in the international community as hegemonistic in its intent.

In the last debate, we have pointed out that the nuclear policy and our foreign policy of this country have been based on national consensus, and the decision of the Government of India to have gone for the second test is a departure from that national consensus.

I had expected that after having committed the kind of a mistake, the Government would, at least, try to bring about a consensus on the strategy to explain the rationale of the test to the international community. That is what I had expected. But that has not been there. We had a debate in this Parliament and the matter ended there. I have also been travelling in different parts of the world and I have also been in touch with the honourable Members of Parliament in different parts of the world. I have also been in touch with our diplomats in different parts of the world. The impression that I had gathered is that 'We have not tried enough to explain our strategy.' It is high time that the Government thinks about it seriously.

I do not understand where is the difficulty in Prime Minister calling the leaders of the Opposition and important political parties and take them into confidence, even on other issues, which I will be coming a little later. For example, on CTBT, what is the talk that is going on between Shri Jaswant Singh and Mr Strobe Talbott?

The honourable Prime Minister, in para 6 of the statement says that dialogue between Shri Jaswant Singh and Mr Talbott was conducted on the basis of a set of comprehensive proposals put forward by India. These are proposals put by India. We do not know whether there are any other counter proposals from the United States of America. But the honourable Prime Minister's statement says as follows:

> These are the proposals put forward by India and these proposals have been spelt out in the statement as including a voluntary moratorium on further tests, willingness to transform the voluntary moratorium into a *de jure* commitment, a joining negotiations on a treaty for ban of future production of fissile material, implementing more stringent control over sensitive materials and technology.

What are the full implications of these proposals? We do not know. The country does not know about it. The full implications of these proposals have not been told to the country. The way these proposals have been put forward by India to the United States of America, to me it appears that you have become very apologetic for what we have done on 11 and 13 May. You have become repentant and you say we are very sorry for what we have done. I said in the previous debate that the intention of the Government of India to have gone for a second test was to equate ourselves with the United States of America. If the United States of America and India are nuclear powers today, where is the question of India going to America and saying here are my proposals and we have done it and what can we do now and please have mercy on us? I think we are not talking from the position of strength. We must talk from the position of strength. I endorse the points which have been made by honourable lady member Smt. Krishna Bose. After what had happened a few days back to Iraq, I will not go into this. I will confine myself to say that India needs to be more cautious. India needs to be more assertive. Anyway, the talks are going on. Six rounds of discussions had already taken place. After six rounds of talks, the honourable Prime Minister tells this nation that USA is turning around to see the viewpoint and concerns of India. Is there anything more in this or that is all? We would like to know some more details.

What is the position after the USA has turned around to see our viewpoint? The sanctions still continue. Two hundred Indian private and public companies are in the US entities list. A large number of Indian organizations, public undertakings, scientific institutions, etc., have been included in the list. Even subcontracting firms have been included in the list and these bodies are subjected to export restrictions. They will be subject to denial of trade, particularly in the matter of technology exports. Of course, I know the Government's stand of *Swadesh* and self-reliance but I am afraid, the realities are different.

We are all aware that on the World Bank assistance to India, the United States Government has taken an official position which is discriminatory. What is the position? The USA has held a position that Pakistan deserved a more lenient treatment in the matter of World Bank assistance than India did. This is the official position taken by the United States of America after six rounds of talks.

I will not speak for long. I straightway come to the Comprehensive Test Ban Treaty (CTBT). In the earlier stages, after the Pokhran tests – I do not know about it but Shri Jaswant Singh will be able to reply – it was widely reported in the media that India might ultimately sign the CTBT on certain conditions. What are those conditions? It was reported widely in the media. I think, some of the honourable Ministers have also made some utterances but I do not want to take their names. The number one condition was that the US should stop restrictions on use of dual-use technology to India. The second condition was exemption of indigenously built reactors from international safeguards mechanism. The third condition was that there should be no curbs on future plans to deploy missiles or weaponize India's nuclear capabilities. I really do not know whether there can be any condition at all.

I was associated – directly or indirectly – with the Uruguay round of talks. I was directly or indirectly connected with the negotiations on WTO. In fact, when the question of social clause came up, I was assigned a duty by the then honourable Prime Minister, Shri Narasimha Rao, to mobilize public opinion around non-aligned and developing countries to oppose the introduction of the social clause. A meeting of the Labour Ministers was convened here and I had one week of sleepless nights during the negotiations. I am quite familiar with the subject. According to me, either you take it or leave it. We have reached a stage where there is the CTBT, whether we sign it or not. I do not know where the scope for putting any condition is.

I would like to know from the honourable Foreign Minister as to whether these parameters are there in his negotiations with Mr Talbott. Nothing is clear from the statement of the honourable Prime Minister which we are discussing today.

In fact, I do not like to go into the details. For example, restrictions on flow of dual-use technology is in fact unrelated to CTBT, and I do not know how it is put as one of the conditions. It is rather related to the Non-Proliferation Treaty (NPT). On CTBT, my colleague and former Speaker, Shri Shivraj Patil, has made our position very clear. Our policy was spelt out at the Pachmarhi Convention. We had cautioned the Government not to be in a hurry. We have time to think over it and we have time to discuss about it. If we wish so, perhaps Shri Jaswant Singh can take some of us into confidence, that is, some leaders of the political parties into confidence. Our only point is that they should not rush through.

FMCT is the second area. I, frankly speaking, could not make out much from the honourable Prime Minister's statement on this. The statement is rather vague. Here again, I wish that the Government had taken some leaders of the political parties into confidence, at least on the parameters of the discussion unless he wants to keep it away from us as a secret.

* * *

Mr Speaker, Sir, the honourable Prime Minister has observed in his statement and I quote:

> The objective of FMCT negotiations at Geneva is ending of future productions of fissile material for weapons purposes.

In this connection, I have a few questions to ask. How are we going to fulfil the superiority of fissile material stocks already secured by P-5 countries. Russia and the USA have stocks to produce 10,000 warheads. How are we going to fulfil the superiority? The second question that I would like to ask is what commitment will we agree to. The third question is what level and kind of verification of our fissile material capability production will we agree to. Will India be prepared to freeze the present asymmetries in fissile material stock holdings of various countries? Before you go to Geneva, I would expect the Government to tell all this to Parliament.

I would like to make two more points. The honourable Prime Minister's statement refers to dialogues which are going on with Germany, France, China, Russia and Japan. The names of these countries have been mentioned in the statement. But nothing has been mentioned about Pakistan. I would like to refer to China, since the honourable Prime Minister has made a reference to China. Could the External Affairs Minister, in his reply, tell us as to what is the progress of dialogue between India and China? The country knows how our relationship had been strained and how the confidence-building exercise between these two countries have been somehow negated by the Pokhran blasts. What are we doing to restore the confidence between India and China? How much progress has been made? I am happy that our relationship with Russia is growing and that the Prime Minister of Russia, Mr Primakov, is here in India. I would like to thank the Government for whatever they are doing to strengthen the relationship with Russia. I am worried about our relations with Pakistan and other SAARC countries. I am particularly worried because the SAARC has a direct impact on the people of North East. I do not know what is the future of the SAARC. North East India is trying to integrate its economy with the neighbouring countries, particularly with Bangladesh. It is only with this objective, two agreements were arrived at, the South Asian Preferential Trade Agreement (SAPTA) and the South Asian Free Trade Agreement (SAFTA). SAPTA is already in force and SAFTA would come into force by AD 2001. This is very very important for the North East. Have you taken up this matter with Pakistan? I would like to know whether Pakistan is going to sign SAFTA or not, particularly after the nuclear blasts. What measures are you taking to ensure that SAARC becomes successful and SAFTA comes into operation by 2001?

Today, we are not debating foreign policy. Today's discussion is limited to Indo-US relations. Our foreign policy is very important. When we were in the Youth Congress, we used to come to New Delhi for leadership training and seminar. It used to be addressed, among others, by Finance Minister and the Foreign Minister. The Finance Minister used to tell us about the economic policies and the Foreign Minister used to explain the foreign policy. I remember, in one of the seminars, the then Foreign Minister, Sardar Swaran Singh, telling us that the position of India in the community of nations is so high that in any international conference, India need not speak.

It is not necessary that India should participate in the debate, speak out in the debate. The mere presence of India in the conference hall is enough. That is the stature of India. That was India. I do not know whether we are the same country. Why had we have that kind of recognition from the world? I think because as far as the foreign policy was concerned, we used to take the national consensus. The whole world used to know that as far as India is concerned, they are unanimous on their foreign policy. Unfortunately, that is no more the case. It is very important. The whole world knew that India was the largest democracy in the world. It is not only the largest democracy, India has functioning democracy, stable democracy and an uninterrupted democracy. It is very important that India used to be respected. And, today we have to ask questions on this.

I am not addressing Shri Jaswant Singh or Shri Vajpayee-led Government. I am addressing it to the whole august House. The way our Parliament is functioning today, are we projecting to the whole world that we are a functioning democracy, a stable democracy? I think it is a very important question. It has a lot to do with our foreign policy. The whole world knew that we had national consensus on many and most of the national issues. The whole country would be one on matters which are of vital importance to this country. I do know whether we are projecting that image today.

This Parliament is not able to function for days together because we are projecting ourselves as a country with differences, as if we have no consensus or unanimity in this country. It is weakening us. So, Shri Jaswant Singh's hands, who is not going to meet Mrs Albright, will be strengthened if we cooperate. I wish him best of luck and success not only in negotiations but also in his career as the Foreign Minister of this great country.

Agra Summit and India-Pakistan Relations*

Madam Chairperson, I am not going to repeat all the points that had already been made very eloquently by the previous speakers, particularly, Shri Madhavrao Scindia. I will try to deal the topic from a different perspective.

After the summit, when Gen. Musharraf arrived at Islamabad, he declared and I quote: 'I have returned empty-handed.' I want to put a question whether it is a true statement. Did Gen. Musharraf return to Pakistan empty-handed? If he is talking about himself, if he is talking about his personal interest or personal gain, I think he is making a wrong statement. If he is talking in terms of the welfare of the people of Pakistan, I think, he is right. He has returned to Pakistan empty-handed for the people of Pakistan.

But, for himself, I think, he got everything. Why did he come here? I really do not know why our honourable Prime Minister invited him. I cannot reconcile that point even now. I asked the honourable Prime Minister whether it was not in haste to invite him. But the invitation from our honourable Prime Minister was such a God-sent opportunity for Gen. Musharraf. He came here not to solve the Kashmir problem. He came here not to normalize or improve the relationship between the two countries. He did not come here to get something for the people of Pakistan. He came here to get legitimacy of his coup, he came here to get legitimacy of his self-proclaimed presidentship of Pakistan, and he got everything from us. He went back to his country with that recognition, with that legitimacy, with that kind of glamour and with that kind of international attention. How could Gen. Musharraf go back to Pakistan with something for the people when he had no intention of getting anything for the people?

He says: 'Poverty is not an issue, peace is not an issue, progress is not an issue, development is not an issue and harmonizing the relationship between India and Pakistan hardly matters. What are you talking about? People-to-people contact! What do you mean by confidence-building

---

***L.S. Deb.*, 1 August 2001 (Spoke while participating in the discussion under Rule 193 regarding the recent summit-level talk held between India and Pakistan at Agra, raised by Shri Mulayam Singh Yadav on 24 July 2001).

measures? Forget about all these. These are irrelevant. What is relevant is Kashmir – step-by-step approach. You recognize Kashmir as a core issue, and then you proceed. If you do not recognize Kashmir as a core issue then everything else is irrelevant.' He is a clever man. I think, he has been able to show to the people of Pakistan that he is concerned about Pakistan. I do not think that he is concerned about the people of Pakistan at all but he is concerned about his chair and he is concerned about his power.

I know Shri Yerrannaidu has just made this point that the people of both the countries want peace; the people of both the countries want reduction in defence expenditure so that poverty alleviation can be stepped up. But Gen. Musharraf does not want it. I have with me the full Budget of Pakistan for the year 2001-2002. They have a deficit Budget of 10.5 billion Pakistani rupees. The debt servicing expenditure is 329.2 billion Pakistani rupees; the defence expenditure is 131.6 billion Pakistani rupees; these two items make 460 billion Pakistani rupees. What is their developmental expenditure? It is 130 billion Pakistani rupees. As against the debt servicing expenditure of 329 billion and as against the defence expenditure of 131 billion, the developmental expenditures in Pakistan for the year 2001-2002 is just 130 billion Pakistani rupees. Does he care for his Budget? He does not.

Well, I do not want to go into so many other points. I do not want to criticize the Government any more but the point which is relevant at the moment is, how do we proceed. The External Affairs Minister has said that the caravan of peace would continue its march.

The honourable Prime Minister said that we have to go on with re-engagement. The point is, how do we proceed with the caravan of peace? How do we re-engage ourselves with Pakistan? I really do not know. After all, Pakistan's bottom line is that there is no cross-border terrorism. It is a freedom struggle. He said, 'It is a freedom struggle.' He says: 'LoC is the problem and not a solution; unless you accept Kashmir as a core issue, I cannot move an inch.' Now, if that is the bottom line of Pakistan, then how do we proceed? I do not see any way that we can proceed. I think the august House has very rightly cautioned the honourable Prime Minister of India in asking him whether he is really making a visit to Pakistan. We are not against his visit. Go ahead. But the point is, what will you do there? One summit has already taken place. Everybody said that it was going to be a historic summit.

When the honourable Prime Minister had taken the meeting of the leaders of the political parties on 9 July 2001 on this summit, I refused to wish the honourable Prime Minister best of luck. If you remember, everybody was saying, 'I wish you best of luck.' I did not see any reason why I should wish him best of luck on that day because I knew what was coming. When I asked the honourable Foreign Minister where was the agenda, the Foreign Minister said, 'Well, we have submitted eight points agenda to Pakistan but they have not responded so far.' On 9 July, there was no agenda. I asked the Foreign Minister what was the composition of Pakistani delegation; how many people are coming? What is our delegation composed of? The Foreign Minister said, 'Our delegation composed of the Prime Minister, the Home Minister, the Foreign Minister, the Commerce and Industry Minister and the Finance Minister.' I think that is all. I am not rebutting. From Pakistan side, they had not disclosed as yet on 9 July, I asked this question. Is it correct that Pakistan delegation will compose of only General Musharraf and Foreign Minister Abdul Sattar? The Foreign Minister said, 'I have no idea.' I said that that was going to be the composition. The Home Minister of Pakistan is not coming. Who is going to talk about cross-border terrorism which is the core issue as far as we are concerned? The Commerce Minister of Pakistan is not a member of the team. Then, who is going to talk about bilateral relations? Economic cooperation is so important. And it so happened that nothing was discussed.

General Musharraf was very proud to say well ninety per cent of their talks was on Kashmir and rest ten per cent must have been on snacks and tea. From that point of view, this is the first time, perhaps, in the history of world diplomacy where a summit between the two heads of Governments was held without preparation and without agenda. What do we do? I do not know what advice to give to the Government.

But I think this Kargil Review Committee Report should be our guidance for future. In Chapter III of the Report, what we should keep in mind is clearly spelt out and I quote:

> Pakistan's behavior has been driven by a desire to avenge its defeat in 1971 and subsequent discomfiture in Siachen.
>
> In this context, Pakistan's strategy *vis-à-vis* India has had three broad inter-connected stands: Undermining the Shimla Agreement and internationalizing the Kashmir issue; waging a proxy war against India to tie up the Indian Army in counter-insurgency operations, and pursuing a nuclear programme to achieve strategic parity with India in using nuclear capability to seize Kashmir at an appropriate opportunity.

This is the approach of Pakistan.

Is the Shimla Agreement not relevant? What did Mr Abdul Sattar say before coming to India in Islamabad? The Foreign Minister of Pakistan said: 'How long does it take for an agreement to lapse – fifty-four years since the UN Resolution or twenty-nine years since the Shimla Agreement? This was what the Foreign Minister of Pakistan said: 'If the UN Resolution has lapsed, the Shimla Agreement has lapsed and Lahore Declaration has also lapsed.' So, what is left now? There is no question of confidence-building measures; no question of bilateral trade, no question of having only a bilateral talk, no question of nuclear disarmament as declared in the Lahore Declaration but only one issue is left and that is Kashmir.

How do we go about Pakistan internationalizing the Kashmir issue? I put this particular question to our honourable Minister of External Affairs the other day, 'If these talks fail and such other future summits that we hold without preparation fail, would it not lead to a third-party intervention?' Of course, the honourable Minister said that there was no question about it. But is it enough to say that there was no question of internationalizing the Kashmir issue? Since 1973, Pakistan has been pursuing this issue in the United Nations. Year after year, they have continued to give notices to the United Nations Security Council to retain Kashmir on the agenda.

I had the good opportunity of being in the Government of India for almost twenty years. I have not only attended but also led many Indian delegations to international conferences. Whether it is UNO, ILO, UNIDO, ESCAP or Commonwealth, I have not come across a single occasion when Pakistan has not raised the Kashmir issue in an international forum; whether it is relevant or not, they would always raise this issue.

* * *

Please do not take things easily. Gen. Musharraf is not a person to be dealt with in an easy way. He is a different type of person. He has been described in one of the newspapers or magazines that I have read as 'merciless cowboy'. I do not know about it but it is true. He is a merciless cowboy and here is a thorough perfect gentleman, so sincere a man. How does it match between Mr Musharraf's cowboy style and the perfect gentleness of the honourable Prime Minister of India? I really do not know how it is going to be.

I think, if Pakistan is very clear on its bottom line and if Pakistan says that the LoC is the problem but not a solution, we should be very clear about our bottom line too.

That is everything that I want to say. What is our bottom line? Our bottom line is the 1994 resolution passed by this august House. What is that resolution? Let me remind the House. We resolved in the House on 22 February 1994 that 'The State of Jammu and Kashmir has been, is and shall be an integral part of India . . . Pakistan should vacate the area of the Indian State of Jammu and Kashmir which they have been occupying through aggression.' This is our bottom line. We must stick to it and we have stuck to it because this is a unanimous resolution passed by this Parliament. This is not the decision of the government of India alone. This is the bottom line which has been set by the august House unanimously.

So, that is our bottom line. I think we have to proceed with that. Ours is a big country. I would like to remind one thing of 1965. In 1965 when Pakistan crossed over to Kashmir, the then Prime Minister, Shri Lal Bahadur Shastri, authorized the Indian Army to cross the international border in Punjab. He said that he was doing it on the basis of an observation of Pandit Jawaharlal Nehru in 1950 that 'an attack on Jammu and Kashmir would be treated as an attack against India, of which it is an integral part.'

Mr Prime Minister, you should not be so humble. You should assert yourself. You are a Prime Minister of one billion people. We are a country of Kautilya who had given us a treatise of statecraft *The Arthashastra*. Let us try to refresh our minds with the lessons that he had given. Let us not be politically naive. Let us not be carried away by the 'Bhai Bhai' sentimentalism. Let us not commit any profanity on the souls of 800 of our Kargil martyrs. I like one statement of the honourable Prime Minister – this is the only statement that I liked – in which he said: 'I focused on the terrorism being promoted in the State of Jammu and Kashmir. I conveyed in clear terms that India has the resolve, strength and stamina to counter terrorism and violence until it is decisively thrust.'

I want to reiterate this determination today on the floor of this august House. That is what the Prime Minister should speak and continue to speak so.

Thank you.

Lessons from Iraq War*

Mr Speaker, Sir, now that the war is almost going to be over and the agreed draft resolution by both the Treasury Benches and the Opposition Benches has been moved by the Chair himself, I am not going into the details of the justification or non-justification of the war. I would only make four points. It is good that we take lessons from this war. I have carefully watched the proceedings of the war and I have come to a conclusion on four areas.

The first point is that the war is not about morals. I think it is clear. It is plainly about the national interest of an individual country. I think you cannot deny that. Otherwise, in this war, there would not have been any differences of opinion in the Islamic world. This is the point I thought I would like to make so that we remember it.

The second point is that the war is about the commercial interest of a country. It is purely commercial. This point has been adequately made by the previous Members as regards the motives of the United States of invading Iraq. This point has been articulately made and I agree that the war is nothing but the commercial interest of the country.

What stands had been taken by France, Germany and Russia before the commencement of the war and what are the stands taken by them now? I think we should carefully see it. Why France, Germany and Russia are now making appropriate noises? President Putin, who opposed the war, has gone to the extent to saying, 'The alienation of USA is not in the interest of orderly international relations.' This is what President Putin has said.

The third point that I would like to make is that this war clearly shows the incapability and the failure of the United Nations system. The United Nations has failed and I think something has to be done about it.

Our defence expert, Shri K. Subramaniam has observed that the United Nations system is indeed anarchic. He has used the word 'anarchic'. India has been one of those countries which have been vociferously advocating to restructure of whole United Nations system so that it become as much more democratic and much more representative. I think, India has to pursue this matter especially after this experience of Iraq War. But the most important point that I would like to make is this.

**L.S. Deb.*, 8 April 2003 (Spoke while participating in the resolution regarding the situation in Iraq).

The fourth lesson that we should learn is about the way the war has been fought. I think Shri Reddy has made this point. The entire Iraq War has gone so much hi-tech. We need to see our defence system itself now. If future wars are going to be hi-tech, are we modern enough to face it? Is the Indian defence system modern enough? I think this is a very very important point.

I am sorry to say one thing here, I found in the last year's Budget that the Defence Ministry could not spend around Rs 6,500 crore, i.e., 30 per cent of the Budget allocated for defence has not been spent.

* * *

The areas where India needs to modernize in defence is self-propelled and air defence artillery guns and night-fighting capabilities. India needs to go modern in the areas of attacking helicopters, surveillance radars, early warning devices, electronic warfare systems, etc., especially when we have a terrorist state as our neighbour. We do not know what will happen when.

The last point that I would like to make is that the United States will perhaps win war in Iraq. But, will they be able to win peace in Iraq? Winning peace in Iraq is much more important. Let Americans understand that winning peace is much more important that winning war in Iraq.

As a nation, I think, on such matters we should not be rushing in our conclusions. It needs to be debated much before. That is my feeling. If you look at the past history, in 1956 when Soviet forces invaded Hungary and replaced the Government of Imre Nagy, we did not condemn the Soviet Union. We voted against the United Nations resolution condemning the USSR. In 1968 when the Soviet Union invaded Czechoslovakia and replaced the Government of Alexander Dubcek, we did not condemn the USSR. Again in 1980, when the Soviet Union went into Afghanistan, we did not condemn it in spite of the fact that Parliament of India was very critical about the Soviet action in Afghanistan. In spite of that, the Government of India refused to condemn it. I was in the Government of India those days. Therefore, I want to say that in war there is no morality. What is more important is national interest and commercial interest.

With these words, I conclude. Thank you.

India's Defence Strategy and the United States*

Mr Deputy Speaker, Sir, I consider this debate very very important in our national interest. International relations are never static. They have their own dynamics driven by the national and international changes in politics, economy and technology. It is everybody's knowledge that today's China is not Mao's China.

The United States and China are very much engaged with each other. Today, Putin's Russian Federation is no more the erstwhile USSR. USA and the Russian Federation are very much engaged with each other on bilateral and global issues. In that scenario, what should India do? The world is changing, and the world will change. India, in our own national interest, will have to change. It is time that we have to get over the cold war syndrome. We cannot afford to blow hot and cold between non-aligned theology and liberal diplomacy. In our own national interest we must be pragmatic.

The honourable Prime Minister's visit to the United States, the joint statement and the statement of the honourable Prime Minister on the floor of the august House are very significant. The honourable Prime Minister's talk with President Bush covered a lot of issues, bilateral and global, which have already been pointed out by the former Prime Minister, Shri Vajpayee. I do not like to go into all these aspects. Perhaps the main focus of the debate is on nuclear agreement. Let me also confine to that.

But before that, let me say about the visit of the honourable Prime Minister to the United States and the joint statement. I do not know whether I should quote Shri Jyoti Basu. He says, 'It was generally all right.' But I personally feel that it is much beyond that. I think, it is very successful visit from India's point of view.

On the nuclear aspect – I think Shri Vajpayee, Maj. Gen. Khanduri and also Shri Suresh Prabhu have referred to it – what is that separation of civil nuclear and military nuclear energy? Is it possible? If it is possible, is it in the interest of the nation? I think, that is the focus of the debate today.

**L.S. Deb.*, 3 August 2005 (Spoke while participating in the discussion under Rule 193 regarding the statement made by the honourable Prime Minister on 29 July 2005 on his recent visit to the United States of America).

I would like to quote Shri K. Subrahmanyam, who is an expert on our defence strategy, and everybody knows him. I think, what he says will be very clear to all our minds. He said:

> It is surprising that there are objections to separating civil and military nuclear facilities. The original suggestion for this came from Dr Raja Ramanna, the designer of the first Pokhran bomb. Ramanna's logic can't be challenged. If civilian and military facilities are not separated . . .

This is the most important point. If they are not separated, then what happens? He said:

> If civilian and military facilities are not separated, it would mean all reactors in India support our military programme.

That is the most important point. Without segregation, without separation, it would mean that all our nuclear inputs would go for military purposes.

That was precisely the reason why America refused to supply uranium to our Tarapur plant. Now, I am surprised why our former Prime Minister had put this question today. It is because it was the NDA Government which approached the United States to segregate this, by saying that we, in India, are going to segregate the civilian energy and the military energy and, therefore, you should not hesitate to supply us uranium. That was the beginning of India pursuing with the United States of America. I am sorry I could not find the exact words. Anyway these technical words are very very difficult for us. We call this as Next Step in Strategic Partnership. This is the word I was looking for. It was on the basis of the NDA Government's initiative that the honourable Prime Minister, Dr Manmohan Singh has been able to carry on further and got the agreement with the United States. Therefore, there is no need to be worried about that.

Mr Suresh Prabhu had asked a question whether the conversion of civil energy and the military energy can take place with that kind of a material. I do not think we should be asking those questions. We should leave it to the scientists to decide about that and we should not be doing that.

Now, Mr Vajpayee had also referred whether the Prime Minister had consulted the scientists before signing this agreement. He had asked whether the scientists were taken into confidence. What is the reaction of the scientists? I have already quoted what Mr Subrahmaniyam has said. I would like to quote Prof. U.R. Rao. What did he say? He says: 'Yes, it is a positive step. Of course, India has not fully depended on US for all technologies but it opens up new areas of cooperation, especially in terms of global positioning system technology.' This is how Prof. Rao has said.

What did Dr Kasturi Rangan, who is also the former Chairman of the ISRO, say? What has he said? He said and I quote: 'I believe this is a milestone in Indo-US relations. Our Prime Minister and the US President must be congratulated. What they had achieved will have repercussions for years to come.' Therefore, I think the scientists in our country, who are engaged in our defence strategy, who have been involved themselves, are so concerned about this. This is the opinion of our scientists. Therefore, I think we, as laymen, should not be worried about that.

I do not believe it if anybody is saying that we are surrendering to another country or it is a sell-out to another country. Are we not an independent country? Are we not capable of deciding for ourselves? Why should we surrender to anybody? Which Prime Minister of any country in this world would like to sell his own country? So, I do not understand this. I think these are allegations which are very, very unfair. Mr Rupchand Pal is looking at me very intensely. The other day I was reading some of the old speeches of leaders and I came across the speech of Mr E.M.S. Namboodripad. When he became the Chief Minister of Kerala, he said this.

He announced that our policy is administration and agitation. My duty is administration as Chief Minister and your duty is agitation. So, agitation and administration must go simultaneously. I think, that is what you are doing today. Anyway, I am not blaming you for that.

* * *

Now, I come to the area of terrorism. I think, we all know that we have been the victims of cross-border terrorism. We have tried to educate and make the United States of America and the other countries of the world understand us. They never understood us. America has not been able to stop cross-border terrorism from Pakistan. Pakistan is continuing to run terrorist training camps. According to the *Times of India*, there are about fifty-five such camps. Their locations have been identified.

All these circumstances led the honourable Prime Minister and the

President of the United States of America to come out with a joint statement that they are going to have a UN Convention on International Terrorism by September. I think, we should welcome that. Hopefully, these are positive steps. Although I have a lot of points to make yet I will conclude now. On one point, I am not very happy with the honourable Prime Minister's visit. That is about his requesting the United States of America for a permanent membership of the Security Council.

I do not know whether we should do it at all. We should not go around the world and say: 'Please make us member of the Security Council.' I have my doubts. I read an article written by Shri Gurcharan Das. He says that we should not do it. He says and I quote: 'Prime Minister's pleading to be in the Security Council is in the nature of an "unseemly campaign". It exposes our lack of confidence and status anxiety.'

Why should we not do a thing we do not have to run after status? Let status run after us. I think, we can do that only when we do everything possible to take our country towards progress and prosperity.

I would like to conclude by congratulating the honourable Prime Minister for the fact that before the Prime Minister went to United States, India was recognized as nuclear weapon State. When he came back, he came back with a recognition of India being a military nuclear power. I think, there is a difference between nuclear weapon State and military nuclear power. The honourable Prime Minister did come back to India with that recognition that India today is a military nuclear power. I congratulate the honourable Prime Minister. Thank you.

PARLIAMENTARY MATTERS

Felicitating Shri P.M. Sayeed*

Mr Speaker, Sir, the world is celebrating the Golden Jubilee of adoption of the UN Charter on Human Rights. According to the Charter, amongst other things social origin shall not be a ground for discrimination. Shri P.M. Sayeed hails from distant sea-bound small region of Lakshadweep. Today, by electing him as the honourable Deputy Speaker, the august House has signalled that in our subcontinent-size democracy, people with origin in distant small regions will not be forgotten. For us, there could not have been a better way of celebrating the Golden Jubilee of the Human Rights Charter than this.

Shri Sayeed is a linguist. He is proficient in Hindi, English, Malayalam, Kannada, Tamil and Tulu. In a sense, he represents the composite culture of our country and is hence eminently suited to hold the high office of the honourable Deputy Speaker.

It was 1996, I went to Lakshadweep to attend a reception that Shri Sayeed had organized in connection with the marriage of his daughter. It was then that I realized the place that Shri Sayeed has in the hearts of his people. His entire village had turned up in his humble house. Virtually all the islanders in the village and nearby places attended the reception. They sat inside his house, in his courtyard, in the seafront and under coconut trees and helped themselves to the very same simple lunch in congregational style. There was no distinction between the rich and the poor, high and the lowly, close relatives and others.

No wonder, Shri Sayeed has returned to this august House nine times over consecutively. In fact, Shri Sayeed and Shri Khagpati Pradhani are the two Members of this august House whose names have been entered

---

**L.S. Deb.*, 17 December 1998 (Spoke on the occasion of felicitating Shri P.M. Sayeed for being appointed as the honourable Deputy Speaker, Lok Sabha).

in the Guinness Book of World Record for having elected to Parliament eight consecutive times.

For him, maturing in our parliamentary democracy through the terms of eleven out of twelve Presidents and eleven out of fourteen Prime Ministers should have been a grand experience. This House has already seen this experience in display in the performance of Shri Sayeed as a member of the panel of Chairmen.

Shri Sayeed is a senior politician, senior to me in politics. Nonetheless, in 1995-96, when both of us were working in the Ministry of Information and Broadcasting, I was the Cabinet Minister and he was the Minister of State. The gentleman that Shri Sayeed is, he never brought our relative political seniority positions to affect our hierarchical relationship in the Ministry. We had excellent relationship. I found that God has gifted Shri Sayeed with a mind and heart which are as serene as the blue lagoon of Lakshadweep.

Thomas Gray, the famous British poet, in his 'Elegy Written in a County Churchyard', wrote:

> Full many a gem of purest ray serene,
> The dark unfathomed caves of ocean bear,
> Full many a flower is born to blush unseen,
> And waste its sweetness in the desert air.

Shri Sayeed is a coral gem, a lily of lagoons. We have fathomed this gem out of the Arabian Sea for us to wear, presented this flower to adorn our House's Chair. We have proved the poet wrong. I am sure he will shine. He will spread fragrance.

Honourable Shri P.M. Sayeed, I wish you all the bounties of God and success in your new assignment.

Demise of Shri Rangarajan Kumaramangalam*

Mr Speaker, Sir, on behalf of my party and on my own behalf, I would like to associate myself with the sentiments expressed by the leader of the House, the leader of the Opposition and other leaders.

Each one of us sitting here in this august House is feeling that we have lost a personal friend. This feeling is prevailing with thousands of thousands of people outside this House. Shri Ranga had tremendous ability to make friends. I knew him as a trade union leader. During my tenure as the Labour Minister of this country for seven years, I had many occasions to interact with him and to argue with him because he used to come with the problems of the working class. He used to come to my office with a large number of delegations. He had such a persuasive power that most of the time I had no choice but to concede to his demands.

I remember one particular occasion when Shri Ranga came with a delegation of about fifty workers. He had a very long list of demands. We had three hours of marathon negotiations. After three hours of negotiations, arguments and counter-arguments, I was shocked when he asked, 'Mr Sangma, may I withdraw all my demands? Will you please allow me to take back this memorandum?' In my tenure as the Labour Minister, that was the only occasion when a trade union leader withdrew the demands on the spot after three hours of negotiations. Such a reasonable man was Shri Ranga.

He was dynamic, he was young, he had tremendous capacity to articulate his views and in a period of three months' time after Shri Rajesh Pilot left us, the country has lost a very bright young politician. I deeply mourn his demise. On behalf of my party and on my own behalf, I would like to convey through you to the members of the bereaved family our heartfelt condolences.

~

*_L.S. Deb._, 24 August 2000 (Spoke while paying obituary references to Shri Rangarajan Kumaramangalam, Member, eighth, ninth, tenth, twelfth and thirteenth Lok Sabha, on 23 August 2000).

Felicitating Shri Somnath Chatterjee*

Mr Speaker, Sir, seven years ago, on 19 March 1997, I had the privilege of conferring on you the 'Outstanding Parliamentarian Award' for the year 1996. On that occasion this is what I said about you, I quote:

> Internally I have always assigned to Shri Somnath Chatterjee the status of my guru.

Sir, today after this unanimous election to the post of honourable Speaker, you have indeed become the maha guru for everyone of us here.

I had the privilege of travelling with you both in India as well as abroad. On more than one occasion, I have told my friends that being with Shri Somnath Chatterjee itself is an experience, knowledge and an intellectual elevation. I do not forget the important role you have played on behalf of Indian Parliament in Beijing in the IPU Conference where you have been unopposedly chosen as the rapporteur of the Conference.

Today, I feel really very happy to see my guru sitting in the Chair. I wish you all the best. I wish you a very successful tenure and I congratulate you from the core of my heart.

May God bless you, Sir.

~

Felicitating Shri Charanjit Singh Atwal†

Mr Speaker Sir, first of all, I would like to congratulate the honourable Prime Minister and the Treasury benches for having conceded this position to the Opposition benches. They have kept the good tradition of the parliamentary democracy. Having conceded this position to the Opposition benches, the BJP, being the largest party in the NDA, could have taken this post to themselves. They did not. This gesture of accommodation and recognition to the smaller partners is itself a very

---

**L.S. Deb.*, 9 June 2004 (Spoke while felicitating Shri Somnath Chatterjee on becoming honourable Speaker, Lok Sabha).

†*L.S. Deb.*, 4 June 2004 (Spoke while felicitating Shri Charanjit Singh Atwal on becoming honourable Deputy Speaker, Lok Sabha).

great thing. Therefore, let me also congratulate BJP, particularly the former Prime Minister Shri Vajpayee, to whom the decision was left. Let me congratulate the Akali Dal for this honour and I thank Akali Dal for having chosen Shri Atwal as their candidate.

I think there are a very few Members in this august House who know Shri Atwal as I do because we had the opportunity of serving as the members of the Executive Committee of the Commonwealth Parliamentary Association for a long time. I have always been proud of Shri Atwal in the international conferences. His dignified way of dealing and presenting things before the CPA Conference particularly in the Executive Committee and whenever I was not able to attend certain meetings because of some other assignments given to me, I was always confident that Atwalji would be there to represent India in a very very dignified manner.

Today, I personally feel proud, I personally feel very happy, because having seen his performance in the international forum, he richly deserves this position.

My heartiest congratulations and I wish him all the best and success.

MATTERS RELATED TO THE NORTH EAST

Railways: Linking the Backward Regions*

Mr Speaker, Sir, the honourable Railway Minister has rightly observed the role of the railway lines as infrastructure in developing the backward areas of the country. He has further expressed his keenness to take up construction of new lines. But it is our misfortune that most of the backward areas of the country – the State like Meghalaya or for that matter the entire North Eastern region – could not find a place in the honourable Railway Minister's map of backward areas.

The State of Meghalaya, particularly the Garo Hills which I represent, is perhaps the most backward area in the country. For centuries past, many places are there where there are no road communications. People in that part of the country have been isolated. They have been completely cut off from the rest of the country. Though it is a backward district, yet it is very rich in mineral resources and forest products. These mineral resources could not be exploited because of lack of communications. Establishment of railway link is the only way to open up the potentialities of exploiting its mineral resources. I suggest that a new railway line from Bongaigoan to Maheshkhola in Garo Hills via Phulbari, Mahendraganj and Baghmara may be laid. This will also cover the south bank of the State of Assam. People are backward there, only because they have not been given the opportunity and because there are no facilities. They are backward in all respects – educationally, socially and economically. Unless special attention and special assistance is given by the Central Government, the area cannot be developed. Besides being a backward area, the State of Meghalaya and especially the district of Garo Hills is very strategic from the point of view of defence. The State is bordering

*_L.S. Deb._, 16 June 1977 (Spoke while participating in the discussion on the Demands for Grants, Railways, 1977-1978).

Bangladesh. So from defence point of view also it should have a direct link with the rest of the country.

In our district, many cash and food crops like oranges, pineapples, ginger and so on are produced and these articles do not get market because of lack of rail link, because they cannot go out of the district. That is why I urge upon the honourable Railway Minister to take up a new railway line from Bongaigaon to Maheshkhola via Phulbari, Mahendraganj and Baghmara which will cover the south bank of Assam. This line should be taken up in this current year's budget.

Railways: A Necessary Ingredient for Accelerating National Growth*

Mr Chairman, Sir, I shall be very very brief. Much had been discussed on the various aspects of the Railway Budget. So, I do not want to enter into those discussions. I would only like to draw the attention of the honourable Minister to the peculiar and specific problems of the people of the area I represent. Before I proceed to make my humble submission, I would like to narrate a small incident, an interesting incident that took place very recently.

On 8 February 1978, I had the occasion to visit a particular area of my constituency. It was about twenty-seven kilometres away from the block headquarter. On my arrival at place I found some thousands of people had assembled there. Generally, in our area it is very difficult to get a gathering of 1,000 people for a meeting because the villages are very much scattered. But on that particular day, I found that 3,000 to 4,000 people had come. When I asked the local leaders as to how they could manage to gather so many people, they told me that these people had come not to see me but they had come to see the jeep by which I travelled. I went in the jeep on a road which was constructed for the first time. This twenty-seven kilometres of route took me about three hours to reach that place. This is the area I am representing. These are the people for whom I am standing here to speak. I can tell you that not

*_L.S. Deb._, 9 March 1978 (Spoke while participating in the general discussion on Railway Budget, 1978-1979).

even one per cent of the total population of my constituency comprising of two districts had seen a train.

Now I want to ask: What provision had been made for the benefit of these people in this particular Budget? The area I represent is North Eastern Area and the name of the State is Meghalaya and the constituency I represent is Garo Hills District.

It had been the policy of the Government, especially of the Janata Government that special attention would be paid to those areas which are backward and hilly. My area falls under both the categories. It is hilly as well as the most backward.

Last year, during the discussion on the Railway Budget, I had also pointed out all these conditions and I was trying to impress upon the honourable Railway Minister that steps should be taken to link this State with the railway line. Unfortunately, nothing has been done. The Ministers, as usual, try to dodge us by saying that due to constraint of resources it cannot be done. I do not know for how many years this constraint of resources will continue. We have seen the constraint of resources for the last thirty years. I do not know for how many years more we are going to have it.

I had put a question last year to know as to how many States and Union Territories in India have not been linked with railways. The answer is that the following States and Union Territories do not have any railway link: they are Manipur, Meghalaya, Arunachal Pradesh, Mizoram, Sikkim, Andaman and Nicobar Islands, Dadra and Nagar Haveli, and Lakshadweep. These are the States and the Union Territories which have not been linked with the railway lines so far. If you look at the list you will find that all these States and most of the union Territories are located in a particular region and that is the North Eastern region. The North Eastern region is a very important region. It has always been said that it was also a sensitive region. The 'railway line' has been defined as a necessary ingredient for the infrastructure of the economic development.

Apart from this, the North Eastern region has a special importance. It borders the international border. On one side, it is the Chinese border; on the other side, it is Burma border and on the third side, it is the Bangladesh border. We may recall that the country had to face the war twice and both times the war took place in the North Eastern region. In 1962, we had to face the Chinese aggression and in 1970, we had to face the Bangladesh war. So, even from the defence point of view, it is very very important that this region has to be linked with the railway line.

Our people in those areas are so poor and so illiterate that it is beyond imagination. There are places where for centuries there is no communication. If the people have to get their daily needs, if the people have to buy a kilo of salt or a litre of kerosene, they have to walk continuously for two or three days in order to reach a particular market. We always talk that special attention will be given to the backward areas. Every year we expect something but nothing comes out. Even this year, we do not find anything in the Railway Budget.

Again, last year, during the Railway Budget discussion, I had demanded that a railway line should be opened from Goalpara up to Maheshkhola along the border. The Minister was kind enough to reply to me saying that the proposal has been looked into and that a portion of the proposed railway line from Goalpara to Mahendraganj has been already surveyed. I also understand that there are two more railway lines in my State where the survey has been completed. They are Gauhati – Burnihat and Jogighopa–Darangiri. These are the three lines where the survey works had been completed. I would, therefore, appeal to the Railway Ministry to see that, if not all, at least one of the lines should be taken up this year so that a stage of 'take-off' can be launched. With these words – since there is no time – I conclude my speech.

Thank you.

Bringing Tribals to the Mainstream*

Mr Chairman, Sir, at the very outset, I would like to extend my sincere thanks to the honourable Minister of Railways, Professor Dandavate, for having shown good gesture to our region that is, North Eastern region, by bringing forward a proposal of constructing new lines in the six Hill States of the North Eastern region. I can assure him that this proposal will bring in the hearts of our people a lot of expectations. But I would at the same time like to point out that considering the long-standing due and neglect shown to our region, this proposal is not at all adequate, if

*_L.S. Deb._, 8 March 1979 (Spoke while participating in the general discussion on the Railway Budget, 1979-1980).

equal justice is to be given to our people. I want to analyse some of the problems and some of the misconceptions that are in the minds of the people here at the Centre, in so far as our region in concerned. The Central leaders have not been able to understand the actual problems of our region. The people in the rest of the country have not yet understood the problems and the conditions under which we are living there. There are people who misunderstand us and the people in other parts of the country accuse us that we have not come in the fold of the national mainstream. If the people of our region have not come to the national mainstream today, it is because we have been compelled to live in isolation. Here I may bring to the notice of the honourable Members an interesting point that a majority of the people in our region have not even seen the train. They do not know what the train is. Not even one per cent of the people in our region have seen other parts of the country. The greatest bottleneck is the transport system and, therefore, every item is so costly in our region. There is another criticism which many people very often speak of us. They say that the hilly States in the North Eastern region, the small States, always ask for more grants from the Centre; they always want Central assistance, and they do not have revenues of their own. I may tell you, Sir, that the cost of development in our region is very high; the people in Delhi or in the rest of the country will not understand that. If one has to construct a small house, even if one kilometre of road has to be constructed by a government agency, everything has to be carried by bullock carts or by human labour. At certain places, these can be carried by trucks, but this is possible at a few places. Therefore, if a road has to be constructed in our region, it may cost ten to twenty times than the cost of construction in the rest of the country. That is the reason we require more money from the Central Government and we have to depend much on the Central Government.

There is another difficulty with us. We do not have proper means of transportation and the result is that we are not in a position to exploit the mineral resources. Our region is very rich in mineral resources, in forest products, but because of lack of means of transport, we cannot exploit them; we cannot do anything there. That is why, I have been trying to impress upon this House – I did so last year also while participating in the Railway Budget and have been saying that from time to time – that it is very important that our region should have proper railway links. I am very happy that the honourable Railway Minister has understood this; this Government has understood this and at least a few kilometres of new railway lines have been given to each of the six hilly States of our region.

While taking up the new schemes, I only wished the honourable Railway Minister would have considered carefully as to which lines should be taken first in my State; surveys have been carried out in respect of three lines. These are: Gauhati to Barnihat, Jogighopa/Pancharatna to Darangiri, and Goalpara to Mahendraganj.

* * *

I wish that the honourable Railway Minister should have taken either of the two other lines. The other two lines seem to me to be more important. These lead to places where mineral resources exist and can be exploited. The railway lines would have scope for further extension also. The Gauhati to Barnihat line which has been taken this year, ends at that point. It cannot be extended further. Economically, it is not very much viable. I wish, the other two lines should have been taken and I would urge upon the honourable Railway Minister to consider this seriously.

Then, I am thankful to the Railway Minister that they are going to construct another bridge over the Brahmaputra. But there was another proposal, and an important proposal. To the best of my information, the honourable Governor of the North Eastern States and the North Eastern Council have made a recommendation for construction of a third bridge over the Brahmaputra at Jogighopa/Pancharatna. This bridge is very important. And to my information, the NEC has recommended that this bridge should be constructed on a priority basis. I would urge upon the honourable Railway Minister to take up the construction of this bridge so that the other parts of the North Eastern region which would depend on the construction of this bridge very much have proper development and many more things can also be done.

With these words, I conclude. Thank you.

Condition of Primary Schoolteachers in Meghalaya*

Sir, I would like to bring to the notice of the Government of India and the august House the problems faced by the lower primary schoolteachers in the East and West Garo Hill districts of Meghalaya for irregular payment of salaries. Sometimes, the teachers do not receive their salary for three to four months. The delayed payment of salary to teachers has become a normal practice in Meghalaya. This is causing severe hardship to the teachers. They face great difficulty in meeting their expenditure. The entire family of the teachers is put to inconvenience. There are nearly 2,500 teachers in these areas where non-payment of salary in time has assumed a serious and grave problem. There is great resentment among the teachers. If no timely action is taken, the situation will get aggravated. The teachers plan to stage demonstrations and adopt other methods to force the authorities to heed their just demands. The Union Government have allotted huge sums of money to Meghalaya State for education. Probably, this money is being diverted on other items by the District Council authorities. The teacher community is suffering from this malady for the last several years.

The teachers are losing interest in their work, and this is having adverse effects on the quality and level of teaching. A dissatisfied and hungry teacher cannot do justice to his pupils. They are on the verge of losing their patience. I request the Union Government to impress upon the authorities of the State to ensure that the teachers get their salaries in time, otherwise, the situation may take an unpleasant turn at any moment. I hope the Government will take early and immediate action in the matter. Thank you.

**L.S. Deb.*, 9 May 1979 (Spoke while participating in the discussion under Rule 377 regarding irregular payment of salaries to the primary schoolteachers in certain parts of Meghalaya).

Status of Scheduled Tribes in the North East*

Mr Deputy Speaker, Sir, the Scheduled Castes and the Scheduled Tribes constitute one-fifth of the total population of this country. The fate and the future of these one-fifth people among the total population of this country has been the subject matter of the debate and the discussion in the Constituent Assembly, after which, certain provisions have been made in our Constitution to protect and to safeguard the interests of these Scheduled Castes and Scheduled Tribes people.

After the Constitution has been enacted, this august House has discussed the fate and the future of these Scheduled Castes and Scheduled Tribes people – I don't know how many times in the last 32 years. Several Commissions have been appointed. Several thousands of leaders have shed their crocodile tears.

* * *

After all that has been done so far, the result according to Report is this. I quote from this Report:

> Three decades of independence and the dawn of freedom is yet to bestow a willing smile on many a hamlet and slums of the Scheduled Castes and Scheduled Tribes. They continue to submit to the decrees of fate rater than have the benefits of the decrees of our basic law. Liberty, Equality and Fraternity, so richly enshrined in the Constitution of the country have still to acquire any meaningful proposition for most of them. Untouchability has been abolished by Article 17 of the Constitution, but those whose article of faith in this pernicious persuasion is superior to an article of the Constitution choose to defy the fundamental law with impunity.

That is law, such as the Protection of the Civil Rights Act, with more stringent provisions to eradicate untouchability, had to be enacted in the thirtieth year of our freedom by amending the Untouchability Offences

---

**L.S. Deb.*, 15 May 1979 (Spoke while participating in the Motion for Discussion regarding the Twenty Third and Twenty Fourth Reports of the Commission for Scheduled Castes and Scheduled Tribes).

Act, 1955, bears ample testimony of the fact that we continue with our sin of denying basic human right to quite a sizeable section of our people.

There are many areas in the country where the Scheduled Castes are denied even common sources of drinking water. At places, they dare not take out funeral processions through the same route on which others do.

The nation's resolve made with due solemnity to secure to all the citizens 'Justice—social, economic', has remained just a promise, honoured perhaps more in breaches in the case of the Scheduled Castes and Scheduled Tribes. Political justice, even if available, loses much of its meaning if it is bereft of the social and economic justice.

After reading the Commission's Report, I thought, today it is the fourth day that the august House is discussing this matter, I could not make up my mind as to whether I should participate in this discussion at all. I say this because of the fact that though discussions have been held, though many promises have been made, though many laws have been enacted, yet, the fate of these people still remains the same. I don't see any useful purpose for discussing this matter when the fate of these people still remains the same. I think it is time for us to examine as to where is the real mistake. If thirty-two years of independence could not give any justice to these people, I think, we should see where the mistake lies. There are laws, but the real problem is the implementation of these laws. Many honourable Members have pointed out the lapses in this connection. Though there are provisions under our Constitution to safeguard and to protect their interests, yet we find that the people who are implementing these laws somehow do not like these laws. So, what is important is the change of attitude. What is necessary and important is the re-education of the administrative personnel, their outlook; what is important is to restructure our social set-up. Any amount of law, any amount of discussion, any amount of shouting on the floor of the House will not change the fate of these people. Unless there is a change of heart in those who are administering the country, in those people who are running this country, the economic and social status of these people will not improve. I would like to give some suggestions in this context, which I think, will to some extent solve the problem. There are two aspects of this matter. One is the social injustice, that is, atrocities done to these people which we are talking about and the other aspect is the economic aspect. I am proud to point out from the Report, Part-2, page 49:

> As regards the atrocities on the *Harijans* and on the Scheduled Castes and Scheduled Tribes, in the year 1974, 1975 and 1976, in the State of Assam, in the State of Manipur, in the State of Meghalaya, in the State of Nagaland and in the State of Arunachal Pradesh, there has been no case of any atrocities on *Harijans*.

I do not know about West Bengal. Maybe in West Bengal also, there were no atrocities during this period. Why I am pointing out this that in the North Eastern region, most of the States like Meghalaya, Nagaland, Manipur, Arunachal Pradesh, etc., the majority of the people are Scheduled Tribes. So, the question of atrocities on the Scheduled Castes and Scheduled Tribes does not arise, because we are ruling our own people. This kind of atrocity is happening only in those States where the majority of the people are the caste Hindus. Where the Scheduled Castes are in minority, the caste Hindus are exploiting them. Therefore, if your want to serve the cause of these people, I think, we should go in for having smaller States so that in those areas where Scheduled Castes and the Scheduled Tribes are predominant, they may be given a separate State and those people are in a position to run the administration according to their own genius. There are demands in Bihar, there are demands in Uttar Pradesh, that these States should be divided into smaller States. Therefore, in a compact area where the majority of population is SC and ST they should be given a separate State so that nobody can have any chance of exploiting those people. Where it is not possible to grant them a separate State, I think some autonomy should be given to those districts where the majority of SC and ST people live. Separate districts can be created within the States for this purpose so that in these districts there could be autonomy on the lines of the Sixth Schedule of the Constitution of India. Now, before small States were created in the North Eastern region, all of us were under the State of Assam. Even then, we were in our own district given autonomy under the Sixth Schedule of the Constitution of India. There was no question of atrocities even at that time. My humble suggestion today is, wherever it is possible, wherever SC and ST live in majority; they should be given political rights and once they are given political rights, social justice will automatically come. The only thing is that we should help them financially so that they may get the economic upliftment. The rulers of the country are taking shelter in the name of protection being given to them and that their welfare is taken care of by giving educational and other facilities in order to raise their economic and social status. Before we talk of protection of the Scheduled Castes and Scheduled Tribes, we should talk about the liberation of these people. We should liberate these people, give them political rights, give them social justice and give them equality and then we should come forward to help them financially. This is only way to solve the various problems facing the Scheduled Castes and Scheduled Tribes.

Assam Agitation: Dilemma between the Ideology of Regionalism and Nationalism*

What is happening in Assam and in the North Eastern region today is a peculiar phenomenon which perhaps has no precedent elsewhere. Many honourable Members who have spoken earlier, have expressed their fear that if the situation in Assam is allowed to continue, then there may be a lot of repercussions, and similar movements elsewhere in the country. Somebody has pointed out that similar sentiments are now being expressed in Orissa, Bengal and some other States like Bihar. I would go a step further and say that such a sentiment may not only have repercussions in our own country; it may also have repercussions in the international arena.

Many things have been said about the nature of the movement. But one thing I want to make this august House to realize is the real feeling that is going on in the North Eastern region. The problem of Assam cannot be studied in isolation; it has to be studied in a broader way taking the North Eastern region as a whole.

What is important to understand in the North Eastern region today is the political trend that is emerging. I would like to draw the attention of the House to a particular statement of All Assam Students Union (AASU). They said that they had no faith on the national parties; national parties cannot solve this problem. If we look at the agitation in Meghalaya which is my State or in Arunachal Pradesh, we find that this is the movement where some national parties are involved but they are using the regional parties of that area as the instrument. Therefore, I

**L.S. Deb.*, 9 June 1980 (Spoke while participating in the statutory resolution on President's Rule in Assam).

would say that it is very important for the rest of the country to understand the political trend that is emerging in our region.

The movement is part of a larger crisis – an ideological crisis that is going on. There is a conflict between the ideology of regionalism and nationalism. There is a conflict between the ideology of living in isolation and joining the mainstream of national life. There is a conflict between ideology of protection and liberation, between safeguard and competition and between culture and modernization. The basic issue that emerges out of the popular slogan of foreign nationals which has almost become a style in the North Eastern region is the preservation of the identity and the culture of people.

There are two schools of thought. The regional parties say that their identity can be preserved by being in the regional parties. Once they join the national parties, more outsiders will come, more foreigners will come; and they will be outnumbered. Therefore, they cannot protect themselves; they cannot safeguard themselves by being in the national parties. There are leaders in the North Eastern region who are national minded, who belong to national parties; and they say that if we want to preserve our identity, it is only by joining the national mainstream that we can safeguard ourselves, because we cannot protect ourselves; somebody has to protect us. It is the Constitution of India which protects us. Take the case of Meghalaya or other tribal areas. It is the Sixth Schedule in the Constitution which provides protection for the tribal people. They have been preserving their identity and culture only because of the Sixth Schedule of the Constitution. If today Parliament which is ruled by the national party decides to do away with the Sixth Schedule of the Constitution, where is their identity? Can a regional party in Meghalaya or Arunachal Pradesh say that their identity can be preserved if Parliament today decides to take away the Sixth Schedule from the Constitution? It is not. Therefore, the tribal leaders of Assam or other parts of the North Eastern region are trying to convince the people in the area that it is only by joining the national parties that they can come up. This is a serious problem in our region. I have told you that the choice is between living in isolation and joining the national mainstream. If we want to go in for development, we do not have people of our own; we do not have engineers, technicians, doctors, etc. If we want development, we have to bring people from outside, then regional parties will say, outsiders are coming in; or identity is lost and that kind of thing. Shall we, therefore, remain backward, remain in isolation or shall we join the national

When the world
was young.

Sangma (third row, seventh from right) with his college classmates.

Another memory from college (Sangma in the front row, second from left).

Sangma with Capt.
W.A. Sangma.

Hand in hand with
newly wedded bride
after the wedding
ceremony.

Sangma with wife soon after marriage.

The then President, R. Venkataraman, administering the oath of office of the Minister of State, Coal (Independent Charge), to P.A. Sangma, at a ceremony at Rashtrapati Bhavan on 21 June 1991.

The then President, Shankar Dayal Sharma, administering the oath of office of the Minister of Labour to P.A. Sangma, at a ceremony at Rashtrapati Bhavan on 9 February 1995.

The then Speaker of Lok Sabha, P.A. Sangma, on his arrival at the exhibition on '50 years of Independence' in the Parliament Annexe on 26 August 1997.

P.A. Sangma inaugurating the exhibition.

P.A. Sangma with Public Accounts Committee chairman Murli Manohar Joshi and others, at the Conference of Chairmen of Committees of Public Accounts of Parliament and State Legislatures held in New Delhi in March 1997.

P.A. Sangma speaking on the occasion of the unveiling of the statue of Netaji Subhash Chandra Bose in the Central Hall of Parliament on 23 January 1997.

P.A. Sangma with the leader of an Australian parliamentary delegation on 26 August 1996.

P.A. Sangma with an Egyptian parliamentary delegation in February 1997.

Speaker P.A. Sangma with the then Deputy Speaker, Suraj Bhan, on the occasion of the inauguration of the exhibition on the Parliament of India on 13 July 1996.

K.R. Narayanan delivering his maiden address as the President of India in the Central Hall of Parliament on 25 July 1997. Also seen are Shankar Dayal Sharma, the outgoing President, P.A. Sangma, the then Speaker of Lok Sabha, Najma Heptulla, the then deputy chairperson of Rajya Sabha, and J.S. Verma, the then chief justice of India.

P.A. Sangma with the then prime minister, H.D. Deve Gowda, and others, after paying tribute to Bal Gangadhar Tilak on his birth anniversary on 23 July 1996.

P.A. Sangma with the then prime minister, Atal Bihari Vajpayee, MP Mamata Banerjee and others, paying tribute to Rabindranath Tagore on his birth anniversary in the Central Hall of Parliament on 9 May 1998.

Shankar Dayal Sharma, the then President, presenting the Outstanding Parliamentarian Award for the year 1996 to Somnath Chatterjee in the Central Hall of Parliament on 19 March 1997. Also seen are K.R. Narayanan, the then vice president of India, H.D. Deve Gowda, the then prime minister, and P.A. Sangma, the then Speaker, Lok Sabha.

With the then prime minister, I.K. Gujral.

P.A. Sangma with a foreign parliamentary delegation.

There are few barriers to reaching out for this gentleman politician.
P.A. Sangma at the Great Wall of China.

P.A. Sangma
and wife with
the former
President of
India, Shankar
Dayal Sharma.

Sangma with wife, Soradini Kongkal Sangma, sons James and Conrad, and daughters Christi and Agatha.

P.A. Sangma showing a lighter side of his personality.

Books are his closest friends.

mainstream? The protection which is given to the tribal areas in the North Eastern area in the Sixth Schedule has not worked very much. We have discussed this with the national leaders, with the honourable Prime Minister we discussed this point recently. The point is: protection is there but people are incapable of protecting themselves. It is something like giving a gun to a person who does not know how to fire. So people belonging to the national parties, people who rule this country should realize that if we want to bring a lasting and permanent solution to the problem in Assam and North Eastern areas, a serious attempt must be made to bring people to the mainstream of national life. If we encourage regional feelings and allow regional parties to come up, this issue can be solved temporarily but I can tell you that there will be no permanent solution. Therefore, my appeal to the national parties will be to keep this point in mind. I was, in fact, surprised when some of the national parties refused to attend the meeting convened by the honourable Prime Minister.

* * *

Prof. Madhu Dandavate is a trade union leader; there are many, we are trade union leaders. We have been in a humble way student leaders and youth leaders and have also been leading some movements. Launching a movement is not a new thing. It was there from the time democracy was born. What is the main idea of demonstration or movement? The main idea or objective of a movement of this kind is to draw the attention of the Government to the problems which we are trying to project. Today the Assam movement has drawn the attention of the Government. The honourable Prime Minister and so many national leaders have repeatedly and categorically stated: we fully appreciate the sentiments of the people of Assam; we understand their problems; we will solve this problem. Their attention has been drawn. Yet the movement is being carried on. Many members have pointed out the effects of this movement on national economy. I do not want to deal with this. The people in the North Eastern region are the worst sufferers in this movement. Arunachal Pradesh, Nagaland, Manipur, Meghalaya, Mizoram and Tripura have to go through Assam to go out or to come in. Even in my state, Meghalaya, two districts, East and West Garo Hills have no direct road link from their headquarters to the state capital. We have to pass through Assam. After the last parliamentary session when

I went to my constituency, the day I reached there, I contacted the district administration. They told me that the rice movement had stopped. For the entire two Garo districts of Meghalaya, the quantity was 137 quintals. We had 1,300 litres of Kerosene for the two districts. There was no diesel. There was no petrol. There was no bus service from Gauhati to Tura, no bus service from Shillong to Tura. Even within the district, there was no transport communication at all. There was no telephone communication because there was no power. Because of shortage of diesel, there was no power in the entire district. From 6.30 to 9.30 there was power. It could not be used in telephone exchange. That time was not enough to charge the battery which was being used in telephone exchange. Postal and telegraph services were completely dislocated. Even to communicate this particular situation to the honourable Prime Minister, I had to take the help of police and paramilitary telecommunication system. There was no communication.

The price of sugar was Rs 10 per kilo. It was not available at all. Salt was being sold at Rs 6 per kilo. The Deputy Commissioner asked me to go to his place and said that there were only 1,300 litres of kerosene. All over the district, the school and college examinations were going on. People were complaining. Law and order had to be maintained. How to distribute 1,300 litres of kerosene? We ultimately decided that we would give one litre each to police station and some to hospitals and whatever was left over we would give to the students appearing in the examination. This was the condition in Arunachal Pradesh, this was the condition in Meghalaya and this was the condition of the people in the rest of the North Eastern region.

In the name of the foreign nationals issue or in the name of any issue, people should not be allowed to die of starvation. Therefore, the immediate solution has to be found out. But, again I want to stress in the long-term measures, the national leaders should think of how to bring the people in the North Eastern region in the mainstream of national life. This was almost achieved during the time of Prime Minister Indira Gandhi before 1977. By 1976, most of the regional parties were convinced that their future lay in joining the mainstream of national life. Therefore, most of the regional parties merged into the Congress party. They were becoming national-minded. What happened in between? A very unfortunate thing happened. Shri Biju Patnaik is not here. He had said that they had not sent army to Assam. They had not done it. Well, they have not done anything. I quite agree with him.

Whatever had been done previously, had been undone by them; whatever had been constructed previously, had been dismantled by them. During the entire two and half years of Janata rule, the entire thing was mishandled in the North Eastern region. Well, I will not blame all the Janata leaders. I will blame particularly the then Prime Minister Shri Morarji Desai. He goes to Shillong and says, 'You have to learn Hindi in one year. If you cannot do that, you go out of India.' I challenged him here on the floor of the august House and said, 'I will learn your Hindi in one year, but you must also learn my Garo in one year.' He went to Nagaland. Six Naga leaders came to see him. The first question he put to them was, 'Are you Indian citizens?' The Nagas were provoked and they said, 'We are Nagas.' Then he said, 'I will not talk to you; you get out.' Then it was reported that he called Laldenga, the Mizo leader, not to solve the problem of Mizos, but only to utter one sentence, 'I don't trust you.' He goes to London, meets Phizo and says, 'I will exterminate the Nagas.' These are the things which go to the root of the sentiments of the people of the area. One character of the tribals which you should understand is that this kind of forcible imposition cannot be accepted by the people that side. You say, 'If you do not learn Hindi in one year, you should go out of India!' I will not blame the entire Janata Party for this. But the then Prime Minister said it. Those who were in the sixth Lok Sabha know that there was a Member by name Smt. Rano Shaiza from Nagaland. She belonged to the Janata Parliamentary Party. When she went to discuss the Naga problem with the Prime Minister, he said, 'You do whatever you like. I do not care for territory. If you want to go away, go away!' Imagine the Prime Minister of the country talking on these lines! Is this the way to handle the situation? If we do not make an attempt to bring these people into the mainstream of national life, I think we cannot have any permanent solution to the problem. There are many people who think in the Centre that the tribal people are very much averse to the national parties. It is not so. I have been in the Congress from the very beginning of my political life. Even during those days when the regional parties used to rule Meghalaya, I have been all along in the Congress party. During the last parliamentary election, in Assam and in Meghalaya there was a movement that there should not be any election until the foreign nationals' names were deleted from the electoral rolls, 500 to 600 students came to gherao me saying, 'You should not file your nomination.' I put them several questions. I asked, 'What is your demand?' They said,

'The foreign nationals' names should be deleted.' I brought the electoral rolls and told them, 'Here are the electoral rolls. Whoever are foreign nationals according to the Government, their names have been deleted. If you have any additional names of foreign nationals, tell me.' They said, 'We do not know.' I said, 'If you yourselves do not know who are the foreign nationals, how can you say that foreign nationals' names should be deleted? Who has given you the power to say that there should not be election? Who has given the power to the 500 students to speak on behalf of six lakh of people in the constituency? If the six lakh people think that there should not be elections, let them not come to the polling booths. This is what I said in every election campaign of mine. But there was 87 per cent to 90 per cent polling in my parts of my constituency out of which my party, Congress-I, got 74 per cent votes of the total votes cast. We have not only won in every Assembly segment, but we have practically won in all the polling booths. The so-called regional parties, who are trying to create problems in my district and also in Meghalaya, they not only lost their deposit but they drew a blank in many polling stations.

It is not a fact that tribal people are not for national parties. We have a Congress-I Government in Arunachal Pradesh. In the last election in Nagaland, out of perhaps thirty-two seats which we have contested, we have won fifteen seats in spite of all the efforts of Shri George Fernandes, being there permanently. We have won the parliamentary seat also in the last parliamentary poll.

I advise the people sitting on the opposite, if you are sincere in solving this problem, please do not try to play with the things which are going on there. Do not try to politicize the issue. Do not try to encourage regional sentiments which are going on in the region. If you do so, then there is no meaning in making long speeches here on national integration or unity of the country. If you are really sincere in solving this problem, then you should not encourage these regional feelings.

With these few words, I conclude. Thank you.

Situation in Assam: Paralysing Normalcy in the North East*

I rise to oppose the resolution moved by honourable Member Shri Fernandes and to support the Bill introduced by the honourable Minister, Shri Makwana.

At the very outset, I would like to place this on record that I fully share the genuine sentiments and aspirations of the people of Assam on the foreign nationals issue. This issue is not confined to Assam alone. In fact, it concerns the entire North Eastern region. So, I know what the real feeling in that area is. But, while appreciating the genuine concern of the people of that area, I must point out to the leaders of the movement in Assam that their purpose has been achieved, that the continuation of this movement is counterproductive to the people and, therefore, they should now seriously think of a solution.

Shri Fernandes and other friends on the other side have opposed this Bill. My honourable friend, Shri Santosh Mohan Dev was very harsh to them. I would like to plead with him not to be so harsh because they are opposing this Bill. The reason perhaps is that they do not know what is actually going on in the North Eastern region.

The nine months' long agitation in Assam has not only affected the State of Assam, it has affected the entire North Eastern region. The august House will remember that on the opening day of this session I had put forward before the House the hardships that were being faced by the people. Shri Santosh has given ample examples to show how the people are suffering there. You are talking about the working class. This Bill has nothing to do with them. It deals with the people of the entire North Eastern region, the starving people there, and you are advocating the cause of the working class. It is not the working class that is suffering there, it is the common people who are suffering. There is no rice, no communication, no essential commodities. The normal life of the people has been completely paralysed and dislocated. I do not understand

**L.S. Deb.*, 3 July 1980 (Spoke while participating in the discussion on resolution regarding (i) Approval of Notification issued by the Assam Government declaring certain services as essential, (ii) Disapproval of Essential Services Maintenance (Assam) Ordinance, and (ii) consideration of the Bill regarding Essential Services maintenance in Assam).

why you talk only of the working class when today we are concerned with the people, not the working class alone.

Do you know there are places in my constituency where if you want to buy a piece of soap, you have to go two days on foot to reach the market? Do you know that in order to reach the police station, one has to walk seven days? Have you ever been in the North Eastern region, have you ever known the people there, have you ever seen the hills there, realized what a difficult life the people are facing there? And you are talking of the working class when people are dying of starvation; do not have the minimum necessities of life? Because of this movement, everything has been stopped. From tomorrow onwards again there will be no train service. You do not know. I am trying to educate you. Why don't you get yourself educated? You must get yourself educated about our region. Do you know how many people are stranded? I have got about 35 boys of an excursion party in my house, who are stranded because they cannot go back to our part due to the bandh in Assam. Do you know that people are seriously ill there, but cannot be brought to Delhi hospitals because there is complete dislocation? Do you know the real sufferings of the people there? They are starving for so many days. Thousands and thousands of students have lost their studies for a year. Can we compensate for the students who are doing technical education, engineering, medical – in every field, who have lost one year? This year, we do not have any colleges where we can send our students. We are trying to impress upon the Government of India that our students, a larger number of them, should be given admission outside the North Eastern region, the medical colleges have been closed because of the movement. How are you going to build the society? A very respectable Assamese gentleman, the other day when the IAS examination results appeared, rang me up and said that there is no Assamese boy who has passed the IAS examination this year. Assamese are intellectuals, there are so many Assamese who had become IAS officers in the last so many years. In fact, the North Eastern region is fed by Assamese intelligentsia, but today, we have no Assamese coming out successful, nobody has appeared for the examination. Is it the way we are going to build our society?

* * *

That is why the present Government is trying to help the people there. In the name of the working class, it is said that this Bill is anti-people.

* * *

Mr Fernandes said: 'I do not know how the Government is being run.' Well, that has been understood by the people of this country and it is precisely because you did not know how to run the Government, that, even though you were voted to power for a period of five years initially, the people have thrown you out of power. If you want to bring normal life in the North Eastern area, if you want to serve the people who have been completely cut off from the rest of the country, who have been denied of bare necessities of life, this bill has become a necessity, in fact, an absolute necessity. I received several telephone calls last night that we are trying to send some coal from our region to the rest of the country; everything has been dumped at New Bongaigon, there are no wagons. Something should be done about this. My friend from Arunachal Pradesh has been telling me that the people, who depend on the export of timber and plywood, have not been able to export these items because of the movement. Our geographical location is such that everything has to come via Assam to our region. Therefore, in order to save the starving people, this Bill is a necessity and I fully support it. Whatever points I had to say, I had already said in the last debate. I have always been saying them. Keeping in view the living conditions of the people there, at present their abject poverty and the lack of essential commodities there, this bill is brought forward to help the people. I do not know why Mr Fernandes said that it is anti-people, to make available the essential commodities like food articles and drinking water to the people there, that this Bill has been brought forward. With these words, I fully support the Bill. Thank you.

Strengthening the North East Administration*

I rise to support the demands for grants in respect of the Ministry of Home Affairs. I was thinking whether I should make a speech at all before I put myself and you, Sir, to embarrassment. I think I will take less time than you have allowed me and leave whatever is left of my time to my friend here, Shri Manoranjan Bhakta, as coming from a Union Territory he wants more time.

Shri Ram Jethmalani spoke very eloquently of insecurity and the uneasy feeling of fear in the minds of people of this country after our government came into being. But I think he left the House without telling the most important thing which he wanted to tell, and that was that during the two and half years of the Janata rule, the people of this country felt very secure and very safe! That part he forgets to tell.

Now he also speaks about the act of irresponsibility by the present government. I want to give only one example of how responsibly the Janata government acted during their regime. Many Members of the opposite side have brought out many points about the atrocities on Harijans and all that. Now, the Belchi incident took place on 27 May 1977 and the hearing of the case started on 5 February 1980, i.e., after two and half years, whereas in the case of an incident which has recently happened in Pipra, the incident took place on 25 February and hearing started on 8 April, that is, only after one and half month. Therefore, I do not know how they are going to justify this that they are acting very responsibly and our government has been acting very irresponsibly.

Mr Jethmalani also spoke that the turmoil in the North East started only after Shrimati Gandhi came into power. I do not know how much he knows about the North East. For his information, the turmoil in the North East region started much before this government came into being. He forgets that except two Members, we do not have any representatives from Assam in this House. This turmoil started before the last Lok Sabha elections. I do not know how he has said that this turmoil started after this government came into being.

We must tell this august House that we the people from the North

*_L.S. Deb._, 21 July 1980 (Spoke while participating in the general discussion on the demands for the Ministry of Home Affairs, 1980-1981).

East region really feel that we have been neglected for many years. But one thing I want to put on record. Whatever status we enjoy today in the political, social or economic field, I must say, is because of Prime Minister Shrimati Indira Gandhi. You remember that we the people in the North East was a component part of Assam. My community never had any representation in this House, so also Mizoram. And it was Assamese people who were representing the entire North Eastern region in this House. But it was Prime Minister Indira Gandhi who gave separate statehood to Meghalaya. It was she who created Mizoram. It was she who created Arunachal Pradesh. It was she who created Manipur and it was also Shrimati Indira Gandhi who gave statehood to Tripura. So, if we have any political status or social status today in this country, it is because of Prime Minister Shrimati Indira Gandhi.

I want to give a few suggestions. As I said, I do not want to take much time of the House. As far as the North Eastern region is concerned, I have some serious suggestions to make for the consideration of the honourable Home Minister. My honourable friend, Shri Chingwang Konya had suggested a few hours back that in order to solve the problem of the North Eastern region, a separate ministry should be created for this part. I support this suggestion. In fact this had been voiced by the people of the North Eastern region for quite some time. Therefore, I would urge upon the honourable Prime Minister to create a separate ministry for the North Eastern region. For some reason or the other, if it becomes difficult for the Government of India not to do so, I would give an alternative suggestion that there should be a separate ministry under the charge of the Prime Minister, for the welfare of Scheduled Caste and Scheduled Tribes and other minorities. In that ministry, there should be a separate cell to look after the North Eastern region because a major portion of that region is inhabited by the people belonging to the Scheduled Tribes.

Another important point that I want to make is this. There are five States in the North Eastern region and for these five States, we have a common Governor. Under the present conditions that are prevailing in that region today, I would earnestly urge upon the Government of India to appoint separate Governors for these five States because it is very difficult for one person to look after such big areas. The population in that part of the country may be less but because of transport bottlenecks, it is really difficult for a single person to look after the whole of the North Eastern region.

Then, there is a difficulty from the constitutional point of view. Mr Chingwang referred to the boundary dispute between Assam and Nagaland, between Assam and Meghalaya and between Assam and Arunachal Pradesh and between Assam and Mizoram. With all these States, we have got boundary disputes. It so happens that the Governor will address the Assam Assembly talking against Meghalaya and in Manipur he may speak against Nagaland and when he addresses the Nagaland Assembly he may speak against the Assam Government and vice-versa. While so doing he may contradict himself in the other Assembly. So, from the constitutional point of view, it is somewhat impractical for all the five States to have a common Governor in the North Eastern Region. Therefore, I would again urge upon the Government to appoint separate Governors for different States in the North Eastern region. Government of India was very kind to constitute the North Eastern Council for looking after the development of the entire region. Somehow, I have doubts about the smooth functioning of the North Eastern Council. Now in many of the regional councils and other bodies, Members of Parliament are associated. But, in this particular North Eastern Council, no Member of Parliament is associated so far.

I would urge upon the Government – Home Ministry – to see if it would be possible to have a representative or two from among the Members of Parliament, belonging to the North Eastern region in that Council.

Many honourable Members have spoken about the Mizoram problem. Well, I am happy that Government of India, the honourable Prime Minister and the honourable Home Minister are taking keen interests in the development of Mizoram. There have been talks in that regard. According to newspaper reports, talks are on between Mr Laldenga and Government of India for finding a peaceful solution to the Mizoram problem. I welcome this move. But, I want to warn the Government of India that there are people who are trying to see that these negotiations do not materialize.

I think that this group is represented by no less a person than Brigadier Sailo himself who is the Chief Minister. Therefore, I would caution the Government of India that there should be no person standing in the way of peaceful negotiations.

One more point I want to make. That is regarding the Constitution (Scheduled Castes and Scheduled Tribes) Orders of 1951 and 1976.

There are many communities who had been recognized as Scheduled Castes and Tribes in one State but they have not been recognized as such in other States. I urge upon the Government to remove this area restriction. For example, my community, Garo community, is recognized as a Scheduled Tribes community in Meghalaya, in Nagaland and even in West Bengal but we are not considered as scheduled tribes in Assam. We have got one lakh population of Garos in Assam but we are not recognized as Scheduled Tribes in Assam. In Assam Hajang are not recognized as Scheduled Tribes but they are recognized Scheduled Tribes in my State. There are communities in my place like Ravas and Koch which have been recognized as Scheduled Tribes in some other places but in my place they are not recognized as Scheduled Tribes. So, I would like the Government to consider this point and bring legislation towards the amendment of this order and remove the restrictions so that everybody is treated on an equal status throughout the country.

With these words, I support the demands of the Ministry of Home Affairs.

Peace through Development in the North East*

Mr Chairman, thank you very much. I am not going to deliver a speech. I will give only four suggestions.

The whole approach to the problem of the North East has to be peace through development. It is because in Delhi there are certain people who take a position that unless peace is restored, no development work can be done. But I do not believe in that. In fact, it has to be the other way round. You have to achieve peace through development. Peace through development should be the concept of the Government of India. That should be the approach of the Government of India

As far as development is concerned, so many points have been raised. I would only request that the packages which have been announced by the three successive Prime Ministers must be implemented and

**L.S. Deb.*, 31 July 1998 (Spoke while participating in the discussion under Rule 193 regarding the situation in the North Eastern region due to insurgency).

implemented effectively. The decision taken by Shri Deve Gowda, the then Prime Minister that every Ministry of the Government of India should earmark ten per cent for North East should be implemented.

It would be good to have more and more of Central Government agencies directly investing in the North East, especially in the area of plantation, commodities and horticulture. The agencies like the Central Rubber Board, the Tea Board, the Coffee Board and the Spices Board can play a very very big role in changing the economic scenario of the North Eastern States. It is because the North East is suitable for cultivation of all these goods.

Infrastructure, of course, is very bad. Some more investments have to be made in the infrastructure sector. I do not know what is the stand of the South Asia Free Trade Agreement (SAFTA), I do not know whether this issue was discussed in Colombo. It is a very relevant issue. I do not know what is the stand of Pakistan after the nuclear tests. But SAFTA is very very important from the point of view of economic development of the North East. So, I would like to know from the honourable Minister of Home Affairs if he has got any information whether SAFTA will come into operation by 2001 or not.

Next, I would request the Central Government to give full support to the State Governments. I am saying this because some of the smaller functionaries of this Government keep on saying a few things which are not at all helpful.

There was one aspect last year during the general elections. The underground people in Nagaland gave a boycott call and they said that the election should not be held in Nagaland. I think, we must be grateful to the Chief Minister of Nagaland, Shri S.C. Jamir, who took a very very firm stand saying that, 'Come what may, election will be held.' Suppose election was not held, then, it would have been a victory for the underground elements. But the Chief Minister took a firm stand and said that the election would be held and election was held. Of course, in many areas, people did not come to vote, that is a different matter. But the courage that has been shown by the Chief Minister himself in conducting the election is great and the nation should be grateful to such leaders. It is from this angle that I am saying that whoever runs the Government of India, as far as the North Eastern States are concerned – whichever Government is running the States in North East, it may be a Congress Government, I have not worded it at all – the Centre must give full support and backing to the Governments in the North East who are fighting against insurgency.

The third point that I would like to make is what should be the role of army. We have heard many unpleasant things today. I also firmly believe that Army should not be used to counter insurgency in the North East. I was very happy to have seen the statement of the Defence Minister, Shri George Fernandes, who has given his reasons also. It is better that we strengthen the local Governments and we get the cooperation of the people themselves there. Through army or through military, I do not think, there can ever be any solution.

Therefore, solution has to be through a dialogue, and I will appeal to the Government to start a dialogue with them.

Repealing the Armed Forces (Special Powers) Act, 1958, in Manipur*

Sir, first of all, I want your permission to speak from here. It is not my seat because I am yet to be allotted a seat. So, I have to get your permission to speak from here.

* * *

Thank you, Sir,

Sir, I want to draw the attention of the august House and through this august House, to the Government of India to the critical condition of Miss Irom Chanu Sharmila, who has been on fast unto death for the last six years. She is demanding for the repeal of the Armed Forces (Special Powers) Act, 1958.

Now, when I say that she has been on fast for the last six years, the House must be wondering how she is still alive. She is still alive because she has been arrested and taken to the All-India Institute of Medical Sciences. She is being forced-fed through her nose. Now her condition has become very critical. Recently, the honourable Prime Minister has visited and there the honourable Prime Minister has offered to amend the law. The people want the repeal of the law and the honourable

**L.S. Deb.,* 12 December 2006 [Spoke while participating in the special mention on the need to repeal the Armed Forces (Special Powers) Act, 1958, in Manipur].

Prime Minister wants the amendment of the law which is not acceptable. Therefore, she has removed her life support. Therefore, I thought it is a matter which is very urgent.

Sir, I am here to support her cause, the cause of the people of Manipur and I also demand that the Armed Forces (Special Powers) Act, 1958, should be repealed. I am demanding it not only to save the precious life of Ms Sharmila but also on its merit. I have gone through the law. If you go through it, you will find that the law does not deserve to exist.

This law was passed in 1958. It is almost 50 years now. When this law was passed, there was only one insurgent group. In 1980, when it was implemented, there were only four insurgent groups. Today, in Manipur alone, there are more than 25 insurgent groups. Therefore, Sir, this law, which is intended to curb the insurgency, has totally failed. Hence, it should be repealed. This Act has become a symbol of domination and repression. The Jeevan Reddy Committee, which was constituted by the Government of India went into it and the report says:

> The Act, for whatever reason, has become a symbol of oppression, an object of hate and an instrument of discrimination and highhandedness.

Further, the honourable Prime Minister himself says that it is an inhuman Act. When the honourable Prime Minister admits that it is an inhuman Act, why should this law be there? Therefore, the conclusion is that the Committee which went into this has specifically said:

> The Committee is of the firm view that the Armed Forces Special Powers Act, 1958, should be repeated.

Therefore, on behalf of the people of the North East, on behalf of the people of Manipur and in order to save the precious life of Ms Sharmila, I demand that the Act be repealed.

With these few words, I conclude. Thank you.

PART IV

Select Speeches in Rajya Sabha

MATTERS RELATING TO COMMERCE, INDUSTRY AND ECONOMIC DEVELOPMENT

Threat to the Survival of Print Media*

Sir, the National Newsprint and Paper Mills Limited, Nepa Nagar is the only unit in the country producing newsprint. The total requirement of newsprint in the current year is estimated to be about 4.1 lakh tonnes, but of which about 50,000 tonnes are being manufactured by the National Newsprint and Paper Mills. The remaining is being imported from different countries by the State Trading Corporation of India.

There is no statutory control on the price of NEPA newsprint but a fair selling price was being determined from time to time in consultation with the Bureau of Industrial Costs and Prices. In December 1978, the Bureau of Industrial Costs and Prices had carried out a Cost Price Study of NEPA newsprint and recommended a fair selling price of Rs 3085 along with an escalation formula for effecting revision in the selling price from time to time based on escalation on the major input factors, such as raw material, power, steam, chemicals, etc. The price of NEPA newsprint was, however, fixed at Rs 3,200 per tonne in April 1979 after allowing some margin on account of the difficulties experienced by NEPA Mills in attaining the capacity assessed by the Bureau of Industrial Costs and Prices. The NEPA newsprint price was further revised to Rs 3,682 effective from 17 March 1980 after taking into account the escalation on the items listed in the Bureau of Industrial Costs and Prices formula.

As the inflationary tendencies persist, the justified price for NEPA

---

*_R.S. Deb._, 8 September 1981 (Spoke while participating in the Calling Attention Motion regarding the reported increase in the price of the newsprints by the NEPA Mills posing a threat to the survival of medium and small newspapers and periodicals).

newsprint in September 1980 worked out to about Rs 4,275 per tonne. However, the figure was very close to the then prevailing price of Rs 4420 for 51 GSM imported newsprint. At this stage the Government took a decision that the future prices for NEPA newsprint will be related to the price of imported newsprint after taking into account the grammage differentials. As a result of this policy decision, the price effective from 25 October 1980 was allowed only at Rs 3886 per tonne.

As a further extension to the revised pricing policy and in order to expedite decision on pricing from time to time, the Government further decided in January 1981 to constitute an empowered subcommittee comprising of Chairman-cum-Managing Director, NEPA Mills, and two Government Directors to fix quarterly selling price of NEPA newsprint in line with the quarterly revision in the imported newsprint prices, after taking into account the grammage differentials.

The prices of the NEPA newsprint were revised as under from time to time by the empowered subcommittee:

Effective Date	*Price per Tonne*
1 January 1981	Rs 3956
1 April 1981	Rs 4277
1 July 1981	Rs 4700

On the last occasion of revision of price, the grammage was also verified by test reports from outside agencies. NEPA Mills had also worked out that according to the BICP formula the admissible price based on the cost of inputs would be Rs 4925 per tonne.

The prevailing prices of NEPA newsprint and the price of imported newsprint from time to time (other than Bangladesh) on high seas basis are summarized as under:

		PRICE PER TONNE *(in Rupees)*
Effective Date	*NEPA newsprint*	*Imported newsprint (during the relevant quarter)*
17 March 1980	3682	4090
25 October 1980	3886	4275
1 January 1981	3956	4365
1 April 1981	4277	4730
1 July 1981	4700	5195

The Indian and Eastern Newspaper Society has been representing that there have been frequent and substantial revisions in the price of NEPA newsprint during the last two years. They have also complained of the inferior quality and higher grammage of the NEPA newsprint. Efforts are being made continuously to improve the quality of NEPA newsprint but taking into account the constraints of the raw material being used indigenously (a mixture of bamboo and local hardwoods), it would be difficult to match the quality of imported newsprint which is based on pulp derived from safe woods. So far as grammage is concerned, due allowance is being made for the difference while determining the NEPA newsprint price.

Despite the revisions of price of NEPA newsprint being carried out from time to time, the mill has been facing various difficulties and its operations in the last few years have not been profitable. The total accumulated losses of the company amount to Rs 3.33 crore as on 31 March 1981. This is partly due to the unsuitability of the raw materials which has nevertheless to be utilized to the optimum extent having regard to the necessity to conserve our foreign exchange resources. The mill has also been experiencing power shortage as well as difficulties arising from operational deficiencies. The mill has undertaken a programme of renovation and it is expected that its capacity utilization would improve thereby leading to improvement in output as well as the financial position.

The Central Silk Board (Amendment) Bill, 1982*

Sir, I beg to move:

> That the Bill further to amend the Central Silk Board Act, 1948, as passed by the Lok Sabha, be taken into consideration.

**R.S. Deb.*, 25 and 31 March 1982 (Spoke while moving the Bill in the Rajya Sabha). The Bill provided for amendment of the Central Silk Board Act, 1948, inter alia providing for a specific term for the Chairman of the Central Silk Board, the method of removal of the Chairman before expiry of his term and also a corresponding right to the Chairman to relinquish his office before the expiry of his term.

Sir, at this stage, I would like to be very brief. Now, this bill seeks to amend Section 4 of the existing Act and also Section 13 of the existing Act. This Board has got 36 members, including the Chairman. The Chairman of the Board, who is one of the members, out of these 36, is appointed by the Central Government, under Section 4 of Act. Now, under Section 13 of Act, under which rules have been framed, the Chairman of the Board enjoys wide administrative and financial powers and the Secretary of the Board, who is also appointed by the Central Government, is to function under the general control of the Chairman. Sir, one important lacuna in the present Act is that there is no procedure indicated regarding the circumstances under which the Chairman of the Board can be removed, or, if he resigns, to deal with his resignation, when submitted. This matter has been broadly indicated in Section 13 of the Act, which deals with the rule-making power of the Board. Under these rules, the Central Government can remove a member of the Board, which includes the Chairman also, if he is convicted of any offence involving moral turpitude. It is now found necessary to incorporate in the provisions of the Act itself, regarding the specific term of the office of the Chairman and the method of his removal before the expiry of his term and also, a corresponding right to the Chairman to relinquish his office at any time before the expiry of his term, as fixed by the Government.

Taking advantage of this amendment, it is also proposed to amend Section 13 of the act, which seeks to provide the rule-laying formula in subsection 3, and this we are bringing strictly in conformity with the principle which has been recommended by the committee on both the houses of Parliament, both Lok Sabha and Rajya Sabha.

As I said, this is a very small amendment, a very minor amendment which only seeks to lay the procedure for removal of the Chairman and since it has been already passed by the Lok Sabha, I do not think the House should take much of its time, and with these words I move that the bill be taken into consideration.

* * *

Mr Deputy Chairman, Sir, I am thankful to the honourable Members, firstly for having supported the Bill, secondly, for having shown great interest in the development of the silk industry in the country. I am also thankful to many honourable Members who have given very good suggestions during the debate. I can assure the august House that all the suggestions which have been given will be examined.

Sir, as I said while moving the Bill for consideration, this amendment has very limited scope, and I described it as a very minor one because it seeks only to lay the procedure for removing the Chairman and for terminating the services of the Chairman. It also seeks to amend Section 13 of the Act, into which one honourable Member has tried to read many things. But this is strictly in conformity with the recommendations given by the Committees on Subordinate Legislation of both the Houses of Parliament, Lok Sabha as well as Rajya Sabha. So there is nothing to be said about that.

Though this Bill is confined to a very limited scope, as I said, the debate has covered the entire aspect of sericulture industry in this country. Though I do not propose to do with everything that has been said on the floor of the House, I do propose to touch upon certain important points which have been raised by the honourable Members.

The first thing which I would like to deal with is that it has been said by may honourable Members that the silk industry in our country has not grown, that Government has not given enough attention to the growing of the silk industry in this country and that the Silk Board had not functioned properly. Sir, this statement will not be completely true, and I must say that during the last three decades the silk industry in our country has shown a steady growth. Our production of raw silk in the country in 1950-51 was 900 metric tonnes, and in 1980-81, the production figure has reached to 5,041 metric tonnes. If we look at the export side of it, in 1950-51, our export of silk was to the tune of just Rs 53 lakh and, in 1980-81, our export figure is to the tune of Rs 53 crore. From Rs 53 lakh it has increased to Rs 53 crore, and by the end of this current year, we hope to reach the target of Rs 65 crore. And I may further say that by the end of the Sixth Five Year Plan our target is to reach Rs 100 crore.

Some honourable Members have also said that the government of India has not given much attention to the development of this industry and that sufficient money has not been invested for the development of the silk industry in this country. Sir, in the First Five Year Plan our allocation for the development of the silk industry was just Rs 45.9 lakh, and during the Sixth Five Year Plan, as the honourable Members are aware, our allocation is Rs 167.37 crore. Therefore, it may not be correct to say that the Government of India has not given any attention to the development of this industry. But I do agree with the honourable Members that perhaps much more could have been done. I do agree with the honourable Members that there is enough potentiality, enough scope in our country to develop sericulture industry, that there are many fields which have not been tapped so far. I can assure the august House that whatever is possible on the part of the Government of India, we are trying our best. But one thing is to be borne in mind that sericulture is a State subject and it is primarily the duty of the State Governments to develop sericulture in this country. Our duty as the Government of India, and function through the Central Silk Board, is to promote the growth of this industry and to extend some help and assistance to the respective State Governments. And I may also add – lest I should forget – growth of the silk industry, I must say that growth of the silk industry a few years ago, in 1978, our position was the fourth in the world in respect of the silk production, and today our position is the third. Once upon a time we were the fifth. From the fifth, we reached the position of the fourth in 1978, and today, we are in the third position.

Another good thing about our country is that ours is the only country in the world which produces all the four varieties of commercially known silk in the world, i.e., mulberry, tasar, eri and muga. As far as tasar is concerned, we are the second largest producer in the world, next only to Cochin. As far as muga is concerned, as many honourable Members have pointed out, we are the only country; we have the monopoly of muga in the world.

Many honourable Members have made some points. I will touch upon them very briefly. Mr Hegde is not here now. He had made only one point that this Bill is a very vindictive one and that this Bill has been brought only to punish a particular person, i.e., the present Chairman. Well, his allegation can be understood. Our intention, the intention of the Government, can be understood by the mere fact that the term of the present Chairman expires on the eighth of next month. Today is the last day of this month, and his term will be expiring on the eighth of the next month. It is just a question of one week. Therefore, I do not know how Mr Hegde has implied his motive in this Bill. I must also remind Mr Hegde that if we really wanted to be vindictive, if we really wanted to deny justice, why should we have given three months' notice? Many honourable Members have pointed out, 'Why are you giving three months' notice? Why can you not dismiss him with one month's notice?' We could have done that. But we did not want to be vindictive, we did not want to do any injustice, and that is why instead of giving one month's notice, the Government is giving three months' notice.

There are many honourable Members who have expressed their sentiment that the Government of India is giving importance to only one part of the country or one area of the country as far as the development of the sericulture industry is concerned. As I have already pointed out, Sir, sericulture is a State subject, and it is up to the State Government or even that of our Central Silk Board. It would not be fair to say that we are giving importance to only a particular State or area. We always try to give importance to all parts of the country, and I may say, Sir, that various development programmes are being implemented to increase the production of raw silk in the country, and the Indo-Swiss Interstate Tasar Project covering the States of Bihar, Madhya Pradesh, Orissa, Andhra Pradesh, Maharashtra, West Bengal and Uttar Pradesh is being implemented from 1981-82 onwards. The outlay on this Project is Rs 10.5 crore, and it is expected that with the implementation of this Project, the tasar raw silk production in the country will go up by 100 metric tonnes. Therefore, we are giving attention to all parts of the country.

Some honourable Members have said that no regional offices exist under the Central Silk Board. At the moment we have four regional offices located in various parts of the country, and I am happy to inform the august House that very shortly the Central Silk Board will be opening Regional Development Offices, one each in Assam, Orissa, Uttar Pradesh, Andhra Pradesh and Tamil Nadu.

* * *

There is already a regional office in Kashmir. That is already there.

And, then, some honourable Members have said, maybe because one honourable Member pointed out that I belonged to Assam, the North Eastern region, that we have not given much attention to the area. Maybe they tried to provoke me. The august House is aware of the importance this Government, particularly the honourable Prime Minister, is giving towards the development of the North Eastern region. It is not only in the field of the sericulture industry or a particular subject that the Government is giving importance to the development of the North Eastern region, but in all aspects.

* * *

I can assure the House that we are giving importance to the development of the sericulture industry, particularly in the field or muga, because, as I see we are having the world monopoly in this.

Sir, we are trying to give importance to the development of this particular variety of silk and we are doing our best for the development of this industry in the North Eastern region.

A point was raised as to why the qualifications have not been prescribed for the Chairman. Sir, the history of the chairmanship of the Silk Board is very long. This Silk Board had the privilege of having as Chairman personalities like Pandit Jawaharlal Nehru himself. Shri Shyama Prashad Mukherjee, who was the Commerce Minister, was the first Chairman of the Silk Board. The practice in the beginning was that the Minister in charge of Commerce used to be ex-officio Chairman of the Central Silk Board. Later on, because the Minister was very busy with so many other things, the practice was that it was chaired by the Textile Commissioner. It was only in 1968 and onwards that we had come up with the practice of having non-official Chairman, and from that time onwards we are having non-official Chairman. As it stands today, the post is a part-time post. The Chairman is not recruited by the Union Public Service Commission (UPSC) or by any other recruiting agency. I do agree with the honourable Members that while appointing the Chairman of the Central Silk Board, we must bear in mind that the person who is appointed to this post must have sufficient background of the silk industry and that he must have knowledge of the industry. This is always taken into consideration by the Government. I can assure the honourable Members that we shall continue to have this aspect in view when we appoint the Chairmen of the Silk Board.

Sir, I do not propose to deal with all the points that have been raised here. I can write to the honourable Members directly regarding some of the points which they have raised. I would appeal to this House to pass this Bill unanimously.

* * *

The honourable Member said about silk politics. The term 'silk politics' is very much unknown to me. I do not know what politics I spoke of. I only gave the figures of production, export, etc., do not know what more the honourable Member wants.

The honourable Member raised the point and actually I forgot to mention that. He said about import of raw silk from China. Many honourable Members have referred to it. Sir, according to the present policy, import of raw silk is banned. That is the import policy at present. But as one of the honourable Members has pointed out this year we had that uzi-fly menace in some of our silk-growing areas and in order to stabilize the price of raw silk, we had to resort to the import of raw silk of 250 tonnes. This is just a temporary arrangement to bring down the prices and to help the weavers. Many honourable Members have referred to the problems of weavers, particularly the Benares weavers. We are aware of the problems of the weavers. We are aware of the Benares weavers. The particular type of yarn that they require has not yet arrived. We hope that within the next couple of months, by April or the beginning of May, it will arrive and as soon as it arrives, we will distribute it to the weavers and we hope we would be able to help them to a certain extent. Thank you.

The Rubber (Amendment) Bill, 1982*

Sir, I beg to move:

> That the Bill further to amend the Rubber Act, 1947, be taken into consideration.

Sir, under the provisions of the Rubber Act, 1947, the Central Government have constituted the Rubber Board, whose duty is to promote by such measures as it thinks fit, for the development of the rubber industry in this country. The Rubber Board consists of a Chairman and twenty-four other members representing different interests. The main functions of the Board are:

(a) Undertaking, assisting and encouraging scientific, technological and economic research;
(b) supply of technical advice to rubber growers;

**R.S. Deb.*, 26 July 1982 (Spoke while moving the Bill in the Rajya Sabha). The Bill provided for appointment of an Executive Director in the Rubber Board and amendment of subsection 3 of Section 25 of the Rubber Act, 1947, to bring the formula w.r.t. the laying of rules before the Parliament in accordance with one which is currently in force.

(c) improving the marketing of rubber; and
(d) securing better working conditions and provisions and improvement of amenities and incentives for workers.

The post of Chairman, Rubber Board, is in the scale of pay of Rs 2,000 to 2,250. The Chairman is the chief executive of the Board and presides over its meetings. The Board has been implementing a large number of developmental schemes for boosting rubber production in the country. The expenditure of the Board is met from out of the releases made by Government every year from the Consolidated Fund of India.

Under subsection (3) of Section 4 of the Rubber Act, 1947, the Chairman of the Rubber Board is to be appointed by the Central Government. In the past, the post of Chairman in the scale of Rs 2,000 to Rs 2,250 had been filled by the Central Government by the appointment of a full-time officer generally belonging to the Indian Administrative Service. On occasion, a non-official was appointed as full-time Chairman.

It is observed that a number of persons who had distinguished themselves in the field of rubber plantations and are fully conversant with the problems relating to the development of the commodity are available in the private sector and from public life. In view of their vast experience with rubber plantations they can make substantial contribution to the rubber plantation industry and guide the affairs of the Board to great advantage. Such persons may not always be available for full-time service as Chairman while they may be prepared to render service in their capacity on a part-time basis Appointment of a part-time Chairman will, however, render it necessary to have a full-time Government officer to discharge most of the executive, administrative and other functions which, at present, are required to be performed by the full-time Chairman. It is in this context that it is proposed to provide for the creation of a statutory post of Executive Director. The Act does not at present, contain any provision for the appointment of an Executive Director in the Board and hence this Amendment Bill.

It has also been proposed to amend sub-section (3) of Section 25 of the Act to bring the formula with regard to the laying of rules before Parliament in accordance with the one which is currently in force.

With these few words, Sir, I would request that the Bill be taken into consideration.

* * *

Mr Vice Chairman, Sir, I am thankful to the honourable Members for having supported this Bill and also for having shown great interest in the rubber plantation industry as well as rubber-based industry in this country. I am also thankful to the honourable Members for having given valuable suggestions regarding the growth of plantation industry in our country. The honourable Members have rightly stressed the importance of rubber in our country. Rubber is a basic and important raw material required for the manufacture of a variety of products which find use in agriculture, transport and household sector. All the honourable Members who have participated in the debate have stressed, and rightly so, the importance and the need of increasing production of rubber in our country. The rubber plantation industry have recorded a commendable progress during the last three decades in our country, that is, since 1947 or since the Act came into being. The area under rubber plantation was 63,000 hectares in 1947. It has increased to 277,000 hectares in 1981-82. The production of natural rubber has also increased from 15,000 tonnes in 1947 to 152,000 tonnes in 1981-82. If we look at the productivity side, the production per hectare has also gone up from 320 kilograms to 800 kilograms due to our successful research work. In spite of that, I do agree with the honourable Members that we have not been able to produce enough rubber in our country. Honourable Members, and in particular Dr Bhai Mahavir, have mentioned about demand and supply. He also mentioned about the state of complete chaos in giving figures. We are aware of all these aspects that we have not been able to produce enough rubber in our country. The Government has been taking many steps to see that rubber production goes up in our country. For increasing the production of raw rubber in our country, the Rubber Board has implemented various developmental schemes. The most important developmental scheme operated by the Rubber Board is the Rubber Plantation Development Scheme for implementation during the Sixth Plan period. Although it is for the Sixth Plan it will operate up to 1993-94 and the financial outlay until then is Rs 49.7 crore. For 1982-83, the scheme has an outlay of about Rs 4 crore. To be precise, it is Rs 3.85 crore. The estimated area that will be benefited from the scheme, as Dr Bhai Mahavir has already pointed out, is about 30,000 hectares each under new plantation and replantation by the year 1984-85. I won't be dealing with all the developmental schemes that the Rubber Board is taking up at the moment, because of the paucity of time. But apart from this particular thing, there are various other schemes that have already been taken up by the Rubber Board. I will briefly mention that under the Rubber Development Scheme, we give a lot of assistance to the growers, such as cash subsidy which is Rs 5,000 per hectare to the small grower and Rs 3,000 per hectare to large growers. There is additional assistance to the weaker sections and small growers identified as those owning not more than six hectares of rubber plantations. This comprises reimbursing of cost of plantation, material used, half cost of fertilizers applied during the maturity period and a subsidy of up to Rs 150 per hectare for the soil conservation works undertaken. Then, under this scheme, long-term bank credit up to a maximum extent of Rs 15,000 per hectare, including the subsidy component, under the ARDC for implementing cash assistance from the Rubber Board is given. The interest on the loan which is normally up to 12 per cent per annum is subsidized by the Board to the extent of 3 per cent per annum. Then, under the same scheme, the Rubber Board also gives free advisory and expansion support to the growers. Then, the Rubber Board also maintains nurseries; the planting material required by the growers is made available partially from the Board's nurseries and partially from private nurseries. The Board has so far established ten nurseries with an annual production capacity of 1.2 million rubber plants per year. Then, we also have a scheme for improving the processing of small holders' rubber. Then, we have a scheme for marketing the small holders' rubber. Then, the most important thing, which many honourable Members have stressed, is the extension of the rubber cultivation in non-traditional areas.

As Dr Adiseshiah has rightly pointed out, rubber cannot be grown anywhere and everywhere. It needs a particular climate and the Rubber Board has undertaken surveys and a study as to which areas could be covered under rubber plantation in our country, and though till now the rubber plantation had been confined to certain States like Kerala, Karnataka and Tamil Nadu, the Rubber Board is now giving importance to extending this rubber plantation to non-traditional areas and the Rubber Board has found that in areas such as Assam, Tripura, Meghalaya, Arunachal Pradesh, Mizoram, Manipur, Maharashtra, Goa, etc., commercial plantation of rubber can be successfully carried out in some of these areas in these States on an extensive scale and we are doing our best to help the State Governments which are also giving importance to this rubber plantation, particularly in the North Eastern region because the States in the North Eastern region had realized that an alternative to the jhuming cultivation can be plantation industry, and that is why they are adopting the rubber cultivation in a big way in those areas. With this idea in view, three regional offices of the Board have been established, and they are functioning at Agartala which is in Tripura, Gauhati in Assam and Konda in Goa.

Then, Sir, during the Sixth Five Year Plan, an outlay of Rs 36 crore has been allocated by the Planning Commission for the development of rubber plantation industry. Now, out of this provision, a sum of Rs 8 crore is expected to be spent during the current year 1982-83. The actual expenditure on plan scheme during 1980-81 and 1981-82 was Rs 3.37 crore and Rs 4.81 crore, respectively. As, again an honourable Member has pointed out, the production target for the Sixth Five Year Plan is two lakh tonnes, we hope to achieve this target within the Sixth Plan period. To be very brief, I would refer to the point raised by some other honourable Members. They referred to the cost of production and they mentioned that something should be done about the welfare of the workers and labourers. We do admit that cost of production in our country is high. The reasons are that cost of inputs is very high, and when I say of inputs, it also includes fertilizers. Then, wages of the workers have to be revised under labour laws from time to time, and because of these reasons, the cost of production is high in the case of rubber production. If we want both, that welfare of the workers should be seen and they should be given more and more facilities and higher wages and at the same time we demand that cost of production should come down, I am afraid, these two things cannot be achieved simultaneously. We have to strike a balance and we are trying our best to see that a balance is struck.

About the figures, there are various figures given by different people. The figure of DGTD, I think, has been quoted from the newspapers. I also read that figure. But I can assure the august House that the figures are assessed by a committee which is inter-ministerial committee, where the Industry Ministry, the Commerce Ministry and the Rubber Board are involved.

Many honourable Members mentioned that during this year 1982-83, the gap between the demand and supply is about 80,000 tonnes. But our official figure is that during 1982-83, the production will be 162,000 tonnes and consumption will be 197,000 tonnes and we have decided to import 30,000 tonnes. So the gap between the demand and supply, according to official figure, is 35,000 tonnes and not 85,000 tonnes.

Regarding the duplication of the posts of Executive Director and Secretary, I can assure the august House that there will be no duplication in the function. Rubber Board is a big organization. The honourable Member asked whether there will be any time when there will be a full-time Chairman and Executive Director. This Bill has been brought to enable the Central Government to appoint a part-time Chairman, if and when the Government thinks it necessary. It is not that we have finally decided to appoint always a part-time Chairman. It is only an enabling provision empowering the State Government to appoint a part-time Chairman whenever it thinks necessary, and if the Government has come with this Bill, it has come with a good intention. After all, Rubber Board represents the growers. Some honourable Members pointed out that it is a technical job and that it is being politicized, and what not. Sir, there is no political motive whatsoever in this Bill. The problem with the opposition Members is that there is no clear perception as to what they want and what they don't. Sometimes they say that the country is being run by bureaucracy who does not know the job, and the people of political stature have no say in the administration, and that bureaucracy is running the Government. When we want to involve the people who have so much knowledge about the industry, for whom the Rubber Board has been created, and when we involve such people to look after the interests of the growers and industry, they say that it is a political move. I can assure the august House that this Bill has been brought with an idea to give recognition to those people and if we find it necessary – again I stress – that in the interest of the rubber industry in the country, it may be necessary for us to utilize the services of a person who has so much of knowledge about the industry, who himself is emotionally involved with the growth of this industry, and it is with this motive that we have come with this Bill. The question of the appointment of the Executive Director will arise only when we ultimately decide to appoint a part-time Chairman. If a full-time Chairman is appointed by the Government, then, the question of appointing an Executive Director will not arise. But when we appoint a part-time Chairman, we thought that it will be necessary for him to have an officer under his disposal who would be able to take charge of the day-to-day administration of the Board. The Rubber Production Commissioner is there and his primary duty is to see the technical development side of it. As you know, Sir, the Rubber Board has four major activities. The four major activities of the Rubber Board are: research, rubber production, rubber processing and administration. These are the four major categories under which the Rubber Board functions, and the Secretary's job will be to look after the household affairs, if I may say so, to record the proceedings of the meetings and so on. There will be no contradiction and there will be no duplicity in the functions of the Chairman or the Vice Chairman, the part-time Chairman or the Executive Director, and I do not think there should be any misconceptions about the intentions of this Bill. Sir, I do not want to deal with all the facts. I think, I have covered most of the major issued raised by the honourable Members. I can only assure the august House once again that we are committed to see that we produce more and more rubber in this country, to look after the interests of the consumers in this country and also to protect the interests of the rubber-based industries.

* * *

Sir, I move,

That the Bill be passed.

* * *

Sir, I did not say that the Bill is meant only for the benefit of the growers. I have only said that the Rubber Board has been constituted for the development of the rubber industry. I did not say that the cost of production has risen because of the wages of labour. I said that the cost of production of rubber in our country is high because of the high cost of inputs like, as I mentioned, fertilizer. Therefore, I have spoken of the input costs. This is one reason. But, I did say about the wages also. I said that because of the periodic revision of wages and grants under the labour laws. It is because of the revision of their wages. That is what I said.

* * *

We strictly follow the labour laws. I have specifically said that revision of wages takes place according to the provisions of the labour laws and it is one of the reasons in addition to the cost of inputs.

* * *

It is not correct to say that we have no scheme for the welfare of the labour. We do have a lot of schemes for the welfare of labour and I can name a few. We have an educational stipend scheme, we have a capital grants scheme, we have a scheme for granting relief to workers in distress in prolonged illness. Like that, we have some schemes for the welfare of the labour.

Another point which the honourable Member raised is that workers have no presentation on the Board. Sir, workers have representation on the Rubber Board. If you kindly go through my concluding speech, you will find that I have said that we have to strike a balance and that we have to see to the conditions of the workers, we have to see to the interests of the growers and we have to see to the interests of the industry based on rubber. This was my concluding remark. I did not say that this is meant only for the growers. Here subclause (d) says, 'Ten members to be nominated by the Central Government of whom two shall represent the manufacturers and four labour.' So, we have representatives from the labour in the Rubber Board. Therefore, there is workers' participation in the Rubber Board, and it is not our intention to exclude them. We are very much concerned about their welfare.

Setting Up of Tripartite Committee to Look into the Problems of Textile Industry*

Mr Deputy Chairman, Sir, honourable Members would recall that my colleague Shri Bhagwat Jha Azad, Labour Minister, had announced in Parliament on 9 July 1982 the setting up of a Tripartite Committee to look into problems connected with the Textile industry generally and in particular to look into the problems arising out of the prolonged strike in the Bombay Textile Mills Industry.

I am glad to inform the august House that the Committee has been set up and the Gazette Notification is being issued today. The Committee

---

***R.S. Deb.*, 13 August 1982 (Spoke while making a statement in the Rajya Sabha regarding setting up of Tripartite Committee to look into the problems of Textile Industry).

will be headed by Shri V.S. Deshpande, who has just retired as the Chief Justice of the Bombay High Court. It shall include five representatives of trade unions. It shall also include five representatives of the employers (cotton textile mills industry owners), two representatives of the Central Government and three of State Governments.

We expect the committee to start functioning immediately and to give its findings on the terms of reference within the stipulated period. On problems relating to badli workers in Bombay, and on grant of conveyance allowance and house rent allowance, the Committee will report in two months or earlier. With regard to wages of Bombay mill workers, the Committee will submit its report in six months or earlier. On other issues, we expect the Committee to report within one year. I do not intend to take the time of the honourable Members in repeating the terms of reference, because they were spelt out in detail in the statement of the Labour Minister, and the same terms of reference have now been spelt out in the Gazette Notification being issued today.

* * *

Sir, this Tripartite Committee has been appointed to go into the entire problems of the textile industry. I want to make that very clear, and Bombay strike or industrial relations is one of the problems which will be gone into by this Committee. One honourable Member has made a charge that this Tripartite Committee is not going to help and that it will lead us nowhere. I must inform this august House that when the intention for appointment of this Committee was announced by the Labour Minister on 9 July, where specific terms of reference and some of the concessions were announced, a number of mills have started working, and as of today I can inform the House that about 27,000 workers have already joined their duty.

About the other point, there is no question of consulting anybody. We have decided to form the Tripartite Committee and we have formed it now. Whoever wants to appear before the Committee is most welcome. This is open for everybody, including Dr Samant, and it is up to those people who want to appear before the Committee and put forward their views.

* * *

We have announced the constitution of the Committee today and in the announcement, we have said that there will be five representatives of the trade unions and the names of the trade unions are (1) Indian National Trade Union Congress; (2) National Labour Organization; (3) All-India Trade Union Congress; (4) Centre for Indian Trade unions; and (5) Hind Mazdoor Sabha. Now it is up to these unions to send their own representatives. We are not going to interfere in the selection of their representatives.

~

The Jute Manufactures Cess Bill, 1983, and the Jute Manufactures Development Council Bill, 1983*

Sir, I move:

> That the Bill to provide for the levy and collection by way of cess, of duty of excise on jute manufacturers for the purpose of carrying out measures for the development of production of jute manufacturers and for matters connected therewith, as passed by the Lok Sabha, be taken into consideration.

Sir, I also move:

> That the Bill to provide for the establishment of a Council for the development of production of jute manufactures by increasing the efficiency and productivity in the jute industry, the financing of activities for such development and for mattes connected therewith as passed by the Lok Sabha be taken into consideration.

Sir, the jute industry occupies a significant position in India's economy today. There are about 69 mills in the country with around 45,000 tonnes accounting for about 30 per cent world export jute goods. The total capital employed in the industry is of the order of Rs 300 crore

---

**R.S. Deb.*, 11 August 1983 (Spoke while moving the Bill in the Rajya Sabha). The Bill provided for the levy and collection, by way of cess, of excise duty on jute manufacturers for the purpose of carrying out measures for the development of production of jute manufacturers and for matters connected therewith, as passed by the Lok Sabha.

generating employment to about 2.5 lakh persons. Besides, the cultivation of jute provides a living to nearly 40 lakh families and the marketing of jute and jute goods and other ancillary activities give yet another sizeable employment to others. For quite some time the jute industry has been facing a financial crisis caused by the shrinkage in the export market and acute competition from the foreign countries and more so from the synthetic substitutes. The export performance has been declining. With decreased demand, the productivity and efficiency of the industry has also remained at a low ebb. Any scheme for revitalization and rejuvenation of the industry would call for vigorous effort towards market promotion, cost reduction, dynamic approach to research and for improvement in techniques, process of production and stabilization of prices.

The existing Jute Manufactures Development Council set up under the Industries (Development and Regulation) Act, 1951, is ill-equipped to perform most of these functions as it does not have adequate funds nor is it constitutionally broad-based with well-defined powers and functions to enable it to make a dynamic view of the promotional and developmental needs of the jute industry. It is, therefore, proposed to provide for the establishment of a new Council to be known in the same name as the existing Council set up under the Industries (Development and Regulation) Act, 1951, in view of the fact that the existing Council has received international recognition over the years. The new Council is proposed to be constituted, among others, with representatives of the producers and exporters of jute manufactures, growers of jute, workmen employed in factories producing jute manufactures, experts in jute technology, research, marketing or economics, representatives of the Ministries of the Central Government dealing with Agriculture, Commerce, Textiles, Finance, Industry, Civil Supplies and Cooperation and representatives of the State Government where jute is cultivated on a large scale. It is proposed to vest the Council with adequate powers to deal with the various aspects of the jute under the Industries (Development and Regulation) Act, 1951. The existing Council will be dissolved as soon as the Council is established under the proposed legislation. A provision has been made in the Bill for the transfer of the officers and staff employed in the existing Council. The finances of the Council will consist of sums provided by the officers and staff employed in the existing Council. The finances of the Council will consist of sums provided by the Central Government from the top of the proceeds of the cess on jute manufactures collected under the provisions of the Jute

Manufactures Cess Bill, Central Government or by any person and sums realized by the Council in the discharge of its functions. The Council shall also have power to borrow on the security of jute fund, set up under the proposed legislation, or any of its assets. Under the Jute manufacturers Cess Bill, Sir, a rate of one per cent instead of the present 0.125 per cent of the value of the jute goods cleared for sale, both for internal and external markets, has been proposed with an enabling provision to raise it up to three per cent depending on the market conditions and other developmental needs. The one per cent cess is estimated to enable the Government to collect about Rs 6.5 crore per annum on an estimated production of jute goods of the order of Rs 650 crore annually. It would be possible with this collection to mount the necessary promotional campaign and give the much-needed boost to the research and development efforts.

Sir, with these short preliminary remarks solving some of the present and persistent problems of the jute industry, Sir, I am sure that the honourable Members will support these two Bills which, if passed, would go a long way in solving some of the present and persistent problems of the jute industry.

Sir, with these short preliminary remarks, I invite a discussion on these two Bills.

* * *

Sir, I am very much thankful to the honourable Members for having taken a very active part in the debate and also for having given a lot of good suggestions, and I am particularly, thankful to Mrs Chatterjee and other Members.

Sir, as I have stated earlier, while moving the Bills for consideration, the jute industry in our country is really passing through a very very critical phase and, maybe, as one of the honourable Members put it, it is the worst period in the history of the jute industry in our country. So, Sir, we as the Government are very much worried about this and we have been trying to solve the problems of this industry. With this end in view, the Government of India appointed a task force in the year 1980 to go into the various aspects of the jute industry and also to suggest ways and means as to how solutions could be found. Now, this task force has given its report and the Government in turn has referred its suggestions and recommendations to the empowered committee. Mr

Surendra Mohan has referred to this particular task force in his speech and he has mentioned that there were about forty recommendations made by this task force and that we have not said anything about these recommendations. In fact, the number of recommendations made by the task force is not forty, but it is fifty-eight. The honourable Member has alleged that the Government has not taken note of any of the suggestions made by this task force and that we have done nothing about these suggestions and recommendations. Sir, for the information of the august House, I may say that the Government has, by and large, practically accepted all the recommendations excepting one or two, and it is because of the acceptance of these recommendations that we have come forward with the present two Bills which are under consideration now.

As I said in the beginning, the crisis in the jute industry is mainly due to the shrinkage in the export market. The well-known economist, Dr Adiseshiah, has said that there is a shrinkage in the export market.

* * *

One reason for the shrinkage is the problem of the market. Now, there are two types of markets. One is the export market and the other is the internal or the domestic market. As far as the export market is concerned, all the honourable Members have mentioned, and I have also initially mentioned, that the export market is going down and it has fallen very sharply.

* * *

Unfortunately, Sir, the honourable Member, Shri Harekrushna Mallick, was not present when I was speaking. He has come at the last moment and he is putting questions. Mr Mallick, if you want to take an active part in the debate, please be present here from the very beginning and try to know what points are made. Our export is very very bad because of the synthetic substitute and also because of the competition from other countries, especially Bangladesh. Now, in this respect, I can assure the House that we have been trying to regain our markets which we had lost or about which we had not been able to do as much as we were expected to do. We do hope that we will be able to regain some of the lost markets. Then, as far as competition from outside is concerned, specially Bangladesh, which is our competitor, as many honourable

Members have pointed out, we have been trying to come to an understanding with Bangladesh to have a joint export market strategy. I may mention, Sir, that a couple of meetings have already been held at the level of the Secretary, one at Dhaka in Bangladesh and another at Bangkok, and we are trying to come to an understanding with Bangladesh so that we can have a joint export market strategy. As far as the domestic offtake of jute goods is concerned, it has gone up, it has not reduced, but it has gone up, because of the various steps that the Government of India has taken. For example, we have taken the decision that the cement industry in the country should use jute bags 100 per cent; so also the sugar industry. We have also tried to impress upon the Department of Fertilizers, so that they also use our jute bags instead of synthetics, which they have been trying to do, and I assure that they may also try to help this industry. Because of these steps we have taken, the domestic offtake of jute goods in the country has in fact gone up. But as I have said, the only problem with us is that we have not been able to keep up our export market.

Another important point which honourable Members have referred to is about the research and development. I do agree with all the honourable Members who have stressed very rightly that we should give importance to research and development. Dr Chatterjee, who has been associated with research and development in this country, has also made a number of points. It has been said that we have done nothing in the field of research and development in our country. We have done quite a number of things. In fact, Dr Chatterjee has mentioned about the technique of blending jute with natural synthetics, polyester, etc. We have already developed this technique, and very successfully, and on many aspects also we have done considerably good job in the research field. But the only problem is that we have not been able to support, perhaps enough, the research institute, because the existing Jute Development Council has very limited resources to give to these research institutes. But I can assure you that with the enactment of these Bills, it will go a long way even in these fields of research and development, because, we hope, that out of the funds generated from this attempt, we will be able to give better support financially for research and development purposes.

Many honourable Members have spoken about the growers, that there is nothing in the Bill about the growers. Sir, the Bill which is before the august House is about the manufacturers.

* * *

I must say that this a manufacturers' Bill. We are going to have this Jute Council, and out of it we will have a jute fund which will be for the overall development of jute, not only jute industry but also the growers, that we have a separate mechanism to help the growers. We have the Jute Corporation of India which gives the support prices to the jute growers. As far as my information goes, at least this year in the present season, there is no problem about the prices of jute. I am told that the farmers are quite happy this year. In case, the prices come down, I can only assure that as our Jute Corporation of India has been doing in the past, we shall always be entering the market wherever the farmers do not get reasonable price. This mechanism is there. Until and unless the jute industry in our country is revitalized, the farmers cannot be helped. We do not export raw jute from our country. Our exports are very negligible. Whatever jute is produced, there has to be an outlet for it. The only outlet is jute manufacturing industry. Therefore, we are making this attempt to revitalize the industry, and it is certainly in the interest of the growers. Even in the Jute Development Council, we have given representation to the growers. Some have asked about the number of jute mills closed down. At the moment, out of 69 jute mills, 24 are closed down and the number of workers comes to 60,000. It is a very very sad situation. I am told that the Government of West Bengal is doing something. Most of the jute mills are in West Bengal and the Labour Minister of West Bengal who is heading the Tripartite Committee, is holding negotiations. Let us hope that he will be successful in his mission and that these mills will be reopened.

Mr Bhattacharjee has mentioned one point. I want to clarify it. An impression has been created through the newspapers and through the questions in Parliament that the West Bengal Government has asked permission from the Central Government to constitute a West Bengal Jute Corporation. To the best of my knowledge, we have not received any proposal whatsoever from the West Bengal Government for the creation of a West Bengal Jute Corporation. As far as my commonsense goes – I have not checked the legal position – I do not think that there is any need to have permission for creating a Corporation in West Bengal. I think the Government can go ahead with it.

These are the main points which have been raised by the honourable Members. I can assure the honourable Members that we are very sincere in your attempt. I hope all the honourable Members will support the two Bills.

* * *

Sir, I beg to move:

That the Bill be returned.

~

Gas Leakage at Shriram Foods and Fertilizers Industrial Plant in Delhi*

Sir, I deeply regret to inform the House that today morning at about 10.30 a.m. a leakage of gas occurred from the precincts of the factory of M/s Shriram Foods & Fertilizers Industries Plant located at Shivaji Marg, Delhi. The leakage resulted from a damage to the outlet pipeline of the petroleum storage tank, arising out of the collapse of the supporting structure of the tank. The plant personnel made attempts to neutralize the leakage with the help of lime and copious quantities of water and formed thick fumes containing steam and possibly gaseous sulphur trioxide which moved in easterly direction. The plant personnel were assisted by the members of the fire brigade which reached there promptly. The Lt Governor and other officials from the Delhi Administration and Government of India also reached the site promptly.

The fumes caused coughing and irritation to the throat and the eyes and breathlessness of the persons exposed thereto. As per available information, the details of persons reported to hospitals are as follows:

S.No	*Name of Hospital*	*Examined/Admitted*
1.	Jai Prakash Narayan Hospital	70 examined/12 admitted
2.	Ram Manohar Lohia Hospital	31 examined/23 admitted
3.	All India Institute of Medical Sciences	43 examined/6 serious admitted
4.	Safdarjung Hospital	25 admitted
5.	Hindu Rao Hospital	31 admitted/3 serious
6.	Ashok Vihar Hospital	3 admitted
7.	Javodhya Hospital	3 admitted
8.	Balak Ram Hospital	2 examined/2 admitted

**R.S. Deb.*, 4 December 1985 (The statement was issued by Shri Sangma as the Minister of State in the Department of States, now the Ministry of Home Affairs, regarding the gas leakage at Shriram Foods and Fertilizers Industries plant in Delhi.

None of the persons working in the sulphuric acid/oleum plant has been affected. The sulphuric acid/oleum plant is closed. The work on neutralization of petroleum is continuing. One General Manager, Plant Manager and Plant Engineer of the company have been arrested. The Lt Governor, Delhi, has taken a decision to order an enquiry into the accident.

* * *

Sir, I fully share the concern of the House regarding the incident that has taken place, and it is really very unfortunate – and, in fact, I myself feel very bad about it – that within a few days I had to come before the House twice to make a statement on the same matter. I also feel very sorry about that. Whatever information I have furnished to the House, I have furnished on the basis of what was available. Most of the queries that honourable Members have raised are very much technical in nature and I am afraid I am not a competent authority to answer all those questions. But as some of the honourable Members have already pointed out, this House had an opportunity to discuss about this particular matter on a number of occasions and especially on the Bhopal tragedy. Whatever queries have been raised today had been raised earlier and the concerned Ministry and the Department had already given those answers. Even I had given a little bit of it last time. I would not like to repeat.

* * *

I won't be able to give a satisfactory answer. I happened to give information because Delhi Administration is supposed to be under our Ministry. But as the nature of the incident or the nature of the industry does not fall under my administrative control, technically, I am unable to answer all the questions. And I would not like to give any answer which I am not myself clear about. That is why I am saying this. But as far as the enquiry is concerned, Professor Lakshmanna asked whether any appropriate enquiry will be conducted. It is precisely because we want to conduct an appropriate enquiry that we have not been able to announce the enquiry committee today, because in my own personal feeling, this enquiry should be conducted or headed by a technical persons because it is a technical subject. So there is no point in just announcing a committee of enquiry. Therefore, the Lt Governor has sought the assistance of the Chemicals Ministry to suggest an expert who can really go into the whole matter.

* * *

It will be a technical expert who will conduct the enquiry. I would not know whether it would be official or non-official. But I will convey to the Lt Governor that this is what you feel. But it will be a technical expert and beyond that I would not be able to say.

* * *

The honourable lady Member and Mr Jain have made a very good suggestion. I shall certainly take up this matter with the Ministry of Information and Broadcasting. What I want to emphasize is that our people around the plant are working. They are combing the area to see whether there are any more people who are affected. Wherever they are finding people affected by this, they are moving them to the nearby hospitals. People are being told not to be very worried about it. About those who are in the hospital, although I have used the word 'serious', I am given to understand that no one is in danger. All of them are out of danger. That much work our people have done. They have been able to go to the spot and neutralize the gas and they are still trying to neutralize more. The affected people have been taken to hospitals. We have certainly taken prompt action from the side of the Delhi Administration. As far as other measures are concerned, as I said, I don't think it will be appropriate for me to say here now anything more than that.

* * *

Sir, I have stated in my statement that the work is going on for neutralization and that work is still on. I have myself put this question to the Delhi Administration and the police people who have been there as to whether the things are under control. They have given me to understand that things are absolutely under control and there should not be any worry about it. This much I can say now. Whether it has been fully neutralized or not, I am sorry, I am unable to say anything about it now. But they say it is absolutely under control. So, these are the main points raised.

* * *

Sir, the investigation is going on and I can assure the House that the law will take its own course. I will not be able to say now as to who will be arrested and who will not be arrested. But I can assure the House that the matter will be inquired into. Thank you.

LABOUR ISSUES

The Dock Workers (Safety, Health and Welfare) Bill, 1985*

Sir, I move:

> That the Bill to provide for the safety, health and welfare of dock workers and for matters connected therewith, as passed by the Lok Sabha be taken into consideration.

Mr Vice Chairman, Sir, the Indian Dock Labourers Act, 1934, the regulation framed thereunder, the Dock Workers' Regulation of Employment Act, 1948, and the schemes framed thereunder, at present deal with the matters relating to the protection against accident of workers employed in loading and unloading of goods in ships and the safety, health and welfare of such workers. These also take care of the ILO Convention concerning protection against accidents of workers employed in loading and unloading of ships.

The 1934 Act applies to workers engaging on board the ship or alongside the ship. This does not cover work done in any other area of the ports and docks. This also does not provide for measures for health and welfare of such workers. Further, the Act does not cover workers engaged in work which is incidental to loading and unloading operations, such as work in relation to preparation of ships for receipt of cargo, including transit sheds, warehouse, yards, sidings, workers engaged in shipping, painting or cleaning and the like. The 1948 Act takes care of safety of all dock workers other than those engaged in ships. The law also does not apply to minor ports. Over the last three decades, the ship

*_R.S. Deb._, 5 and 10 November 1986 (Spoke while moving the Bill in the Rajya Sabha). The Bill provided for the safety, health and welfare of dock workers and for matters connected therewith, as passed by the Lok Sabha.

cargo-handling processes have changed considerably. Mechanization has come into operation in a big way. The nature of cargoes has changed. There are cargoes which are dangerous and toxic. There are oil tankers, heavy machinery, etc.

There is no proper system for reporting of accidents, conduct of enquiries, fixing of responsibilities, as there are ship owners, employees of ship owners who act as agents and other principal employees. The powers of the Inspectors of dock safety are not adequate.

They have to be given powers for prohibiting handling of cargo when the condition in the workplace is dangerous to life, safety or health of dock workers.

In these circumstances, the Government had considered it necessary to bring out a comprehensive legislation to cover all aspects of safety, health and welfare of dock workers. We have also taken care to provide for stringent penalties for violation of law. This law, when given effect to, will make enforcement easier, check the occupational risks involved in dock work and a proper machinery would be available for going into accidents in ports and docks.

The honourable Members are aware that this Bill was discussed earlier in the Lok Sabha and there was unanimous support for the measures that we are bringing out in the interest of safety, health and welfare of workers engaged in loading and unloading of goods in ships and workers entrusted with incidental work in the ports and docks area. I would request the honourable Members to cooperate with us in bringing out this important legislation in the interest of safety and health of the dock workers.

I would request the honourable Members to cooperate and support this Bill. With these few words, I commend the Bill for consideration.

* * *

Madam Vice Chairman, I am grateful to the honourable Members for having welcome and supporting this Bill unanimously.

Madam, at the moment, there are mainly two Acts which govern the safety, health and welfare of the dock workers: the Indian Dock Labourers Act, 1934 and the rules framed thereunder, and the Dock Workers (Regulation of Employment) Act, 1948 and the rules framed thereunder. In the course of the implementation of these Acts, Madam, loopholes have been noticed. The National Commission on Labour went into the working of these Acts and the rules framed thereunder and made specific recommendations and suggested that there should be a comprehensive law to deal with the safety, health and welfare of the dock workers. Therefore, it is a result of this report of the National Commission on Labour and also the experience gained in the last many years of the implementation of these Acts that the Government has come forward with the comprehensive legislation.

Some of the honourable Members have pointed out that this Bill is not comprehensive enough. I thought it was quite comprehensive. But I do admit that there could be some loopholes here and there. As we go on implementing the Act and as we come across the defects, we will be willing to come back to the House and rectify those defects, as Mr Matto has rightly pointed out.

Madam, this Bill deals purely with the safety, health and welfare of workers working in loading and unloading process in the ports. So it is limited to that activity. Honourable Members while participating in the debate had gone much beyond the scope of this Act to suggest quite a few things regarding the minimum wages, regarding housing schemes, regarding medical facilities, regarding casual nature of the work, i.e., the contract labour. All sorts of things have been mentioned during the debate, but as I already pointed out, this act confines only to the safety, health and welfare of workers while they are working in loading and unloading of goods.

As I have mentioned it while making the preliminary remarks in the beginning that this Act has attempted even to widen the scope and definition of dock work and dock workers. In my view it is very comprehensive, but I am not saying this what the honourable Members have said here are irrelevant. They are very very relevant. I think it is an occasion for us to discuss about the problem in general that have been faced by the dock workers. It is not that the Government is not doing anything in those areas. In fact, there are many other Acts, which govern those aspects. We have contract labour Regulation and Abolition Act and we have the Minimum Wages Act. Many other Acts are in operation and they do look after the aspects which have been pointed out by the honourable Members.

As far as the welfare measures that are being carried on are concerned, I must mention that there are a number of welfare measures which are already in force like minimum wages are guaranteed for them in a month, there is an attendance allowance which is 1/68th of the monthly wage, there is a weekly off with wages, leave with wages and holiday with wages. Pension or a contributory provident fund is also in operation. Gratuity is also in operation for them. They are entitled to free medical aid. They also are entitled to house rent allowance. They also have canteen facilities, uniform facilities, games and sports facilities. The children of the dock workers get education scholarships and school uniforms. Like that there are many other schemes of welfare activities which are already in operation.

Regarding the provisions of the Act, quite a few things have been pointed out. One point where the whole House was unanimous was about too much of power having been given to Inspectors and we normally talk about Inspector raj. I am inclined to agree with the view of the House that Inspectors should not be given too much of power. In this Bill, it has been said no complaint can be lodged, no case can be proceeded against without the permission of the Inspector. That provision has already been made.

As Mr Reddy has already pointed out this Bill was passed by the Lok Sabha last year and after one year we are coming to the Rajya Sabha. During the last one year, many things have happened even in the thinking of the Government. If you kindly recollect the Bill on the Child Labour (Abolition and Regulation) Act, I have pointed out in the august House that powers of the Inspectors have been taken away and the powers of the Inspectors have been given to every citizen of the country. Like that there is another Act which is coming as an amendment to Equal Remuneration Act or some other Acts particularly in the unorganized sector where we have progressively taken away the power of the Inspectors. But since this Act was drafted more than a year ago and passed by the Lok Sabha, I can only say I am inclined to agree with the august House that we should not have given that much power to the Inspector. But let us see how it goes. Depending on how it goes we will come back, maybe if necessary, even to remove the power of the Inspector in future.

* * *

Well, it takes some time, it has to undergo certain procedure. I do not want to explain that. But I am admitting that. In other laws which we have brought in the last one year, especially since when I have been in this Ministry, this has been done away with in many of the Acts. Now one specific question was asked: what will happen to the Directorate of Dock Safety? Whether there will be duplication of work? Will the Directorate of Dock Safety continue? Madam, the powers of the Inspectors which are contemplated in this Bill shall be vested with the Inspectors in the present Directorate of Dock Safety.

One honourable Member has asked about the safety and wanted to know the present position. Madam, the incidents of reportable accidents in our ports in various part of the country, fortunately, have been coming down in the last few years. In 1983, the reportable accidents that took place in the country was 1,500; in 1984 it came down to 1,155. I hope with the passing of this Bill today, the incidents of reportable accidents will come down because we have provided for more stringent punishments than it was there in the earlier Act. It is with this hope, I can assure honourable Members that we will implement this Bill with all earnestness.

With these few words, I once again thank the honourable Members who have participated in the discussion on this Bill. Thank you.

Unemployment and Industrial Lockouts*

Sir, there has been a marked improvement in the industrial relations situation in the country during 1985 compared to 1984. The number of disputes (strikes and lockouts) declined from 2,094 to 1,716, the number of workers affected from 19.5 lakh to 10.7 lakh and the man-days lost from 56.03 million to 29.37 million. Similarly, the number of layoffs in industrial units has come down from 847 in 1984 to 665 in 1985 with the number of workers affected also steeply declining from 1.4 lakh to 0.99 lakh. Though the number of industrial closures (due to reasons other than industrial disputes) has marginally increased from 188 in 1984 to 203 in 1985, the number of workers affected has sharply decreased from 72,000 to 31,270 during the same period.

According to the provisional estimates, this declining trend has been maintained even during 1986 (January–August) with number of disputes

---

**R.S. Deb.*, 27 November 1986 (Spoke while participating in the Calling Attention Motion regarding unrest and unemployment due to increasing incidents of lockouts, lay-offs and sickness in Industrial sector).

standing at 986, workers affected at 9 lakh, loss of man-days at 14 million and the number of industrial closures with workers affected at 145 and 15,000, respectively. During January–June 1986, the number of units laying off and the workers affected were 242 and 34,000 respectively.

Available data on industrial sickness indicate that the number of large and medium sick units has come down from 1832 in December 1984 to 1778 in June 1985, although the number of sick small scale industrial units during the same period has increased from 93,282 to 97,890. Government have taken a series of steps to combat industrial sickness and rehabilitate sick industrial units through a package of assistance extended by the banks and financial institutions.

In the light of the foregoing facts, Government do not consider that there has been increasing labour unrest and unemployment due to increase in the incidence of industrial disputes, lay-offs and closures.

Government have been keeping a close watch over the industrial relations situation in the country. Potential areas of labour unrest and disputes are being continuously monitored in order to see that preventive action is taken to resolve disputes and remove the causes of industrial unrest at the incipient stage. The industrial relations machinery both at the Centre and in the States continue to make efforts to settle industrial disputes through preventive mediation, conciliation, adjudication and arbitration as provided for under the existing labour laws. Emphasis is being laid on holding tripartite consultations before major issues concerning labour policies and programmes are formulated. A number of tripartite industrial committees for industries such as coal mines, non-coal mines, engineering, jute, cotton, textiles, chemicals, cement, plantations, leather goods, construction and road transport have been re-constituted. Important issues of immediate concern to the maintenance of harmonious industrial relations are being discussed in these tripartite fora from time to time.

It has been the endeavour of Government to improve industrial relations not only by taking industrial relations, not only by taking steps to prevent labour unrest but also by maintaining a constant dialogue with employees and employers.

* * *

Madam, I am grateful to the honourable Members who have highlighted the problems of the working class in our country, the health of the industry and thereby the economy of the country.

At the very outset, I want to make one thing very clear that I am being complacent about the whole situation, some allegations have been made. I am not. And no responsible citizen of this country can be complacent about any situation that happens in our country, which is not in the interest of any section of the people. The fact is that there were 665 lay-offs in 1985 – I have furnished the figures – affecting 99,000 workers. The fact is that 203 units were closed down in 1985 affecting 31,270 workers. The fact is that there are 99,668 sick units, large, medium and small, Rs 3,805.17 crore from the financial institutions are locked up. This is certainly a matter of great concern for all of us, not only to the Labour Minister of this country. The whole House has expressed it.

What I stated in my statement is that there has been no increase in the labour unrest in our country. This is what I have stated. And for that I have said that if we look at the figures of lay-off, the figures have come down. Not that I am happy with the figures that have come down.

* * *

There has been an increase in the loss of man-days due to lockouts. I have made the point in the statement. I have told this on a number of occasions in the august House. In fact, in the last session of Parliament, we had a full-fledged discussion on the working of the Labour Ministry. And your point is very right that the number of man-days lost due to lockouts have gone up compared to strikes. So, this is the trend. This is the fact.

* * *

I am a Congress man . . . I am not supporting strike at all. I am only saying that, comparatively the number of man-days lost due to lockouts has gone up. But, both are not desirable for this country at all.

* * *

As regards the observations of Vajpayeeji on complementing labour, yes, I am complimenting the labour. Why not? I am complimenting the labour. In fact, because there has been an improvement in the labour relations situation in the country and because our working class has worked, this has found expression in the growth rate of the industrial production in our country. In the last ten months of this year, there has been 6.5 per cent increase in the industrial production as against 5.8 per cent of the all-India figure during the Sixth Five Year Plan, the whole of the Plan. Therefore, it has found its expression. So, 6.5 per cent was the growth in the ten months against 5.8 per cent during the Sixth Five Year Plan. So, I am only making a statement that looking at the figures comparatively in the last two years, which, have given, even if you look at the figures in the last five years, you find that there has been a progress in the industrial relations in our country. The number of man-days lost and the number of disputes have considerably come down. This is a very good trend. I should say. We should be happy. But that does not mean that everything is all right. There are a lot of things which need improvement. I would like to make only one point, which, I think is very important. The maintenance of industrial relations in our country is primarily the job of the respective State Governments. It is the duty of the State Governments to create an industrial climate and a better atmosphere in their respective States. I cannot do it. The Central Government cannot do it. So, the industrial situation, whether it is in the case of lockouts or in the case of strikes or in the case of any other method, the primary responsibility lies with the respective State Governments. It is they who have to manage it and it is they who have to create a conducive situation.

* * *

I am not quoting a figure of West Bengal . . . If I quote West Bengal figures, I know you will not sit down. Therefore, I will not quote it.

* * *

I am very happy that Shri Gurudas Das Gupta has raised a very important question of agricultural labour in our country. Out of 296 million working force in our country, 194 million belong to agriculture labour. And we have not paid our attention to that. I have been making this statement repeatedly. In fact, in the last Consultative Committee meeting on the suggestion of the honourable Member Shri Gurudas

Gupta, we decided to discuss only this problem in the next Consultative Committee meeting to be held on 3 December. It was on your suggestion, Mr Das Gupta. I am happy that you have made this point here again. We are all for it, particularly for the implementation of the Minimum Wages Act, which has found place in the newly structured 20-point economic programme.

So many individual points have been raised. The NBCC point has been raised. I know this problem. I am not going to say what I am going to do about it but I may tell you that I am aware of the problem and am trying to find a solution. There are other matters which Mr Ashwani Kumarji has raised. He has come to me a number of times. He knows how much we have been trying to sort out this problem.

I think Mr G. Gopalasamy will not leave me if I do not answer to him. It is regarding closed mills in Tamil Nadu. I must make it very clear that as far as the policy of the Government of India is concerned, there is no question of any discrimination with any part of the country. In fact, I had two sittings with the Finance Minister of Tamil Nadu. He was the Finance and Labour Minister at that very time. He had also met the then Textile Minister, Mr Khurshid Alam Khan. The honourable Member posed a question: while Gujarat could be helped, why Tamil Nadu could not be helped? If I remember very correctly, I am not very sure of the latest situation, when we offered to the Tamil Nadu Government the Gujarat pattern of package, unfortunately, they said that it would not be workable in Tamil Nadu. So, it is not our fault. We have offered it but the Tamil Nadu Government had reservations. At least the Finance Minister told me he was not sure if it would be workable. It is not that we have not offered them; we have offered them.

* * *

They have given a proposal which, I think, the Textile Ministry is considering. Actually, the Finance Minister of Tamil Nadu wanted my interventions. He gave a press statement and then he came over here. He wanted my intervention. I intervened in the matter. This is how the discussion came up and we had two sittings.

* * *

I know this problem very well. There were workers who were on hunger strike and they were at a very critical state. I received a lot of telegrams saying that these people will die if they go on for one more day of hunger strike. They wanted me to intervene and I intervened in the matter. I requested them not to go on hunger strike and they gave up hunger strike and they are still alive today. I am very happy about that. So I know the problem and I have been personally involved in this matter.

Madam, most of the cases which the honourable Members have raised, I know personally many of these cases. But I do not think we have time to reply to all these because lunchtime is already over.

Regarding comprehensive Bill, some honourable Members have raised about it. We had a tripartite meeting on 22 and 23 September and yesterday also I had a sitting for half a day with all the Central Trade Union leaders on this. Hopefully, we will be able to finalize our proposals very soon and should be able to come to the Parliament with amendments to the Industrial Disputes Act and the Trade Union Act during the next session.

Once again, I thank all the honourable Members.

The Labour Welfare Fund Laws (Amendment) Bill, 1986*

Sir, I beg to move for leave to introduce a Bill further to amend the Mica Mines Labour Welfare Fund Act, 1946, the Limestone and Dolomite Mines Labour Welfare Fund Act, 1972, the Iron Ore Mines, Manganese Ore Mines and Chrome Ore Mines Labour Welfare Fund Act, 1976, and the Beedi Workers Welfare Fund Act, 1976.

Sir, I introduce the Bill.

* * *

**R.S. Deb.*, 4 December 1986 and 9 March 1987 (Spoke while moving the Bill in the Rajya Sabha). The Bill provided for the Amendment of the Mica Mines Labour Welfare Fund Act, 1946, the Limestone and Dolomite Mines Labour Welfare Fund Act, 1972, the Iron, Manganese and Chrome Ore Mines Labour Welfare Fund Act, 1976, and the Beedi Workers Welfare Fund Act, 1976.

Madam Deputy Chairman, I beg to move:

> That the Bill further to amend the Mica Mines Labour Welfare Fund Act, 1946, the Limestone and Dolomite Mines Labour Welfare Fund Act, 1972, the Iron Ore Mines, Manganese Ore Mines and Chrome Ore Mines Labour Welfare Fund Act, 1976, and the Beedi Workers Welfare Fund Act, 1976, be taken into consideration.

Madam, this is a very small amendment and the whole idea of amendment is that funds which are available for the welfare of workers can be spent only for the limited purposes which have been specified in the Act. Now, on 5 September 1986, the Minister for Family Welfare, Shri P.V. Narasimha Rao convened a meeting when it was decided that the family welfare funds and the labour welfare funds which are available with the Government of India should also be spent for family welfare activities. Because, under these welfare funds, we already have some infrastructure of hospitals and dispensaries all over the country and since population growth is a major challenge to our country, we are seeking this amendment to enable the Government to spend a portion of the money which is available for family welfare activities. Since the aim of this bill is so good, I was expecting that this could be passed even without a discussion. But if honourable Members are keen to discuss it, I have no objection. But it is a very limited issue enabling the Government to spend money for family welfare activities.

* * *

I am grateful to the honourable Members for having supported the Bill; and also for having given very good and constructive suggestions. As I mentioned in my preliminary observations, this amendment is with a limited purpose of enabling the Government of India to spend a portion of its welfare fund for family planning. Population growth has been a major problem for our country and population control is our national objective and we all realize that all-out efforts are required to tackle this problem. The honourable Minister of Health and Family Welfare is taking a lot of steps in this direction and in that process, our honourable Minister, Mr P. V. Narasimha Rao said that thrust may have to be given sector-wise, if possible. He convened a meeting of the employers and the employees, trade union leaders and the Labour Ministry. There we discussed as to how this message of population control can be taken to the workers, among the industrial workers, where also we emphasized that this message has to be taken across to the workers through the media like the television, radio, newspapers, and as honourable Member, the first speaker pointed out, it can also be done through informal education, through trade union leaders and particularly, through the Central Board of Workers' Education. It was talked that under the social security scheme, Labour Ministry administers a number of welfare programmes, particularly, the ESI hospitals that we have all over the country, and the hospitals and dispensaries which are available under the welfare fund. As far as ESI hospitals are concerned, there is no difficulty, we are doing the job. But about the four welfare funds that are available with us, the Act specifies as to for what purpose a fund can be utilized. It specifically says that it can be utilised for health, it can be utilized for education of the workers, it can be utilised for the housing schemes for the workers and it can be utilized for water supply scheme. Therefore, the purposes for which the money can be spent have been specifically laid down.

In regard to the health programme, we already have six hospitals and 215 dispensaries spread all over the country under the welfare funds. Since the doctors, hospitals, and dispensaries are already available and this particular aspect of family planning cannot be undertaken in these hospitals, it was thought that as part of our campaign, we can expand our activities to family welfare.

* * *

As regards the ratio of population to doctors, I am sorry, I do not have this figure. Now, we have the social security scheme for the industrial workers mainly for the organized sector and we operate this scheme through the Employees State Insurance Corporation. As far as this scheme is concerned, I am sure, we have not reached that ratio, proportion. We are trying to reach that. I do not remember exactly. We have the figure as far as the organized sector is concerned. But as far as the funds are concerned, I am not sure, I am not at all sure whether we have reached that ratio or not. I am sure we have not reached that.

As I said, we have six hospitals, and 215 dispensaries. But we are now thinking of expanding our activities. In this, we have adopted a particular policy. The question is whether we should go in for a big hospital which may cost about Rs 2 or Rs 3 crore, which may cover a population of 25,000 workers. I am trying to meet the point raised by honourable Members just now. The question is whether it is better for us to go in for a 50 or 100-bedded hospital, which may cost, as I said about Rs 2 or Rs 3 crore, or whether it is better for us to spread it and go in for smaller dispensaries with three or four of five doctors at a cost of say, Rs 15 or Rs 30 lakh. In order to give more coverage, we have come to a deliberate decision that in future, we will not go in for hospitals; on the other hand, we will go in for dispensaries and spread them all over the country so that the benefit can reach a large number of workers. Once we implement this, we will be able to reach nearer the ratio which the honourable Member talked about.

Mr Matto wanted to know how much money is going to be spent. Our limited purpose is, since we have the infrastructure available already, when we have the hospital and dispensaries, we must utilize them for the specific purpose. This is a limited thing. As far as the funds are concerned, they are not very much, I wish we had more funds. I will give you the figures. As far as mica is concerned we have Rs 201 lakh, iron ore, manganese and chrome ore, Rs 222 lakh; beedi, it is somewhat more, Rs 761 lakh; limestone, Rs 284 lakh. But one thing has to be understood that the welfare schemes which we are undertaking are only a supplement to what the respective State Governments and employers are doing. It is not that we have taken up the sole responsibility in this regard. This is only a supplement to what is already being done by the State Governments as well as by the employers. In this connection, I am happy to say that as far as the public sector employers are concerned, they are contributing quite a lot. Well, in the private sector, it is not a happy situation, though there are people who are doing very good in that sector also. All of them are not doing very well at all. Majority of them, by and large, are not very much forthcoming. Even in our own sector, we need the cooperation of the employers and I would solicit more cooperation from them.

Some honourable Members have raised the question about other welfare activities. I have already mentioned about that. The housing we do, the water supply we do, we do education and medical health, but even here we only supplement, as I said. As far as housing is concerned, we have started giving emphasis to housing. Last year, we tried to do something but it is from this year that we would take off and we will be doing much more on the housing side. The number of houses that we have been able to build for the workers is about 16,335 and it is not correct to say that the houses are in a bad shape or they have been badly constructed. Somebody pointed out about this. I had myself gone to see some of the houses and I can confidently certify that those houses are really very good. Water supply scheme, we have completed in 35 places. On the education side, as far as 1985-86 year is concerned, we have awarded scholarships to 26,254 students and the money that we spent last year was Rs 7,586,000. I have also instructed that this year we must reach the figure of rupees one crore because here is the area where, I think, we can do quite a lot. Then, the honourable Member was mentioning that the labourers' children remain labourers. I do not think it is so. I can confidently tell that under our scheme, particularly in the beedi sector, I have myself come across a number of doctors and engineers who are the children of the workers and who have become doctors and engineers because we have helped them. It is because we have helped them. It is because of our efforts and the welfare fund that they have become engineers and doctors. Yet, I must say that the result that we have achieved are at all not satisfactory. To say that nothing had been done will not be correct but I will certainly say that the success is not at all satisfactory. I can only assure that the policy of the Government of India is to give more emphasis towards unorganized sector than the organized sector, to which Shri Kalpanathji has already referred that there are people who are getting more and more and on the other side there are people who are getting nothing. I think our duty is to those who are getting nothing.

* * *

As regards the yearly income and expenditure, I have got the figure, but I will have to dig out the papers. Well, if it is mica, for example, it was about Rs 96 to 97 lakh last year, yearly income. For limestone, it was Rs 71 lakh total income in 1985-86. It is accumulative and we have Rs 14 crore. That is why I am saying that it is a very small amount and with that amount you cannot expect us to do much.

* * *

Well, of all the sectors, we have been giving more importance to beedi workers. At the moments we have more money with the Beedi Welfare Fund and we will be getting more money because the cess that we have imposed from 1 March this year is 30 paise for thousand beedis as against 10 paise which was there earlier. We hope that we will be able to get more money as far as beedi is concerned. The question of identity cards has been raised by some honourable Members. I am glad to say that out of 30 lakh, which is the official figure of beedi workers, we have already issued identity cards to 20 lakh beedi workers. The responsibility of issuing identity cards to the beedi workers is that of the employer. In this Amendment Bill, we have brought in a provision that if an employer fails to issue an identity card, he shall be punishable. So a penal provision has been brought in here for the first time. We hope we should be able to do more. As the august House is aware, we have also extended the application of provident fund for the beedi workers, and I am happy to say that it is not doing very bad, it is doing quite all right. We have now started collecting some money for them.

I do not think there is any other important point that has been raised as far as this particular Bill is concerned. So, Sir, with these few words, I once again thank all the honourable Members and request that the Bill be taken into consideration.

* * *

I beg to move:

> That the Bill, as amended, be passed.

~

National Policy on Child Labour*

Mr Vice Chairman, Sir, yesterday, during Question Hour, I promised that I will make a statement on the Child Labour Policy tomorrow. I have come one day ahead of my commitment. The statement which has been circulated, I am told, is a statement to be made in the Lok Sabha but the copy which I am holding is for the Rajya Sabha. Maybe there has been some mistake and the Lok Sabha copies have come to the Rajya Sabha and the Rajya Sabha copies have gone to that side. So, it should be taken as a statement made in the Rajya Sabha.

**R.S. Deb.*, 12 August 1987 (Spoke while making a statement and participating in the discussion regarding the National Policy on Child Labour in the Rajya Sabha).

The Child Labour (Prohibition and Regulation) Bill, 1986, the objective of which was to prohibit the employment of children below 14 years in certain occupations and processes and regulate the employment of children in others, was passed by Parliament in December 1986. During discussion of the Bill, a point frequently made was that the legislation would not be sufficient to tackle the problem of exploitation of child labour. In particular, many honourable Members felt that it was necessary to suitably rehabilitate the children who would be withdrawn from the prohibited employments and to provide welfare inputs like education, health care, skill development, etc., to the children working in permitted employments. At that time, Government had given a commitment in Parliament that the Policy on Child Labour would be formulated to take care of these aspects. I am happy to inform the august House that the National Policy on Child Labour has been approved by the Government.

The policy consists of three main ingredients: (1) Legal Action Plan, (2) Focusing of general welfare and development programmes on child labour and their families; and (3) a project-based Plan of Action.

Under the Legal Action Plan, emphasis will be laid on strict and effective enforcement of the provisions of the Child Labour (Prohibition and Regulating) Act, 1986, the Factories Act, 1948, the Mines Act, 1950, the Plantation Labour Act, 1951, and other Acts containing provisions relating to employment of children.

The second aspect of the policy will be to utilize the ongoing development programme for the benefit of child labour and their families. Various national development programmes exist with wide coverage in the areas of education, health, nutrition, integrated child development, and income and employment generation for the poor. These programmes will be utilized to create socio-economic conditions in which the compulsions to send the children to work will diminish and the children are encouraged to attend schools rather than take wage employment.

Under the Project-based Plan of Action, ten projects are proposed to be taken up in areas of child labour concentration, which are as follows:

1. The Match Industry in Sivakasi, Tamil Nadu.
2. The Diamond Polishing Industry in Surat, Gujarat.
3. The Precious Stone Polishing Industry in Jaipur, Rajasthan.
4. The Glass Industry in Ferozabad, Uttar Pradesh.

5. The Brassware Industry in Moradabad, Uttar Pradesh.
6. The Handmade Carpet Industry in Mirzapur–Bhadohi, Uttar Pradesh.
7. The Lock Making Industry in Aligarh, Uttar Pradesh.
8. The Handmade Carpet Industry in Jammu and Kashmir.
9. The Slate Industry in Markapur in Andhra Pradesh.
10. The Slate Industry in Mandsaur in Madhya Pradesh.

The following action will be taken in each of these areas:

(i) Stepping up the enforcement of the Child Labour (Prohibition and Regulation) Act, 1986, the Factories Act, 1948, the Mines Act, 1948, and such other Acts within the project area. If necessary, special enforcement staff will be created for the purpose.

(ii) Coverage of families of child labour under the income employment generating programmes under the overall aegis of anti-poverty programmes.

(iii) Formal and non-formal education of child labour and stepping up programmes of adult educations for the parents of the working children.

(iv) Setting up of special schools for the child workers where provisions of education, vocational training, supplementary nutrition, health care, etc., will be made. If necessary, stipends will be given to children taken out from the forbidden employment, to compensate their loss in earnings.

(v) Creation of awareness through social activist groups and by other means, so as to educate and convince people regarding the undesirable aspects of child labour.

Certain infrastructure will be created for the projects, with a Chief Executive Officer in charge of each project. There will be a Child Labour Project Board for each project, with the local Collector as its Chairman, and with officials, non-officials and representatives of voluntary organizations as members, to ensure coordination of the inputs by various Departments. There will also be a high-level Monitoring Committee set up at the Central level with representatives of the concerned Ministries, Departments and State Governments on it.

Each project will be carefully drawn up in consultation with the State Governments and the Central Ministries concerned to ensure proper coverage and intermeshing of programmes of the Central and the State

Governments. In the first phase, the ten projects are together expected to cover up to 30,000 child workers. The likely expenditure on the projects is expected to be of the order of Rs 11 crore annually.

* * *

Sir, I quite appreciate the views of the august House that this statement that I have made does not look very attractive. It does not look so attractive because I did not want to come before the House with the attractive statement which it would not be possible to fulfil.

* * *

I am not clever, but I am being honest.

* * *

Sir, I have come to announce a project which I think will be possible. Now, I have said in my statement that ten projects have been selected and Rs 11 crore have been earmarked for this year. Now, for the 1987-88 financial year, we are already in the middle of it. By March 1988, the financial year will be over. Now, within this period of five to six months, spending of Rs 11 crore on these ten projects is a very big task for me. Therefore, I have come to the august House to tell what I am going to do in these five months. Shri Narayanasamy has raised a question why the brick-kiln industry has not been included. It shall be included but not this year. It will be included in the next year's project. That is the reason why I have come with a modest proposal.

Now, the number 30,000 looks very small when the total child labour force of the country is 70 million. Therefore, when I have given the figure as 30,000 it looks ridiculous. But I want to clarify that these 30,000 children which I have mentioned will be those children who shall be rescued from the prohibited areas and then they will be exclusively looked after by us. I have not come out with a figure who would be benefited by our other programmes, programme number one, and programme number two. For example, Sir, the Sivakasi question has been raised. In these ten projects, Sivakasi is also included. The number of working children in Sivakasi is about 25,000 to 30,000 and all these twenty to thirty thousand children are going to get benefit by the project of Rs 14 crore. But I have not included these 30,000 children from Sivakasi because out of these 30,000 I will be selecting a few who are very unfortunate, really helpless, and I will be bringing them up. That is why I have come with a small number of 30,000 for one year. I will be very happy as Labour Minister if I can pick up 30,000 children, rescue them and bring them up. Ferozabad is included in this project and the total number of working children there is 6,000. But I am not going to pick up all the 6,000. They will no doubt be getting the benefit of the project indirectly as in education and some other things. But 30,000 will be the selected children. In Bhadohi and Mirzapur, the ultimate cost of the project is Rs 24 crore and there are almost one lakh of children working in that area. And all these one lakh children shall be benefited out of the Rs 24 crore project. But out of them, I will be selecting a few who will be totally looked after by us and I will bring them up. That is why the number 30,000 looks very small. But the actual beneficiaries from the working children will be many more. But I must make it very clear that the problem of child labour in our country is very large, very very big and if we think of wiping out this problem in one year or two years, I am sorry, we will not be able to do it. We have to fight this problem for some time to come. But the fact is that we have started.

* * *

Policy of the Government has been incorporated in the Act itself which the august House had discussed. What came out of the debate when the Act was passed was that mere legislation will not help; we must also have rehabilitation programmes. So I have come out with a statement for rehabilitation programme, besides other programmes. That is what I would like to clarify and say that the problem of child labour has been recognized by the Government; it has been taken as a national challenge and we are going to meet this challenge. I must make it very clear that this battle will not be over in one year or two or three years; we have to fight it and I hope that now that this Act had been passed and we have sanctioned projects, other project will also be taken in the years to come and we will be able to go a long way in helping these unfortunate children.

~

Constituting National Commission on Rural Labour*

Mr Vice Chairman Sir, honourable Members are aware that the Prime Minister in his Budget Speech for the year 1987-88 had announced the constitution of a National Commission on Rural Labour. Accordingly, a Resolution has been issued constituting the Commission. Shri Jinabhai Darji will be the Chairman of the Commission and following persons are its members:

1. Shri H. Hanumanthappa, MP
2. Shri R.P. Panika, MP
3. Shri Keyur Bhushan, MP
4. Dr P.C. Joshi
5. Dr Pradhan H. Prashad
6. Shri Suresh Mathur, Member Secretary

I also place on the Table of the House a copy of the Resolution No. U-24012/1/87-RW dated 11 August 1987 which gives the terms of reference, names of member, and other essential information.

* * *

Mr Vice Chairman, Sir, I am grateful to the honourable Members who have raised very valid points. I accept, the points raised by you are very valid. As far as the terms of reference are concerned, since it was lengthy, I thought, instead of taking the time of the august House reading the terms of reference, it would be better to lay them on the Table of the House. If the House desires, I will read. Otherwise, tomorrow morning you will get all the copies. I assure you that whatever points have been raised, whatever suggestions have been made about the terms of reference have been included in the terms of reference. For example, whether the question of land reforms has been there or not.

* * *

**R.S. Deb.*, 13 August and 9 September 1987 (Spoke while making a statement in the Rajya Sabha regarding the constitution of the National Policy on Rural Labour).

The terms of reference is so exhaustive and it covers all aspects of rural labour, I do not think there is any more scope to include any other thing. If you read it, I am sure, you will be satisfied. It includes land reforms, rural indebtedness, employment generation, housing, forestry, water, social security, choice of technology, training programmes for farmers and minimum wages. There is specific emphasis laid on child labour, woman labour and bonded labour. It includes everything and I am confident that you will be satisfied.

* * *

Regarding the composition of the Committee and the number of members of the Committee, I think the points made by the honourable Members are very valid. You have said there is no member from the Opposition. It is a very valid point. You also said there is no woman member; when the Commission is going to deal with specific women's problems, there should be a woman member. That is also a valid point. But unfortunately, when we offered membership to a Member from the Opposition who happens to be a woman, she declined to be a member of this Commission. I only thought that it had become as established style and policy of the Opposition to dissociate itself from whatever committees Government forms.

* * *

I am happy that you are willing to cooperate in this Commission. I will take it that way and you have my assurance, there will be representation of the Opposition and I am grateful to you that you have agreed for it. I have come here without the Opposition Member and the women because if I start going to other people and then they refuse it, if I repeat this process, there will be delay and I did not want to delay it. Whoever has accepted membership, I have announced it and some members will be added to this Commission. There is no problem in it.

I am sorry, Mr Das Gupta made some uncharitable remarks about the members of the Commission. I do not think we should make such kind of remarks. Every member of the Commission whom Government has selected is a distinguished member in his respective field, all the members are distinguished members in their respective fields and I have full faith in them, including the Chairman. They are all distinguished members and I do not think it is charitable on our part to make such kind of remarks.

As far as a discussion on the terms of reference is concerned, it is not in my hands. If the Business Advisory Committee so desires, if the Chair so desires, I have no problems at all for a discussion, on the terms of reference to this National Commission. I would rather welcome it so that I get more ideas on how to go about it. It will be a pleasure for me to have a debate. But it is not in my hands. It is in the hands of the Business Advisory Committee.

Then, two specific points were made. One is whether it will also include the workers in the urban sector. Well, it is a National Commission on Rural Labour. The Census of India has specific criteria to decide which is rural and which is urban. We have kept it open in the terms of reference. It is for the Commission either to accept the criteria adopted by the Census of India or to have their own definition of rural areas. It has a specific reference to migrant labour and, therefore the Commission will certainly have jurisdiction over those labourers who have migrated from rural areas to urban areas and, to that extent, the Commission will have jurisdiction. In the terms of reference, since the Commission may not be able to do the entire work itself, we have also said that the Commission can commission studies if they do desire. So, they can also take, what you call, the expertise from the experts in different fields. So, this power has been given to them and they can even appoint some consultants if they so require. So, the terms of reference are very wide and we have said that they should give their interim report as soon as possible – Shri Matto raised this question – but the life of the Commission will be three years. This is all about the Commission. Thank you Sir.

* * *

Mr Vice Chairman, Sir, I am grateful to the honourable Members who have participated in trying to get clarifications on the statement that I made on Friday last. I am sorry, and I must apologise to the House, that the statement did not contain the salient features of the recommendations. Had those been given, perhaps, it would have been a much more meaningful discussion – I do admit. I am told the copies are available in the library – not one but three. But I do concede, even three copies are not enough. However, I would like to remind the Starred Question

No. 174, where an exhaustive reply was given on the National Commission of Rural Labour. But I hope that we will have some more occasions to discuss this report in full detail.

* * *

If you think the session should be extended for this, I do not think so.

Sir, in 1985, when the late Prime Minister Shri Rajiv Gandhi addressed the ILO at Geneva, he gave a call that we must pay our attention to the unorganized labour, because, particularly in India, the unorganized labour constitutes about 90 per cent of our total workforce. And it appears that we are paying more attention to the organized labour and less attention to the unorganized labour. When I took over the Ministry of Labour, he wanted me to go round the country and find out the conditions of the rural labour, which I did. I am grateful to many of my colleagues, Members of Parliament, who on many occasions accompanied me to several places. In 1987, when Shri Rajiv Gandhi was presenting the Budget, he made an announcement that the National Commission on Labour could be constituted. Accordingly, the Commission was constituted in August, 1987. The report was substituted on 31 July and I am sorry that from 31 July to 9 September is not yet two months as claimed by my very very good friend Mr Das Gupta, who should have been replying to the clarifications because he is practically the author of the report.

In any case, the report was submitted on 31 July 1991, and it is a very voluminous report containing a lot of recommendations. I must thank the Commission for its having done a very good job. Many useful and concrete suggestions and recommendations have been made in the report. I would like to assure the House that we would put all the efforts under our command to see that the recommendations are studied quickly. Whatever consultations are to be made, we will make them quickly, and wherever possible, we will not lag behind in implementing these recommendations. But we have to follow certain procedures.

Actually, now we have written to the State Governments to study them. We propose that these should be discussed in the Consultative Committee.

The recommendations, their acceptance and the method of acceptance as well will certainly be available in the House. But before we come to that conclusion, it has to undergo certain stages. We have to call a meeting of the Indian Labour Conference. After all these, we will make up our mind. We will certainly come to the House, and the House can discuss it.

* * *

We intend to call a meeting of the Indian Labour Conference in November 1991, where it will be discussed thoroughly.

* * *

Since the House was deciding that it should come back to it again, I thought that it would not be necessary for me to react instantly to some of the points. I can, however, react to some of the points very instantly. For example, the main point is whether we are going to have a Central legislation for protection of the agricultural labour. That is the main issue which the Commission has recommended. I have personally, when I was the Labour Minister, made it very much known to Mr Das Gupta that I am in favour of this. I have said so. Now that the Commission has recommended that there should be a Central legislation for the protection and welfare of agricultural labour, I think there should be no difficulty on the part of the Government to accept this recommendation. But we will have to go through certain procedures.

Secondly, there was a suggestion that the minimum wages should be raised to Rs 20 per day. As of now the minimum wage as prescribed is Rs 15 per day. I do not think there will be any difficulty for the Central Government to accept this recommendation. In fact, we are coming forward for the amendment of Minimum Wages Act, where some major changes will be there. For example, according to the Minimum Wages Act, 'The minimum wages will be revised every five years.' Now, we are going to make it 'every two years'. Like that there are many things on which I can react but I thought, perhaps, I will react to those points while replying to the debate on the working of the Labour Ministry. Then I will touch some of the points. Thank you.

The Payment of Wages (Amendment) Bill, 1987*

Mr Vice Chairman, Sir, I am grateful to Mishraji and all the honourable Members for this useful discussion. I do not have much to say on this Bill. The Payment of Wages Act was enacted in 1936 and this was meant to protect the welfare of the workers. This is meant for protection against non-payment of wages to the workers, against delayed payment of wages or sometimes unauthorized deductions from the wages. That was the main intention when this Act came into being. Now, Section 9 of this Act deals with conditions under which deductions can be made by the employer for (1) ordinary absence, and (2) concerted absence. As far as ordinary absence is concerned, I think there is no quarrel at all. In regard to subsections (1) and (2) of Section 9, there is no quarrel at all. What Mr Mishra seeks to achieve through this Bill is to delete the provisions in subsection (2) of Section 9. I think, there has been an impression that for one day's absence, eight day's wages will be deducted. The position is that in order to enable an employer to deduct wages for eight days for one day's absence, there must be three conditions fulfilled. Somebody – I think, Shri Tridib Chaudhury – has pointed this out. The three conditions are: (1) there must be ten or more persons acting in concert to absent themselves, (2) they absent themselves from work without due notice, and (3) they must absent themselves from work without any reasonable cause. Unless these three conditions are fulfilled, wages for eight days cannot be deducted from the worker. Otherwise, it has to be governed by subsections (1) and (2) of Section 9.

Now, the question is, whether this is an arbitrary provision or whether it is against the interests of the workers. Somebody raised the question about the constitutional validity of this provision. This provision has been challenged. There have been cases. It has gone to the honourable high court; even up to the honourable Supreme Court. For the kind information of the House, I would like to point out that the constitutional validity of this provision has been upheld by the judiciary. They have

R.S. Deb., 20 November 1987 (Spoke while participating in and replying to the Private Member's Bill moved by Shri Chaturanan Mishra in the Rajya Sabha which provided for deletion of the subsection 2 of Section 9 of the Payment of Wages Act, 1936).

not said anywhere that, constitutionally, it is invalid. But there are cases where eight days' wages were deducted. In one case, the Supreme Court brought it to one day. They said eight days' wages is too much; you deduct one day's wages. But the Supreme Court have not said that it is constitutionally invalid. This is the point I wanted to clarify.

Now, as somebody pointed out, this Act has been in existence for 51 years. But the question is, on how many occasions this particular provision has been used or misused? This is the point. Mr Mishra who is a trade union leader himself must have had some experience and that is why he has come to the august House with this Bill seeking to delete this provision. But he himself admitted, while moving the Bill, that this provision has not been used and yet he wants that this should not be there. Actually, I was expecting that in this debate honourable Members would come forward and give me specific instances where this provision has been used or misused. The only example which came out was that of the Coal India. I will answer that. The Coal India strike took place on 21 January 1987. They went on a one-day strike. The company management served notice on the workers asking why eight days' wages should not be deducted. Questions were raised in Parliament on this. In the Consultative Committee of the Ministry of Labour, this issue was discussed. Members of Parliament pleaded with me that I should talk to the Energy Minister and sort out this point. I talked to Mr Sathe. Some honourable Members also talked to Mr Sathe. In the meantime, the Eastern Coalfields workers went to the Calcutta High Court. My information is, till now, eight days' wages have not been deducted from the wages of the workers of Coal India for the 21 January strike. Therefore, even this example is not correct.

Unless we have any specific cases where it has been used or misused against the workers, unless we have some experience gained, where this provision has gone against the interests of the workers, I do not see any reason why we should, at this stage, go in for a review of this provision. But I can assure the House that if there is any case of victimization or misuse of this provision, if this provision has gone against the interests of the workers, if there has been arbitrary exercise of this provision, I am prepared to look into it and I am prepared to review it. But as of now, I must submit to the august House that I do not see any reason why we should review it.

There is one point raised by Shri Chitta Basu which I want to answer, though it is not connected with the subject. The point related to the interim relief which was agreed to. Shri Chitta Basu said that West Bengal has been discriminated. I must submit before this august House and for the information of Shri Chitta Basu that West Bengal has not been discriminated because it is not on the basis of States. NTC means all over India, and all over India we have not paid. At 4.30 hours, I had to meet the delegation of IDPL, Rishikesh, who have not received the interim relief. I will go from here to meet them. BALCO has not received it. So, it is not a discrimination against one State. That impression he should never get. On the 31st I have met the trade union leaders in Calcutta. I have discussed with them this issue thoroughly and I have promised that I will take up the matter with the Ministry of Industry. Unfortunately, from Calcutta I had to go to Nagaland and from there I came back yesterday only. In the meantime, our officers have been in touch with them. So, I would appeal on this floor that this sort of matters should be sorted out across the table. We have always been for that and there is no necessity for going on strike. I would appeal to them to call off the strike on the 21st and I am prepared to talk to them any time they want to talk to me.

With these words, I request the honourable Member to withdraw the Bill.

* * *

I forgot to mention one more point. One honourable Member made a point about lockout vis-à-vis strikes. Now, the Government policy on lockouts and strikes is under review and I have promised that a new legislation will be coming in. Industrial Relations Act will be brought in to replace the Industrial Disputes Act. About this particular provision, I have said that we will review the situation. That is why I have said that in case there has been any discrimination or arbitrary action against the workers as result of this provision, I am prepared to review it. So, let the honourable Member give me specific instances or history of it. However, all the labour laws are always under constant review and I have no difficulty in reviewing this.

Raising the Problems of Journalists*

Mr Vice Chairman, Sir, some honourable Members had raised in the august House the issue relating to steps being taken by the management of the Times of India Group of Newspapers and in particular in respect of publication of the *Nav Bharat Times*. A section of the press had also reported that M/s Bennett Coleman and Co. of the Times of India Group had decided to close down the News Bureau of the *Nav Bharat Times* and to convert it into a translated version of the *Times of India*. The report also stated that a number of news persons would be retrenched. Some of the journalist bodies too reportedly have protested against the developments.

The management of the *Nav Bharat Times* has also, following the above, come out with a clarification in the press that the newspaper reports were 'unfounded'. The management have further stated that they have only sought sharing of group editorial resources across the group publications to enhance the value of each publication in the group while continuing to retain its identity. While the Government would not wish to intervene in the internal matters of newspaper establishments in the interest of freedom of the press, should there be any violation of law, it shall ensure due action as may be specifically called for.

* * *

Well, Mr Vice Chairman, Sir, I am officially the Minister of Coal. But I have been looking after Labour for some time. In any case, whatever answers we give, that is from the Government; and we have the collective responsibility as everyone of us is aware.

Regarding the statement, Sir, I am inclined to agree with Mr Padmanabhan and other colleagues here that this statement does not carry much of information.

* * *

I have to explain to you the background. This issue was raised on the floor of the august House.

**R.S. Deb.*, 13 December 1991 (Spoke while making a statement and participating in the discussion regarding the Times of India Group of Newspapers).

That is why I will explain the position.

Sir, the matter was raised day before yesterday on the floor of the august House. Some honourable Members demanded that some information should be given. Then, yesterday, the matter was raised on the floor of the Lok Sabha, and the Chair gave a direction that the Government should come with a statement. That is the reason why I have to make a statement. And once I make a statement in the Lok Sabha, our practice is that we should also make the same statement in the Rajya Sabha. So, it is a matter of direction from the Chair that this has to be done. I pleaded that I should be allowed to make the statement on Monday because I do not have information. But then I was told that I have to make the statement here today itself.

* * *

I am only saying about my concern that as far as the administration of journalists and other newspaper employees' conditions of service is concerned, it is administered by the State Governments. It does not come under our purview. The Times of India Group establishment has headquarters in Bombay and therefore, the appropriate Government is the Government of Maharashtra. As far as the *Nav Bharat Times* is concerned, it is located in Delhi and the appropriate Government is the Delhi Administration.

* * *

Only when there is an industrial dispute, then we come into the picture. We have checked up both from their Delhi office as well as their Bombay office. There is no industrial dispute case; there is no industrial dispute pending before us and, therefore, it is very difficult for me, and I must admit that I am not in a position to give many information which the honourable Members would have liked to know. However, whatever information we could collect, I have tried to inform this House.

Yesterday, the representatives of the Bennet Coleman's employees union met me and they also met the honourable Minister of Information and Broadcasting, Mr Ajit Panja, today and they have submitted a memorandum. In that memorandum, they have brought out a lot of information to us. Since this memorandum was submitted to the

Information and Broadcasting Minister today jointly addressed to Mr Panja and myself, I have had practically no time to check on the information that has been given here. But I have no reason to disbelieve, and it is because of this background that the delegation has told us that Bennet Coleman & Company has in recent years stopped publication of *Dinman Times, Sarika, Kala Bharati, Parakh*. All these are Hindi papers. They have also closed down the *Youth Times* which is published in English and they have also closed down the *Evening News of India* which is published from Bombay. As a result of these closures, it is alleged here that one hundred journalists and non-journalists have been retrenched.

* * *

That is why an apprehension in the minds of the journalists is that since the *Times of India* management have already closed down a number of newspapers, the *Nav Bharat Times* may also be closed down. Of course, the management have denied it. They have issued a press note saying that it is unfounded. We could not get it in writing. Somebody here asked whether there has been any communication from them. We talked to them on the telephone and they have told us on the telephone that whatever has been stated in the press is correct; that is the correct position and they have no intention of closing down the *Nav Bharat Times* and that its identity would be retained. That is what they have told us on telephone.

* * *

On translation also, we asked them and they say – and I am giving you their version – that occasionally what they would like to do is that some of the editorials from English paper, the *Times of India* – if it is a very good one and is in the interest of people – would be translated into Hindi and published in the *Nav Bharat Times*. Similarly, if there is an editorial, if there is a good editorial . . . in the *Nav Bharat Times*, which is a good one, they would translate it in English and publish it is in the *Times of India*. This may be very rare.

* * *

It is not a question of believing or not believing. Since these matters came up, we talked to them. This is the explanation they gave. I am just informing the House.

Another point raised here was that the management is recruiting journalists on contract basis. The delegation told us that the *Times of India* has already 30 journalists on contract basis, the *Economic Times* has 50 and the *Nav Bharat Times* has eight. Unfortunately, the legal position is, the Contract Labour (Abolition and Regulation) Act does not apply to journalists. It only applies to workmen who are earning Rs 1,600 and less. Journalists do not come under the purview of this Act. Of course, Shri Kapil Verma wanted to know whether the law would be reviewed. I have noted his suggestion.

* * *

Sir, the position is, I do not have much information with me now. But I would invite the attention of the august House to the last sentence in my statement, wherein I have said: '. . . should there be any violation of law, which goes against the interests of working journalists, it shall ensure due action as may be specifically called for.' I have said that we shall ensure that due action is taken. This is my assurance to the august House.

* * *

Whatever responsibility is cast on us, for the protection of the interests of the journalists, we shall discharge it.

The Coal Mines Nationalization (Amendment) Bill, 1992*

The Constitutional provision lays down that a Money Bill cannot be introduced in this House. A Bill which is a Money Bill cannot be introduced in the Upper House. It has to be introduced in the Lower House. Article 117 of the Constitution of India clearly lays down as to

**R.S. Deb.*, 15 and 21 July 1992 (Spoke while moving and participating in the discussion on the Coal Mines Nationalization (Amendment) Bill, 1992, in Rajya Sabha).

what is a Money Bill. If you look at Article 117 or rather 110, which my learned friend just read on, it is very clear that this Bill does not come under the purview of the Money Bill. In fact the provision says, 'dealing with all or any of the following matters: (a) the imposition, abolition, remission, alteration or regulation of any tax'. Now, clause no. (2) says, even if it is an imposition of tax by the local authorities that will not be deemed to be a Money Bill. This particular Bill merely deals with empowering the Government of India to allow private coal mining for captive end use for purpose of power generation and iron and steel sector or any other sector which the Government may from time to time notify. Therefore, it has nothing to do with a Money Bill.

* * *

Let me explain Article 110 (1) (e) which the honourable Member has referred to say, 'the declaring of any expenditure to be expenditure charged on the Consolidated Fund of India or the increasing of the amount of any such expenditure to be expenditure'. This financial memorandum only deals with the restructuring of an office which is already in existence. We will administer the implementation of the amendment. What we are saying is that as of today, we do not expect any additional expenditure on the office of the Coal Controller. But it may so happen that sometimes you may have to add one LG assistant or one UG assistant more. But we do not want any additional funds from the Government of India.

* * *

Mr Vice Chairman, Sir, I am grateful to all the honourable Members who have participated in this short debate and also extended support to this Bill. The necessity for bringing this amendment Bill has been spelt out in the Objects of the Bill and initial remarks by the Deputy Minister while commending this Bill for the consideration of the House. The Eighth Five Year Plan envisages an additional power generation to the tune of 30,538 MW. Out of the 30,538 MW of additional power to be generated during the Eighth Five Year Plan as much as 20,156 MW is to be generated from the thermal sector, that is coal and lignite.

If 20,156 MW of additional power is to be generated during the Eighth Five Year Plan, then the demand for coal by the end of the

Eighth Five Year Plan will be 311 million tonnes. But as of today we will be able to produce only 298 million tonnes. So, by the end of the Eighth Five Year Plan, there will be a gap of 13 million tonnes of coal. This is one aspect.

* * *

The demand will be 311 million tonnes but our production will be 298 million tonnes. So the gap will be 13 million tonnes of coal by the end of the Eighth Plan. If coal is to be supplied for generating 20,156 MW then the total amount of money which is required by us, by our Department, Coal India Ltd, Singareni, Neyveli altogether, is coming to the tune of Rs 19,374 crore. This is the money required which we have projected to the Planning Commission. But ultimately, the Planning Commission has brought it down to Rs 11,320 crore. Of course, it is yet to be finalized.

* * *

Sir, the plan allocation is going to be Rs 11,320 crore as against our projected demand of Rs 19,374 crore. So we have a clear-cut gap of Rs 8,000 crore in order to generate 25,156 MW. Now, even Rs 11,320 crore, which more or less will be approved by the Planning Commission for the Eighth Five Year Plan, the budgetary support that is given by the Government of India is very very minimal. At the time of nationalization, we used to get 100; even 1985 it used to be at least 90 per cent budgetary support. But this year our budgetary support has come down to just 19 per cent. Taking all these factors into account we were really in difficulty. We had a lot of discussions among ourselves in the Ministry and we have only three alternatives before us. One alternative is: if I am required to produce 311 million tonnes of coal by the end of the Eighth Five Year Plan, then I must get the money that I require from the Government of India as budgetary support, which is not available. The second alternative is that the power stations or the consumers who will take coal from us, they will give the money to us to develop new mines and with their money we will develop new mines and supply them coal. That is the second alternative available to us and we know that this is not possible because you know even today I have got Rs 18,000 crore as arrears from our consumers. So there is no question of the consumers giving us advance money for developing new coal mines. And the third alternative is that we lease out some specific mines purely for captive purposes: 'we require so much of coal, we do not have the money to develop the mine so you develop it.' This is the most acceptable solution that we found and it is precisely because of this reason I have come to this august House to seek this amendment. I can assure the august House that the government of India has no intention as of now to denationalize the mines.

There is no proposal at all. There is no such proposal under the consideration of the Government. Those who are going to have the lease of new mines, it is going to be purely for end-use purposes. They cannot and they will not be allowed to use that coal for some other purpose or to market it or to sell it to others. Mr Dayanand Sahay made a very emphatic point, that is the marketing part of it. All the coal will be with the Coal India Limited and we are not going to give it to others. It is only for captive purposes for their end use that we come to seek this amendment. The reasons I have already explained.

* * *

Sir, if everything was said before, then the Minister would have nothing to speak after the debate. So we did not want to give all these figures. The second aspect of the amendment is to allow the setting up of washeries by the private sector. On the floor of this august House there was no question, there was no way, when coal was discussed and the question of quality was not addressed. The maximum complaint that we get in the Ministry from the honourable Members of Parliament and in the discussions that take place on the floor of both the Houses of Parliament is regarding the quality of coal. I have very frankly admitted both in the Lok Sabha as well as this august House that unless and until we are able to supply beneficiated coal, the complaint on quality will be there. We will not be able to give quality coal. The only way to supply quality coal is to beneficiate the raw coal and for that purpose came the question of resources. We do not have the money with us. Therefore, we are going to allow the private investment as far as setting up of washeries is concerned so that we can achieve two things. One is that we are able to satisfy our consumers on quality and, secondly, we bring down the pressure on transportation. As some of the honourable Members have rightly pointed out, it so happens that sometimes the raw coal which is going to the consumers contains 25 to 30 per cent ash and if the raw coal is washed and transported, then the pressure on railways will also come down and we will be able to supply and transport more. As the position stands today, the Railways are having a lot of problems in transporting materials, goods, etc., and, therefore, sometimes even if we have the coal with us, because of transport problems we are not able to satisfy the demand. And I have the details of what type of washeries we are contemplating; I do not know by what time. I don't think it is wise for me to waste the time of the august House in giving these details. We will notify these details. There are a few individual points that were raised.

Mr Hanumanthappa has referred to the closure of a thermal plant four days after my departure from Bangalore and where I had given an assurance that coal would not be a problem. Coal is available, I am given to understand, Sir, that the power plant was shut down not because we did not supply coal. The august House is aware that from 1 October 1991, we have introduced the cash-and-carry system. We do not supply coal any more on credit. Their credit today stands at Rs 20 crore and perhaps it was because of this reason that there has been a temporary suspension of supply of coal.

As far as Tamil Nadu is concerned – my friend has asked about Tamil Nadu – all the three thermal power stations in Tamil Nadu are linked to Singrauli Coalfield and the Western Coalfields, and it will continue to be so. There is no question of the existing power plants having to depend on the private mines. No power plants will be made to depend on the private mines because I have explained that the private mines will be absolutely for the end use and for captive purposes. Therefore, the existing arrangements for all the thermal plants all over the country will continue. With these few words, Sir, I once again thank the honourable Members for having given support and given us the ideas and I request that the Bill be taken into consideration.

* * *

Sir, as of now, Section 5 of the Mines Act debars investment in the coal sector. Therefore, the investment that we are talking of, as of today, is intended only for domestic investment and not for foreign investment. If foreign investment is to be brought into the mining sector, then Section 5 of the Mining Act has to be amended. Not before that.

INTERNAL SECURITY

The Citizenship (Amendment) Bill, 1985*

Madam Deputy Chairman, I beg to move:

> That the Bill further to amend the Citizenship Act, 1955, as passed by the Lok Sabha, be taken into consideration.

As the august House is aware, on 15 August 1985, the representatives of the Government and the leaders of the All-Assam Students Union and the All-Assam Gana Sangram Parishad signed a memorandum of Settlement which was laid on the Table of the House on 16 August 1985. Assam Accord is a political settlement of which the core is the clauses relating to the foreigners issue. Accordingly, it is proposed to enact the Citizenship (Amendment) Bill, 1985, to give a legal shape to the clauses 5.1 to 5.4, 5.6 and 5.7 of the Accord relating to the foreigners issue. The proposed legislation which is by way of amendment to the Citizenship Act, 1955 and seeks mainly to insert a new Section 6-A in the Principal Act deals with the following two categories of persons of Indian origin who came from erstwhile East Pakistan, now Bangladesh, to Assam:

(i) Those who came prior to 1 January 1966; and
(ii) Those who came between 1 January 1966 and 24 March 1971 (both days inclusive).

The salient features of the proposed legislation are as under:

> It has been provided that all persons of Indian origin who came before 1 January 1966 to Assam from Bangladesh (including those whose names were in the 1967 electoral rolls) and who have been ordinarily

---

**R.S. Deb.*, 2 and 3 December 1985 (Spoke while moving the Bill in the Rajya Sabha) The Bill provided for Amendment of the Citizenship Act, 1955, as passed by the Lok Sabha.

resident in Assam since the dates of their entry into Assam shall be deemed to be citizens of India as from 1 January 1966.

For every person of Indian origin who came to Assam between 1 January 1966 and 24 March 1971 from Bangladesh and who has been ordinarily resident in Assam since then and who has been detected to be foreigner, following provisions have been made:-

(i) He shall register himself in accordance with the rules framed for this purpose;

(ii) If his name is included in any electoral roll in force on the date of detection, it shall be deleted from the electoral roll;

(iii) Every person so registered shall have all rights and obligations as a citizen of India (including the right to obtain a passport), but shall not be entitled to have his name included in any electoral roll before the expiry of a period of ten years from the date of his detection as a foreigner.

(iv) After the expiry of a period of ten years from the date of detection as a foreigner, every person so registered shall be deemed to be a citizen of India for all purposes.

(v) It has been expressly provided that in determining whether a person seeking registration fulfils the requirements of registration as indicated above, the registering authority shall act in conformity with the opinion of the tribunal constituted under the Foreigners (Tribunals) Order, 1964.

The proposed amendment will not affect any person who, prior to the commencement of this enactment, is a citizen of India. The benefits of the proposed amendment will not be available to such persons who have been expelled from India under the Foreigners Act, prior to the commencement of this Act.

The Bill, inter alia, stipulates that persons of Indian origin who came to Assam from the erstwhile East Pakistan (now Bangladesh), between 1 January 1966 and 24 March 1971, both days inclusive, shall be detected in accordance with the provisions of the Foreigners Act and the Foreigners (Tribunals) Order, 1964. Following detection, these persons will have to be registered in accordance with the rules to be made by the Central Government in this behalf. This will require strengthening of the Government machinery which will involve some expenditure from the Consolidated Fund of India. For various reasons, it is not possible at this stage to precisely quantify the expenditure likely to be incurred on this account.

With these words, Madam, I commend the Citizenship (Amendment) Bill, 1985, for the consideration of this august House.

* * *

Madam, I thank the honourable Members for giving us this very interesting debate on this very important Bill. The debate yesterday started with self-contradictory statements by our honourable friend Mr Mohanan. We also witnessed a very emotional speech by Mr Hashmi, very impressive speech by my honourable friend, Mr P. Babul Reddy, and a very good speech by Prof. Lakshmanna.

Madam, Assam Accord is a political accord. As I stated earlier, this Bill only seeks to give a legal shape to a portion of the settlement which relates to the foreigners.

This Assam Accord has been widely welcomed in the whole country. It has been welcomed by this august House and the other House. It was very clear in this debate that every honourable Member had welcomed the Assam Accord. As my honourable friend Mr P. Babul Reddy has very rightly pointed out yesterday that those who have welcomed this accord cannot oppose this Bill; and those who are opposed to this Bill cannot support this accord. It is in this context, I have said that our honourable friend was little contradictory when he said that we welcome the accord but oppose the Bill. I think those who welcome the accord has no room to oppose this Bill.

Now, a number of points have been raised about depriving the minorities or disenfranchisement and all sorts of things. Madam, I want to make it very clear that this Bill does not deal with the minorities of any kind. This Bill deals purely with a matter relating to the foreigners. When we talk about foreigners there is no room for us to discuss about minorities, whether it is religious or linguistic.

A foreigner is a foreigner. He may be speaking any language; he may be professing any religion. But a foreigner is a foreigner. We are dealing, in this Bill, only with matters relating to foreigners. Secondly, it must be made very clear that we are not discussing about taking away anybody's right. There is no question of deprivation. There is no question of taking away anybody's right here. On the other hand, we are conferring rights on the foreigners who have come to our country and whom we are accepting. This Bill deals with two categories of people. One is, those people who had come on or before 1 January 1966 and we are conferring citizenship on these people by the Act at a stroke. They do not have to go through any process. Therefore, it is conferment of rights that we seek to do. There is no question of taking away anybody's rights. The second category of people are those who have come between 1 January 1966 and 24 March 1971. This is the second category of people on whom we are going to confer citizenship after ten years from the day they have been detected as foreigners. Where is the question of taking away anybody's right? Where is the question of disenfranchising a large number of people, as somebody had alleged? There is no question of disenfranchising anybody. This is a question of giving citizenship rights with retrospective effect, that is from 1 January 1966 and conferring citizenship rights with prospective effect, that is, after 10 years from the day they have been detected as foreigners. This is very simple.

Now, the question is whether Parliament has the authority, has the right to confer these rights on the people. So many points on the constitutional validity or the constitutionality of this Bill have been discussed. I think many honourable Members from this side and the other side including, I think, Mr Babul Reddy himself have pointed out that Parliament is competent to decide on all matters relating to citizenship. And this has been very clearly, very expressly, unambiguously, put forward in Article 11 of the Constitution of India. It says:

> Nothing in the foregoing provision of this Part shall derogate from the Power of Parliament to make any provisions with respect to the acquisition and termination of citizenship.

I want to underline this: 'and all other matters relating to citizenship'. Therefore, the constitutionality of this Bill cannot be doubted. The power of Parliament to enact such a Bill cannot be challenged at all. Now one pertinent question, of course, remains. As allegation has been made that this Bill is creating two types of citizenship. I do not know where are the two types of citizenship. Those people who had come on or before 1 January 1966 will become citizens immediately when this Bill comes into force. And those people who have come between 1 January 1966 and 24 March 1971, both days inclusive, will become citizens of this country after ten years from the day they have been detected as foreigners. Where is the question of two types of citizenship? The question is, till they become citizens of India after ten years from the day of detection, what will happen to them; whether they will be able to enjoy all the rights, since they are not citizens, since they are going to become citizens after ten years. This is a pertinent question.

* * *

I am discussing the constitutionality, whether Parliament has the right to confer other rights of these people till they become full-fledged citizens. And this provision has also been made very clear in Section 12 of the Citizenship Act, which I would like to quote for the benefit of the honourable Members. Section 12 reads:

> The Central Government may, by order notified in the Official Gazette – by a simple order – make provisions on a basis of reciprocity for the conferment of all or any of the rights of a citizen of India on the citizens of any country specified in the First Schedule.

The First Schedule lists the members belonging to the Commonwealth. Bangladesh was not added in the First Schedule at that time because it has come only recently; otherwise, this could have been done by a mere notification under this provision. Therefore, there is no question of having two categories of citizens as has been talked about. Even, for the sake of argument, if you concede about the right to franchise, it is one thing to be a citizen of India and it is quite another thing to be a voter. It is not that all citizens of this country are entitled to vote. It is only when one attains the age of 21 under Article 326 that one is entitled to franchise. But do you mean to say that those who are below 21 are not citizens of this country? I am just talking about the legal points.

Another point made is that this agreement has been reached in spite of the international commitment, which obviously refers to the Liaquat–Nehru Pact and the Mujibur–Indira understanding, etc. I must inform the august House that all these aspects have been fully taken care of before this Agreement has been reached. Para 4 of the Accord says:

> Keeping all aspects of the problem, including constitutional and legal provisions, international agreements, national commitments and humanitarian considerations, it has been decided to proceed as follows . . .

Therefore, all these aspects have been taken into consideration.

Another point made was that the Government has gone back from what Mrs Gandhi promised, that Mrs Gandhi said that 1971 should be the cut-off year. Of course, this point was very effectively answered by my senior colleague, Mr Baharul Islam that Mrs Gandhi had never agreed that 1971 should be the cut-off year. What she had always said was that we could start with 1971, that 1971 could be a starting point. This was what Mrs Gandhi had said. So there is no question of going back from what Mrs Gandhi had said.

Many other points have been raised, particularly by the professor. It has been a very, very, well-argued speech yesterday and the professor has been very kind to point out many other provisions of the Accord and why the Government has not been doing anything in that respect. One particular thing which he quoted was para 6 where it says:

> Constitutional, legislative, administrative safeguards, as may be appropriate, shall be provided to protect, preserve and promote the cultural, social, linguistic identity and heritage of the Assamese people.

In a written answer to one of the Parliamentary questions, I think, I had given a background of this whole thing. During the agreement, during the discussions, during the negotiations, it was agreed that the AASU leaders will submit a proposal as to in what manner they want their rights and their culture, their heritage and identity to be preserved. They are supposed to give us a proposal and we are waiting for their proposal. As soon as their proposal comes, we will certainly examine it. Either my answer was not seen by him or it did not give the background clearly. You have every reason to misunderstand it. I think it is my fault, it was not your fault.

* * *

I can only assure the august House and the people of Assam that we are committed to the all-round development of Assam. We have full commitment to every provisions of the Accord and we are going to implement it in letter and spirit and this I can say on the floor of the august House. There is no question of not implementing any provisions of the Accord. Every provision of the accord will be implemented and we have already taken a number of steps, and if I go on telling what steps have been taken against each para of the Accord, it will take a long time. But I can only assure the august House that we are committed to the development of Assam and, in fact, if you look at the figure for the Seventh Five Year Plan, you will see that the Seventh Plan outlay for

Assam has been finalized at Rs 2,100 crore as against the Sixth Plan figure of Rs 1,115 crore. So, the Seventh Plan outlay is almost double that of the Sixth Plan.

* * *

In the case of the most of the backward States, it is so. I think it is true of most of the North Eastern States because a special effort is being made to develop them. It is not confined to Assam alone but it applies to some other States of the North Eastern region. To that extent, Madam, the professor is right.

Another point that is to be noted is that out of this amount of Rs 2,100 crore, Central assistance will be to the tune of Rs 2,065 crore, which means that practically the whole of the Seventh Plan is being financed by the Central Government. I am giving a little illustration only to show that we are certainly committed to the development of Assam and for that matter, all parts of the country. But we are making special efforts to develop Assam in view of the promises that we have made in this Accord.

With these words, Madam, I once again thank all the honourable Members and request that the Bill may be passed.

* * *

Madam word 'undivided' has been used in the Citizenship Act 1955, and that word has been defined in the Act itself. Therefore, we cannot substitute this word at this stage because the main Act itself defines that word. So it is not possible for us to accede to this.

* * *

Madam, I move:

> That the Bill be passed.

PART V

Felicitating P.A. Sangma on Becoming Speaker

Shri Atal Bihari Vajpayee (Prime Minister): Mr Speaker, Sir, I feel extremely happy while felicitating you as the Speaker of the Lok Sabha. You have been elected unanimously. It is indicative of your popularity. But at the same time, it also signifies the fact that in spite of political differences, Indian democracy and this highest representative institution of the Indian democracy can unite on important matters and can take decisions unanimously.

Mr Speaker, Sir, you have the privilege of being born in independent India. You belong to that part of India which is known as North East. This region is an important part of India but somehow feels itself neglected. Sometimes, people living there feel that they are not only far from Delhi but are far from hearts also. There is no reason for nurturing such a feeling. I am sure that your election will help in lessening this feeling.

You have shouldered many responsibilities. We have seen you working in many capacities. Perhaps, there has been no such issue related to the Central Government which has not been solved with your skill. You have been popular as the Labour Minister and even your opponents have appreciated you. You have also been the Chief Minister of Meghalaya. Your election has enhanced the dignity of this august House. You are a devoted follower of the great religion, Christianity. Your sense of tolerance, feeling of fraternity and quality of taking all together are the assets which will now be available at national level. I am confident that under your leadership, the rights of this august House as well as that of the Members will be protected. People of India have elected their representatives. Now, it is the turn of these representatives to prove their mettle. As I said, Lok Sabha is the highest representative body, we have to maintain the dignity of this august House and keep the democracy intact. I have noticed that some of our old friends have been re-elected. Now, their charm to move towards the middle of the

---

L.S. Deb., 23 May 1996 (The Prime Minister and honourable Members spoke while felicitating Shri P.A. Sangma as he was elected Speaker, Lok Sabha).

House, instead of sitting in their seats will certainly be less. There is a need to run the House with dignity. Wherever we deviate, you can guide us to the right path. You have to take all together. We wholeheartedly wish you success. We assure you of our best cooperation. I once again congratulate and felicitate you.

~

Shri P.V. Narasimha Rao: Mr Speaker, Sir, I feel extremely happy that you have been unanimously elected as the Speaker of the august House. Unanimity is the essence for this election and I would very much welcome the spirit of unanimity which gives you a lot of manoeuvrability, a lot of power and a lot of scope to come to conclusions which otherwise would have been very difficult.

I have seen you in many capacities and perhaps more than anyone else, I have had the opportunity of appreciating your work in whatever capacity you have been working. As the Chief Minister of Meghalaya, I remember the very difficult situation which you faced. As the Labour Minister of India, I very well know through what holes you were dragged sometimes. But you came out unscathed and you proved to be one of the most successful Labour Ministers of India because the time when you became the Labour Minister was so crucial – everything was touch and go – that the whole policy would have collapsed if we not had a Labour Minister of your calibre. So, I feel very happy that you are at the place where your talents will be required in great measure and I am sure they will be available in adequate measure.

I welcome you and I beseech the honourable Members of the House to help you in maintaining the dignity of the august House as, I am sure, you would like to maintain the dignity and conduct the business of the House in the best possible manner and in the best traditions of Parliamentary democracy. I welcome you once again.

~

Shri Shivraj V. Patil: Mr Speaker, Sir, it is indeed very heartening to know that the leaders of all parties and, in fact, all Members of the House have shown sagacity in choosing the Speaker unanimously and choosing you, Shri P.A. Sangma, as the presiding officer of the august House of the People of this country, which has the greatest democracy in the world. They all deserve appreciation of all the people who believe in the practice of parliamentary democracy.

You, Mr Speaker, appear to be young, but you are a very experienced leader who had innings in responsible positions at the State level and the national level and are very humane, intelligent, cooperative, balanced and pragmatic politician and you are bound to protect and enhance the dignity of the august House and to strengthen the democratic and parliamentary system in India. In this responsible and onerous task, you may need the cooperation of this House which, I am sure, would be given to you in ample measure.

The Speaker has to deal with legal, political, economic, social and psychological matters and has to respond to matters which arise suddenly and abruptly. An approach which is sympathetic, unbiased and correct can help in all these matters. The tradition of this House so far has been to adopt an approach of that kind and, I am sure, it would be adopted by it in future also.

I would like to pray for the successful tenure of yours as the Speaker of the eleventh Lok Sabha and to give you my very sincere and very warm congratulations on your elevation to this prestigious and high position.

~

Shri Sharad Yadav: Mr Speaker, Sir, it is a matter of pride for the entire nation that after the constitution of the eleventh Lok Sabha, this House, the highest institution of this country, has expressed its faith in you at such a crucial time when the country is facing a number of challenges.

I have been in this august House for several years. You have been performing your duty with efficiency, skill and wisdom in this House and have been solving our ticklish problems easily. Though we were in the Opposition, we too used to be convinced with your logic on many occasions, though on coming out of the House, we used to feel that that was not the correct thing. The efficiency, skill and wisdom shown by you in the House have really been praiseworthy.

We are followers of Late Dr Lohia. He used to call North East region as 'Sagarmatha' of India. In the region where you hail from, 'the Himalayas are called 'Sagarmatha'. Today, you are sitting on the 'Sagarmatha' (peak) of this august House. Under your leadership, this nation will achieve great heights and in this Parliament, more powers will be bestowed to make this poor, hopeless and helpless country a strong nation. You would guide this nation in resolving all the future problems. With your election as the Speaker, the poor of India has felt a sense of pride and it has strengthened the unity of the nation. Besides, the way your name has been unanimously agreed upon is unprecedented in the history. On this occasion, I would also like to thank the former speaker for his five years' successful tenure in this House. On several occasions, he handled the situation very tactfully and had shown great efficiency.

With these words, I, on behalf of my party and all the honourable Members of this august House, congratulate you on this historic occasion and hope that you would be able to give a new turn to the future history.

~

Shri Murasoli Maran: Mr Speaker, Sir, it is an honour and privilege for us in the House to have you in the chair as the Speaker of this august House and the head of this great Parliament of India. The fact that you have been unanimously chosen speaks not only about the present-day political equation inside the House but also your admirable qualities which made you acceptable to all of us.

Sir, you have shouldered many responsibilities with great distinction. You had been a teacher, an advocate and more than anything else, you belong to my tribe – you are a journalist. You had been a very good Chief Minister of Meghalaya, not only a Chief Minister but also you acted as the leader of the Opposition for two years. Therefore, I think I need not remind you about the feelings of the Opposition. So, I am sure, you will be fair to the Opposition.

Sir, the House would congratulate and compliment the small little man of India who went into the small little polling booth and got the small little ballot paper and made a mark, a small little mark on it and elected all of us. All glory to that small little man, the common man, the great citizen of India who has allowed us to retain the reputations that we are the largest democracy in the world.

Sir, you have got very difficult task before you. The people, in their wisdom, have given no majority to any single party. This makes your task all the more difficult because nobody wants that the country should plunge into another election. This presupposes that this House and you, Sir, should conduct the affairs in such a way that the burning problems are given attention and care. This I want to remind you.

Sir, when I promise cooperation, I cannot say that we will keep our mouth shut and will keep the decibel level at the lower possible level because if there is an uproar, it is not just one voice but the voice of the lakhs of people whom we represent. I would like to submit that if a voice is raised from any corner either from the front bench or from the back bench demanding your attention to their plight, I appeal to you, Sir, that you must listen to it. We are here to justify our election, to justify our presence. Therefore, I seek your help in this matter.

Sir, there is always a question whether the Speaker should belong to a party or not. Sir, I am reminded about the speech of the first Speaker of the Lok Sabha, Dr Mavalankar. Sir, he had stated very clearly: 'It is obviously not possible in the present conditions of our political and parliamentary life to remain as insular as English Speaker so far as political life goes. But the Indian Speaker acting as such will be absolutely a non-party man meaning thereby that he keeps aloof from party deliberations and controversies. He does not cease to be a politician merely by the fact of being a Speaker.' Therefore, it is very clear that Speaker may not be non-political but he should definitely be a non-party man. I do hope that nobody will bring him down to a party level. He is above party level.

Sir, the Speaker is here not to run the country. The Speaker is here to run the House efficiently. So I hope you will rise to the occasion and do justice to all of us.

Sir, there are rules and regulations to guide us. But as the former Speaker has just explained, they are not enough because the composition of the House is so different that the rules may not help you. But I think, you should not be a skylark. Only conciliation and accommodation should solve the problem. Therefore, I want you to be firm and at the same time, I want you to be fair. It is not very difficult. I think it is Aristotle who said: 'Man is a political animal.' But we are not political beasts. We have been political adversaries at the best but most of us here have got the highest respect for each other as political beings and personalities and we want to have a proper, healthy discussions and debate. Sir, we are at the threshold of major challenges; we are at the crossroads of history and I hope this House in its collective wisdom will work in a determined manner to face the challenges that the nation is confronting us.

Therefore, Sir, I offer you all our cooperation and, I think, we will make it a great success; the eleventh Lok Sabha will be a great success.

Shri Somnath Chatterjee: Mr Speaker, Sir, it is with greatest pleasure that I stand here today to convey my greetings and felicitations to you.

Your unanimous election to this august office is a clear recognition of the qualities of your head and heart and it is a fitting decision by all the parties here to agree to this unanimous election.

Sir, I have had occasions to watch your performance as also achievements as a Member of the House and also as Minister. And what has always impressed us is, apart from your admirability, that you have had always an open mind to hear others and if necessary, to change your decision if good arguments were offered. I also remember with great pleasure your active and competent participation in the deliberations of the Committee on Subordinate Legislation where you were a Member and I had a great honour to be the Chairman. And, I remember your hospitality when we went to Meghalaya. As a Member you could organize that and we had a very profitable time from more senses than one.

Mr Speaker, Sir, today you are occupying a seat representing a part of our country which has been feeling a sense of alienation from the mainstreams for various reasons and coming from eastern India also, I have great pleasure that today we have come into the reckoning and all over India there is a clear acceptance to the role you have been playing in projecting the problems and the issues of eastern India as well, apart from all-India issues.

Sir, we know that composition of the present House is such that there may be problems and we hope we shall be able to solve them under your guidance and under your leadership. We have great traditions to maintain and uphold.

This is a House where Members have to articulate the urges and the aspirations of the common people of this country. There are Members of the House who occupy the back benches, but they have also to perform their duties and functions as Members of the House, as the elected representatives of the people. Naturally, I am sure that under you, all sections of the House, particularly the backbenchers, as they are called, will get full opportunity to project their points of view and to refer to the problems in their own areas.

We have seen here turbulent times. But that also reflects the problems that are faced by the people outside. Turbulence here does not necessarily mean disrespect to the chair but sometimes we have to adopt methods that may not seem to be quite appropriate in this august House. I am very confident, knowing you as I do for so many years and having had the great privilege of working with you in Committees, that you will fully justify the faith that we have all shown in you and will be one of the outstanding Speakers of this august House.

Sir, on behalf of my party and myself, I pledge our full cooperation and I am sure that you will be able to conduct the deliberations of the House with all success and you will have a glorious tenure. Mr Speaker, Sir, you have our very best wishes.

~

Shri P. Chidambaram: Mr Speaker, Sir, I rise to offer my congratulations and good wishes on your election as Speaker. This perhaps was the most unusual election of a Speaker. The 500-odd Members gathered here have witnessed a very unusual election. I do not wish to comment on the election because we all know the circumstance under which you have been elected as Speaker.

In a sense this reflects the very complex mandate that the people have given in this election. Today and the days that will follow, we will all speak on the mandate, the meaning of the mandate, the various interpretations that are possible. Yet, one thing is clear; no one, no party, no leader can arrogate to himself or itself the sole authority to decide the course of this nation. If political parties were slow to gather this message, the people were ahead of us and in a very resounding manner they have declared that all of us must work together. We may have fought elections against each other; but the mandate is to work together, to sit down and negotiate, talk to each other, find ways in which we can agree rather than we can disagree. That, however, will not make the eleventh Lok Sabha any less stormy than the tenth or ninth Lok Sabha. I cannot promise that we will not raise our voices. No one here can promise that we will not rush to the well of the House occasionally.

No one here can promise that we will not question your ruling; no one here can promise good behaviour. But I can promise, Sir, knowing you as an old friend that you will enhance the reputation of the chair that you sit on because by nature you are a conciliator, you are a negotiator. By nature, you are a man who makes peace with his worst enemies. So, you will bring a healing touch to the very stormy House that I envisage over the next five years.

Sir, my colleague reminded me of the tradition of the leader of the

House and the leader of the Opposition conducting the Speaker to the chair. I believe, the tradition began when no one was willing to be the Speaker and therefore, the Prime Minister and the leader of the Opposition had to drag the Speaker to the Speaker's chair. That is the old British tradition which we have modified and we have a very civilized manner in which we take you to the chair. The Speaker does not speak: he hears, he listens, he brings about an unspoken consensus, he urges the House to reach this consensus, he urges the House to reflect the wishes of the people.

Sir, I salute you for another reason. I believe, Sir, you will be the youngest person to have been elected to this chair. You also represent a generation to which I belong. A young generation has now taken the reins of this country and your elevation to this chair, I believe, will herald that change. And perhaps, you are the first Speaker who may have been born just after the struggle for independence, but on the eve of Independence. If you were born a year later, you would have qualified to be called 'Midnight's Child'. You were born just on the eve of Independence.

Coming from a State which joined the mainstream many years later, a State which is peaceful, beautiful and has wonderful people, I think, Sir, you, more than anyone else, will articulate the views and the aspirations of the forgotten small India. There are millions of them all over the country, belonging to small religions, small communities, small States but each one them adds to the greatness of this country in your elevation in your election. Sir, I think, we salute that small India, people belonging to small States, people belonging to small tribes, people belonging to small communities, people who have very small voice, a very small note because of circumstances. In honouring something which is small, we really honour all that is great in India.

Once again, Sir, on behalf of my party, the Tamil Manila Congress, I offer you my congratulations, felicitations and our promise of the fullest cooperation.

~

Shri Bolla Bulli Ramaiah: Mr Speaker, Sir, I wholeheartedly congratulate you on my own behalf as well as on behalf of my Telugu Desam Party, on your unanimous election to this august post of Speaker of Lok Sabha. Earlier you have been a Chief Minister of Meghalaya. Also a Minister for Labour and Minister for Information and Broadcasting, all these being very difficult jobs, you were able to conduct yourself very well. I hope and I am confident that you will succeed in running this House which is the highest legislative forum, in a most dignified manner, giving opportunities to all the sections of the House to ventilate their views. I assure you, Sir, on my behalf and on behalf of my party, we will extend our cooperation to you in running the House.

~

Shri Indrajit Gupta: Sir, I consider it a matter of gratification and privilege that accidentally it happened that I was called upon to declare you elected to this high post, which you may occupy with the unanimous choice of this House.

There is a proverb, as you know, which says that a cat has nine lives. Perhaps, I am reaching now that end of my career.

And, therefore, it is doubly happy for me that at this stage, you Sir, have been chosen unanimously by this august House and today I feel, of course, it is a matter of pleasure for the entire country, particularly the people of the North Eastern region. I am sure they are filled with happiness, joy and pride that the Parliament of India has made, I consider it to be the gesture towards the federal spirit of this country. That was very necessary and very important. Apart from the fact that you belong to a minority community, a tribal community, Christian community, all the matters are very very important. And today at a time when our country is facing a very difficult crisis of the identity, identity of a common nation, it was very necessary in my opinion that the House should make this gesture. And I am, therefore, grateful to all sections of the House, including our friends on the other side that they have cooperated in this decision that we have taken. Sir, I do not wish to dwell in too much detail on your qualities of head and heart. I am a trade unionist in the better part of my life and I know the working class also today in this country. They will be happy to find that the Labour Minister like you who showed himself to be champion of the rights of the working men has been elevated to this high office. As somebody said just now, you have to play the role of a conciliator and mediator in many disputes, in so many cases, where you proved yourself to be a very adept, very accommodative, very affable, very friendly and a friend of all the people who wanted you to help them to solve some difficulties. I hope you will play a similar type of role in this House. Latterly, we have been, in this country, facing what is known as judicial activism. Some people like it and some people do not like it. This judicial activism has come into play recently. We should admit it partly at least because of the failure of the legislature and of the executive to play their due parts. As a result of which the judiciary in many cases has stepped in and taken the initiative, sometimes with good results and sometimes maybe not with good results. But we are Members of this august House. We are Members of Parliament and we do feel proud when our Parliament can play its due role, its sovereign role in this country's structure. I hope, Sir, that you will be able to guide us and help us so that we can be worthy of the responsibility which the electorate has given to us. I would like to point out that, roughly speaking, I may not be quite exact in my calculation, roughly about half of the electorate has not voted. What this is due to is something which we should ponder over. We should discuss whether there is a feeling of apathy for various reasons gripping the minds of large numbers of people, maybe it is partly due to the loss, growing loss of credibility of this institution itself.

If that is so, then we have to do some introspection and find out how far we are to be blamed for it. There is time to correct oneself; there is time to restore this Parliament to its original glory and pride.

We hope that with you in the chair as Speaker we are going to offer you our fullest cooperation for this – you will be able to guide the Parliament along a path which is historically and constitutionally destined to travel.

We assure you of our cooperation and we wish you all success. On behalf of myself and on behalf of my party, you have our best wishes on your success.

~

Shri Mulayam Singh Yadav: Mr Speaker, Sir, we as well as the entire House are happy on your unanimous election. We congratulate you and extend our warm wishes to you on the occasion of your taking over the responsibility of the world's greatest democratic institution. I am sure you will certainly deliver the goods. The unanimous support of the whole House on your candidature clearly shows the ability and experience that you possess, to execute this great responsibility. Since I have been elected as a Member of Parliament for the first time, it is my maiden experience to witness an unanimous election of a candidate of Opposition to this post. It shows your capability and worthiness.

So far as your experience and ability is concerned, you have had the opportunity of working with several Prime Ministers. Besides holding the portfolio of the Ministry of Labour, you have adorned several other posts too. Therefore, you have a vast experience of labourers' problems. I hope that we will get your cooperation in solving these problems through this august House. I, on my own behalf as well as on behalf of my party, promise to extend full cooperation. I am sure that while executing this great responsibility, you will also safeguard the rights of the Members of this august House.

Several such occasions will come when you will feel that the House is not functioning according to your wishes or an honourable Member is adamant on expressing his views. On such occasions, I hope, you will never link it to any sort of distrust in you or the post held by you. To give vent to the feelings and aspirations of the people we represent becomes the greatest responsibility of the honourable Members. Their duty is not to put forth the problems of the people but also to fight for them. I hope you will never lose your patience on such occasions.

The crisis the country is facing today is not a political crisis; it is, in fact, a process through which a strong force will emerge before the country. We have not lost hope, it hardly matters whether a single party has got the majority or not, all the parties should work together. I know, during this process, a strong force will emerge in the country, which will solve the problems of the country and fulfil the hopes and aspirations of the poor, which they have been cherishing since independence. Such a force will provide opportunity to the downtrodden and the people belonging to the minorities. I am happy that you hail from Meghalaya, the North East region, which once considered itself neglected. Now the area will feel that it also has importance in India and it also has the responsibilities and rights. Yours is a dignified key post where one works without fear and favour. I assure you, Sir, we will extend our full cooperation in execution of your responsibility. With this promise, we again congratulate you and extend our good wishes.

~

Shri Chitta Basu: Sir, I raise to join the honourable Prime Minister and other distinguished Members of this august House to offer my hearty felicitations to you on the occasion of your elevation to the office of the Speaker of this great democratic institution.

Sir, we have seen you in various capacities in the State and also at the national level. We, as trade unionists and workers who have been working in the factories, mines and otherwise, cannot forget the role you did play when you had been the Labour Minister of our country. It has been rightly pointed out that your role has always been the role of a conciliator. Your role has always been the role of uniting the people, the working class, and not dividing them. Here, in this House, the complexion is very varied. There are big national parties; there are small parties; there are also other small parties and tiny groups. There are conflicts of interests; there are conflicts of class interests; there are various conflicts which are always reflected on the floor of this House. This floor is the mirror of different segments of the society and we cannot ignore this mirror. If we ignore this mirror, we ignore the nation as a whole. The working class of today is faced with great crisis and I expect that, in the coming days, the working class will have to work upon a massive struggle and those struggles are to be reflected here. With your experience in the past, I hope, believe and I am also confident that those movements and agitations of the working class and trade unions outside, in defence of their rights – economic, political and others – would also get sufficient attention of this House, particularly Sir, of your good self.

Sir, I think, you may be quite well aware of the millions of our tribals working in different parts of India; they are toiling; they are sweating and living hard lives. Sir, on your election to this exalted position, those teeming millions belonging to the tribals and minorities will feel greatly encouraged and enthused to build up their struggle and reach their right to live with honour and dignity of which they are deprived.

Sir, you also represent an important religious minority. Minorities, Sir, cannot be hushed up. Minorities have also their rights. A great democracy, the character of a democracy depends upon the degree of the guarantee to the minorities. I hope my friends sitting on this side would realize the importance of the minorities in our society. Ours is a society which is composite in nature and has got no unitary role to play. Society is multiple in nature and multifarious aspects are also there to be looked into.

Sir, I would say that North East is really the most important strategic area of our nation. We feel today that the people of the North Eastern region are getting increasingly alienated. Your elevation to this position would also bring them to realize that India needs them and they also need India.

India also takes into account the hopes and aspirations of the millions of people in the North Eastern region. I hope and I believe that with your being in this exalted office, this process of alienation of the North Eastern region would stop.

Sir, I represent a very small group in this august House and naturally we are sometimes aggrieved, aggrieved because we do not find adequate time to give expression to our feelings; to give expression to our views. Views are views. It is not regional; it is not partial; it is not small; it is not big. Views are views and views are to be expressed freely and fairly.

Sir, I hope and I believe and I am confident that with your nature, smiling all the while, we would also have smile on our face when we feel rejected, disappointed and suppressed. I hope that we would build up the traditions of this House and help us to maintain the decorum in this august House. Once again, on behalf of my party, I convey my felicitations to you.

~

Shri Birendra Prasad Baishya: Mr Speaker, Sir, I am extremely happy today to wholeheartedly congratulate you on my behalf and on behalf of my Party, the Asom Gana Parishad. For the first time in the political history of India, the honourable Speaker of Lok Sabha has been elected from the North Eastern region.

Sir, today is the most significant day for the North Eastern region. The post of the Speaker is a neutral one. So, I am hundred per cent confident that each and every honourable Member of this august House would get an equal treatment from the honourable Speaker. We belong to the North Eastern region of our country. Our region is an extremely backward region and so I would like to request you to give special attention towards the solutions of the various problems of the North Eastern region.

~

Shri Narayan Dutt Tiwari: Mr Speaker, Sir, I congratulate you from the core of my heart on your unanimous election to this highest post. After the constitution of eleventh Lok Sabha, you have been elected as the sentinel of democracy. I would like to congratulate the honourable Prime Minister, honourable leader of Opposition, the leaders and the Members of other parties for this political unanimity that has evolved in the beginning of eleventh Lok Sabha itself, in spite of the large-scale political differences. Today, we have demonstrated to the world our ability to solve the issues, which was speculative about our finding a solution to the national problems in the present political, social and economical scenario. This august House, through you, has tried to give a befitting reply by taking unanimous decision in the beginning itself and for all this, the honourable Members of the House deserve congratulations.

Sir, today, different political hues are clearly visible in the House, but we should have a belief that even in such a situation, the House will be able to take unanimous decisions on the burning issues. This belief is generated by your election. Sir, I have been fortunate enough to watch ups and downs of your life and see you transformed from a worker to a Member of Parliament and then rising high on the political scene. Since you hail from Meghalaya, the abode of clouds, I know you are blessed with the quality of patience and humility, treating all equally and you can deliver the goods amid all odds. I am sure you will be impartial in giving your rulings, irrespective of different ideologies the Members may believe in.

Sir, this House has its own experience, traditions and conventions. There are rules, rulings, concepts and traditions which have been laid down by different honourable Speakers like Shri Mavalankar, Shri Ayyangar, and even by Shri Vitthalbhai Patel before the freedom of the country, which will help you in fulfilling your responsibility in the present Lok Sabha. I am sure that, by dint of your experience, you will follow the parliamentary traditions even in odd circumstances. There are Members who have been serving the House for decades and have grasped full knowledge of the conventions of other Parliaments too. They have been extending their fullest cooperation in smooth functioning of the House. Such intellectuals are there in every party. I am hopeful that you will get cooperation of younger generation of MPs also who too are expert in parliamentary practices and conventions.

Sir, many new Members have vast experience of Legislative Assemblies and many of them have been the Chief Ministers and Ministers in their States. They have contributed a lot to Assemblies, Committees, Municipal Corporations, Zila Parishads and Village Panchayats and in this way, though new, they too have the knowledge of rules and possess experience of Parliamentary practices. I am sure you will get cooperation from all of them. Sir, I am also sure that the eleventh Lok Sabha will live its full life under your speakership and present before the country and the world new parliamentary democratic norms and conventions and thus reach new heights and horizons.

With these words, once again, I congratulate you from the core of my heart.

~

Shri P.C. Thomas: Sir, I congratulate you on your unanimous election as the Speaker of this august assembly. Sir, with your long experience in the fields of politics, administration and Parliament and Legislative Assembly, I am sure, you will become one among the best Speakers we have had. I am sure you will be able to get the support of each and every Member of this august House. We find a very good quality in you – as has been expressed by most of the Members here – that is, you are a good mediator and a negotiator. Above all, I feel you are a very good gentleman. Cardinal Newman once defined the word 'gentleman' and according to him a gentleman is one who does not inflict pain on others. I do not think you can be that gentle to fit in that definition. If you are so gentle, honourable Members of this House will have to be more gentle so as to cooperate with you in a manner to make this august House a big success. I am sure, with your long vision and wide experience, you will be able to take into confidence all the Members of this House.

Views expressed by every section of this House are important, whether they come from large parties, small parties, Opposition or Treasury Benches. As has already been mentioned by Shri Chitta Basu and others, views of the Members belonging to small parties may also be considered because they also represent one constituency. I am sure there are more small parties like mine. As a Member of the smallest one-Member party, Kerala Congress (M), I pray and beseech you to give an honouring look to the Members of small parties.

Sir, as has been expressed, there are many problems faced in the North East and there are many problems faced in the other areas also. I come from the southernmost part of this country. We also have many problems. I am sure you will give us the opportunity to depict the problems of farmers, the problems of workers, the problems of the poor faced in that area.

Sir, I would like to once again congratulate you. Lastly, I have a word to say, not to you alone but to the House as a whole. It is my wish and the wish of all of us sitting here that you should have a long life of five years as the Speaker. I am sure that in saying this, I represent the mind of each Member of this august House.

Shri Surjeet Singh Barnala: Mr Speaker, Sir, on my behalf and on behalf of my party, I congratulate you on your unanimous election to the post of Speaker of the eleventh Lok Sabha.

We have all come to this House with problems, problems of our constituencies, problems of our States, problems of our regions and national problems, of course. They will all be discussed here from time to time and important decisions will have to be taken by you. This time the elections have thrown a very complex pattern in this House. No party is in absolute majority. No party is even in a comfortable majority as compared to the other parties. It is a very difficult situation which you will have to face and that is why everyone who felicitated you has stated that your duties in the House will be quite difficult. But I am sure you will be able to surmount all those difficulties because of your long experience in political life – in your life before you entered politics and thereafter as the Chief Minister of your State, as a Minister in the Government of India and also in the Opposition for some years. You have all the experience needed to take appropriate decisions in the House.

It was very nice of all the political parties to have taken a unanimous decision in electing you in a situation that has arisen in the country, nobody is sure of what is going to happen tomorrow. Nobody is clear about it on this side as well as on that side.

* * *

My suggestion, Sir, will be that all the eminent leaders of the nation from various political parties who have been elected should sit together and unanimously form a Government which could run for five years. A unanimous view on the formation of a Government on the pattern of a national Government, or something like that, should be thought of.

That is necessary. Otherwise your position here will become very difficult all the time. We are hopeful that decisions taken by you will be independent, unbiased and in consonance with the wishes of the House. We again congratulate you heartily.

~

Shri Nitish Kumar: Mr Speaker, Sir, I on behalf of my party and myself would like to congratulate and greet you on being elected unanimously.

Nothing more can be said in your praise than what has been said in this House. Therefore, none can attract your attention by just praising you. I have seen you working as a Minister and have always found you in happy mood. You are a cheerful person and I hope that you will maintain your sense of humour while sitting in this chair and will never deprive the honorable Members of the opportunities to express their views. The present composition of the House is such that on many occasions you may have to face the heated exchanges in the House and sometimes you may face even adverse situations but you will have to handle all these situations tactfully. Therefore, we hope that you will handle these situations without losing your sense of humour. We also hope that the backbenchers like me would also be given opportunities. It should not happen that in your cheerful mood, we may lose the opportunity. However, we hope that you will remain in a mirthful mood even when you do not give a chance to the honourable Members and also we are confident that you will scold them less. It is expected that the person occupying the chair of the honourable Speaker will make all efforts to ensure that this House continues for a maximum period of time but the way they are speaking, no one can tell whether the House will complete its full tenure. If they really want that the House should complete its tenure, then there should be unanimity on allowing Vajpayeeji to continue for the next five years on the pattern of the unanimous election of the Speaker. If such an opportunity is not given, then I am sure that this House is not going to last even for few days. Though we have full hope, yet no one can say so surely. We hope that with your able guidance and competence, you will make all efforts to prolong the duration of the House to the maximum extent and like the former honourable Speaker, Shri Shivraj Patil, you will also complete full five years' term as Speaker.

Mr Speaker, Sir, with these words I assure you of my full cooperation and hope that you will uphold the dignity of the House. With these words, I once again felicitate you on this occasion.

~

Shri Madhukar Sarpotdar: Respected Speaker, I, on behalf of my party Shiv Sena and myself, congratulate you for occupying this highest office in the parliamentary system. This House has unanimously passed this one motion. It directly indicates that this democracy has got a very bright future.

I am sure you have got sufficient experience. You worked as the Chief

Minister of Meghalaya State. As you know, the name itself indicates that Meghalaya means clouds. When there was an accumulation of clouds, being the Chief Minister of that State at that time, you found out certain methods and eventually that State functioned very smoothly. Sir, the present situation in this country and in this particular House is like that. Clouds are all around and amidst these clouds, now you have been elevated to this position. I have heard so many people here praising you. Eventually, everyone was expecting that he should get justice, he should get an opportunity to express his viewpoints and the House should function peacefully. And on top of that this entire House should function for the next five years.

Sir, I remember that the Speaker of the First Lok Sabha was Shri P.G. Mavalankar and the Speaker of the Tenth Lok Sabha was Shri Shivraj V. Patil who is present here in this House. The traditions which have been maintained in this august House should continue to be maintained and the dignity of this House should not be allowed to be lowered. That is our expectations. I am sure you will not allow that situation to change.

Sir, you worked as a trade union leader. You were the Labour Minister of this country and I being one of the trade union leaders of this nation know that there are multiple problems being faced by the working class. Some of the veteran trade union leaders have mentioned in their speeches that difficult days are not far off for the working class and when those days come, at that time, it will be a real test for the Speaker to handle the situation. It is very necessary that you should treat all the newcomers impartially. I have a very little experience of the chair when I was in the panel of Chairmen in our State. I have an experience how this House functions. In view of this position, we expect from you the best performance and that too with a smiling face.

I know that some of the honourable Members said that the things are not clear. According to me, the things are very clear in everybody's mind and the result is likely to come. But everyone is having a desire that this House should survive for the next five years. That is a very important thing. Although difficult days are ahead, yet you will be in a position to tackle that situation and each and every Member in this House, even the newly elected or one who is having a tremendous amount of experience also, will get same treatment from you so that this House runs very smoothly.

On behalf of my party, Shiva Sena, and also on behalf of all the

Members of my party, I congratulate you heartily and wish you a grand success in the next five years of your tenure.

~

Shri Kanshi Ram: Mr Speaker, sir, I would like to congratulate you on behalf of my party and myself on your unanimous election. A lot has already been said in your appreciation and on present-day atmosphere, I would not like to speak anything more. I, on behalf of my party and myself, would like to assure you of our fullest cooperation.

~

Shri G.M. Banatwalla: Mr Speaker, Sir, on behalf of my party, the Muslim League, I extend to you my heartiest felicitations on your unanimous election as the Speaker of this august House. Sir, you have assumed the mantle of the Speaker at a very critical and crucial time or turn in the history of parliamentary democracy in our country.

Your unanimous election as Speaker is a shining and a unique response to this critical nature of the history of parliamentary democracy in our country, as Speaker represents a glorious response for the world democracies in the world also to follow.

Mr Speaker, Sir, today, the entire House rejoices. Some of us also turned into poetic language while felicitating you on your unanimous election to this exalted position. You are today elected as the custodian of democracy in our country and I am sure, you will uphold the highest traditions of parliamentary democracy in which, insha-Allah, you will have all our cooperation.

Mr Speaker, Sir, as I said, the entire House rejoices, the country rejoices because your election as the Speaker reflects the unity and integrity of our country in its varied form. The House rejoices, the country rejoices, the minorities also rejoice today especially at a time when they were feeling apprehensive in various respects. I therefore, rise on behalf of my party to extend to you our heartiest felicitations and to assure you of our fullest cooperation. We also know very well that from you, every section of the House will have due justice. Wish you all the best, Mr Speaker.

~

Shri Madhavrao Scindia: Mr Speaker, Sir, let me congratulate you on your unanimous election to the august office of Speaker of the Lok

Sabha. I think, the United Front, the Congress Party, the Bharatiya Janata Party, all other parties and other Members of Parliament involved in this exercise also deserve congratulations for this unanimity that was evolved and I am sure this augurs well for the future of this House.

Mr Speaker, Sir, you bring to this chair a most affable, tactful and charming personality. I have always considered you as one of the bright stars on the Indian political scene and you have a reputation for impartiality which I am sure will hold you in good stead in exercising the duties of your office. What is astonishing is that the Information and Broadcasting Ministry which has been the island, which has been the shipwreck of many a reputation for impartiality, yet you very dexterously steered your ship through the tempestuous and shark-infested waters that surround the Information and Broadcasting Ministry and brought it safely to the shore. I am sure this was the result of your efficiency and your dexterity and, maybe, you are fortunate that your tenure in the Information and Broadcasting Ministry was also a very short one.

Mr Speaker, Sir, I have had the privilege of working with you as a colleague. I have always respected the quiet, efficient and the low-profile manner in which you have handled your various portfolios. I am absolutely confident that the dignity of the office of the Speaker will certainly be upheld by you. I am especially happy that you are a brother citizen from the North East. Our country is a mosaic. As the late Shrimati Indira Gandhi had always said, it represents unity in diversity. If anyone tries to stifle that diversity, that will weaken the unity. The only way to strengthen the unity is to recognize that diversity. Mr Speaker, Sir, you represent that stream of thought, that spirit, and I am sure that your tenure as the Speaker will greatly strengthen the unity of this very great country.

Mr Speaker, Sir, a very onerous duty has devolved on you. Sir, you have been in several Lok Sabhas. I am sure that you understand what a simple, straightforward and easy set of people, all of us whom you are to handle. I am sure that you will not be daunted by that task. I would just like to assure you of my unstinted cooperation and that of my party and wish you well in bringing new laurels to this very august office.

~

Shri Sultan Salahuddin Owaisi: Mr Speaker, Sir, I congratulate you on behalf of my party, Majlis-e-Ittehadul-Muslimeen, and myself and hope that your tenure will prove to be a revolutionary one. The poet will play hide and seek and swing from one side to another, but I am sure that your tenure will be a historical one in which the poet will comment:

Aye bhi woh, gaye bhi woh,
Khatam fasana ho gaya.

Mr Speaker, Sir, at present I would like to submit that the Muslims who are the largest minority group in our country have several problems and have been plundered continuously even after independence. I hope that their problems will be solved through you in this august House and the language in which I am congratulating you will get its due right.

Lastly, I would not fail to mention the name of our former Speaker, Shri Shivraj Patil, who worked very patiently. Really, whatever he has done is praiseworthy. I used to observe silently that he never got annoyed and worked very patiently. Therefore, I think that he deserves to be applauded for it. I hope that you will also provide us opportunities and will execute your responsibility with the same fortitude.

~

Dr Jayanta Rongpi: Mr Speaker, Sir, your journey from the job of a teacher to a separate Hill State movement, then to the chair of the Chief Minister, then to the responsibility of the Union Minister and now to the chair of the Speaker is a remarkable one and a fantastic individual achievement. On my own and on behalf of my party, Autonomous State Demand Committee, and also on behalf of each and every individual of the North East, I congratulate you on your elevation to Speaker.

Mr Speaker, Sir, the unanimity of your election – in spite of the background and the political compulsion prevailing upon the major political formations – I am sure, will make each and every individual of the North East proud.

Mr Speaker, Sir, the nation has given a fragmented opinion and I am sure that you will ensure that each and every set of opinion gets the fullest of expression in this august House. North East, having a large number of problems, sent a small number of representatives leading to a peculiar problem which you are well aware of and I have no doubt in my mind that you are seized of the matter and you will take necessary steps to address this issue.

You are the first tribal Cabinet Minister of this country for which the tribal people of this country had to wait more than four decades. And now today with a double crown you have become the first tribal Speaker of this nation. So I congratulate you again and extend my fullest cooperation. Thank you.

~

Kumari Mamata Banerjee: Respected Speaker, Sir, today is your day and you deserve congratulations from all the sides. Sir, I only want to add one thing that the need of the hour today is to restore value-based politics. This is the highest forum of democracy and I think, from the chair, you can direct for the value-based politics. The message should go to the people of this country that the day-by-day deteriorating political situation should be stopped. And to restore the value-based politics, this House should work unanimously and conscientiously for some value-based issues at least. With these words I want to tell you one thing. Ours is a very vast country. Different languages are spoken. So I want to say that:

Tyag ka naam Hindu hai, iman ka naam Musalman,
Pyar ka naam Isai, Sikh ka naam balidan,
Ye hai Hindustan.

We have to restore this unity and integrity of our country.

~

Shri Sanat Kumar Mandal: Sir, on behalf of my party, RSP, and on my own behalf I take the opportunity of congratulating you, the Speaker of the eleventh Lok Sabha. I assure you of all necessary cooperation in running the business of the House and I request you to do justice to the small-party Members in the highest forum of democracy of the country. I also appeal to you to act impartially and judiciously in the extraordinary political scenario that is prevailing in the House presently, in order to hold high the democratic values and essence of the Constitution.

~

Shri Jai Prakash: On my behalf and on behalf of Haryana Vikas Party, I welcome you and all the honourable Members of Parliament. No party has got the majority in the House. In spite of all this, the honourable Members and leaders of the different parties have elected you unanimously. Therefore, I am very grateful to all my colleagues and the House.

Our colleague, Shri Nitish Kumarji was saying that this convention should continue. Today, a debate is going on in the national and international media on the life of the eleventh Lok Sabha. I request you to ensure the dignity of the House and conduct its proceedings in the same manner as has been adopted by all the honourable Members of Parliament in electing you unanimously. The people of the country have placed immense responsibility on your shoulders. All the honourable Members sitting here represent 900 million people. Therefore, I would like to request all the honourable Members to let the House complete its five years' term, respecting the mandate of the people. Otherwise, the people of this country would say that these Members were sent to run the Parliament for five years but they have failed in their task and have come back to them because of mutual differences. The entire nation is today looking at you. There are people who would try not to let the Lok Sabha complete its term. The new Members and those who have been re-elected as well as all others want that the Lok Sabha should complete its full term of five years.

Mr Speaker, Sir, ours is a very small party and I hope you will give us equal time as is given to the major parties.

~

Shri P.A. Sangma: Thank you, I know that many honourable Members would like to participate in this, but we are already crossing the Lunch Hour. I thank everyone of you and I thank everyone who has already congratulated me.

Honourable Members, the people of our great country who represent about twenty per cent of the humanity have returned this eleventh Lok Sabha through peaceful elections. The honourable Members of the House have done me a unique honour by electing me as their presiding officer in an unprecedented gesture of unanimity cutting across the entire political spectrum, regional and cultural differences and even power equations. I offer my salutations to all of you.

I am overwhelmed too by the generous sentiments expressed from all sections of the House.

Even as we are at the close of the present millennium, many countries of the world are still in the process of transition to democracy, often facing painful social and political convulsions. As we have assembled here, we have reaffirmed our commitment to democratic roots.

As I take this chair, I pay my tributes to the great leaders of our nation, veterans like Shri Vitthalbhai Patel and Shri Dada Saheb

Mavalankar, who shaped the traditions of this august House. And, no doubt, I shall be drawing my inspirations from them.

The Lok Sabha is a hallowed hall of democracy. The ideal for all of us, therefore, should be to give it the sanctity of a place of worship. In the House there should be debate and dissent with dignity, compromise with courtesy and respect without rancour.

The mandate as well as the basic term of reference for us in this House is legislation. It is through legislation that we reflect the will of the people, lay down the policies and establish the rule of law. Time being the constraining factor, we should deploy the same to produce optimum results in terms of good governance.

We are people from the grass roots, represented in all sections of the House. We have a feel for the pulse of the people. I am sure that we will enrich the proceedings of the House by bringing our collective wisdom and experience to bear the dignity and quality of our debates.

The verdict of the people as reflected in the composition of this House has given rise to aspirations as well as apprehensions amongst them. I am sure that all of us will collectively discharge our responsibility so as to fulfil their aspirations and allay their apprehensions.

I shall assure you in this context that while conducting the proceedings of this House, I shall endeavour my utmost to be guided by transparency and impartiality in my actions and provide equal opportunity to all in giving expression to their views.

Parliament business is serious but need not be tense. Tension would need not be tempered by a sense of wit and humour. We would have to draw inspiration from eminent parliamentarians of yesteryears with a sense of humour, like Pandit Nehru, Shri Piloo Mody, Shri Balraj Madhok, Shri Mahabir Tyagi and Shri Jagjivan Ram, etc. Humour spawns camaraderie and camaraderie enhances understanding.

The secretariat of the Lok Sabha does play a crucial role, though behind the screen, in facilitating the smooth and orderly conduct of the proceedings of the House. I shall be drawing upon the experience and cooperation of the secretariat too in the effective discharge of my duties.

The media is the interface between the House and the people. I would seek their cooperation in objective presentation of the proceedings of the House to the people.

Honourable Members, all of you have chosen to give the care of this House to my trust. On my part, I would assure you that I shall endeavour my best to rise up to this trust and meet your expectations.

PART VI

From the Speaker's Chair

HOMAGES/OBITUARY REFERENCES

Demise of N. Subha Reddy, Dr Manoj Pandey and Yagya Dutt Sharma*

Honourable Members, I have to inform the House with profound sorrow of the sad demise of our former colleagues, Shri M. Subha Reddy, Dr Manoj Pandey and Shri Yagya Dutt Sharma.

Shri M. Subha Reddy was a Member of the eighth Lok Sabha representing Nandyal parliamentary constituency of Andhra Pradesh during 1984–89. Earlier, he had been a Member of the Andhra Pradesh Legislative Council during 1958–72 and the Andhra Pradesh Legislative Assembly during 1972–78. An agriculturist by profession, Shri Reddy was an able and active parliamentarian. He took keen interest in focusing the attention of the House to agrarian problems and issues relating to rural development. Shri Reddy lost his life in tragic circumstances when he fell victim to a bomb attack on 20 June 1996 in Kurnool town in Andhra Pradesh at the age of 82 years.

Dr Manoj Pandey was a Member of the eighth Lok Sabha representing Bettiah parliamentary constituency of Bihar during 1984–89. An agriculturist and a medical practitioner by profession, Dr Pandey was an active political and social worker. He worked ceaselessly for the upliftment of the poor and weaker sections of the society. He rendered free medical service to the people and imparted free education to the children belonging to poor and backward classes of the society. Dr Pandey actively participated in the proceedings of the House. He passed away at Hilton Hospital in London on 3 July 1996 at young age of 45 years.

Shri Yagya Dutt Sharma was a Member of the fourth and sixth Lok Sabhas representing Amritsar and Gurdaspur parliamentary constituencies of Punjab during 1967–70 and 1977–79. He also served as Governor of

*_L.S. Deb._, 10 July 1996.

Orissa. An ayurvedic physician by profession, Shri Sharma dedicated his entire life to the improvement of indigenous system of medicine and vigorously strove for promotion of the Ayurvedic system of medicine. During the famines of 1943 in Bengal and Kangra–Kulu Valley in 1945–46, he along with a team of doctors from Punjab provided succour to the famine-stricken people. He also worked for the relief and rehabilitation of refugees in 1947 and rendered medical assistance to the sick.

An able parliamentarian, Shri Sharma lost no opportunity to focus the attention of the House to the problems faced by the peasants and the deprived sections of the society. He was member of various parliamentary committees. Shri Sharma passed away in New Delhi on 4 July 1996 at the age of 75 years.

We deeply mourn the loss of these friends and I am sure the House will join me in conveying our condolences to the bereaved families. The House may stand in silence for a short while as a mark of respect to the deceased.

Homage to Victims of Atomic Bombs Dropped in Hiroshima and Nagasaki*

Honourable Members, fifty-two years ago on this day the Japanese city of Hiroshima was destroyed by an atom bomb. Three days after, Nagasaki, another Japanese city suffered the same tragic fate. Thousands of people were killed and millions maimed, depicting to the world how dangerous could be the wars and how harmful were the unbridled ambitions of human beings and nations. To date, the after-effects of radioactivity released by the two atomic bombs continue to haunt the survivors of Hiroshima and Nagasaki.

Hiroshima and Nagasaki stand as reminders to the world's conscience that weapons of mass destruction such as nuclear weapons should never be used. The dangers of the nuclear weapons and modern devices of war now have multiplied. If the nuclear arsenal that exists in the world today is not reduced and eliminated, the human race cannot become free from the fears of devastating destruction.

Since independence, disarmament has been an important component

**L.S. Deb.*, 6 August 1997.

of India's foreign policy. We have repeatedly emphasized that nuclear weapons must be eliminated from the earth. The principles that can be adopted to reduce and eliminate nuclear arsenal and other conventional weapons of mass destruction should be non-discriminatory and reassuring of prosperity and peace for all people of the world. The tragedy caused by the atom bombs should make us all compassionate, just and humane so that these qualities inform us in handling human affairs.

This House may now observe a minute's silence in memory of the victims of the atomic holocaust of Hiroshima and Nagasaki.

Homage to Martyrs of the Freedom Movement*

Honourable Members, the House observe in solemnity today, the fifty-fifth anniversary of the Quit India Movement.

As you are aware, on 9 August 1942, the leaders of the freedom struggle, under the guidance of Mahatma Gandhi, gave a clarion call to the men and the women, the young and the old, the rich and the poor from all parts of the county to launch the Quit India Movement to liberate the country from the yoke of alien rule and for ushering in Swaraj and sovereignty. Mahatma Gandhi exhorted them to do or die for freedom. The entire nation rose like one entity and resolutely resisted the repression that followed. The unique struggle was characterized by non-violence. The twin tools of ahimsa and satyagraha, espoused by Mahatma Gandhi, were adhered to even in the face of grave provocation. This determination shook the foundations of the colonial rule and sounded its last post.

The sacrifices made by the freedom fighters ultimately led to the dawn of freedom on the horizon of India. It is our sacred duty to pay respectful obeisance to the memory of all those patriots. We can endeavour to repay our debt to them by strengthening the unity and integrity of the country.

The House may now stand in silence for a short while in memory of the martyrs of freedom movement.

**L.S. Deb.*, 8 August 1997.

Demise of Dwarka Nath Das*

Honourable Members, I have to inform the House of the sad demise of one of our friends, Shri Dwarka Nath Das. Shri Dwarka Nath Das was a sitting Member of Lok Sabha representing Karimganj parliamentary constituency of Assam. He had represented the same constituency during the tenth Lok Sabha also from 1991 to 1996.

A teacher by profession, he had served as a principal in a school in his native district. A well-known social worker, Shri Das contributed a lot towards socio-economic development of South Assam Barak Valley. He had special interest in the field of education, psychology, economics and philosophy.

An active parliamentarian, he served as a Member of Standing Committee on Petroleum and Chemicals and Select Committee on the Constitution (Scheduled Tribes) Order (Amendment) Bill, 1996. He also served as a Member of Committee on the Welfare of Scheduled Castes and Scheduled Tribes in 1994–96.

Shri Dwarka Nath Das passed away at Calcutta on 18 August 1997 at the age of 68 years. We deeply mourn the loss of this friend and I am sure the House will join me in conveying our condolences to the bereaved family. The House may stand in silence for a short while as a mark of respect to the deceased.

Demise of Babunath Singh†

Honourable Members, I have to inform the House of the sad demise of one of our friends, Shri Babunath Singh.

An agriculturist by profession, Shri Singh was an active social and political worker. He worked vigorously for more than two decades for the welfare and upliftment of the Scheduled Castes and Scheduled Tribes. During his long parliamentary career, he focused the attention of the House to the problems faced by the underprivileged and the downtrodden.

**L.S. Deb.* 26 August 1997.

†*L.S. Deb.*, 27 August 1997.

Shri Babunath Singh passed away on 18 July 1997 at Surguja at the age of 89 years. We deeply mourn the loss of this friend and I am sure the House will join me in conveying our condolences to the bereaved family. The House may stand in silence for a short while as a mark of respect to the deceased.

RULINGS/ANNOUNCEMENTS

Constitution of a House Committee to Inquire into Alleged Misconduct of Member

Honourable Member, Shri Ram Naik had given on 26 August 1996 notice of a motion for constituting a special House Committee to inquire into the alleged misconduct of Shri Sukh Ram, a Member and former Union Minister.

The notice given by Shri Ram Naik rests broadly on two grounds, viz., (i) that the Central Bureau of Investigation recovered huge amount of cash in raids conducted at the residence of Shri Sukh Ram which according to Shri Naik is presumably unaccounted money; (ii) that Shri Sukh Ram failed to intimate the Lok Sabha secretariat about his foreign visit.

In view of the seriousness of the matter, I caused copies of Shri Ram Naik's notice to be forwarded to Shri Sukh Ram for furnishing his comments for my consideration. I also called for a factual note from the Department of Personnel and Training.

I have since received a factual note from the Department of Personnel and Training intimating that two criminal cases under various provisions of the Prevention of Corruption Act, 1988, and the Indian Penal Code have been registered against Shri Sukh Ram and the same are under investigation. The Department of Personnel and Training have also invited my attention to the observation of the honourable Supreme Court in ISRO Spy Case, SPL (Crl.) No.942/1995 that interference at a premature stage of investigation may derail and demoralize the investigation.

A fax message from Shri Sukh Ram from London has also been received on 11 September 1996 confirming the receipt of our communication and intimating: 'I am still not keeping well and therefore I will be sending my reply in due course of time. Please bear with me.'

As regards the observation of the honourable Supreme Court, to which the Department of Personnel and Training have invited our attention that interference at a premature stage of investigation may derail and demoralize the investigation, I feel that discussion in the House on any matter may not be termed as interference in investigation. Moreover, as per the well-established parliamentary convention, in criminal cases, the rule of sub judice has application only from the time a charge sheet is filed. That stage has not yet reached in this case.

In view of the gravity of the matter and the far-reaching implications it has for the honourable Member as well as for the dignity of this august House, I am of the considered opinion that the principles of natural justice should not proceed hastily without considering to and we should not proceed hastily without considering the comments of Shri Sukh Ram. I am, therefore, inclined to keep the matter pending for the present.

~

Seating of Breakaway Group of Samata Party*

Honourable Members, I have another small announcement to make.

Honourable Members, I have to inform the House that on 2 August 1996, I received a jointly signed letter from Sarvashri Chandrashekhar, Ram Bahadur Singh and Bhakta Charan Das, honourable Members of Parliament intimating me that at a meeting of the Samata Party held on 2 August 1996, the said three members had 'unanimously decided to constitute a group representing a faction which has arisen as a result of spilt in the Samata Party'. The honourable Members had requested me to give recognition to their faction which has arisen as a result of split in original Samata Party.

I caused a copy of the said letter to be forwarded to Shri George Fernandes, Member of Parliament and leader of the Samata Party in Lok Sabha.

After giving a careful consideration to the matter, particularly in the light of the Constitution and the rules made thereunder, I have decided

**L.S. Deb.*,12 September 1996.

to seat the said three honourable Members separately in Lok Sabha for the purposes of functioning in the House. This breakaway group of Samata party shall be known as Samajwadi Janata Party (Rashtriya).

~

Constitution of a Special House Committee to Enquire into the Conduct of Shri Sukh Ram, Member*

Honourable Members may recall during the previous session, on 26 August 1996, Shri Ram Naik, a Member, had given notice of a motion for constituting a special House Committee to enquire into the alleged misconduct of Shri Sukh Ram, a Member and a former Minister. I had decided, vide my ruling dated 12 September 1996, to keep the matter pending as Shri Sukh Ram, who was then undergoing in treatment abroad has requested me to grant him some time to furnish comments on Shri Ram Naik's notice.

I have since received Shri Sukh Ram's comments.

To recapitulate, the notice given by Shri Ram Naik rests broadly on two grounds, viz., (i) that the Central Bureau of Investigation recovered huge amount of cash in raids conducted at the residence of Shri Sukh Ram (which according to Shri Ram Naik is presumably unaccounted money); and (ii) that Shri Sukh Ram failed to intimate the Lok Sabha Secretariat about his foreign visit.

Shri Ram Naik has contended that it amounts to a misconduct on the part of Shri Sukh Ram. He has, accordingly, requested that an enquiry into the said misconduct of the Member.

The Department of Personnel and Training have confirmed that two criminal cases under various provisions of the Prevention of Corruption Act, 1988, and the Indian Penal Code has been registered against Shri Sukh Ram and the same are under investigation.

Shri Sukh Ram has, in his comments, explained the emergent circumstances under which he has to undertake the foreign visit at a very short notice due to which a formal information could not be sent to the Lok Sabha Secretariat.

**L.S. Deb.*, 3 December 1996.

As regards the allegation of recovery of huge amount of money from his residence during his absence, Shri Sukh Ram has stated that the matter is still under investigation by the CBI and that he may ultimately be called upon to defend himself in a court of law. Shri Sukh Ram feels that his defence is likely to be compromised or even frustrated if he were to comment at this juncture on the allegation of recovery of cash from his residence. He has, therefore, chosen not to offer any comment on this point

I would dispose of the second ground of Shri Ram Naik's notice first.

Shri Sukh Ram has explained to my satisfaction the circumstances of and the urgency behind his sudden foreign visit. Moreover, the requirement that the honourable Members should intimate the Lok Sabha Secretariat before undertaking a foreign trip is solely for the convenience of the Members themselves. It enables the Secretariat to make necessary arrangements for assistance, etc., for the members during their stay abroad. It is not obligatory on the part of the Members to intimate the Lok Sabha Secretariat before proceeding on foreign visits.

I am, therefore, of the view that no misconduct is made out against Shri Sukh Ram on that score.

Reverting to the first ground of Shri Ram Naik's notice, I feel that the entire matter has to be seen in a broader perspective and a clear distinction has to be made between the allegation of conduct unbecoming on a Member of Parliament against Shri Sukh Ram and the allegation of involvement in criminal offences against him. The notice given by Shri Ram Naik states that the recovery of huge amount of money from Shri Sukh Ram's residences as the only ground for constituting a special House Committee to enquire into the alleged misconduct of Shri Sukh Ram. A separate enquiry or the investigation arising out of the same facts is already being conducted by the CBI.

The allegation of conduct unbecoming of a Member of Parliament is thus incapable of standing on its own legs. It derives sustenance from the allegation of involvement in criminal offences. If the allegation of involvement in criminal offences is ultimately proved, the allegation of misconduct will automatically be established. If, however, the allegation of involvement in criminal offences falls through, the very foundation for the allegation of misconduct would crumble.

Under these circumstances, even if a House Committee were to be constituted, it would be called upon first to enquire into and establish the commitment of criminal offences before it could arrive at any conclusion about the misconduct of the Member. With the threat of prosecution in a court of law hanging upon the Member, I cannot perhaps fault Shri Sukh Ram in taking the stand that he has taken in offering no comments in the matter.

I am of the firm view that the investigation into offences of criminal nature is within the exclusive domain of the investigation agencies and that the courts are the proper forum for establishing the guilt or the innocence of an accused in criminal cases. It would not be proper if Parliament were to arrogate to itself the jurisdiction of either the investigating agencies or the court. The founding fathers of our Constitution had, in their wisdom, clearly demarcated the jurisdictions of the three organs of the State viz., the legislature, the judiciary and the executive. Each of these three organs should strive to strengthen the fabric of the democratic set-up by refraining from encroaching upon the domain and jurisdiction of the other organs and by having healthy respect for them. Under these circumstances, I think that it would not be in the fitness of things to constitute a special House Committee to enquire into the conduct of Shri Sukh Ram at this point of time.

As I cannot, perhaps, reject Shri Ram Naik's notice on merits, I am inclined to keep it pending till a final verdict is given by the court in criminal cases against Shri Sukh Ram.

~

Commemorating the Twenty-fifth Anniversary of Liberation Day of Bangladesh*

Honourable Members, today is the Twenty-Fifth Liberation Day of Bangladesh. Today we are reminded of the historic event of the joint action by the Bangladesh freedom fighters and the Indian armed forces which resulted in the emergence of an independent sovereign state of Bangladesh. The services rendered by our army, navy, air force and the Border Security Force during this event were truly consistent with their great traditions. The people of India will always recall with great pride and gratitude the sacrifice of those who had laid down their lives.

**L.S. Deb.*, 16 December 1996.

Respect for territorial integrity and sovereignty, peaceful co-existence and non-alignment, adherence to democratic values and human rights are the basic tenets which both countries profess and practise. It is indeed this common ground which guides the friendly and good-neighbourly relations between the two countries.

I am sure, the House will join me in commemorating the event on this day of its silver jubilee and in conveying its greetings to the people, Parliament and Government of Bangladesh.

Issue of Admissibility of Notice of Motion Under Rule 184 for Constitution of a Parliamentary Committee to Go into All Aspects of Bofors Gun Deal

On 24 February 1997, Shri Jaswant Singh, an honourable Member of Parliament had given a notice of Motion under Rule 184 of the Rules of Procedure and Conduct of Business in Lok Sabha for constituting a committee of both the Houses to go into all aspects of the documents received from the Swiss authorities and to consider the Government's response thereto.

The question of admissibility of the Motion tabled by Shri Jaswant Singh and the scope of constituting another Parliamentary Committee was discussed yesterday, 25 February 1997, in the Zero Hour. I have heard the valuable views expressed by honourable Members as well as the Government's view expressed by Shri Ramakant D. Khalap, honourable Minister of State in the Ministry of Law and Justice, referring to the undertaking given by the Government of India to the Swiss authorities. The Minister stated as under:

> There are many more investigations which are going on and there are solemn undertakings between the two sovereign countries. If today we violate the undertaking given to the Swiss authorities, with what face could we go again and ask for further documents?

Informing about the conditionalities attached, the Minister stated as under:

> The document transmitted and the information contained therein may be used for investigatory purposes or as evidence only in the interest of the prosecution regarding an ordinary criminal offence. Any other use of this document and the information contained therein is subject to the explicit and previous authorization of the Federal Office for Police matter.

The Minister added:

> Therefore, anticipating that such a question would be raised here, we requested the Swiss authorities whether they would allow us to disclose these papers. We have received last night a fax message from them saying that they cannot agree to this proposal of placing these documents on the Table of the House.

The honourable Law Minister, on being asked, as to whether the CBI had disclosed the names, stated as under:

> There was a lot of kite flying going on. The newspapers were publishing so many things . . .
>
> Therefore, the CBI thought it proper to inform the country that these were the entire set of names which they have received.

When asked to specify those names, the Minister added:

> They are before everybody.

There is no doubt that it is as much incumbent on the Parliament as on the Government to honour international commitments and abide by the conditionalities mentioned by the honourable Minister. It is, however, not clear why the CBI took an inconsistent stand and thought it proper to disclose the names, which the Parliament, as it turns now, is not entitled to know. This is, therefore, a serious matter to be taken note of by the Government and appropriate action taken by them under intimation to the House.

It may be recalled that a Joint Parliamentary Committee to enquire into the Bofors contract was constituted in 1987. The Committee held 50 sittings taking 140.25 hours in its deliberations. I mentioned it yesterday. The Report of the Committee was presented on 26 April 1988. The Report of the Joint Parliamentary Committee was discussed in the House on 5 May 1988. Apart from this, the Bofors issue was discussed in one form or the other during the eighth and ninth Lok Sabhas for about 60 hours.

After going into all the aspects of the matter, I am of the opinion that no useful purpose will be served in appointing another Parliamentary Committee. I am, therefore, not admitting the notice.

~

Issue of Admissibility of Notice of Motion Under Rule 184 Regarding Failure of Constitutional Machinery in Uttar Pradesh

I have received notices of Motion under Rule 184 from Shri Atal Bihari Vajpayee, Shri Jaswant Singh and Shrimati Sushma Swaraj for recall of the Governor of Uttar Pradesh for the failure of the constitutional machinery in Uttar Pradesh. I have also received notices of Motion Under Rule 184 from Sarvashri Atal Bihari Vajpayee, Murli Manohar Joshi, Jaswant Singh, Rajendra Agnihotri and Shrimati Sushma Swaraj, Members of Parliament for recall of Governor of Uttar Pradesh for his failure to control the deteriorating law and order situation in Uttar Pradesh.

The thrust of the first set of notices for recall of the Governor is that the Governor has failed in taking appropriate steps to form a Government in Uttar Pradesh after completion of the election process which has resulted in the failure of the constitutional machinery in that State.

Honourable Members will recall that this issue was also sought to be raised in the House during the previous Session by way of notices of Adjournment Motion given by several Members. I had on 27 November 1996 withheld my consent to the notices on the ground that the matter was pending before the Allahabad High Court.

The matter is at present pending before the honourable Supreme Court. There is no material change in the situation in as much as the highest court of the land is now seized of the matter. The issue involves interpretation of a number of complicated legal points on which the court has yet to give its final verdict.

In view of this, I am disinclined to admit the notices of Motion under Rule 184 on the ground of failure of constitutional machinery in the State.

Reverting to the second set of notices, they rest broadly on the logic that the deteriorating law and order situation in Uttar Pradesh merits the recall of the Governor.

The Ministry of Home Affairs, to whom copies of notices were forwarded for furnishing a factual note, have forwarded a note on the law and order situation in Uttar Pradesh. The note, while giving break-up of various categories of crimes in the State of the past five years, states that the law and order situation in the State cannot be said to have worsened after the imposition of the President's Rule. It is, however, admitted that 'it is true that there have been some sensational cases of kidnapping and murder in recent past.'

The matter was also raised in the House on 24 February 1997. Almost all the honourable Members who participated in the discussion were of the view that there was total breakdown of the law and order situation in the State. The Home Minister is on record having admitted that Uttar Pradesh was 'heading for anarchy, chaos and destruction'. If that be the perception of the honourable Home Minister of the country regarding the state of affairs in Uttar Pradesh, I feel that the honourable Members are justified in demanding a discussion.

The question is whether the discussion should necessarily be under Rule 184. In this context, honourable Members may recall that the honourable Minister of Home Affairs, while replying to supplementaries to Starred Question No. 43 on 25 February 1997, had stated that 'wherever any State is brought under the President's Rule, an Advisory Committee consisting of representatives of different political parties is constituted for acting during the period of the President's rule. Unfortunately, in the case of U.P. such a Committee has not yet been constituted as there is some technical and legal hitch. We are trying to overcome that as soon as possible so that an Advisory Committee is set up.'

Considering the entire facts and circumstances of the case, including the above assurance given by the honourable Home Minister and his genuine and candid concern for the State and also further taking into account opportunities that may be available to the honourable Members at the time of passing of Uttar Pradesh Budget, I find that a detailed discussion under Rule 193 should be adequate. I am, therefore, inclined to admit a Short Duration Discussion under Rule 193 and allow it accordingly.

Let me also hasten to direct that the Government should immediately establish an Advisory Committee of the Parliamentarians of Uttar Pradesh, truly representative of the various political parties so that the Uttar Pradesh Governor is fully informed of the ground realities as perceived by the people's representatives.

Discussion on the Report of the Justice Jain Committee on Rajiv Gandhi Assassination

I am giving the ruling with a lot of pain and anguish. Honourable Members, the interim report of the Justice Jain Commission on Shri Rajiv Gandhi's assassination along with Action Taken Report was placed on the table of the House by the Government on 20 November 1997, the very first working day of this session. This was in pursuance of the commitment given by the Government for the purpose in the meeting of the leaders of political parties which I held on 10 November 1997. Notices have also been received in due process of rules for discussion of the reports. The Business Advisory Committee has also decided that the House would discuss the Report on 25 November 1997.

In the meantime, Congress (I) Party has demanded that the Ministers belonging to DMK should be dropped from the Government. They have made the demand on account of certain findings of the Jain Commission which they have considered as amounting to their indictment.

In pursuance of the demand, honourable Members of the Congress (I) Party have shouted slogans and demonstrated in the House on 20 November 1997, 21 November 1997 and today. Other Members of Parliament, including those in the Treasury Benches have also indulged in slogan shouting and demonstration. This has rendered transaction of business as per schedule impossible. Consequently, the House has had to be adjourned repeatedly without transacting any business including Question Hour business.

I do understand that the issue is emotional for the honourable Members of the Congress (I) Party. I respect their sentiments. The emotional response of the honourable Members of Parliament of the DMK is also understandable. However, slogan shouting, demonstration and continued disruption of the business of the House is a sad breach of the Resolution of the Golden Jubilee Session of the House held from 26 August 1997 to 1 September 1997, as far as it concerns commitment in respect of an orderly conduct of business. It is also a mindless mockery of the people who have returned this House and appalling situation of the very institution of Parliament which I may not permit.

I have, therefore, decided to adjourn the House sine die. The House stands adjourned sine die.

PART VII

Midnight Speech on the Golden Jubilee of India's Independence: Achievements and Milestones

Honourable Members, it is with a great sense of pride that we have gathered here for the special session of Lok Sabha to commemorate the golden jubilee of our Independence.

As you are aware, I have had prolonged discussions with leaders of parties and groups about the format of the discussion to be held during the special session. It was ultimately decided to have the discussion on a Motion as listed in today's List of Business. It was also decided that no formal business will be transacted during the special session.

Honourable Members will appreciate that the Motion has been drawn in very wide terms and has a very large canvass. I would rather not lay down specific guidelines for the discussion but it would be my earnest appeal to all sections of the august House, that it would not be necessary for each speaker to try to dilate on all the aspects of the Motion.

In order to have a meaningful discussion within the time at our disposal, the honourable Members would do well to concentrate while speaking only on one of the subjects listed in the Motion which may be area of their special interest. This, I feel, will minimize repetition and at the same time provide opportunity to a greater number of honourable Members to participate in the discussion.

I may further inform the House that it was also decided during deliberations in meetings with the leaders that the discussion on the Motion may not be on party lines. Free and frank expression of views with constructive criticism as well as appreciation, wherever called for, and concrete suggestions for improvement would, therefore, best set the tone for the discussion. For enabling as many honourable Members as possible to speak within the limited time available, it has been agreed at

---

L.S. Deb., 26 August and 1 September 1997. Spoke while addressing the joint sitting of the Houses on the occasion of Golden Jubilee of India's Independence on the Motion moved by Shri Atal Bihari Vajpayee on 'The State of our Democracy and Democratic Institutions, the Economic Situation, the Positions of Infrastructure, the Achievements and Potential in the Field of Science and Technology and State of Human Development in the Country' and the Resolution regarding 'Agenda for India' moved by Honourable Speaker.

the leaders' meeting that the time limit for each honourable Member may be restricted to ten minutes. Leaders would, however, be allotted more time. The decision in the morning is that the leader of each political party will get twenty minutes besides Shri Vajpayee who will move the Motion. I do not want to limit time for him. Others will be confined to within ten minutes.

I solicit kind cooperation of members in sticking to the time schedule. The entire proceedings of the special session are being telecast live. In order that the daily schedule news bulletin in Hindi, English and Urdu which are telecast from 2 o'clock to 2.35 p.m. are not disturbed, it has been decided that the House may observe lunch time from 1.35 to 2.35 p.m. instead of from 1 p.m. to 2 p.m. . . . It has also been decided today that in order to enable more honourable Members to participate, the House will sit one hour more everyday, that is up to 7 o'clock. I may also add that it becomes a duty of each one of us to maintain the dignity and decorum of the august House during the special session to enhance the solemnity of the occasion.

* * *

It is going to be my maiden speech and since it is my maiden speech, I am sure, I will not be disturbed.

Honourable Members, let me first place on record my deep gratitude to all of you in having granted me the indulgence of remaining in the chair and taking the floor for the first in the history of this House.

We are assembled here in this special session organized as part of the Golden Jubilee Celebrations of our Independence – to take stock of our achievements since becoming free, introspect on our inadequacies and set for ourselves an agenda for future.

POLITICAL LIFE

Popular elections and sustenance of democracy

Since Independence, we have had eleven General Elections and over 300 State Elections. Transfer of power to successive Governments has been smooth and peaceful. This is not mean achievement. We can be proud of being a true democracy, when the world, cutting across of regions, is dotted with countries where access to power is often through *military coups and revolutions*. The voter turnout averaging at around 60 per cent since 1984 as against 45 per cent during the first General Elections of 1952 reflects the increasing political awareness of our people. Our style of practising democracy has also proved that political consciousness is not necessarily a function of literacy.

Conduct of business of the House

While universal adult suffrage has been a resounding success, the grass-root signals I have been receiving as the presiding officer of this popular Chamber about the conduct of our business indicate that generally the people are deeply concerned. They are highly resentful of frequent bouts of pandemonium in the august House. Honourable Members collectively rising to attract the attention of the chair, repeated marches into the well of the House, cross-talk and interruptions of Members' interventions, etc., and feel that the expenditure on Parliament of the order of about Rs 7,000 per minute of its time is a costly luxury that our country can ill afford. It is quite understandable that the complexion of this eleventh House is significantly different in that a large majority of them are the real sons of the soil in their constituencies and first-timers as well, and that they are impatient to improve the lot of the masses they represent and hence their tumult and tempestuousness. Our political parties have a great role to play in this context. They need to organize pre-electoral training for the aspirants for positions in this august House.

Accountability

The interface between the Parliament and the executive has, no doubt, been by and large one of mutual understanding and complementarity. Nonetheless, of late, people have increasingly tended to seek adjudication in courts of law on issues of public grievance against holders of public offices through a spate of public interest litigation. The presiding officers of legislative bodies of India went into this question in a symposium towards the end of the last year. They found that the root cause of the problem concerns accountability. They observed:

> The chain of accountability of the civil service to the political executive, of the political executive to the legislature, and of legislature to the people, has got snapped all the way. Accountability should be restored at all echelons.

So, let us collectively reinstate accountability, making it part of our style of working.

Probity and standards in public life

Accountability is also an issue of probity and standards in public life. This is not merely a problem of the political world. It is as well of the world of civil servants, the professionals, holders of public offices and of those who interact with them including non-governmental organizations. It is even a problem of the world of business. A group of honourable Members, having taken the initiative proactively, are seized of this issue. My suggestion is that the term 'holder of public office' be given a rather broad definition as Lord Nolan of the British Parliament has done in a report submitted to the House of Commons by a committee headed by him. All those who come within the ambit of such a definition should be held to be accountable in their respective domains through mechanisms that we should evolve to prevent errant behaviour.

Ensuring probity and standards in public life is nested for carrying credibility with the public, apart from its importance for its own sake. Credibility is to be carried by demonstrable action rather than public pronouncements. Actions such as enactment of the Lok Pal Bill and securing exemplary conviction of a few errant holders of public offices through successful prosecutions in due process of law rather than blanket public self-denigration are the surest ways to carry credibility, apart from being fair to quite a good crop of our leaders who have spent all their lives in selfless service to the public.

The problem should also be handled where it originates. Punitive action for devious behaviour is ex-post facto in nature. The Symposium of Presiding Officers of the Legislative Bodies of India, about which I have made reference earlier, kept this in view when they advised that the political parties would evince care in the right choice of candidates, including with reference to their antecedents, their education and training. They also emphasized the need for the people themselves to exercise their franchise with great caution and return to the legislative bodies candidates reputed for their probity and aptitude for public service. Political parties have to take up the tasks as well of educating the electorate in this regard, organization of electorates being one of their prime functions.

Societal peace, violence and insurgency

Societal peace is the basic requirement for bringing about socio-economic development. Having won our freedom non-violently under Mahatma

Gandhi, known the world over as 'AHIMSA MURTHY' we find violence, terrorism, insurgency and societal tensions surfacing in many parts of the country. We need to seriously introspect and go to the root of the problem, identify the motivations for these phenomena and eliminate them. Broad reviews of the present situation in the country has reflected the following causes for these phenomena:

Societal exclusion based on castes, communities and religions.
Economic exclusion attributes of which are seen as unemployment, underemployment, iniquitous income distribution, poverty and exploitation.
Perceived political exclusion by denial of regional aspirations.
Lack of adequate sensitivity in management of ethnicities.
Frustration of youth leading to political extremism.
Demonstrable fall in standards in public life, i.e., of those in the establishment.
Cross-border subversion.
Disenchantment of the expatriates.
Excesses by those wielding State power.
Perceived denial of human rights.
Imbalance in media projection.
Inadequacies in strategic thinking and intelligence. I want to emphasis on this – inadequacies in strategic thinking and intelligence.
Inadequacies in the system of rendering criminal justice.

The United Nations observed its Golden Jubilee in 1995 by organizing the World Summit for Social Development at Copenhagen. The summit called for social integration by basically addressing the problems of social, political and economic exclusion into which all the above factors are subsumed. India was a significant partner in the summit. We would do well to follow up on the summit declaration and programme of action.

Empowerment of women

We need to remind ourselves that about two years back, at the UN Fourth World Conference on Women, we were the first to subscribe, without any reservation whatsoever, to the Beijing Declaration and Platform for Action. We also made a commitment to establish a National Policy of Empowerment of Women. I would request the Government to bring before the august House in this Golden Jubilee Year, the draft policy which seems to have evolved through wide-ranging and nationwide consultations since the Beijing Conference. The Parliament, on its part, has already established a Joint Committee on Empowerment of Women.

Administration

We have a highly flawed system of management of administration. It is a highly centralized administration, away from the people. A billion people and a vast subcontinent that we are, there is no escape for us from our administrative management being meaningfully decentralized. This is the very sprint behind the Constitution 73rd and 74th amendments. Four years have passed by since these amendments. Can we claim that we have really shared power and made the Panchayati Raj system a reality on the ground? We need to search our conscience.

Our administration including the police force, regretfully, has got significantly politicized. The civil service which is designed to be neutral being pressed into the service of political masters and use of the police force for setting political scores have become facts of life today. This is not conducive to the rule of law. The administration should be depoliticized and made responsive to the public and responsible only to the rule of law.

POPULATION

Our country is rich but our people are poor. This is significantly due to unceasing population explosion. The route to finding solutions to most of our problems – food security, employment, underemployment, poverty, inequities, in fact, management of our economy in all its social and political dimensions – is to be seen in successfully addressing this simple but basic problem. If we can only contain our population within the country's carrying capacity, we will turn it into a productive human resource well nourished and insulated against morbidities. Let us take Dr M.S. Swaminathan Group report on population from the shelves and do some hard thinking about implementing it.

EDUCATION

Employment orientation of education

This stock of the illiterate amongst us is a mind-boggling 460 million, Speaking at the Chatham House, London, in October 1931, and lamenting the damage done to our educational system, Mahatma Gandhi said:

> I say without fear of my figures being challenged successfully that today India is more illiterate than it was fifty or a hundred years ago . . . I defy anybody to fulfill a programme of compulsory primary education of these masses inside of a century.

Gandhiji has proved prophetic. He also suggested a solution, that of *Buniyadi shiksha* or Basic Education. The philosophy behind it is simply that education should be relevant to the world of work. So long as this underlying issue of employment relevance is not addressed at all levels of education – primary, secondary and tertiary – and people don't have faith in the worthwhileness of education, universalization of elementary education and access for people to employable skills and employment will remain a mirage, whatever be the quantum of financial resources deployed for education.

Resources for higher education

The National Policy on Education adopted by this august House over a decade ago concludes:

> The main task is to strengthen the base of the pyramids, which might come close to a billion people at the turn of the century. Equally, it is important to ensure that those at the top of the pyramid are among the best in the world. Our cultural well-springs had taken good care of both ends in the past, the skew set in with foreign domination and influence, it should now be possible to further intensify the national effort in human resource development with education playing its multifaceted role.

In order that this sound policy is implemented equitably, even while earmarking resources liberally for universalization of elementary education from the public exchequer, for strengthening the apex of the educational pyramid, can we raise internal resources in the higher education sector by adopting a depoliticized strategy of rationalizing the fee structure which would stipulate cost recovery from the well-to-do sections and scholarships for the poor?

AGRICULTURE

Food self-sufficiency and Green Revolution complacency

Through the Green Revolution we have not merely achieved food self-sufficiency since the 1970s, but have become a net exporter of foodgrains. This revolution has been spectacular considering the phenomenal growth of population. But, I am afraid that we are getting lulled into Green Revolution complacency. Application of the Green Revolution technologies has been feasible only in the irrigated areas. Seventy per cent of culturable lands is situated in, and over forty per cent of foodgrains production in the country comes from arid and semi-arid regions. For farmers and people in these regions, life is still an ordeal. Technology has not come to their rescue yet, despite deployment of financial and physical resources in dry farming.

Plateauing agricultural growth rate

Agricultural growth rate has also plateaued at an annual compound rate of 1.7 per cent since 1990-91. The impact of population growth on the sizes of landholdings, the economic viability of intensive agriculture in suboptimal landholdings, and stagnation in productivity levels which are quite below international standard are disturbing and require deep investigation.

Inorganic cultural practices and their implication

Our agricultural lands receive about 33 million tonnes of chemical fertilizers, apart from 61,000 tonnes of pesticides a year. Long-term sustainability of intensive agriculture based on inorganic cultural practices would also need detailed scrutiny. Such agriculture also has implications for food quality, protection of environment and preservation of biodiversity, environment protection, and quality and safety of food, apart from self-reliance, need to be seen as essential elements of food security.

Agriculture, civil supplies and farm exports

The interface of the agro sector with domestic civil supplies sector and export front requires skilful management. The farmer has to receive remunerative prices so that the same would be a self-triggering mechanism for increasing private investment in agriculture. At the same time, the people need to access essential commodities at affordable prices. A stable export presence is to be ensured as well, if we are to exploit the enormous export potentiality of our agro sector. Can we relieve the farmers of strangulating controls on production, movement, marketing and prices of farm produce to ensure the economic viability of farming? How do we find the colossal resources required for public investment in agricultural infrastructure? How do we harmonize the interests of domestic consumption and export trade in farm products? These are crucial issues which need careful examination.

PUBLIC DISTRIBUTION

Freedom from hunger

While we have achieved freedom from famine, freedom from hunger is not given to all. While our foodgrains production has quadrupled since 1950-51 and per capita net availability of foodgrains is about 500 grams per day, food availability is not matched by food access for all, for sheer want of purchasing power of those living below poverty line. At present, through the public distribution system, we are providing subsidized rations to those living below poverty line and even to those above poverty line. While targeted supply management at public expenditure to benefit those below poverty line is appropriate and necessary, in the long run, or even in the medium term, lasting solution to the problem of food security can be found only vesting the weaker sections with purchasing power through gainful employment.

Delivery of services

Efficient and leakage-free delivery of services in the public distribution system, as long as it is run, is indispensable. Pilferage of essential commodities and tampering with their quality in the public distribution system should be construed as heinous crimes and met with drastic penalties.

INDUSTRY

Past and future

Since 1948, we have had six Industrial Policy Statements. Planned growth of industries, mixed economy with the public sector having the commanding heights, licensing regulations and controls, domestic industry protection, and protection of the small scale sector were the features of these policies. These policies were relevant to and consistent with the bygone years of a nascent economy. We have had positive as well as negative consequences. On the positive side, we have developed an infrastructure of basic industries and indigenous entrepreneurship. On the negative side, we have low inflow of foreign capital, monopolistic trends and lack of international competitiveness. To face the challenges of international market competition, we have had to liberalize since 1991. Delicensing and deregulation have had to be carried out; investment restrictions dismantled; private sector allowed access to areas previously reserved; and flow of foreign technology and foreign capital rendered easier. New corporate structures through mergers and amalgamations, modernization and absorption of new technologies and new managerial styles seem indispensable. Our corporations themselves are slowly becoming transnational and multinational. What should be our strategy to harmonize the cross-border thrusts of our corporate sector with protection for domestic industry built up on our own factor strength over the years, in the face of capital starvation and technological obsolescence? The august House may like to go into this in some depth.

Rehabilitation of sick Central public sector enterprises: Its inevitability and human dimensions

About sixty of our Central public sector enterprises are chronically sick. We need to take a hard look at them. We do, of course, have several proposals for rehabilitation and turnaround of some of these corporations. The process of decision making in regard to the future of these corporations has been marked by inordinate delays. Quick and bold decisions are needed in regard to this matter. Such decisions call for strong political will and support, apart from very patient and sustained industrial relations exercises.

Restructuring and rehabilitation of enterprises is always a very painful process. Liberal separation compensations and retraining and redeployment of redundant employees will have to be organized wherever feasible. Until conclusive decisions are taken one way or the other, in regard to restructuring of public enterprises, labour payments cannot be allowed to fall into arrears. On 31 July 1997, Central public sector enterprises coming under seventeen Ministries of the Government of

India had an outstanding labour payment arrears of Rs 605 crore. Out of this, Rs 435 crore are statutory dues under provident fund, ESIC and gratuity laws. Some of these defaults also carry with them criminal liabilities. A demoralized and dehumanized workforce is likely to backlash on the very process of economic reforms.

Industrial sickness is not merely a problem of the public sector in our country. It has become endemic to the country's industry as a whole. The financial and economic dimensions of the sickness have been vividly presented in the working document for this session. The session may like to address the problem in its entirety.

A new work culture

There needs to be a sea change in the managerial and industrial relations styles in our country. As our veteran trade union leader Shri Ramanujan has advised, bipartisan as means of industrial conflict resolution should replace tripartism as industrial relations tend to get politicized and impacted by extraneous factors under the latter modality. A new work culture for the managerial as well as other employees should be developed, the hallmark of which should be emphasis on productivity. We compare very poorly in productivity vis-à-vis some of our neighbouring countries. Beyond a level, wage enhancements may have to be linked to productivity enhancements. Many successful private sector enterprises do have productivity-linked wage structures negotiated with trade unions. We could make efforts to universalize this practice. Our working people, be they managers or others, need to come to terms with the truth that the surest social security, or shall I call it job security, for them is the commercial viability of their enterprises. Governments and trade unions also need to devote more attention than before to improving the lot for the unorganized workers who constitute ninety per cent of the workforce of our country.

In the past, we had not necessarily opted for export-led growth like some of the South-East Asian and East Asian economies. But we do have significant achievements in exports. Exports amounted to Rs 108,478 crore in 1996 as against mere Rs 647 crore in 1951. In the 1950s, primary products accounted for 85 per cent of our exports. Now, manufactured products constitute more than 75 per cent of our exports. However, some of the striking factors to be noted in respect of our export scenario are:

> Five products, gems and jewellery, ready-made garments, cotton yarn fabrics, marine products, drugs and pharmaceuticals, constitute 40 per cent of our total exports in value terms. Sixty-nine other products constitute rest of the exports. Since 1969-70, while the unit value index of our exports went up by eleven times, volume index went up by only five times. Nearly 50 per cent of our exports go to European countries, USA and Japan. Our share in world export is less than one per cent.

The lesson to be drawn from this fact is that virtually, we do not matter in world exports. Our export production base has to expand; our export products as well as their direction have to diversify; and exports in terms of volume also have to be significantly enhanced. In the phase of globalization of economies, our economic survival and prosperity depend, to a significant extent, on the expansion of exports. This can happen only if there is an expansion of imports as well. This itself is one of the justifications for economic reforms and liberalization.

ECONOMIC REFORMS

Wealth generation

Economic reforms is simply a matter of living within means. Means can be created only by generation of wealth. Wealth will not get generated unless our resources are deployed efficiently. Even Peoples Republic of China has come to accept this position and hence their adoption of the socialist market economy. If we raise our resources through taxation and if their investments do not yield adequate returns, growth will only be stagnant or negative. Again, if our resources are distributed in terms of subsidies without consideration of their potential for stimulating wealth generation, consequence will be the same, viz., stagnation and negative trends and growth. For the first time, a transparent and comprehensive presentation of our subsidy regime has been made by the Ministry of Finance. I hope the august House will take the occasion of this session to reflect on this presentation as well. Maybe, we can examine the scope for phased removal of at least non-essential subsidies. Of course, we can borrow domestically and from abroad. But for servicing the borrowals and the repayment of loans, our investment policies should be prudent and capable of generating wealth. This has not been happening in the past. We should make it happen now, particularly because our external debt service ratio is twenty six per cent of our GDP. Our per capita external debt is Rs 3,286 which is thirty-five per cent of the per capita income of Rs 9,321. We are indeed in a debt trap. The State Governments also are caught in an internal debt trap, their revenue generations significantly getting absorbed by their debt service liabilities vis-à-vis the Government of India. The entire concept of foreign direct investment is based on the fact that it is non-debt creating. Corporate bodies receiving investments are expected to earn enough to give returns to the investor.

FOREIGN DIRECT INVESTMENTS (FDIs)

People do have apprehensions that because of the so-called 'overheating' of the economy due to large flows of foreign capital, we may be confronted with problems like those faced in Mexico and Thailand. So long as we ensure that the flow of foreign capital is channelled to priority sectors like infrastructure for the development of which we cannot find our own internal resources of any realistic scale for a long time to come, follow prudent investment policies and take adequate safeguards against fly-by-night operations of foreign investors and have a vigilant monetary policy, we will not go the way Mexico and Thailand have done.

We would also need to bear in mind that our country as yet, does not attract as much flow of foreign funds as other countries like China and our South-East Asian neighbours do. Our share in foreign direct investment inflows into all developing countries is less than three-fourths of one per cent. Flow of foreign capital and their volatility will be as much favourable to us as the investment climate we generate in our country. We also need to significantly reduce the time gap between clearance of foreign investment proposals and commissioning of projects. My first-hand information from China is that between the clearance of investment proposals and commissioning of projects, time gap is not more than three years.

Investments, like water, will flow by gravity. Gravity is towards areas where there is ready-to-build infrastructure. Bulk of our investments are flowing towards Maharashtra and Gujarat, particularly metropolitan areas. This does create problems of regional disparities and in-country economic migrations in search of employment. This problem of regional disparities is experienced intensely in the Peoples Republic of China where they have opened up coastal regions and certain Export Processing

Zones for industrialization. We would do well to learn from the experiences of other reforming economies as well in the context of analysing our experiences in this regard.

Our employment scenario since 1951 till now has been dominated by reliance on agricultural sector. Ratio of employment in industry has remained stagnant, only services exhibiting increasing trend in employment. Casualization of employment because of excess supply of labour relative to demand is also increasing. The impact of economic reforms on quality of employment is yet another aspect deserving serious examination. Nearly three decades have lapsed since the first National Labour Commission gave its report. The employment scenario, labour standards, technology inflows and skill requirements have undergone a sea change since then. Establishment of the Second National Labour Commission is long overdue.

SCIENCE AND TECHNOLOGY: INDUSTRY ORIENTATION

Science and technology services, like education, should also be relevant to the world of work. While pure science and laboratory-based researches are important, they are primarily in the domain of the academic world – colleges and universities. A new thrust has to be given for industry and enterprise-based researches as a means of removal of technology obsolescence of our industries and constantly updating the industrial technologies.

ENVIRONMENT AND ECOLOGY: RESTORATION AND PROTECTION

Our agricultural and industrial practices, ever-growing urbanization, in-country migrations and lifestyles of the people have taken an incredible toll on our forests, environment and ecology. We have, no doubt, taken significant measures to handle this problem. Many of the environment and ecology restoration measures are capital intensive. Modalities of finding resources for rectifying the damages already done should be gone into. Protective measures for the future should stem from readjustment of our lifestyles and thinking processes.

INTERNATIONAL COMMITMENTS

Our country is reputed for its excellent track record of honouring commitments made in terms of international covenants and agreements, be they in United Nations or in specialized agencies under the United Nations system. Before entering upon these commitments in international fora, no doubt, widest possible national discussions and debates would be appropriate. But once commitments are made, we need to honour them. We can ill afford to be seen as a nation reneging on our commitments. Such commitments should be properly and duly followed up by national legislative action, wherever needed. While even failure of such legislative action would be understood and appreciated by the world community as a matter of democratic compulsion, dithering and inaction in this regard would only project India as an untrustworthy customer in running international relations in a civilized manner.

The issues I have attempted to present, in essence imply the need for a *second freedom struggle* – this time the struggle should be for *freedom from our own internal contradictions* between our prosperity and poverty, between the plenty of our resources endowments and the scarcity of their prudent management, between our culture of peace and tolerance and our current conduct sliding towards violence, intolerance and discrimination. If we succeed in this second freedom struggle, there is no reason why in the ensuing millennium, we shall not be amongst the top nations of the world.

Thank you for your attention.

* * *

Honourable Members, this session, an extension of the fifth session of the eleventh Lok Sabha has been historic on several counts.

It was convened in commemoration of the Golden Jubilee of our Independence.

I had the privilege of addressing the august House for the first time in its history under Rule 360.

Again, for the first time in the history of this House, the motion for debate was piloted by leader of all parties and groups together. There was no business of the Government or of private Members. The business was that of all, of the Government, the Opposition, of every honourable Member, of the nation as a whole.

Unbroken telecasting of the proceedings was watched by the people not merely during the day but nights also, as far as I have gathered. The media has been objective in its assessment and, by and large, it has appreciated our effort in this Session.

Maybe, the speech delivered and the statements laid on the table by the honourable Prime Minister could be the longest ever delivered by any Prime Minister.

The debate surpassed many previous records.

An unprecedented 209 honourable Members including Ministers took the floor.

One hundred three honourable Members laid their speeches on the table of the House which shall, of course, form part of the proceedings of the House.

Therefore, in effect 312 honourable Members participated in the debate. I know many honourable Members were keen to participate, as has just now been demonstrated. I tender my apologies in not having been able to give time to all.

The debate lasted for six days with extended sittings and through two nights, spanning 64 hours and 29 minutes.

The previous record of debate which has now been surpassed was the debate on Railways, the Demands for Grants for Railways which lasted for five days from 6 to 13 March 1997, spending 26 hours and five minutes.

Transaction of business was non-partisan and without political rancour or recrimination. Not a single minute of the House time was lost in interruption or disorderliness. The level of thinking was quite high as reflected by the speeches of the honourable Members. In his famous 'Tryst with Destiny' speech delivered on the midnight of 14–15 August 1947, Pandit Jawaharlal Nehru observed and I quote: 'Freedom and power bring responsibility. That responsibility rests upon this Assembly.'

Without doubt, during this session, we have risen up to the ideals of Panditji. Let this become the regular style of our work.

Let me thank everyone of you – the leaders of the political parties, the Chief Whips of the political parties and the entire staff of the Lok Sabha Secretariat – who have toiled for making this session a success.

Let me also present my compliments to the presiding officers who shared my task by taking the chair. Shri P.C. Chacko deserves our special compliment in having created again another history by presiding over the august House continuously for seven hours and fifty-four minutes.

Before we meet again for the Winter Session, we would have celebrated Durga Puja and Diwali, the Festival of Lights. Let me conclude by praying to God that the future of this House, the future of the people, the future of our country, be as splendorous as the Festival of Lights.

There has been a suggestion from a number of honourable Members of Parliament. Since the session has been a historic one and every Member has demonstrated his commitment to the nation, to the cause of the nation, as a token of our commitment to the welfare and the progress of this country, the Members could consider contributing their daily allowances of this one-week session to the Prime Minister's Relief Fund. I hope that it has the approval of the whole House.

I now present the resolution before the House:

> We, the Members of Lok Sabha, meeting in a specially convened Golden Jubilee Session of both Houses of Parliament, to commemorate the completion of half a century of freedom;
>
> Having remembered with gratitude the great sacrifices made and the salutary service rendered by our freedom fighters;
>
> Having recalled with deep satisfaction and pride the maturity of our people in vigilantly preserving democracy and safeguarding the unity of the nation and the valour of our soldiers, sailors and airmen, including ex-servicemen in service in the country.
>
> Having then specifically deliberated upon matters concerning our current political life, state of democracy in the country, our economy, infrastructure, science, technology and human development;
>
> Do now solemnly affirm our joint and unanimous commitment to the issues hereinafter mentioned, and we also do solemnly resolve and direct that they be adopted as minimum tasks, constituting our 'Agenda for India' on this historic occasion;
>
> That meaningful electoral reforms be carried out so that our Parliament and other legislative bodies be balanced and effective instruments of democracy; and further that political life and processes be free of the adverse impact, on governance of undesirable extraneous factors including criminalization;
>
> That continuous and proactive efforts be launched for ensuring greater transparency, probity and accountability in public life so that the freedom, authority and the dignity of Parliament and other legislative bodies are ensured and enhanced, that more especially, all political parties shall undertake all such steps as well attain the objective of ridding our polity of criminalization or its influence;
>
> That the prestige of Parliament be preserved and enhanced, also by conscious and dignified conformity to the entire regime of Rules of Procedure and Conduct of Business of the Houses and directions of the presiding officers relating to orderly conduct of business, more especially by:

- Maintaining the inviolability of the Question Hour,
- Refraining from transgressing into the official areas of the House, or from any shouting of slogans, and
- Invariably desisting from any efforts at interruptions or interference with the address of the President of the Republic;

That a vigorous national campaign be launched by all political parties to combat economically unsustainable growth of population, recognizing that such growth lies at the root of most of our human, social and economic problems.

That education at all levels be made employment-relevant, special attention being given to quality; that achievement of the constitutional mandate of universalization of elementary education be closely monitored; and that universal primary education be achieved by AD 2005;

That the national economy be prudently managed, with emphasis on:

- Efficient use of resources and avoidance of wastes,
- Priority attention to development of infrastructure,
- Generation of wealth as a sustainable means of achieving full, freely chosen and productive employment, of elimination of poverty and of securing equity and social justice, and
- Balanced regional development;

That continuous efforts be made for achieving in a time-bound manner, marked improvement in the quality of life of all citizens of our country with special emphasis on provision of our minimum needs – food, nutrition and health security at the household level, potable water, sanitation and shelter;

That gender justice be established in the spirit of the Declaration and Platform for Action of the UN Fourth World Conference on Women (1995) and be practised as a way of life, with particular emphasis on education of the girl child;

That consistent efforts be made in terms of inculcation of values and adjustment of the life and working styles of our people to secure protection of environment and preservation of ecology and biodiversity;

That science and technology be primarily anchored in the creation of a scientific temper, be developed by promotion of governmental as well as non-governmental efforts and be pressed into service not merely for economic development but human development in all its dimensions;

That finally, the essence of participatory democracy be seen in the inculcation of our national spirit of self-reliance, in which our citizens are equal partners in all spheres of our national endeavour, and not simply the beneficiaries of governmental initiatives.

This is the resolution that I present before the august House. Shall I take it that this is unanimously passed?

The resolution is unanimously passed.

In the meeting of the political parties, it was decided that this declaration should be signed by honourable Members of the House. It will not be feasible for every honourable Member of Parliament to sign it before the house adjourns. So, it was decided that Speaker may selectively choose senior leaders as a token to sign it on the table of the House and the rest of the members after adjournment of the House. They may kindly be seated in their respective seats. The signature slips will be distributed to each bench and they can sign them. But, before we adjourn, ceremonially, I have chosen nine honourable Members including myself to sign it. It will be signed by the Speaker, the Prime Minister, the leader of the Opposition Shri Atal Bihari Vajpayee, Shri P.V. Narasimha Rao, Shri Somnath Chatterjee, Shri Ram Vilas Paswan, Shri G.M. Banatwala, Sardar Surjit Singh Barnala and the Deputy Speaker. After this, we will adjourn the House.

* * *

The verbatim proceedings of the House of the entire debate will be brought out as a commemorative publication. It will be given to all the honourable Members of Parliament. The second publication will be that each Member's points will be scrutinized thoroughly, all the good suggestions that they have made will be brought out separately. On each page one Member's important suggestions will be published. So, it is not only the verbatim report, but your selective concrete suggestion will also be brought out separately.

* * *

I thank you once again.

Honourable Members may now stand up for '*Vande Mataram*'.

PART VIII

Select Speeches in Conferences and Seminars

Address at the 60th Conference of Presiding Officers of Legislative Bodies in India*

I have great pleasure in welcoming all the Presiding Officers of Legislative Bodies in India to this Conference.

The Standing Committee of the All India Presiding Officers Conference has enabled me to set out for the Conference, an agenda of considerable significance in the present political context of our country. The Conference is to deliberate on orderly conduct of business of legislative bodies which is vital for the growth of democracy, parliamentary surveillance of the executive through the committee system, relationship with the press and electronic media and coverage of the proceedings of the legislatures.

We, the presiding officers of legislative bodies, are meeting at a time when politics is becoming kaleidoscopic, parties are becoming fragile and governance is increasingly through coalitions. In this environment, Governments of the day get driven to the razor's edge, their legitimacy coming under frequent test and the power of the chair being temptingly invoked in the process. The chair in the legislative bodies, whether occupied by the Speaker himself or by the Deputy Speaker or any other for the moment, is a highly sanctified institution. Its occupant would do well not to yield to undesirable temptations and should specially take care that the exercise of his authority does not disrupt the due processes of the Constitution and the law.

In the statement I made in the Lok Sabha in response to felicitations on my election to the chair, I observed that the House is a hallowed

---

**The Journal of Parliamentary Information*, Vol. XLIII, No. I, March 1997. Pages 12–15, 40–41. Spoke while Addressing the 60th Conference of the Presiding Officers of Legislative Bodies in India held in New Delhi on 10–11 October 1996. The Conference held detailed discussion on various issues of topical concern as far as the legislatures are concerned.

place where what should prevail is debate and dissent with dignity, compromise with courtesy and respect without rancour. The means to achieve this is orderly conduct of business in the House.

The Rules of Procedure and Conduct of Business in the Houses is not a book of empty rituals. It is a Code of Conduct for decorous and orderly transaction of business. Continuous conformity to it needs to be elegantly ensured by the presiding officers.

How is orderly conduct conducive to the growth of democracy? The matter should not be too literally construed. It does not refer merely to the demeanour of individual members in the House. It refers to the totality of conduct of members inside and outside the House, their collective self-regulation in time management in the House; conformity to parliamentary party discipline; adherence to decisions of the Business Advisory Committee; compliance with conventions; cooperation in decentralized style of functioning; respect for private Members' business; and making good governance, in its broad sense, possible.

Articles 105 and 194 of the Constitution vest the Houses and the legislatures with enormous powers, privileges and immunities. It is also the role of the presiding officers of the Houses to defend the liberties and privileges of the Members. Particularly in view of this, the righteous conduct of the Members outside the Houses assumes special significance. It is in this background that both the Houses of the US Congress came to establish Ethics Committees in the early 1970s in an attempt to force basic standards of probity on the Members. No doubt these committees have not been an unqualified success. Nonetheless, it is worth examining whether in the Indian context we can form such committees and make them work.

We, the presiding officers, do have a serious problem when it comes to time management of the Houses. In the Lok Sabha, for example, within a six-hour working schedule, the 545 members get 40 seconds of time per capita. Matters of urgent public importance, which the representatives of our multitudinous population want to raise, and very legitimately at that, are incredibly large in number, and often unquestionable in their gravity. Members, naturally, clamour for projection of their problems on the floor of the Houses taking recourse to all permissible modalities – Starred Questions, Zero Hour, Half-an-Hour Discussions, No Day Yet Named Motions, Short Duration Discussions, Calling Attention, Adjournment Motions, etc. The demand on and supply of time do not simply match. Members cannot be satisfied. This is the root cause of difficulties in securing orderly conduct of business in the Houses. Members who do catch the Speaker's eye, which has been described as 'the most elusive organ that nature has ever yet created', and up indulging in tedious repetitions causing breaches of order, unparliamentary expressions and disorderly conduct; the presiding officer rises and is not heard in silence as expected. The situation calls for enormous patience and understanding on the part of the presiding officers. They may have to draw on all their inner resources of conciliation and personally interact with the dissatisfied Members in the lobbies every now and then.

In this context, the parliamentary parties have a significant role to play; the presiding officers will have to build up rapport with the party leaders to hold their rank and file on leash and bring home to them the inevitability of time management.

The presiding officers will have to learn the art of transacting business through consensus. The Business Advisory Committee is a device to build up consensus; it should be taken recourse to as frequently as needed. It is inherent in the role of the Opposition that it selectively attempts to delay transaction of business with implications for time management on the floor. And it is inherent in the role of the Government too, to get its business through to the maximum extent feasible. The presiding officer has to secure a balance by application of his negotiating skills in the Business Advisory Committee meetings.

The whips of the parties are essentially business managers in the House. The presiding officers will do well to take time off to liaise with them as well to facilitate smooth flow of business on the floor.

Often, stormy situations are created on the floor of the Houses for want of respect for conventions. For example, it is the convention that the members do not mention individuals who do not have the opportunity to defend themselves in the House. When this convention is breached, some members are likely to react strongly. Firm but elegant invitation to compliance with conventions would be needed in such circumstances.

The Parliament has come to establish an elaborate committee system. There are 35 committees at present. Some States have also established Subject Committees. Examples are Kerala, Karnataka, Orissa, West Bengal, etc. The merits of the committee systems are:

* On account of time constraint, the plenary of the Houses are not able to transact all business to the extent desired; individual committees having as many as 45 members, function as mini-

Parliaments, in essence the committees facilitate decentralized functioning of the Parliament.

* Demands for grants get mandatorily remitted to committees for detailed scrutiny; even the demands which would get guillotined in the House would have received detailed scrutiny in the hands of the committees.
* Scrutinizing annual reports of ministries, as they do, implementation of the developmental programmes of the Ministries gets closely monitored, often repetitively.
* Budget scrutiny and monitoring of implementation of programmes facilitate accountability of the executive to the Parliament being enhanced.
* Bills, as may be referred by the presiding officer to the committees, get scrutinized in detail; this facilitates sober examination of legislative proposals in comparatively cooler environment; and members of the committee are able to bring to bear on the laws their practical wisdom flowing from their grass-roots experience.
* The committee system is comprehensively participative and democratic in the sense that every member functions on one committee or the other.

Of course, there is a certain degree of overlapping between the functions of the departmentally related committees and the traditional Finance Committees. Innovative operational styles will have to be evolved to eliminate overlapping of jurisdiction. The committee system, of course, is quite expensive, committees do want to undertake field visits to make their reports and recommendations. Correctional tools for concurrent removal of inadequacies in administration, maybe, orderly transaction of business in the committees could be made cost effective despite expenses. And the committees, in effect, can become powerful budgetary, legislative and evaluating engine rooms.

It should, however, be urged that the committees do not become groups that keep minutes but lose hours. Indeed, time is the essence of the business of legislatures.

Orderly conduct of business in the Houses would suffer from a serious inadequacy if private Members' business, whether in terms of Bills or resolutions, is not taken seriously. Private Members' business received considerable sanctity even during colonial days. We have had experience in the matter for nearly nine decades. Flowing, as it does, from matters of general public interest, it is as important as the other business of the legislatures, including Government business. The objective served through the mechanism of private Members' business, in the least, is obtaining an expression of the opinion of the legislatures. Members of the legislatures on the Treasury side have to be particularly brought to treat private Members' business as serious and not as ritualistic routine.

Article 361A of the Constitution gives constitutional validity and sanctity for the interface of the media, including electronic media, with the legislatures. On the statutory side, the Parliament Proceedings (Protection of Publication) Act, 1997, has also been enacted. The presiding officers should keep this in mind and facilitate the media to play an effective role as the intermediary between the legislatures and the public. It is also common knowledge that several debates in the Parliament are influenced by what is projected by the media. Meaningful systems of access for the media to important areas of the legislatures – Press Galleries, Central Hall, etc. – should be facilitated. I would even suggest that, in the matter of interface with the media, the traditional conservative approaches of the legislatures would need to be relented.

Before I conclude, in order to bring home that in the transaction of business of the legislatures, we should keep national integrity as the foremost concern in our democratic system, particularly in the present context, I would quote Edmund Burke, who told the electors of Bristol: 'Parliament is a deliberative Assembly of our nation. You choose a member indeed, but when you have chosen him, he is not the member for Bristol, but he is Member of Parliament.'

Let this philosophy of Burke guide us in our actions.

Thank you, Jai Hind.

* * *

After the Special Address by the Prime Minister, the Conference came to a close at a solemn function in the Plenary Hall of the Vigyan Bhavan.

Preliminary observations by Speaker at the concluding ceremony of the conference.*

In his preliminary observations at the concluding session, the Lok Sabha Speaker and President of the Conference, Shri P.A. Sangma, commented

*Concluding Remarks.

the IPU Council for the design of the Conference which was unique.

Shri Sangma said that the deliberations at the Conference pointed to the fact that women themselves are halting and hesitant in entering politics and consider it an unclean domain. But politics is one of the most beautiful human activities. The legitimacy of this activity has to be carried home to women. Men need to be prepared for adjusting themselves to the new role they have to play as women get inducted into public service, particularly in the context of the sea change overtaking the institution of family.

Shri Sangma observed that political participation is a pervasive process. Political training of women needs to be continuous and lifelong, even commencing from the school stage; it should be at all levels too – local, provincial, national and international. Academic, specialized and party institutions should be involved in the training process.

Establishment of quotas for women's political participation is legitimate and practical as proved by experience. Electoral reforms could be considered for eliminating the disadvantages faced by women in political participation.

There is apprehension that mobilization of finances from private sources may create dependence and obligations. The solution to the issue is transparency in mobilization of funds, expenditure and accounting for it.

The media's role has been traditionally one of reflecting some striking aspects of the status quo and trends. If the media is to play an active role, women themselves should devise direct and institutional mechanisms for networking with the media.

The IPU should continue to survey the status of political advancement of women, monitor it and promote it. There needs to be a summit of heads of Government on political participation of women. Candidly speaking, politics is power and perquisites as well, apart from public service. Men, who are in a majority in politics, could be reluctant to be deprived. If this scenario is to change, political commitment should follow from the heads of Government, Shri Sangma stressed.

Address at Fiftieth Anniversary of the First Sitting of the Constituent Assembly*

Respected Rashtrapatiji and Distinguished Guests.

This day, fifty years ago, was historic. Beginning was made in these premises for the establishment of the supreme law of our land, our Constitution. It is a matter of great pride, of honour for us, to commemorate that beginning. Let me first of all pay homage, on this occasion, to all the departed members of the Constituent Assembly.

Dr Shankar Dayal Sharma, our honourable President, by his own right, is a legal luminary, a constitutional expert and a renowned exponent of the rule of law. Sir, you symbolize everything that the framers of our Constitution visualized in the holder of our presidency. You belong to the very generation of our special guests of the day, members of the Constituent Assembly who are present here. It is a matter of historic coincidence that you would be honouring them. Sir, I have great pleasure in welcoming you.

Vice-President, Shri K.R. Narayanan, with his strong background in professional diplomacy and hailing as he does from the State of Kerala, the land of literacy, equity and social justice, has distinguished himself in the office of the Chairman, Rajya Sabha, which has been vested with special dignity by the Constituent Assembly. His presence today with us is a matter of special encouragement for all of us. I extend a hearty welcome to him.

One of the public debates today concerns the future of parliamentary form of Government in our country. Opinions are being often voiced now that the presidential form may, perhaps, be more suited for us. The framers of our Constitution did give serious thought to the matter. They opted for a parliamentary form on the conviction that in our conditions, responsibility of the executive should be given the paramount consideration. We have had successful examples of governance through coalition which have proved that responsible Governments can be stable as well. The task before the honourable Prime Minister, Shri H.D. Deve

---

**The Journal of Parliamentary Information*, Vol. XLII, No.4, December 1996. Pages 365–367. Spoke while addressing a function to commemorate the Fiftieth Anniversary of the First Sitting of the Constituent Assembly held in the Central Hall of Parliament House on 9 December 1996.

Gowda today is one of providing stability through responsibility. I welcome him to this function with great pleasure.

Dr (Smt.) Najma Heptulla, the Deputy Chairman of the Rajya Sabha, not merely represents the aspirations of the women of India today, she has brought laurels to the Indian Parliament in her capacity as a dynamic member of the Executive Committee of the Inter-Parliamentary Union. My special welcome to her as well as to my able and worthy colleague, Shri Suraj Bhan, the Deputy Speaker, Lok Sabha.

The heritage handed to us by the Constituent Assembly is priceless. This heritage is of a secular, democratic, republican model, characterized by universal adult franchise, guarantee of Fundamental Rights, linguistic balance, equity and social justice, parliamentary form, independence of the judiciary and recognition of unity in diversity in which the federal principle is subsumed. All these features are enshrined in the historic 'Objectives Resolution' moved by Pandit Jawaharlal Nehru and adopted by the Constituent Assembly. President Andrew Jackson of the United States observed about his country's Constitution: 'Perpetuity is stamped upon the Constitution by the blood of our fathers.' This is true of our Constitution as well. It is with these feeling flowing from my guts that I welcome the eight members of the Constituent Assembly present here with us today. These members are Begum Aizaz Rasool and Saravashri S. Nijalingappa, C. Subramaniam, Chowdhari Ranbir Singh, Motiram Baigra, Kusum Kant Jain, Balwant Singh Mehta and Bhagwan Din. Let us honour them with a hearty and standing ovation.

There are other members of the Constituent Assembly who are not present here with us today – Shrimati Renuka Ray and Shrimati Malati Chowdhuri and Sarvashri R.B.Kumbhar, M.R. Masani, B. Gopala Reddy, L. Krishnaswami Bharati and M.A. Sreenivasan. Let us felicitate them in absentia.

I welcome all the honourable Members of Parliament, many of whom have, over the years, dedicated themselves to, and toiled for, the preservation of our Constitution and its underlying ideals. Let me welcome everyone to whom I have not made specific reference and is present here to honour the special guests.

Dr Ambedkar stated in November 1949, and I quote:

> If hereafter things go wrong, we will have nobody to blame except ourselves. There is great danger of things going wrong. Times are fast changing. People including our own are being moved by new ideologies.

They are prepared to have Government for the people and are indifferent whether it is Government of the people and by the people . . . Let us not be tardy in the recognition of the evils which . . . induce people to prefer Government for the people to Government by the people. I am confident that we will not fail Dr Ambedkar. Thank you for your kind attention. Jai Hind.

Address at the Unveiling of the Statue of Netaji Subhash Chandra Bose*

Rashtrapatiji, Upa-Rashtrapatiji, Prime Minister, Shri Kshiti Goswami, honourable Minister for PWD, Government of West Bengal, Relatives of Netaji Subhash Chandra Bose and Distinguished Guests.

The colossus of India's freedom movement, Netaji Subhash Chandra Bose has today come to take his place in these hallowed premises of the Parliament of our country, though not in flesh and blood. He is immortal in a living sense too. He lives in the hearts of millions of our countrymen. His ideals are timeless too.

Most often, it is experience that makes a revolutionary. Netaji was born as such. He rebelled against academic establishment as a student leader, against the British even against the moderation and passivity of Mahatma Gandhi's non-conformism. He came to symbolize the radical and militant dimension of the freedom movement. He was an enigma for all. His ideals and vision transcended his contemporary times.

Gurudev Rabindranath Tagore, while showering tributes on him characterizing him as DESH NAYAK, said: 'Subhash Chandra, I have watched the dawn that witnessed the beginning of your political SADHANA. In that uncertain twilight there had been misgivings in my heart and I had hesitated to accept you for what you are . . . You have come to absorb varied experiences . . . enlarging your vision so as to embrace the vast perspectives of history beyond any narrow limits of territory . . .'

**The Journal of Parliamentary Information*, Vol. XLIII, No. 1, March 1997. Pages 4–5. Spoke while addressing the function at the unveiling of the statue of Netaji Subhash Chandra Bose on 23 January 1997.

Netaji was a human being of rare versatility. He was a philosopher. Philosophy was indeed his major in higher education. He imbibed the thoughts of Aurobindo Ghose and Swami Vivekananda. No surprise, then, that with an incredible sense of other-worldliness, he denied himself the security of civil service and opted for the rigours of a soldier of our Independence movement, suffering prison life repeatedly.

For the British rulers of India, Netaji was a fugitive from law. But for the people of India, he was the ambassador of their cause of freedom. The Provisional Government of Azad Hind established by him abroad to end British rule was a moving epic. Writing to Mahatma Gandhi, Netaji said that the sole objective of the Provisional Government was liberation of India and once that mission was achieved, he and his comrades would like to retire.

His alliance with the Japanese in fighting the British stemmed from his diplomatic skill. He was quick to see that the enemy's enemy is a friend and he saw the Japanese in that mould.

Netaji professed and practised secularism. In his secular world, the Hindus, the Muslims, the Christians and the Sikhs were comrades without conflicts.

Three weeks from hence our Rashtrapatiji will be inaugurating an International Conference of Parliamentarians from all over the world in which political participation by women will be discussed. More than half a century back, Netaji had made women's political participation a reality by organizing the Rani Jhansi Regiment of the Indian National Army.

Today is the 100th birth anniversary of Netaji. Let us dedicate ourselves to live by his ideals of selflessness, patriotism, national unity and integrity, secularism and impatience for change so that in the millennia to come, we can hold our heads high and live in dignity.

My special compliments to Kartick Chandra Paul, the sculptor for his lifelike recreation of the DESH NAYAK.

With these words, I welcome all the distinguished guests.

Jai Hind.

Address at the Inauguration of the Eighth Conference of the Chairmen of Public Accounts Committees of Parliament and State Legislatures*

Dr Murli Manohar Joshi Saheb, honourable Chairmen of Public Accounts Committees, Shri Shunglu, Comptroller and Auditor General of India, Distinguished Guests.

I have great pleasure in participating in this Conference of the Chairmen of Public Accounts Committees.

I should compliment Dr Joshi for having taken the initiative in organizing this Conference. In fact, he wanted a Conference of Chairmen of PACs in SAARC countries to follow this Conference. As some of the important SAARC countries had problems in participating in such a Conference around this time, it has not been possible to organize the same. In any case, we are in touch with the SAARC country Parliament Secretariats in our efforts to organizing this Conference sometime in April 1997.

Having been a Union Minister holding different portfolios over the years, I have had the opportunity of knowing many senior civil servants in the Government of India who keep meeting me often. Some of them have had opportunities to appear as witnesses before the Public Accounts Committee currently headed by Dr Joshi.

The impression I have received from these civil servants is that Dr Joshi is both a feared and admired person. Feared, on accounts of his absolute thoroughness; admired, for his absolute fairness. It is this combination of thoroughness of issues and fairness in assessment of Government action which should be the hallmark of the Chairmen and members of Public Accounts Committees.

The Public Accounts Committee is perhaps the most crucial institutional mechanism for securing parliamentary control over the executive. At the Central level, the institution of the Public Accounts Committee has completed 75 years.

**The Journal of Parliamentary Information*, Vol.XLIII, No.2, June 1997. Pages 171–174. Spoke while inaugurating the Eighth Conference of the Chairmen of Public Accounts Committees of Parliament and State Legislatures held in New Delhi on 15 and 16 March 1997.

The special feature of the Public Accounts Committee is that it has the support of the highly professionalized services of the Comptroller and Auditor General (C&AG) and his establishment. The staff of the C&AG at various levels go through some of the toughest in-house tests for securing elevations at various levels of their hierarchy. Their audit is based on documents maintained by the Government establishments in the ordinary course of business. The audit paras are prepared in a participative manner. Before the paras are finalized, the department heads are invariably asked to give their comments. In fact, it is in this respect that the PACs are also different from many other committees of legislative bodies. Committees support in guiding their scrutiny of executive actions.

In terms of mandate, the Public Accounts Committees examine:

* whether funds exhibited in the Finance Accounts as having been spent were legally available for expenditure;
* whether the expenditure was duly authorized by competent authority and conforms to the authorization;
* whether reappropriations are consistent with the relevant provisions.

Over the years, administration has undergone a sea change. The Welfare State model having been adopted by our system of governance, developmental administration which is highly complex has come to be the principal role of the Government. A wide range of subjects have consequently become matters of immediate interest to the PACs – subjects relating to State Corporations, trading and manufacturing schemes, developmental projects, etc.

At the Central and State levels, a large number of autonomous and semi-autonomous bodies of a specialized nature fully or predominantly funded by the Government have also come to be established so that such bodies are able to implement programmes without being hamstrung by government routine. Wherever such bodies come under the audit of the C&AG, their accounts also come under the purview of the Public Accounts Committee.

I understand that since the year 1960, the Public Accounts Committee of the Parliament has presented more than 1,000 reports. It is our experience that these reports have significantly contributed to ever-increasing demand for propriety in Government's financial transactions. Very many improprieties have also come to be projected before the Parliament and the public. The special role of the Public Accounts

Committees has also ultimately impacted on public perceptions about successive Governments, creating an overall environment of desirable public vigil. Today's public demand of transparency in governmental actions and probity in public life are, to my mind, in no small measure due to vibrant and active Public Accounts Committees.

Having been exposed to the preparation of audit reports by the establishment of the C&AG and subsequent scrutiny by the Public Accounts Committee, while being within Ministries, I have the perspective of the executive as well which, I think, I should share with you now. Government functionaries do have to conform to a fairly rigid regime of rules and regulations. Decision making is a multi-point process. Expenditure proposals go through different hands up the hierarchy. The problems of procedures, processes and personalities cause, very often, inordinate delays. Funds voted are not spent. Serious shortfalls in expenditure occur. Because of delays, there are also inevitable cost overruns. In certain inevitable circumstances, expenditure incurred is also in excess of authorization. Those who are in charge of audit, whose reports go before the Public Accounts Committees, should have an empathetic understanding of the disabilities of the decision makers behind the hard core of the regime of rules and regulations. If this understanding is missing, we may not be fair to the executive. It is my experience that decision makers who are just inactive and who are sticklers to the mere letter of the rules and regulations, are faulted less often. Those who are innovative and dynamic and try to achieve and show results, taking decisions in good faith, are faulted more often. I shall give an example.

In implementing a distress relief programme for fisherwomen in a particular State, a decision was taken to allow expenditure on purchase of a bus to be given to a fisheries cooperative. Audit took objection on the ground that this expenditure would provide relief in terms of employment only to three or four persons – the driver and cleaners. The decision maker had to present almost a battle in defence of the decision explaining that the fisherwomen could go to their marketplace for sale of their goods more often and faster and in larger numbers so that they could get real value for their fishery items on sale. Decisions taken in the executive, in the ordinary course of business, should not be too technically viewed. It is desirable that bona fide and rational decisions taken by meaningful and constructive interpretation of rules and regulations are not questioned in audit.

The Public Accounts Committee, by the very nature of their functioning, scrutinize expenditure after they are incurred. Therefore, they always have the benefit of hindsight. And, foresight of the decision makers can never be as accurate as hindsight. This realization should also inform the Public Accounts Committees.

Members of the establishment of the C&AG, in essence, are professionals like doctors and lawyers. Even as clients of doctors and lawyers take them in trust and expose themselves fully, the executive exposes itself to the trust of the C&AG's establishment during audit. Because of this, it is desirable that every care is taken to see that audit reports do not get to be known to the public until they are laid before the legislative bodies and come under the scrutiny of the Public Accounts Committees. This will help in preventing avoidable politicization of audit reports.

Reports of action taken by the Government on the recommendations of the Public Accounts Committees are as important as the original recommendations of the Committees. Such Action Taken Reports are the only means of monitoring implementation of recommendations without which the accountability of the executive to the legislature cannot be secured in the real and lasting sense.

I am sure that under the enlightened guidance of Dr Murli Manohar Joshi and Shri Shunglu, whom I have personally known as an outstanding civilian, this Conference would facilitate very fruitful exchange of experiences across the country and shall also pave the way for the success of the forthcoming Conference of SAARC Public Accounts Committees.

With these words, I am immensely pleased to inaugurate this Conference.

Thank you,
Jai Hind.

Address at the Conferment of the Outstanding Parliamentarian Award, 1996, on Shri Somnath Chatterjee, MP*

Respected Rashtrapatiji, Respected Upa-Rashtrapatiji, honourable Prime Minister, honourable Deputy Chairman, Rajya Sabha, Shri Somnath Chatterjee, honourable Members of Parliament and Distinguished Guests.

It is a matter of great honour and pride for me to be associated with this solemn function to confer on Shri Somnath Chatterjee, the 'Outstanding Parliamentarian Award 1996' of the Indian Parliamentary Group (IPG).

Inwardly, I have always assigned to Shri Somnath Chatterjee the status of my guru. In 1997, I was member of the Parliamentary Committee on Subordinate Legislation headed by him. In this capacity, I also travelled around with him in the North East. He made me feel that just being with him was education and assimilating his ideas was intellectual elevation.

Public service as parliamentarian and legal practice as professional are matters of family tradition for Shri Somnath Chatterjee. His father, late Shri N.C. Chatterjee, had also served our nation as a Member of Parliament and had practised law, in the apex court of India as Shri Somnathji does now.

Though Shri Somnath Chatterjee has had an aristocratic lineage and Western education, including for being a barrister, he embraced communism for his political faith and has been a steadfast practising communist for about three decades.

When Shri Somnath Chatterjee joined us in the eleventh Lok Sabha, it was for the seventh time that he was returned to this august House. This at once speaks volumes for his image amongst his electors, his standing in his party and his stature as a parliamentarian and a national leader.

Shri Somnath Chatterjee, throughout his parliamentary career was also naturally sought after on account of his expertise to be Chairmen

---

**The Journal of Parliamentary Information*, Vol. XLIII, No.2, June 1997. Pages 153–155. Spoke while addressing a function on 19 March 1997 in the Central Hall of Parliament House for conferment of the Outstanding Parliamentary Award, 1996, on Shri Somnath Chatterjee, MP.

and member of many committees. He served with distinction as Chairman of the Committee on Subordinate Legislation as well as Committee of Privileges. He was also a member of several Joint Committees and Select Committees, particularly ones requiring expertise in law. As a barrister, and as a senior lawyer, he brought his legal acumen to bear, with considerable impact, on shaping legislation in a diversity of areas – areas of corporate, fiscal and commercial laws and constitutions and criminal laws. His enlightened advice was also available to the Ministries of Law, Finance and Home, in the Parliamentary Consultative Committees of which he has had occasions to serve. His earlier service as Chairman of the Departmentally Related Standing Committee on Railways and his service currently as Chairman of the Committee on Communication, has helped in balanced and constructive scrutiny of the performance of these Ministries.

The Government of West Bengal has also understandably secured, over the years, the benefit of his chairmanship in several State Public Sector Corporations.

His debating skill will turn any legislator green with jealousy. His depth of subject, knowledge, the diction and propriety of his vocabulary and elegant humour of his presentation, as I have often seen from the presiding officer's chair, almost invariably makes his political opponents speechless and helpless.

When Shri Somnath Chatterjee is on his legs, he demonstrates an incredible awareness of national and international issues, simply by emoting from his experience. I was closely following his statement on the floor of the House, on 25 February 1997, on the Motion of Thanks to the President's Address. In the sweep of his statement, he effortlessly traversed a wide-ranging ground – the rationale of governance through coalition, separation of power, federalism, secularism, liberalism, national integration, macro and micro-economics, employment situation, poverty alleviation, welfare administration, regional development and South Asian regional issues.

Trade unionism is natural to Bengalis. Combining in himself his Bengali moorings, syndicatism which he should have imbibed during his youthful days as Barrister and Marxian dialectics, as a practising communist, he has been an inevitable leader of the working class. He has been giving mature leadership to several major trade unions in West Bengal. I am also aware that he is now doing his best to harmonize working class aspirations with the dictates of a globalizing and liberalizing world.

Nor is Shri Somnath Chatterjee confined to the world of politics, Parliament, law and the working class. In the State of West Bengal and at the national level, he is associated – as President or Member – with a significant number of organizations rendering service in the areas of civil liberties, academics, arts and sports. This profile is that of a resplendent humanist.

Shri Somnath Chatterjee's performance in the Conferences of the Inter-Parliamentary Union (IPU) has always had stunning impact on the international audience. Last year, I had the privilege of getting the support of human rights issues in the IPU Conference in Beijing. As the rapporteur on the Committee on Human Rights, his contribution in harmonizing a plethora of amendments from several countries for hammering out a resolution on human rights was widely complimented.

In terms of the conformity to the rules of procedure and conduct of the business of the House, and of protecting the collective dignity of the House, and dignity of the individual parliamentarians, he is a copybook model.

The towering personality which Shri Somnath Chatterjee is, literally and figuratively, by accepting the Outstanding Parliamentarian Award of the Indian Parliamentary Group for the year 1996, is indeed honouring every one of us in the Parliament, even as he is being honoured. He fulfils every parameter stipulated for nomination of parliamentarians for this award. I heartily felicitate him. I wish him long years of public service to the people of his constituency, to West Bengal, to the Parliament and the people of India and to the international community of parliamentarians.

Thank you for your attention.

Jai Hind.

Address at the Birth Centenary Celebrations of Late Shri V.K. Krishna Menon*

Respected Rashtrapatiji, Respected Upa-Rashtrapatiji, honourable Prime Minister, honourable Guests, Ladies and Gentlemen.

It was three days back that we observed the 101st Birth Anniversary of Late Shri V.K Krishna Menon. He hailed from Kozhikode in the Malabar district of British Madras Presidency. On his father's side, he had a princely lineage. On his mother's side, he could trace his lineage to one of the most celebrated Dewans of the State of Travancore.

He had his education up to the pre-degree level in the modest but time-honoured educational institutions of Kozhikode. Having taken history major, naturally, he took keen interest in the British system of parliamentary democracy. He was fascinated by the political philosophies of John Locke, John Stuart Mill, Thomas Hobbes, Rousseau, Marx and Engels.

Having done his graduation in the Presidency College in Madras, he was attracted by the Theosophical Movement of Dr Annie Besant and her Home Rule League. He also came to be associated with the Indian National Boy Scouts Association. In 1924, he went to UK with Dr Arundale.

Thereafter, he lived there for 28 years. He started his life there as a teacher at the St Christopher School, Letchworth, Herfordshire. He did political science in the London School of Economics where he became a student of Professor Harold Laski. By 1934, he had taken MSc degree, after advanced studies in economics, politics and psychology and also completed the law course and became barrister, Middle Temple.

He came in contact with the great intellectuals of the day, Beatrice Webb, Sir Stafford Cripps and Bertrand Russell. He was also an active Labour Party worker, member of the Socialist League and participated in the local government.

The struggle for India's independence had to be fought both on the

---

**The Journal of Parliamentary Information*, Vol. XLIII, No.3, September 1997. Pages 256–259. Spoke while addressing a function held in the Central Hall of Parliament House on 6 May 1997 as part of the Birth Centenary Celebrations of Late Shri V.K. Krishna Menon.

Indian and the British soils. On our land, the struggle was carried on for six decades commencing from the first session of the Indian National Congress in 1885 under the presidentship of W.C. Bannerji. The struggle on the British soil was spearheaded by Shri V.K. Krishna Menon. Having been initiated by Dr Besant in the Home Rule Movement in India, he continued to work under the Commonwealth of India League in UK. With untiring dedication, he shaped the minds of the British people, parliamentarians, intellectuals and decision makers in the cause of India's freedom.

In 1930, the Commonwealth of India League was covered into the India League with the exit of Dr Besant. This development was also brought about on account of Shri Menon's close cooperation with the Indian National Congress which passed the 'Poorna Swaraj' Resolution at its Lahore Session.

During Shri Menon's struggle for our Independence on the British soil, highlights after 1930 were the India League's Parliamentary Delegation to India in 1932 and his deputation to the World Peace Congress in Geneva in 1935. The report of the parliamentary delegation back in UK was a major milestone in creating significant awareness amongst the British about the validity of India's cause for freedom. Shri Menon also struck a bond of personal friendship with Pandit Jawaharlal Nehru which later on developed into strong political partnership between them. He assisted Mahatma Gandhi during the first Round Table Conference. Having parted company with the Labour Party for a while on the issue of self-determination for India, Shri Menon joined the Party again in 1945. He was, thereafter, closely associated with negotiations on transfer of power. After the Second World War was over, he got the Labour Party to commit itself to self-determination for India.

After India attained Independence, he became the first High Commissioner to UK from 1947 to 1952. He was the Chairman of the Indian delegation to the United Nations General Assembly from 1953 to 1962. He made outstanding contributions in the United Nations. Termination of the Korean War, vacations of British, French and Israeli occupation of Egyptian territories, including the Suez Canal, repatriation of Korean prisoners of war, termination of the Indo-China war, etc., were some of the more important matters on which Shri Menon's personal contribution was very significant. He projected to the world that whichever be the power of the nation, human rights violations were unacceptable and that self-determination was an inalienable right of colonized countries. He established that Kashmir was an integral part of the Sovereign Indian Republic and by sheer perseverance shifted Kashmir out of the multilateral agenda of the United Nations and made it a bilateral issue between India and Pakistan.

As Defence Minister, from 1957 to 1962, he laid the foundations for the self-sufficiency of our defence forces. Laying stress on capacity utilization of the ordnance factories, production of heavy vehicles for the army and modernization of the air force and the navy were his contributions. For him, the takeover of Goa from Portuguese was a simple issue of wiping out the last vestiges of colonialism in India.

Following upon Chinese aggression in 1962, Shri Menon had to lay down the office of the Defence Minister. Several reasons have been attributed to the country's performance in the face of the Chinese aggression. But Shri Menon did demonstrate candidness and intellectual integrity in admitting that he had banked on diplomacy rather than military measures in dealing with the Chinese.

Having been a Member of the Rajya Sabha initially from 1953 to 1957, he was Member of the second, third and fourth Lok Sabhas from 1957 to 1962, from 1962 to 1967 respectively.

Shri Menon looked upon the Constitution as an instrument for securing economic development, distributive justice and political pluralism. He saw no contradictions between individual liberty and socialist society, so long as the articulation of individual liberty did not result in exploitation, Shri Menon as a federalist, he believed that State autonomy was not a matter of condescending concessions but he cohesive force for ensuring national unity and integrity. He clearly saw the divisive and destabilizing potential of religion, language, castes and communities and wanted these forces to be strongly discouraged.

The Constitution, the electoral laws, political parties and inner-party democracy within political parties, according to Shri Menon, were closely interrelated. He felt that democratic contours of political parties were not internal to the parties, but were a national matter.

Shri Menon cautioned about external assistance for economic development, including industrialization. This caution was not based on any dogma, but on this basic concern for economic independence. He was immensely aware of our technology shortfalls and in fact wanted external technology and expertise without giving room for imperialism through the economic route.

Shri Menon was one of the architects of the policy of non-alignment. He believed in national autonomy in decision making, each country taking its decisions in its own national interest. Non-alignment for him, therefore, was a means of reflecting nation's policies in international relations. Joining power blocs, Western bloc or the Soviet bloc, according to him, would have compromised national sovereignty and autonomy. Shri Menon viewed it as a policy of peace, steering clear of the military dependence. He did not have any pretensions of power. But, then and now, non-alignment survives. It has survived through the politics of power blocs, through détente. It is alive today during unipolar trends. It is here to stay.

We have half a century of experience in trying to alleviate poverty. Shri Menon visualized that peace, development, economic strength and respect in the world at large were not capable of being achieved by us unless the gap between the rich and the poor was eliminated. Social justice, according to him, was one of the motives for our Independence struggle and was the first pledge to the redeemed. He believed in the Welfare State model in which there would be social security for the masses.

Shri Krishna Menon was indeed a very colourful personality and a giant amongst Indian leaders. He symbolized intellectual integrity from which flowed the courage of his convictions. In India and abroad, it is that courage which spawned his detractors and made him friendless. His almost single-handed and incredible contribution to India's Independence with his base on the British soil and his phenomenal performance in international politics with his base in the United Nations were overshadowed by the developments of 1962. Cooler minds of later years will, however, not fail to assign him the place rightfully due to him in the history of our nation.

Thank you for your attention.

Jai Hind.

Address to the Conference of the Chairmen and Members of Public Accounts Committees in SAARC Parliaments*

Honourable Dr Murli Manohar Joshi, Chairman of the Public Accounts Committee, Distinguished Delegates from SAARC Parliaments, Shri Shunglu, Comptroller and Auditor General of India, Ladies and Gentlemen.

Many of you may be wondering what has the Speaker of the House of the People of India got to do with this distinguished gathering of the public accounts specialists from SAARC countries. I can only attribute it to Dr Murli Manohar Joshi who, though an intellectual and scientist by his own right, is not without his cruel sense of humour. Though I am no financial expert of public accounts specialist, he has insisted on my presence here. I tried to quote my preoccupation with the ongoing Golden Jubilee Session of the Parliament, but I could not resist the affectionate persuasion of Dr Joshi. Of course, I do feel honoured to be amidst you. The best I could do is to share a few of my ringside experiences in finance and accounts acquired in my earlier roles as the Union Minister in Government of India and the Chief Minister of my State Meghalaya.

All over the world today, in political life, ensuring accountability seems to be the priority. Preparation of budgets of financially sound principles and authorization of resource mobilization and appropriation of funds for public expenditure through legislative process are common features of all democratic societies. When these processes are gone through, people do expect those in positions of power to be accountable for acting on the budgets. This accountability also is secured by the Parliament itself with authority vested in them by the Constitution. Public Accounts Committees are the mechanisms through which this accountability is sought to be ensured. Usually, these Committees are professionally advised and supported by the institution of the Comptroller and Auditor General enjoying constitutional status.

**The Journal of Parliamentary Information,* Vol. XLlll, No., 4, December 1997. Pages 398–401. Spoke while addressing the Conference of the Chairmen and Members of Public Accounts Committees in SAARC Parliaments held in New Delhi on 30–31 August 1997.

Parliamentary control over finance is basically anchored in the budget documents presented to the Parliament, that is, the Annual Financial Statement of estimated receipt and expenditure of the Government. The items of expenditure are broadly categorized as 'voted' and 'charged'. The charged items of expenditure like, for example, the emoluments and allowances of the honourable President, honourable Vice-President, the Speaker, judges of the Supreme Court, Comptroller and Auditor General of India, apart from certain other items, do not come under detailed scrutiny in the Parliament, they being charged to the Consolidated Fund. The Parliament can also legislate on other items to be so charged. Often, of late, concern is being expressed about expansion of charged items.

Preparation of the budget itself is largely a bureaucratic exercise, though extensive consultations do take place with various interests – industrialists, farmers' groups, trade unions, social scientists, economists, etc. Once the budget is presented in Parliament, its scrutiny gets involved in a lot technical parameters. Cut motions on the basis of which the budget could be criticized are symbolic in nature. On a cut motion in regard to a demand for agriculture, for example, there could be long-winded statements and speeches about floods and droughts. The Parliament debate ultimately does not bring about any significant change as such on the size of the budget. Of course, we do have mandatory scrutiny of the budget by the departmentally related committees. The committee reports again do not immediately impact on the size of the budget though they may have implications for the future on the future budget exercises in terms of allocation of resources or implementation of programmes.

The budget documents also tend, in certain circumstances, to reflect a vast gap between people's aspirations for development and ability to raise resources. The Planning Commission, while preparing the Five Year or Annual Plans, is confronted with disproportionately huge demands from the Ministers and State Governments, though broad indications are given with reference to expected resources about the desirable size of the Plans. The ultimate consequence is that the budget documents are full of token provisions for several activities which may or may not be enhanced midway through the processes of implementation of programmes. New programmes and activities are also taken up midway through financial years without having been planned out earlier at the time of budget preparation. The cumulative effect of budget practices of this nature is that resources get thinly spread. They also get suboptimally provided. Many projects get implemented at a snail's pace over many years resulting in cost escalations, wastages and non-provision of adequate funds for the cost-effective implementation of a limited number of prioritized programmes.

Public spending has been described humorously as 'the most delicious of all privileges: spending other people's money'. The same prudence which is exercised in private life to avoid expenditure on avoidable activities is not exercised in the dispensation of public money. Activities once undertaken become self-perpetuating and interminable.

As those involved in public expenditure scrutiny, you may be aware of the concept of zero-based budgeting. It was Jimmy Carter of the United States, as Governor of Georgia and a presidential candidate, who pioneered it. The concept is simply that every government programme has to be justified afresh for each financial year.

Our financial experts and budget specialists are never inadequate in acquiring modern tools in management. Some years back, when I was a Union Minister, I remember that Jimmy Carter's zero-based budgeting became a mantra chanted with professional perfection and wisdom in the corridors of all Ministers, the lead of course having come from the North Block where resources are to be found and from the Planning Commission where the resources are allocated. Dictats were given to all Ministers to analyse every activity to judge on the relevance of its continuance. And, laborious exercises were indeed carried out. I am not aware of any activity having been discontinued. What continues is the concept of zero-based budgeting in the textbooks of public finance in the schools of management.

Many economies go out of gear because of failure in balancing the budget. How is the budget balancing exercise done? Resources, whether they be of tax or non-tax origin, have to be raised as planned and expenditure contained therein. This does not often happen because neither resources are actually raised as planned nor expenditure contained within limits. Often mobilized resources are also not deployed efficiently. This is even worse than failure to mobilize the planned resources because inefficient use of resources cuts into even existing resources. If a million rupees are invested in an enterprise the result of which is only earning of a loss, leave alone earning of any profit, the gap to the extent of the loss has to be filled by drawing on existing resources. In circumstances like this also, because Governments are not families, sophisticated tools of economic analysis are promptly pressed into service to justify failures.

All of you would only be too familiar with the enigmatic tool of understanding called 'cost-benefit analysis'. By handling, rather mishandling this tool, any economic or commercial loss could be proved result in social benefit; that is, loss can be projected as an economic cost, justifying a social benefit.

We also have the interesting innovation called the Performance Budget. This is a document expected to be presented to the Parliament along with the Demands for Grants. I have always felt that this document is a misnomer. Though it is titled as Performance Budget, it often reads like a 'Doomsday Book' of non-performance. Usually, it is authored by Financial Advisers who make it an uninspiring catalogue of shortfalls in achievement of physical targets. It was Shri C. Subramaniam who as Union Finance Minister, introduced, of course, with the very good and laudable intension of speedy dispatch of Government business, the system of the so called 'integrated finance'. Under this system, the Financial Adviser has a dual responsibility, that is, to the Minister in charge of the concerned portfolio as well as the Finance Minister. For the Minister in charge of the portfolio other than Finance, working 'integratedly' with the Financial Adviser is like sleeping with the enemy. Each shortfall in achievement of the physical targets, chronicled by the Financial Adviser, would carry behind it a story from which rich lessons could be learnt for streamlining public expenditure.

As a practitioner of public finance with very limited experience, I may suggest the following for consideration by this Conference:

* Go into the rationalization of charged items of expenditure.
* Scrutinize the scope for prescribing limits on thin spread of resources, particularly because inefficient provision of resources may not even come within the scope of audit and even it is does, audit is ex post facto because of which responsibilities cannot be fixed in respect of defaults and inadequacies of earlier years.
* Examine modalities of effective and meaningful implementation of zero-based budgeting.
* Carefully scrutinize 'cost-benefit' justification of executive.
* Streamline performance budgeting.

I am sure that this Conference will be a delightful experience for all of you under the guidance of Dr Murli Manohar Joshi who is reputed for his scientific approach, thoroughness, objectivity and fairness.

Thank you for your kind attention.

Address at the 61st Conference of Presiding Officers of Legislative Bodies in India*

Honourable Speaker, Himachal Pradesh Vidhan Sabha, Shri Kaul Singh Thakur, Chief Minister of Himachal Pradesh, Shri Virbhadra Singh, Presiding Officers of the State Legislative Bodies, Officials of the Parliament Secretariats and of State Legislative Bodies, Ladies and Gentlemen.

I am immensely pleased to cordially welcome you all in this beautiful and historic city of Shimla. I thank the Himachal Pradesh Chief Minister, Shri Virbhadra Singh, his Government and the honourable Speaker, Shri Kaul Singh Thakur, for hosting this Conference.

This Conference of the Presiding Officers is of special significance. This is the second major event of the legislative arm of governance in our country during this Golden Jubilee Year of our Independence, our democracy. The first one was the Special Session of the Parliament from 26 August to 1 September 1997.

The agenda we have set for ourselves consists of two main subjects – our democratic experience and discipline and decorum in legislative bodies.

Our democracy is unique. It is the largest in the world. It has been successful. It has been uninterrupted over fifty long years. It has stood the test of the incredible pluralism of our society. It has coexisted with different shades of ideology from extreme right to extreme left through a multiparty system. Our democracy, nonetheless, faces several challenges. We need to manage these challenges vigilantly to make a continued success of our democracy.

Our country is geographically too vast, demographically too large, socially too pluralistic. These factors by themselves constitute a powerful challenge. The only way to meet this challenge is by the decentralization of governance. For the purpose, a legal framework for a three-tier decentralization has been given through the 73rd and 74th constitutional amendments. It is for us now to make it a reality on ground.

**The Journal of Parliamentary Information*, Vol. XLlV, No. 1, March 1998. Pages 3–7. Spoke while Addressing the 61st Conference of the Presiding Officers of Legislative Bodies in India held in Shimla, Himachal Pradesh on 21–23 October 1997.

Our democracy can survive in the long run only by the strengthening of our federal structure. And, there can be cooperative federation only by meaningful devolution of powers to the States. In fact, during the Special Session of the Parliament, inviting attention to the Sarkaria Commission's recommendations, several Members of Parliament expressed serious concern about the lack of adequate devolution of powers to the States.

A clearly discernible trend in our multiparty system is the emergence of regional parties at the expense of national parties. Hung legislatures are becoming increasingly common. Consequently, governance through coalitions becomes necessary. Coalitions, by themselves, need not cause concern, while ideally Governments of individual parties with adequate majority would be preferable. Indeed, in today's world, about 60 countries are run by coalition Governments. For the safety of our democracy, however, political parties need to develop consensus on basic socio-economic issues confronting the nation, like population control, education, employment, infrastructure development, etc. Some of the most prosperous countries of today are those which have made socio-economic development neutral to party politics. Consequently, political instability does not necessarily have impact on development. We should also evolve modalities of strengthening our parliamentary democracy to ensure political stability, despite multiplicity of parties. Turning the emergence of even regional parties to advantage, we can get them to develop a national outlook.

Forty per cent of our people, nearly 400 million, live below the poverty line after fifty years of Independence. This level of poverty is the gravest danger for our democracy. So poverty elimination has to be high on our national agenda.

Unsustainable growth of population, beyond the carrying capacity of our country, is the root cause of our poverty and very many other economic problems. This is a complex issue having implications for food security, nutrition, health, education, employment, infrastructure needs and environment. The technology for control of population is, of course, available. Nor are resources for the purpose really a problem. The problem is really one of cultural attitudes. If the attitudes are changed, population is controlled; if population is controlled, poverty is eliminated making our polity safe for democracy. I call upon all the MPs, MLCs and MLAs in the country to launch a sustained campaign amongst the people in their constituencies for bringing about the required attitudinal change amongst them to accept the small family norm and thus contribute to population control.

Illiteracy is yet another challenge that we face. Illiteracy causes lack of skills which in turn causes unemployment and poverty, endangering democracy. The stock of illiterate people in our country is 460 million. Investment in education is the solution to the problem. Our national resolve is to set apart six per cent of national income for education. This should be duly reflected in our financial resource allocations, through Plan and non-Plan budgets and through involvement of the private sector. I personally feel that we may even have to go for investment of more than six per cent of GDP in education. Education also needs to be made relevant to employment, as I have been urging in every given opportunity and in all fora.

The youth power of the country has to be mobilized for making it continuously safe for democracy. This can be done only by giving them hopes for securing their future. Otherwise, they are likely to become candidates for terrorism, drug running and other social evils.

There is a perceived sense of economic exploitation amongst sections of society within States. It is this sense which gives rise to local and regional demands for autonomy. This has to be addressed with great sensitivity and practical solutions found, lest local and regional aspirations deepen into fissiparous tendencies and endanger our democracy.

Market has become the decisive factor all over the world, including East Asia, Central Asia and East Europe. Political systems have changed and ideologies are getting relegated to the backseat. The challenge of the market is a challenge for democracy too in all countries, including India, which have been accustomed to highly regulated economies. Deregulation poses serious problems of transition. Economic transition does involve present sacrifices for future welfare. Present sacrifices have social costs. As industries and capital and financial markets get opened up for investors from economically powerful countries in the process of transition, forces tending to destabilize the economy, as reflected in the present South-East Asian crisis, could come into operation. The pain of current sacrifices during economic transition has to be mitigated. The social costs have to be equitably borne. Trends of economic destabilization have to be checkmated and prevented. In short, the whole process of economic transition – inevitable as it is in the present-day world – has to be prudently managed. Otherwise, what is likely to get destabilized ultimately is democracy itself.

Probity and standards in public life have become a matter of universal concern in several countries. This is true of our country as well. We are going to have a full day's symposium on issue relating to constitution of Ethics Committees. I shall deal with this matter in some detail on the day of the symposium.

Our legends and epics have given a very high place for women in our society. Many women of India have made history. Indira Gandhi was not merely a Prime Minister of our country but her memory is cherished all over the world long after her demise. We have had eminent women Chief Ministers, apart from judges and other professionals. But we continue to be a male-dominated society. The contribution of women to national economy does not even feature in our National Income Accounts. They have to be given their due place in decision-making positions, including at the political level. This, indeed, is the significance of the 81st Constitutional Amendment Bill. We need to achieve true partnership between men and women in politics. Otherwise, we would suffer from democratic deficit. The modalities of securing women's partnership in politics are a matter of detail. Be that as it may, we should achieve this partnership. Constitutional and legal framework for this need to be established earlier than later. And, more importantly, practices should be brought in conformity with whatever constitutional and legal framework we may get to establish.

Legislative bodies can and should play an effective role in addressing all these issues I have referred to. After all, it is their mandate to secure accountability of the executive in evolving appropriate policies for the purpose and implementing them. The Parliament does play a very vibrant role in this regard through fairly lengthy sessions lasting for substantial part of the year and through the elaborate committee system that has been established. My impression is that State legislative bodies meet for comparatively lesser number of days in a year. The scope for bringing about improvement in this respect needs to be gone into.

We do in the normal course of House business discuss national issues in legislative bodies. But such discussions take place in a rather fragmented way and discontinuously, thanks to the pressure on time from several standard items of business. It is because of this that the Special Golden Jubilee Session of the Parliament was organized to exclusively discuss the basic national issues. I would urge that in the course of this Golden Jubilee Year, all State legislatures too may hold such exclusive sessions. They may also endeavour to adopt the unanimous resolution adopted by the Parliament of India.

All of us are immensely aware of the discipline and decorum we maintain and the orderly conduct of business that we facilitate when we meet in the Conference of the Commonwealth Parliamentary Association. Why not we ensure these standards in our legislative bodies? In most Parliaments of the world, Members appreciate the value of the House time and respect each other's time. They avoid cross talk, interruptions, repetitions and misconduct. Our legislators need to be guided and trained in this respect. Political parties have the primary responsibility in this regard. I have urged them to organize training courses for their Members. The presiding officers also may like to do so in their States.

Let us strengthen our democracy by addressing the basic national issues; let us set our economic house in order and strengthen it; let our legislative bodies become powerhouses feeding energy to our Governments.

I have taken more than the usual time I like to take in important conferences like this. Being our conference of the Golden Jubilee Year and considering the gravity of the task before us, I anticipated your indulgence. Wish you fruitful discussions. Thank you for your attention. Let us give a big hand to our very hospitable hosts, the Chief Minister and the Government of Himachal Pradesh, Honourable Speaker, Shri Kaul Singh Thakur and all those involved in organizational work for this conference.

Address at the 61st Symposium on the Need for Constitution of Ethics Committees in Legislatures*

Honourable Chief Minister of Himachal Pradesh, Shri Virbhadra Singh, Honourable Speaker, Himachal Pradesh Vidhan Sabha, Shri Kaul Singh Thakur, Presiding Officers of the State Legislative Bodies, Honourable Members of Parliament and Members of Legislative Assembly, Officials of the Parliament Secretariats and of State Legislative Bodies, Ladies and Gentlemen.

**The Journal of Parliamentary Information*, Vol. XLIV, No. 1, March 1998. Pages 8–12. Spoke while addressing a symposium on the 'Need for Constitution of Ethics Committees in Legislatures' held in Shimla on 23 October 1997.

Ethics in governance is a matter which has come to hold the attention of people today universally. The issue of what has come to be referred to as 'good governance' is even being suggested by multilateral and their agencies as a qualifying parameter for countries to seek financial aid from them. What these agencies simply mean 'good governance' is that, inter alia, aid provided should be used for the purpose for which it is given. There should be no corrupt practices. Modalities and procedures for use of aid should be transparent. There should be accountability in achieving the targets and objectives. We are, and should be, concerned with ethics in governance for its own sake and proactively.

People's representatives are holders of the trust of their constituents. Naturally, the electors expect that the care of this trust is not abused. The electors are persuaded by political parties to return their candidates to legislative bodies based on much publicized election manifestoes. When they return particular candidates, they trust what the parties have stated in the manifestoes. They trust that the candidates returned by them will also work by the manifesto promises. But it is our experience that many manifesto promises are breached by the political parties as well as the candidates. Manifestoes have largely become populistic promises unethically made. The first principle of ethics in our democracy should be that political parties and legislators stand accountable to the people in terms of their manifesto promises.

When we met in October 1996, we deliberated on accountability. Our finding was that the chain of accountability had come to be broken all the way, that is, accountability of the civil service to the political executive, of the political executive to the legislature, of the legislature to the electorate. There is need for an introspection by our political world on this situation and for corrective actions. The civil service in our system is expected to be politically neutral. Often this neutrality itself is neutralized because of the politician–civil servant nexus. Mass-scale transfers of civil servants are made whenever new Government takes charge in some States. In the result, they stand intimated, demoralized and politicized very often, many crucial civil service posts in the Governments and in the field remain unfilled, bringing implementation of development programmes to a standstill and destroying the stability of administration. Frequently transferred officers don't develop professional expertise in their jobs. Above all else, this clone of politician–civil servant will come to wield authority without responsibility or accountability, undermining the very basis of our parliamentary democracy. Political ethics demands that there should be understanding amongst all political parties for the abolition of this 'mass-transfer industry'.

I feel compelled to make a special mention about politicization of the police force, the members of which are also expected to be neutral civil servants. The police force symbolizes the coercive authority of the State. If its neutrality is broken and is made to serve political masters, what breaks down is the rule of law itself, because it has implications in terms of violations of human rights and State terrorism.

The manner of financing of elections in general has implications for relations between legislators and those in positions of authority in the Government on the one hand and the election financiers on the other. The activities of the Government having become complex over the years, embracing several crucial aspects of the common man's life, the community of holders of public office has become rather large in size and diversified in its role and authority. The interface between holders of public office and providers of various kinds of service has intensified. When service providers also become financiers of elections, corrupt practices become rampant. It is in this background that the ethical dimension of the nexus between politicians and industrialists and businessmen gets projected to public view. It is permissible under the Company Law for corporate bodies to make contributions to political parties. But the problem is that there is no transparency about the extent of contributions. The consequence is that there could be quid pro quo between industrialists and politicians which may ultimately militate against equality before law, largesse being given to favoured industrialists. In effect, individual industrialists may even come to influence Government policies. The problem has to be addressed by electoral reforms.

The third nexus is between politicians and criminals. History-sheeters get to be preferred candidates of political parties in running for offices because they are seen as winning candidates. The Election Commission is since barring such persons from electoral contests. The laws relating to qualifications for, and disqualification of, members of legislative bodies on the ground of criminality, including the constitutional provisions, the Representation of People Act, the Prevention of Corruption Act, etc., should be comprehensively reviewed and re-established, leaving no scope for doubts and interpretations or for arbitrary exercise of powers by election officials. Prevention of entry by criminals into, and of their continuance in, legislative bodies by law is only a technical aspect of the matter. More important is the role that the political parties themselves have to play in this regard as well. Aspirants for membership may not have been subjected to convictions. But the electorate does have clear assessment of the track record of aspirants for public offices in terms of their public service and their general reputations for probity, integrity, criminality, etc. Political parties should make conscious and proactive efforts at sensing this assessment of the electorate and based on that, exclude from their candidatures persons with questionable track records.

We have been making efforts for nearly three decades to enact the Lok Pal Law to bring public functionaries, including those in high places, under the surveillance of exalted and independent statutory authority. We have not so far succeeded. We should expedite the enactment of the law.

One of the positive measures that need to be considered to prevent recourse to unethical practices by the legislators in the discharge of their duties is to provide them salaries and allowances consistent with their status and responsibilities. According to the Warrant of Precedence of the Government of India, Members of Parliament occupy positions above the Secretaries to Government.

The proliferation of political parties and consequent 'hung legislatures' put a premium on defections. Defections, by their very nature, are unethical. Of course, the Tenth Schedule to the Constitution which is the law on defections has been established. Our experience with invocation of the Tenth Schedule, however, has thrown up a number of practical problems in handling issues relating to disqualification of members on account of defections. Time has come for us to review the Tenth Schedule in the light of our experience and perfect it.

Discipline and decorum in legislative bodies are not mere matters of Rules of Procedure and Conduct of Business of the Houses. Rules are the means for securing discipline and decorum which, in turn, stem from a basic consideration of ethics. What is the consideration? It is simply that every second of the time of the Houses shall be used by the Members in serving their electorate, the people at large. Undisciplined conduct of Members, including slogan shouting, avoidable interruption of debate, long-winded speeches exceeding the time granted by the presiding officers, etc., result in wastage of valuable time meant for transacting business in service of the public. It also results in wasteful public expenditure. I would call upon all the presiding officers to establish a strict system of time use and implement it. All of you would also agree what a delight it has been for us over the last two days to have facilitated orderly conduct of business, strictly conforming to time limits for statements. I would further recall upon the presiding officers to calculate the cost of each second of their House time and give wide publicity for the same so that public awareness about, and resentment against, wastage of House time is generated.

It is well established that undisciplined conduct in the Houses amounting to criminal acts do not come within the scope of parliamentary privileges and immunities. The presiding officers, in my opinion, would do well – cases of such acts – to initiate privilege proceedings *suo motu* and take them to their logical conclusion, including expulsion of the guilty members in due process without prejudice to other actions under the relevant penal and criminal laws of the country.

The various issues of ethics that I have referred to have implications directly or indirectly for the privileges of legislative bodies. The question that could be naturally raised in this context is whether the Privileges Committees in their present form cannot handle ethics issues. My understanding is that 'ethics' is a larger issue in which privileges are subsumed. This apart, there is a preventive dimension to the ethical standards of conduct of holders of public office. The Rajya Sabha has already established an Ethics Committee in March 1997. There are Ethics Committees in countries like UK and the United States and Australia. A Group of the Committee of Privileges of the Lok Sabha has studied Ethics Committees in these countries. This symposium is going to have the pleasure of participation by the members of this group. I am sure interaction between the presiding officers and the members of this group will help the Lok Sabha take meaningful decisions on the need for Ethics Committees and on their structure and functions, if the need for the same is going to established finally. I shall desist from suggesting any framework for the Ethics Committees and limit myself to pointing out some of the practices that exist in other countries for ensuring ethical standards of conduct which are registration and declaration of interests of Members, periodic declaration of their assets, norms for receiving of gifts and hospitalities, norms for advocating specific causes, etc.

The Lok Sabha Secretariat has circulated a self-contained paper for use by the presiding officers in this symposium. A few models of Ethics Committees have also been suggested in this paper for favour of your information.

I shall conclude now. On my own behalf and on behalf of all the presiding officers, I express my grateful thanks to honourable Shri Virbhadra Singh, Chief Minister of Himachal Pradesh for very graciously inaugurating the symposium, apart from personally monitoring arrangements for the last two days' conference and today's symposium as told to me by the honourable Speaker, Himachal Pradesh, Shri Kaul Singh Thakur. Thank you one and all.

Address at the Training Seminar for Secretaries of Legislatures of the Asia Region of the Commonwealth Parliamentary Association*

Honourable Chief Minister of West Bengal, Shri Jyoti Basu, honourable Speaker, West Bengal Legislative Assembly, Shri Hashim Abdul Halim, Director, Administration, CPA, Shri Raja Gomez, Distinguished Delegates, Ladies and Gentlemen.

I am pleased and honoured to participate in the inaugural of this seminar for the Secretaries of the Legislatures of the Asia Region. The seminar is indeed consistent with the mission of the CPA (Commonwealth Parliamentary Association), namely, promotion of knowledge and understanding about parliamentary democracy among its members. Secretaries of legislatures are very crucial functionaries. Training them and exposing them to an exercise in sharing of experiences in a seminar like this is a significant and effective way of fulfilling the CPA mission. Let me compliment the CPA and the West Bengal Branch of the Association in organizing the seminar programme. Earlier this year, in the month of April, the CPA conducted a Regional Conference at Kohima, Nagaland, for the legislators of the North East of our country. Repeated programmes of this nature signify the importance that the CPA assigns to the Asia Region in general and India in particular.

**The Journal of Parliamentary Information*, Vol. XLIV, No. 1, March 1998. Pages 13–17. Spoke while addressing the Training Seminar for Secretaries of the Legislatures of the Asia Region of the Commonwealth Parliamentary Association (CPA) held in Calcutta from 11 to 15 December 1997.

The subjects of the seminar, I find, are rather wide-ranging and include parliamentary culture, the concept of parliamentary privileges, accountability, administration, management, modernization of services, etc.

Parliamentary culture is a broad expression in which several aspects of representative democracy are subsumed. Parliament reflects people's power. We follow the Westminster model of parliamentary democracy. Oliver Cromwell's victory in the English Civil War created an all-powerful image for the Parliament. The Earl of Pembroke declared in 1648, I quote, 'A Parliament can do anything but make a man a woman and a woman a man.' The primacy as well as the supremacy of the Parliament in democratic governance, according to me, are fundamental to wholesome parliamentary culture. Along with the executive and the judiciary, the legislature is expected to participate in governance.

How does the legislature participate in governance? It performs its function, primarily by making laws. The laws should reflect the collective will of the people. They should reflect and be consistent with what is understood as the common law or natural law which is distinct from the statutory law. For example, human rights and fundamental freedoms like freedom of association, freedom of speech, etc., are natural and axiomatic and are, therefore, construed as part and parcel of the natural law.

Legislatures should also perform the function of securing the accountability of the executive. It is the job of the executive to run the Government on a day-to-day basis. In running the Government, the executive wields enormous powers. Decision makers in the executives are in the nature of guardians of public interest. But the question that has always been asked since the days of Plato and Aristotle is 'who will guard the guardians'. Legislatures being constituted by the representatives of the people, they are indeed to guard the guardians. This gives rise to the principle of accountability.

The executive is expected to be accountable to the legislature. That is how Article 75 of India's Constitution provides that the Council of Ministers is collectively responsible to the House of the people. Wholesome parliamentary culture, then, is one that ensures the accountability of the executive. There is a whole lot of procedures and mechanisms through which this accountability is sought to be ensured – the Question Hour, Calling Attention Motions, Notices on Matters of Public Interest, Adjournment Motions, Confidence and No-confidence Motions, etc.

These are not to be seen as mere procedural rituals but very significant links in an overall design for ensuring accountability of those who wield power in the executive.

Voting of grants for various governmental activities and monitoring of expenditure of those grants are also vital functions in the performance of which the role of legislatures in governance is to be seen. The established mechanisms for the purpose are the Annual Financial Statements and the Financial Committees, i.e., the Estimates Committee, the Public Accounts Committee and the Committee on Public Undertakings. There are practical limitations to parliamentary control over finance. The principal limitation is the availability of time in the House. Budget documents are invariably the creations of the Government, conditioned by availability of resources. Parliamentary debates on Budget are normally through Cut Motions. Cut Motions are only symbolic. They are not used for the purpose of significantly reducing or enhancing the Budget. They are rather used for the purpose of drawing attention of the Government to inadequacies in policies and in implementation of policies. Nor are the Parliaments in a position to take up detailed discussions on all the demands for grants for sheer want of time. All of us in this gathering are well aware of the process of guillotine, details of which I don't have to go into. Committees on Estimates only give recommendations. They can only serve the purpose of broad guidelines and perhaps for laying down priorities of expenditure. Public Accounts Committees and Committees on Public Undertakings largely perform ex post facto functions. It is in the background that we in India have created the system of departmentally related Standing Committees which mandatorily go into the detailed scrutiny of demands for grants, examination of Annual Reports and Performance Budgets of Ministries. This committee system is of fairly recent origin. Nor do all State legislatures have this system. It is worthwhile to universalize this system and further perfect its working.

The legislators themselves are accountable to the public at large. Stated differently, each parliamentarian or Member of a Legislative Assembly is accountable to his electors. Of course, the electors hold the parliamentarians accountable at the time of elections. This again can only be ex post facto. We don't have the system of recall of legislators with whom the electorate is not satisfied. Hence the ex post facto exercise in securing accountability of their representative by the electors. This brings us to the question of orderly conduct of business in the Houses by the parliamentarians.

The time of the Houses being limited and expensive, parliamentarians should observe rules relating to orderly conduct of business. Cross talk, attempting to speak without being recognized by the chair, collective efforts at attempting to draw the attention of the chair, repetitive arguments in the course of speeches and statements in the Houses, shouting of slogans and demonstrations on the floor of the Houses, etc., are in the ultimate analysis, serious breach of accountability of the parliamentarians to the people who return them.

Disorderly conduct of business is largely due to lack of experience on the part of the parliamentarians. In the eleventh Lok Sabha, out of a total of 543 elected members, 284 were first-timers. Many of them have not even had experience in political life at the State or sub-state level. In their anxiety to be demonstrably and perceptibly active on behalf of their electors, parliamentarians often used to indulge in disorderly conduct. Live telecasting of parliamentary proceedings, they believed, perhaps, helped them in their activeness in the Parliament being seen by their electors on the television. It is yet to be seen, through the result of the next General Elections, whether the electors have really appreciated their idea of activeness in the Parliament.

Legislators, particularly the first-timers, need to be trained in the Rules of Procedure of the Legislatures. This would go a long way in facilitating orderly conduct of business in the Houses. Secretaries of legislatures, interacting with the parliamentarians as they do on day-to-day basis and having long experience could make significant contribution in the matter of this training.

Many parliamentarians do also look forward to significant level of information support for the purpose of discharging their duties in the Houses. In the Parliament, we have a Library and Reference, Research, Documentation and Information Service. We also have a Newspaper Clipping Service. Normally, this service makes available to the parliamentarians documents required by them within a day or two. To render this service effectively, Secretaries of legislative bodies should themselves undergo training. They could keep track of the highly informative publications of the CPA and bring them to the notice of the parliamentarians. They can draw on CPA's Parliamentary Information and Reference Centre (PIRC). The CPA has advanced a lot in recent times into the use of modern technology. The CPA Secretariat is now equipped with email facilities. The CPA Home Page has also been established on the World Wide Web. Secretariat would also do well to access the World Wide Web and network with the CPA systems.

Independence of the judiciary is yet another principle which is always respected in the conduct of Parliamentary proceedings. Matters which are sub-judice are not to be discussed in the Houses. Judges, as presiding officers of the judicial bodies, are also not to be discussed. All over the world, parliamentarians do complain about the so-called judicial activism. On account of developments in the judicial process like public interest litigations and litigations involving he probity and standards of peoples' representatives, not to speak of issues of public concern like environment protection, judicial intervention is sought by the people more than ever before. Particularly in the context of these complexities, Secretaries of legislatures would need to be aware and be updated with developments in the area of legislature–judiciary interface. The inviolable principle, however, is respect for the autonomy of the legislatures and the judiciary in their own areas of competence. Detailed knowledge about this should always be helpful in providing information and advice that may be tendered by the Secretaries to their presiding officers.

Secretaries should also be aware of the rights of the media vis-à-vis the legislatures. In India, the media has a constitutional right of access to parliamentary proceedings. While providing access to the media, the officials should make the media aware of the implications of colourable use of parliamentary information to parliamentary privileges.

Parliamentary privileges are based on the principle of avoidance of molestation, that is, parliamentarians should be in a position to discharge their parliamentary functions without fear or hindrance. Anything and everything stated in the House or any factum of voting in the House cannot be questioned in a court of law. For the parliamentarians, to claim privilege, there should be clear nexus between their work in the Parliament and the alleged breach of privilege. Privileges can be claimed only in the realm of civil law. Criminal actions can never be the basis for claim of privileges and immunities. Most importantly, all over the world, people do not take kindly to the abuse of privileges and immunities. These are the basic facts and principles which should always inform the Secretaries in their work.

I am sure that this seminar with its fairly comprehensive agenda is going to be highly rewarding and enlightening for the participants. I wish the seminar all success.

Thank you for this opportunity to share some of my thoughts on the seminar subjects with you. Thank you too for your kind attention.

INDEX